A Cloud of Witnesses

PROFILES OF CHURCH LEADERS

Edited by
J. C. Wenger

WIPF & STOCK · Eugene, Oregon

Acknowledgements

The chapters on Peter Chelčický and Comenius were written in German and published in Přemysl Pitter, *Geistige Revolution im Herzen Europas* (Zürich und Stuttgart: Rotapfel Verlag, 1968), translated for this volume by Elizabeth Horsch Bender, and somewhat condensed editorially. Used by permission.

The chapter, "Logic and Fantasy: The Word of C. S. Lewis," by Clyde S. Kilby, was first published in *Christian Action*, The Methodist Publishing House, 201 Eighth Avenue, South, Nashville, TN 37203, January 1969. Copyright © 1968 by Graded Press. Used by permission.

Wipf and Stock Publishers
199 W 8th Ave, Suite 3
Eugene, OR 97401

A Cloud of Witnesses
Profiles of Church Leaders
By Wenger, J. C.
Copyright©1981 by Wenger, J. C.
ISBN 13: 978-1-5326-0265-8
Publication date 7/28/2016
Previously published by Eastern Mennonite Seminary, 1981

To the Memory of
CONRAD GREBEL, c. 1498-1526

Initially a Convert of Zwingli
and Subsequently
Founder of the First Modern
FREE CHURCH
I Dedicate this Book

*Published through the generosity
of
Allen W. and Donna Burkholder Graber*

Preface

The preparation of this volume has been a rather slow process. The plan was to use only well-educated writers—most of them have earned doctorates—and such persons are usually busy. And busy they proved to be. There were many delays. It is therefore a matter of gratitude that a total of 72 essays have been brought together. Any collection of such essays is necessarily selective, if not downright arbitrary, but the book does include such major figures as Tertullian, Cyprian, Augustine, Luther, Zwingli, Calvin, Cranmer, Wesley, Kierkegaard, Finney, Machen, Barth, and C. S. Lewis. Each writer was selected as a scholar who could sketch a true portrait of these theological giants and interpret them fairly. Many readers will also enjoy making the acquaintance of other men of God, perhaps less famous, but who also served Him faithfully and effectively—including Anabaptists, Friends, Baptists, and Mennonites—such persons as Boniface, Waldo, Chelčický, Grebel, Sattler, Riedemann, Menno, Fox, Backus, A. T. Robertson, John A. Broadus, Geo. R. Brunk, I, and Harold S. Bender. A few of the 72 were selected because they exerted considerable influence in the history of Christian thought, although they held views not acceptable to evangelicals. I made a serious effort to use only writers who were sound and capable interpreters, able to discern the elements of strength and weakness in the persons of whom they wrote.

The book is weighted in favor of the era from the Reformation to the present. Only eighteen of the subjects preceded Luther. About the middle is R. Barclay, whose definitive exposition of Quaker doctrine, the *Apology*, appeared three centuries ago (1676). But if the very heart of the Reformation was the rediscovery of God's Word, together with the centrality of Christ and His salvation, perhaps the weighting of the essays in favor of the last four centuries is justified.

It would be only fair to mention that the end of the Reformers' efforts was intended to be renewal, not schism. They were striving to bring the church back to full faithfulness to the revealed Word of God, to the principle—as they put it—of *sola scriptura*, that is, the sole authority of holy Scripture. But in the sixteenth century the prelates of Rome would have none of this, clinging instead to the old two-authority formula, Scripture *and tradition*.

Perhaps it is also right for the editor to report that he is not only a member of the Evangelical Theological Society, but also a convinced Free Churchman. The Reformation, unfortunately, did not restore the church to its original situation of complete independence from the state, dependent only on the Word of God and the Spirit of God for its effectiveness, and even for its very survival. On the contrary, the Reformers were ready to maintain and defend the old so-called Constantinian synthesis of church and state, formalized by the joint edict of the Eastern and Western emperors, Theodosius and Gratianus, of February 28, 380. The post-Reformation formula which summarized this unfortunate territorial church system was *cuius regio, eius religio.* In plain English this succinct Latin phrase meant that the ruler of each territory determined the required religion of his subjects—with dissenters facing the alternatives of (1) emigration or (2) the possibility of arrest and imprisonment—even of death! In support of such unchristian persecution the state churchmen pointed to the Mosaic directive that heretics were to be put to death!

It was the Free Churchmen who called for separation of church and state, for religious liberty, and for voluntaryism in matters of faith. They insisted that only Christ was to be Lord of the conscience. They insisted on their right to freely preach the gospel, and they held that persons hearing the Word ought to have the freedom to respond to gospel preaching in repentance and faith, freedom to seal their vows of voluntary discipleship with water baptism, and freedom to unite with a congregation of likeminded believers. The Free Churchmen, in spite of persecution unto the death, proceeded to set up tiny congregations of converted and baptized believers, some of which have survived to this day: the largest body of sixteenth-century Free Churchmen were the Mennonites. Later the Baptists, the Society of Friends, the Church of the Brethren, and other Free Churches became champions of many of the same tenets of faith. From its very inception as a nation the United States has guaranteed all of the basic freedoms to its citizens—although these freedoms were in practice often denied to its minorities. The legal granting of these basic freedoms has made this nation historically an object of worldwide admiration. The voices of such men of God as Chelčický of Bohemia, Grebel of Switzerland, and Menno of Friesland—as to the futility of war—have not been generally heeded, however.

It should be stated frankly that there was no effort to whip each of these essays into a one-man style. It was felt rather that the variety of styles would actually enhance the attractiveness of the volume. The only concern was for clarity—such clarity as well-educated men should be able to effect! The goal was to produce a book which the general public would read with interest and appreciation.

It is a pleasure to thank each of the contributors, as well as two friends who gave professional counsel along the way: Dr. Cornelius J. Dyck, Director of the Institute of Mennonite Studies, Associated Mennonite Biblical Seminaries, Elkhart, Indiana, and Dean A. J. Klassen of the Mennonite Brethren Biblical Seminary, Fresno, California. I am also deeply indebted to two other scholars who helped in the final preparation for the press: Dean George R. Brunk III, of Eastern Mennonite Seminary, and Ken Reddig, Conference Archivist, Center for Mennonite Brethren Studies in Canada.

The reading of this book should both instruct and warn. It should alert to error and establish greater soundness of faith. Most of all, it should be an appetizer to more extended reading in the history of Christian thought. To this end I send it forth with a prayer for the united blessings of our triune God: Father, Son, and Holy Spirit. *Soli Deo gloria!*

J. C. WENGER
Associated Mennonite Biblical Seminaries
3003 Benham Avenue, Elkhart, IN 46517
November 13, 1980

Contents

1	Ignatius of Antioch	John M. Drescher	9
2	Montanus	Howard H. Charles	13
3	Tertullian	Robert D. Sider	16
4	Cyprian	Cornelius J. Dyck	21
5	John Chrysostom	Erland Waltner	25
6	Augustine	Linden M. Wenger	29
7	Gregory the Great	Gerald C. Studer	33
8	Boniface	S. F. Pannabecker	37
9	John of Damascus	Paul Peachey	42
10	Peter Abelard	Ed. G. Kaufman	45
11	Peter Lombard	Daniel Hertzler	49
12	Bernard of Clairvaux	Willard M. Swartley	52
13	Waldo	Leonard Verduin	56
14	Duns Scotus	Paul M. Lederach	59
15	Peter Chelčický	Přemysl Pitter	63
16	Thomas a Kempis	Delbert Grätz	67
17	Savanarola	LeRoy Kennel	70
18	Erasmus	David Ewert	74
19	Martin Luther	Peter J. Klassen	78
20	Philip Melanchthon	John S. Oyer	82
21	Ulrich Zwingli	Robert Holland	86
22	Conrad Grebel	J. C. Wenger	89
23	Thomas Müntzer	Franklin H. Littell	93
24	Michael Sattler	Myron S. Augsburger	97
25	Peter Riedemann	Leonard Gross	102
26	Menno Simons	Cornelius Krahn	106
27	John Calvin	J. C. Wenger	109
28	Martin Bucer	John H. Yoder	113
29	Thomas Cranmer	Walter Klaassen	116
30	Richard Hooker	Dwight Y. King	119
31	Blaise Pascal	Owen H. Alderfer	122
32	John Bunyan	Jacob J. Enz	125
33	John Davenport	Howard J. Zehr	129
34	Comenius	Přemysl Pitter	131
35	George Fox	Lewis Benson	135
36	Robert Barclay	D. Elton Trueblood	139
37	Philipp Jacob Spener	Orlando H. Wiebe	143
38	Gottfried Arnold	Donald F. Durnbaugh	147
39	William Law	John R. Mumaw	150
40	Jonathan Edwards	Keith L. Sprunger	154
41	John Wesley	J. C. Wenger	157
42	Immanuel Kant	Elmer A. Martens	161
43	Isaac Backus	T. B. Maston	165
44	Schleiermacher	Marlin E. Miller	168
45	Søren Kierkegaard	Arthur M. Climenhaga	172
46	Charles G. Finney	J. J. Toews	176
47	Horace Bushnell	George G. Konrad	181

48	Albrecht Ritschl	G. Irvin Lehman	184
49	John A. Broadus	W. R. Estep, Jr.	186
50	William James	H. R. Baerg	190
51	Walter Rauschenbush	Clarence Hiebert	194
52	B. B. Warfield	C. Norman Kraus	198
53	Ernst Troeltsch	J. Lawrence Burkholder	202
54	Geo. R. Brunk I	J. C. Wenger	205
55	A. T. Robertson	W. R. Estep	212
56	Louis Berkhof	Geo. R. Brunk II	216
57	Lewis Sperry Chafer	Henry H. Harder	218
58	J. Gresham Machen	Grant M. Stoltzfus	222
59	A. H. Unruh	A. J. Klassen	226
60	Karl Heim	H. D. Burkholder	230
61	Karl Barth	Clarence Bauman	233
62	Rudolf Bultmann	David Schroeder	237
63	Christian Neff	Gerhard Hein	241
64	Thomas R. Kelly	T. Canby Jones	245
65	Reinhold Niebuhr	John H. Redekop	250
66	C. S. Lewis	Clyde S. Kilby	255
67	Florence Friesen, M.D.	J. C. Wenger	263
68	Harold S. Bender	Guy F. Hershberger	266
69	A. J. Muste	J. R. Burkholder	272
70	G. C. Berkouwer	Archie Penner	276
71	Wolfhart Pannenberg	Helmut Harder	279
72	Women in the Anabaptist-Mennonite Tradition	Esther K. Augsburger	282

"Let no man do aught of the things pertaining to the church apart from the bishop."

1
Ignatius of Antioch
Approx. 40-110

John M. Drescher

His Life, Writings, and Death

Around the start of the second century an aged prisoner named Ignatius was traveling across Western Asia Minor chained to a guard of Roman soldiers. He was ordered from Antioch in Syria to suffer martyrdom by the wild beasts in the arena at Rome.

Ignatius, second or third bishop of Antioch, is known as Ignatius "the Martyr." Born about AD 40, legend says he knew and perhaps was a disciple of Peter or John. He was sentenced to death in a period of persecution sometime during Trajan's reign, AD 98-117. What is of particular interest is that although Ignatius had great fame due to his death, his previous life is utterly blank. Even his death is described by his words of anticipation but is nowhere recorded. As Goodspeed writes, "Ignatius flashes into the field of Christian literature like a bird out of the night and, after a few days, flashes out again into the obscurity from which he had come."

It can be said with some degree of certainty that Ignatius was a native of the East, probably Syria and particularly Antioch. He applies to himself the statement used by Paul that he was of an "untimely birth," which likely means he was not born of Christian parents and was probably converted in adult life. His condemnation to the wild beasts suggests that he was not a Roman citizen.

Ignatius must have been a leader of great prominence because, as he was taken to Rome, Christian communities along the way sent delegations to meet him. By means of these delegations he sent letters back to the churches. These seven letters or epistles are the only memorial given us of his extensive labors.

John M. Drescher was editor of the *Gospel Herald* for many years, the organ of the Mennonite Church. He was moderator of the Mennonite General Conference, 1969-71. He received the AB from Eastern Mennonite College, and the BD from Goshen Biblical Seminary. He was a pastor at Rittman, Ohio, for eight years. He is the author of numerous books, including *Meditations for the Newly Married* and *Heartbeats*. He now resides at Harrisonburg, Va., where he is coordinator for campus church at Eastern Mennonite College.

Of these seven epistles five are addressed to the Christians at Ephesus, Magnesia, Tralles, Philadelphia, and Smyrna. One letter was addressed to Polycarp of Smyrna. A letter some consider his most important was written to the Christian community at Rome. In all of his letters he refers to himself by the additional name of Theophorus, which means God-borne or God-bearer.

Polycarp alludes to Ignatius in his epistle to the Philippians. Irenaeus quotes a passage from his letter to the Romans. Origen twice refers to him, both times quoting him and naming him.

Some scholars rate the writings of Ignatius among the most interesting and important of all the early church fathers. No other writings of the early church fathers have had more discussion than these which came from a leader of the community where believers were first called Christians.

His Theology and Major Contribution

The writings of Ignatius are of particular importance because this period of church life left few preserved documents. Without these we have few landmarks to help us understand the church at that time, its doctrine, discipline, and its organization.

C. T. Cruttwell writes in *A Literary History of Early Christianity:* "The spiritual value of these letters has always been highly esteemed. They form, indeed, no unworthy successors to the epistles of the New Testament. The fervent piety of the man, his transparent singleness of purpose, his unfeigned humility, his enthusiasm for the Lord he served, are indeed common to him with many another Christian writer. But the peculiar intensity of his style, cast in an Oriental mold, lavish with exaggeration, yet totally free from rhetorical artifice or mere word-painting, gives an almost weird power to his words which the more cultivated periods of a Chrysostom or a Basil attain; while the calm strength of his convictions, the loftiness of his ideal, and his firm consciousness that the Divine Spirit is with him, lend a solemn grandeur to his witness for Christ, which is felt increasingly with every fresh perusal" (p. 91).

Ignatius was the first Christian to define and oppose the Docetic position—that Christ's suffering was not real but only a "semblance," so that Christ only seemed to suffer. It denied the reality of Christ's human body. His denunciation of this docetism is similar to the statements of Paul and particularly of John. In fighting this false doctrine Ignatius stresses the passion of Christ as the peak of Christian doctrine. He had a holy horror of heretical teaching and calls heretics the "herbage of the devil."

Both the divinity and humanity of Christ are clear in the Christology of Ignatius. God prepared mankind for salvation in Judaism— which found its fulfillment in Christ. "Christ is of the line of David according to the flesh, and the Son of God by the will and power of God; was really born of a virgin and baptized by John in order to comply with every ordinance." When Ignatius speaks about the divinity of Christ he speaks of Christ's descent from Mary and the Holy Spirit. When he speaks of Christ's humanity he stresses the Davidic descent and his baptism to fulfill all righteousness. He refers to Christ as God more often than any other early Christian writer.

No other early Christian writer is as eloquent on the "imitation of Christ." Ignatius continually dwells on this Pauline concept of his being linked by a divine union, being in Christ and being found in Christ. A favorite theme is to be "inhabited" by Christ.

From his concept of resemblance or imitation of Christ sprang the ardor and enthusiasm for martyrdom so that he might follow Christ perfectly and as he says be "a genuine disciple."

Through these letters we see something of the fight against heretical teaching which was leading to schism. In Philadelphia there was a Judaizing movement. Smyrna was rife with the Docetic heresy. And out of his great concern for unity we see the next major emphasis of Ignatius—that of obedience to church leadership.

Over the years problems as to the genuineness of these letters arose since it was difficult to believe that a hierarchical organization was so well formed by the beginning of the second century. Opponents of episcopacy labored hard to overthrow the authenticity of these epistles while advocates of episcopacy made every effort to defend any passage which suggested their cause.

In these letters is the first clear representation of the threefold ministry—bishop, presbyters, and deacons. Ignatius stresses the supremacy of the bishop in each church and the duty of implicit obedience to him. He speaks of the bishop presiding in the place of God. God's voice is expressed through the bishop. Without the bishop's approval no services are to be held or actions taken. One has the feeling that this strong push for central authority was designed to meet the heresies hitting the church.

Many believe however that there is no clear doctrine of apostolic succession here. The authority of church leaders is not derived from a chain of teaching chairs such as for Irenaeus later, or from a succession of ordinations argued by Augustine, but from the fact that the offices are the earthly antitype of a heavenly pattern. The bishop represents God; the presbyters, the apostles; and the deacons, Christ (Magnesia 6:1). We do get a clear picture of a local congregation, governed by a single bishop, supported by a council of presbyters and assisted by deacons.

We are indebted to Ignatius for a number of expressions of primary importance. The word "Eucharist" used in the sense of holy communion occurs first in his epistle to the Philadelphians. The word "Christianity" is first used by him, not in an external designation of belief, but in its spiritual meaning as a state of heart and life. The expression "Catholic church," meaning universal or the faithful collectively, was first used by Ignatius. He is the only one among the apostolic fathers who refers to the virginal conception.

Over the years the writings of Ignatius have been criticized for what seems to some an exaggerated teaching in the direction of authoritarianism; for a deficiency in regard to the Holy Spirit and the gifts of the Spirit; for his stress on becoming a martyr for Christ and thus to "reach God"; for the comparative neglect of the doctrine of God as Creator and Governor of history; for the absence of reference to sin and the sinner; and the lack of teaching on justification of faith, for "faith" to Ignatius seems to signify primary conviction.

When one sees these writings, however, as communications from one who was headed for martyrdom in the face of threatening heresy and disunity, it is not difficult to understand why Ignatius touched at particular points on that which spoke to the immediate situation and why he could not, in these seven epistles, cover an entire system of theology.

The writings of Ignatius are spiritual, personal, and popular. They reveal a man, and are not in any sense philosophical. They are the expression of a real person sharing his deepest thoughts and concerns in a time of crisis.

Bibliography

Cruttwell, Charles Thomas, *A Literary History of Early Christianity.* Cureton, William, *Corpus Ignatianum.* Cureton, William, *The Ancient Syriac Version of the Epistles of Saint Ignatius.* Dirksen, Aloys, *Elementary Patrology.* Fremantle, Anne (edited by), *A Treasury of Early Christianity.* Goodspeed, Edgar J., *A History of Early Christian Literature.* Grant, Robert M., *The Apostolic Fathers,* Vol. 4. Lightfoot, *The Apostolic Fathers,* Part II. Magill, Frank N., *Masterpieces of Christian Literature in Summary Form.* Quasten, Johannes, *Patrology.* Wesley, John. *The Epistles of the Apostolic Fathers; The Ante-Nicene Fathers,* Vol. I; *Early Church Fathers; Writings of the Apostolic Fathers.*

*"Do not hope to die in bed . . .
but in martyrdom."*

2

Montanus

Howard H. Charles

Montanus was a native of Ardabau, a village on the border between Phrygia and Mysia in Asia Minor. His dates of birth and death are unknown. He was a convert from paganism and may originally have been a priest in the cult of Cybele. His rise as a prophet in the church is dated by some scholars ca. 172, although others would put it about fifteen years earlier. He is believed to have died before 180. Closely associated with him were two women prophetesses, Prisca (Priscilla) and Maximilla. This trio gave rise to the movement known as Montanism which survived in Asia Minor until the sixth century.

At his conversion or subsequently the Spirit "fell" on Montanus. As a result he had periods of ecstasy during which he prophesied. He is said to have regarded such pronouncements as the direct utterance of the Spirit. According to his own analogy he was the lyre and the Spirit was the plectrum. The product was the very word of God. Furthermore, he believed that Jesus' promise of the coming of the Paraclete (Holy Spirit) had been fulfilled in himself. The Paraclete had taken up bodily residence in him. Just as the age of the Father had been followed by that of the Son, so now the age of the Spirit had begun. He and his women associates believed that this period would be very brief. It would shortly be consummated by the second advent. Maximilla said, "After me there will be no more prophecy, but the End."

They believed not only in the imminent end of the age, but also in the millennial kingdom. This was to be set up at or near Pepuza, a Phrygian village which apparently was the headquarters of the movement in the early days. This village (and/or Timion close by) was referred to as the New Jerusalem. Here many of the adherents gathered to await the anticipated descent of the heavenly city.

Montanus and his immediate associates were essentially orthodox. He accepted the fundamentals of the apostolic faith. In certain details, however, especially in the area of conduct, Montanus believed that the apostolic gospel might be corrected or supplemented by new

---

Howard H. Charles is Professor of New Testament in the Associated Mennonite Biblical Seminaries, Elkhart, Ind., and a minister of the Mennonite Church. He received the BA from Goshen College, the BD from Union Theological Seminary (Richmond), the ThM from Princeton Theological Seminary, and the PhD from the University of Edinburgh. He wrote *The Bible and Alcohol* and *God and His People.* In 1980 he was presented with a *Festschrift* entitled *The New Way of Jesus,* Faith and Life Press.

revelations given by the Spirit through him and his prophetesses. Attention was focused on three matters. (1) *Fasting.* By the time of Montanus the church had already adopted set fasts. An increased emphasis was now placed upon fasting. Two additional weeks were added to the annual paschal fast and the period for the two weekly fasts was lengthened by several hours. (2) *Marriage.* The early leaders appear to have rejected marriage. Both Prisca and Maximilla separated from their husbands when they became prophetesses and were given the status of virgins. In later times the opposition to marriage took the form of a ban on second marriages. (3) *Post-baptismal forgiveness of sins.* The church's practice of granting absolution for grave sins committed after baptism was opposed. Forgiveness was not said to be impossible, but it was God's prerogative to grant it and not that of the church officials.

The "New Prophecy," as the movement came to be called by its critics, also tended to underscore *asceticism.* The more rigorous ethic was an attack on what was felt to be a growing laxity on matters of conduct in the church. It was supported by vivid expectations of the imminent coming of Christ. It was accompanied by a tendency to court martyrdom. "Do not hope to die in bed," said Montanus, "nor in abortion, nor in languishing fevers, but in martyrdom, that he who suffered for you may be glorified."

It was once thought that Montanus wished to restore to the church of his day the primitive enthusiasm of the apostolic era. He was seen to be an exponent of the freedom of the Spirit in the face of a growing institutionalization of the church. But Montanus cannot be considered as being anti-institutional. His movement soon became highly organized. It had not only its recognized leaders but also an efficient system for the collection of "offerings" and the dispensing of support to its prophets. His purpose was not to democratize prophecy or ecstasy, but to bring the Word of God to bear more effectively upon the life of the Christian community. Prophecy was the medium for the discharge of that ministry.

In order to understand the Montanist movement several factors should be kept in mind. (1) The Phrygians by long tradition were inclined to ecstasy. Phrygia was the home of the cult of Cybele, whose worship was characterized by wild frenzy. Both the origin and the appeal of the movement may owe something to this local predisposition. (2) The strong eschatological expectations were encouraged by the severe distresses that accompanied the wars of Marcus Aurelius. There was fear that the German tribes to the north would invade the Roman Empire. Various bishops were predicting the imminent end of the age. (3) There was the growing threat of Gnosticism. This heresy not only set aside the traditional eschatological beliefs of the church but also frequently encouraged moral laxity in conduct. (4) Prophets and prophecy were firm elements in the church's memory both of the apostolic era and the more immediate past. Montanus had predecessors who were recognized and honored.

Although Montanus and his female associates believed themselves to stand in the succession of the Christian prophets from the days of the apostles onward, they also differed from these earlier figures. The point at issue was not so much the matter of prophetic utterance as the manner of prophesying. Does a true prophet deliver his message while in an ecstatic trance? The Montanist prophets attempted to justify their form of prophesying by appealing to such passages as Peter's experience on the housetop in Joppa, where the Greek word for ecstasy occurs (Acts 10:10). But their critics clearly had the support of the New Testament behind them. Regardless of the manner in which the Christian prophets received their revelations from the Lord, they spoke them in full command of their rational faculties. The Montanist prophets resembled the dervishes of the desert and of the pagan shrines more closely than the Christian prophets.

The activity of the Montanist trio caused no small stir in the churches of Phrygia and the surrounding areas. Many converts were soon won. As the movement grew the bishops in the Asian churches became alarmed and met repeatedly to consider and finally to condemn it. Various considerations led to this action. The Montanist doctrine of the Spirit was regarded as extravagant. Moreover, the claim to a divine revelation that could correct or supplement the apostolic tradition was regarded as heretical. Furthermore, the movement was divisive in times that called desperately for Christian unity.

In spite of its condemnation by the local church the movement spread into other parts of Asia Minor and beyond. Before the end of the century it had reached Antioch in Syria. Already by 177 it had come to the attention of the church in the west. The Roman church was inclined to a somewhat sympathetic view of the movement until a vigorous opponent of Montanism arrived in Rome and persuaded the bishop to condemn it. In North Africa it won (about 207) its most famous convert in the person of Tertullian, who was attracted by its puritanical spirit. Constantine sought to suppress it. It was not until the sixth century, however, that the movement was finally stamped out in Phrygia by the emperor Justinian.

In the perspective of Christian history the repudiation of Montanism by the church would seem justified. If it had triumphed it probably would have opened the door to the development of Christian doctrine and practice under an irrational "spiritualism" that ultimately might well have severed the church from its historical rootage. It is fortunate also that in condemning Montanism the church did not listen to those voices that wished to repudiate the Johannine writings (Fourth Gospel and Revelation) from which it drew strong support.

Bibliography

For primary sources drawn from ancient anti-Montanist writers see Eusebius *Ecclesiastical History*, V. 16.1-V. 19.4. A convenient collection of utterances by Montanus, Prisca, and Maximilla is given by R. M. Grant, *Second-Century Christianity* (London, 1946), pp. 95 f. For Tertullian's defense of Montanism see his work *Adv. Praxean, The Ante-Nicene Fathers*, Vol. III. A quite full discussion of the movement is found in *A Dictionary of Christian Biography*, ed. by W. Smith & H. Ware (London, 1882), III, 935-945; a shorter treatment is in the *New Schaff Herzog Encyl.* (New York, 1910) VIII, 485-487. One of the best brief accounts is H. Lietzmann, *The Beginnings of the Christian Church*, Vol. II, trans. by B. L. Woolf (London, 1938), chap. 8.

"What has Athens to do with Jerusalem?"

3
Tertullian

Robert D. Sider

Born in Carthage of pagan parents, Tertullian (ca. 160-220/30) was the first in a distinguished line of Africans to force pagan culture into the service of Christian literature. Indeed, it is almost exclusively as a writer that Tertullian deserves our attention. He did not, like Cyprian and Augustine, fellow Africans, ever achieve the dignity or power of the episcopal office. Not that he would have offered a purely scholarly disdain to such an elevation; on the contrary, there is good reason to believe that he tried to play a fairly active part in the ecclesiastical movements of his day. He appears to have engaged in a successful campaign for the support of the African clergy against Praxeas, who was peddling unacceptable notions of the Trinity, and when adultery was declared to be a sin the church could forgive, he openly attacked the powers then ruling the church for their leniency. But Tertullian's cold logic and rigorous morality could have won him but few friends, and, finding a formal support for his fiery and intransigent personality in the harsh discipline and prophetic novelties of Montanus, he eventually (ca. 207) broke with the Catholics, and joined the Montanist group. It is not certain that he found there the satisfaction he craved, for we hear later of a group of Tertullianists in Africa, and it has been surmised that their founder was our Tertullian, departed not only from the Catholic but now from the Montanist church as well.[1] Thus, in spite of apparently active and often belligerent efforts to mold the policies of the church, Tertullian failed as an ecclesiastical statesman. Not so as a writer. His brilliant and caustic pen has won general admiration for many centuries.

A child of the second century, Tertullian lived at a time when rhetoric was "queen of the sciences" and oratorical power the end of knowledge. There can be no doubt that Tertullian was educated in the typical rhetorical fashion of his day. With the skills he had thus ac-

---

Robert D. Sider is Professor of Classical Studies in Dickinson College. He received his BA (Honours Classics) and his MA from the University of Saskatchewan, and the BA, MA, and D. Phil. from the University of Oxford. In 1971 the Oxford University Press published his monograph, *Ancient Rhetoric and the Art of Tertullian*.

quired it is almost certain that before his conversion in the last decade of the century he was employed as an advocate[2] in the courts of law. Since he had lived in this way until he was nearly forty,[3] conversion meant for him not merely a new religious creed but a "baptism" of the culture which had become a part of him and which he was unable to reject. Consequently, nothing looms so large in the writings of Tertullian as the dominant and pervasive influence of rhetoric.

Indeed, Tertullian has importance as a theologian only because he brought his rhetorical training to bear on traditional theology. Theologically, Tertullian made no attempt to break new ground. He shows no interest in creating, in the manner of Origen, an absorbing theological synthesis.[4] He repeatedly disavows all attempts to offer fresh theological answers, and here we can accept his word as the literal truth, since many of his major theological ideas are patently lifted almost directly out of the pages of Justin and Irenaeus. Thus Tertullian's claim to distinction lies not in any novel and imaginative grasp of theological issues, but in the rhetorically effective statement of his theological heritage.

Three factors, all of them rhetorical, combine to give to Tertullian's work a genuine theological distinction. There is, first, a brilliant rhetorical style which provided sharp, accurate, and memorable formulae for the traditional theology whose tools of definition had still to be perfected. Second, Tertullian learned from his rhetorical education an effective mode of argument. He knew how to bring to theological argumentation the kind of empirical evidence that would be convincing in a court of law, and especially to treat the Scriptures with the same kind of touch analysis that might be applied to documentary evidence in legal disputes.[5]

In the third place, Tertullian had learned from his rhetorical practice the clever disposition of his material. This brought a fundamentally new approach to the whole problem of theological debate. Irenaeus, it seems, had depended for his persuasive power upon "theological architectonics": a massive structure held together by a central theological theme, around which the individual doctrines of the church could find support. The strength of this method lay in its possibilities for thematic resonance and imagistic reverberations; its weakness, in its inherent inability to force to a self-contained and cogent climax the truth of any one particular doctrine. Irenaeus' weakness was Tertullian's strength. Conscious of the power of rhetorical climax, he devoted one treatise to each of the cardinal Christian doctrines, and forcing the wealth of Christian thought into neatly defined boundaries, brought to a sharp and effective focus the Christian statement of each truth.

Of the theological treatises, a few are, quite justly, of special fame. The treatise *Against Marcion*, Tertullian's longest and most ambitious work, offers for us today not merely an argument for the Christian paradox of the mercy and justice of God, but an unusually rich resource for the study of the Marcionite sect. In his work *On the Prescription* Tertullian sets in sharp relief the argument that gets lost in Irenaeus' more rambling work, that the Scriptures and their interpretation belong to the church alone, while the church is defined by faithfulness to the tradition handed down by a succession of bishops from the time of Christ. It is here, too, that Tertullian forbids wild speculation in philosophy, demanding disdainfully what Athens has to do with Jerusalem. The treatise *On the Flesh of Christ* is marked by another famous antithesis, "I believe because it is absurd," but this treatise has greater importance because it elucidates what eventually became the standard Christological definition. Finally, in *Against Praxeas* Tertullian enunciates what has been called by a recent critic the first truly theological statement of the doctrine of the Trinity in Christian thought.

From these treatises three points of major theological interest arise. There is, first, the question of Tertullian's definition of the church. If the church is to be found only where its tradition has been guarded by an unbroken succession of bishops, do we not have here a very mechanical theory of apostolic succession? It is likely that Tertullian did not really intend to encourage the idea of the special and unbroken grace of the episcopal office. He was arguing rather that the definition of the true faith is not to be determined by irresponsible individual arbitration, but only in continuity with the historic community of the people of God. It is upon the continuity of truth to be found in God's people that he insists in his definition of the church.[6] Second, Tertullian has often been ridiculed as the champion of revelation over reason. In reality reason and revelation are not opposed in Tertullian.[7] The two are, for example, set in a careful and intricate balance in the treatise *On the Resurrection of the Dead*. It may also be pointed out that if the treatise *On the Flesh of Christ* pays an individual tribute to blind faith ("I believe because it is absurd"), it is, nevertheless, this very treatise which is built at every point upon the best methods of rational empirical investigation then known. Finally, Tertullian's treatise *Against Praxeas* must be regarded as more successful in its statement than in its exposition of orthodox Trinitarianism. Tertullian's powerful rhetoric could give splendid verbal shape to the church's paradoxical experience of God; but it failed to bring to that shape those luminous images which might have bestowed clear and expansive meaning upon it. The treatise *Against Praxeas* is distinguished rather by the brilliance of its formulations than by the clarity of its exposition.

In addition to the major theological works Tertullian wrote many other treatises of an apologetic and disciplinary nature. His *Apology* is rhetorically the most skillful exposition and defense of Christianity up to his day, while his disciplinary treatises, often harsh and unlovely, are nevertheless a mine of information about the practices of the early church.

The lasting importance of Tertullian may be suggested by four points. (1) Our picture of the life of the early church is enormously enhanced by the interesting and varied details which appear, often incidentally and therefore with the greater verity, in the pages of Tertullian. (2) There can be no doubt about the solid contribution of Tertullian to the development of Christian theology. Earlier claims, it is true, pressed unduly his work as a theological originator. It appears now that he was not, as was formerly thought, the creator of a Latin theological terminology, and that he was not solely responsible for the Western tendency to view the doctrines of sin and of reward and punishment in legalistic terms. But his gift for the accurate formula, for the skillful appropriation of evidence, for the sense of literary structure which gave to each Christian doctrine an independent and self-sustaining proof, made it possible for him to be, at the appropriate moment in Christian history, an effective force in refining theological thought and methodology. Indeed, as we have seen, even as late as the fifth century the church drew upon the writings of Tertullian for its final precise formulation of the doctrine of the nature of Christ. (3) But it is perhaps even more important that Tertullian's writings exercise upon our own generation, as upon many previous ones, a powerful fascination. We may not go to them for the great illuminations of Augustine, but we do respond to the creative artistic form they give to the convictions and experience of historic Christianity. (4) Finally, if we remember that all of these achievements sprang almost entirely out of Tertullian's devoted use of secular culture, we have a suggestive paradigm for the contemporary church, a witness to the power that can spring from the "baptism" of secular culture—to the fact, ironically enough, that Athens does have very much to do with Jerusalem!

Bibliography

Barnes, Timothy D. *Tertullian: A Historical and Literary Study*. Oxford, Clarendon Press, 1971. This fundamental study sets the work of Tertullian in the context of his times, discusses all the major issues in a century of scholarship, adds an extensive bibliography and creates a fresh, if somewhat romantic, picture of Tertullian. The best introduction to Tertullian available.

Evans, Ernest. *Tertullian's Treatise Against Praxeas*. London: S.P.C.K., 1948.

――――――. *Tertullian's Treatise on the Incarnation*. London: S.P.C.K., 1956. In these commentaries, Evans has done work, readable by the general layman and fundamental for the scholar, on Tertullian's discussion of the doctrines of the Trinity and the nature of Christ.

Greenslade, S L. *Early Latin Theology: Selections from Tertullian, Cyprian, Ambrose and Jerome*. Library of Christian Classics. Philadelphia: Westminster Press, 1956. A brief but excellent evaluation of Tertullian's place in the history of theology is followed by a representative selection of Tertullian's writings, in a good translation.

O'Malley, T. P. *Tertullian and the Bible*. Utrecht: Dekker & Van de Vegt N. V. Nijmegen, 1967. A useful summary of the abundant scholarship on Tertullian's use of the Bible, with some fresh and interesting insights on the subject.

Daniélou, Jean. *The Origins of Latin Christianity*, trans. David Smith and John Austin Baker. Ed. by John Austin Baker. Philadelphia: The Westminster Press 1977. Daniélou devotes a substantial part of this volume to the theology of Tertullian. He argues that Tertullian's theology is shaped by his firm rejection of Judaeo-Christian thought then prevalent in the church. Daniélou also believes that Tertullian did indeed attempt to systematize theological thought and he undertakes to expound the "system."

Footnotes

1. Some scholars believe that Tertullian remained a Catholic throughout his life, but formed a "church within the church," which became independent only after Tertullian's death. Cf., for example, D. Powell, "Tertullianists and Cataphrygians," *Vigiliae Christianae*, 29 (1975) 33-54.

2. The Roman advocate was distinguished from the lawyer in that he was not an expert legal adviser but an orator who pleaded cases for his clients in the courts.

3. We have no clear evidence of Tertullian's age at the time of his conversion. It is only from the manner of his writings that we assume a maturity suggestive of a man approaching forty. Timothy Barnes, *Tertullian: A Historical and Literary Study*, Oxford, 1971, 58-59, has argued for conversion at a much earlier age.

4. But for a different view see the note in the bibliography in Jean Daniélou, *The Origins of Latin Christianity*.

5. Tertullian's historical-empirical approach to Scripture offers some striking similarities to modern biblical exegesis and of itself compels an abiding interest in his work. For his method see my *Ancient Rhetoric and the Art of Tertullian*, pp. 63-73 and 85-100.

6. For this view see S. L. Greenslade, *Early Latin Theology*, Philadelphia, 1956, 28-29. In a highly suggestive study which summarizes the major scholarship on the subject R. Verstagen, "L' Église dans l'oeuvre de Tertullian. Pour une reinterpretation," *Bijdragen*, 35 (1974) 393-410, has argued that Tertullian saw the church as an image of the Trinity and interpreted accordingly the biblical verse "where three are met together, there am I."

7. For a further discussion of the faith-reason problem in Tertullian, see my note "Credo quia absurdum" in *The Classical World* 73 (1980) 417-419.

"He who does not have the church for his mother, cannot have God for his Father."

4
Cyprian

Cornelius J. Dyck

In the New Testament the word *episkopos* was usually not a title but a description of the function of the elder as overseer, guardian, or superintendent as in 1 Peter 2:25, Hebrews 13:17, Acts 20:28, or 1 Timothy 3:2. This included all the work of the ministry in the church. These functions were many and varied, and the equipment for fulfilling them are the *charismata*. By the time of the mid-third century, however, *episkopos* had acquired the now familiar connotation of an administrative unity and function. This historical shift in the meaning of *episkopos* is important because it involves the whole relationship between structure and spirit in the life of the church. In contrast to many Protestants, for example, Roman Catholicism has always affirmed that the Spirit became office (hierarchy), just as the Word became flesh.

Whenever historians consider the rise of the episcopate or the origins of the papacy, and with it the entire question of church order, they focus their attention quickly on Cyprian, the bishop of Carthage in North Africa. During the twelve short years of his life as a Christian, ten of them as bishop, the issues of church discipline and church order were his primary concerns. We have from his pen during this period thirteen treatises and fifty-nine letters, among which *On the Unity of the Church* may well be the most central. It is here that he coined the now classic phrases "Outside the church there is no salvation," and "He who does not have the church for his mother cannot have God for his Father." Protestants tend to read this document as favoring episcopacy, Roman Catholics as favoring papacy.

Cornelius J. Dyck is Professor of Anabaptist & Sixteenth Century Studies in the Associated Seminaries. For many years he was Director of the Institute of Mennonite Studies. He is a Mennonite minister, and author of various books, including *An Introduction to Mennonite History* and *A Legacy of Faith, The Heritage of Menno Simons*. He received the AB from Bethel College, the AM from the University of Wichita, and the BD and PhD from the University of Chicago. He is a member of the Center for Reformation and Free Church Studies, Chicago Theological Seminary.

Life and Martyrdom

We know very little about Cyprian's life before his conversion in 245-246 at the age of forty-seven. A brief biography of him by Pontius, a deacon who lived with him, is too enthusiastic about his many virtues to be fully reliable. We know that his full name was Caecilius Cyprianus, but that he was also known as Thascius. He was raised as a pagan, was well educated in rhetoric, and, until middle age, taught rhetoric, and occasionally practiced law in the courts. He was quite wealthy, but turned most of his property over to the church for the poor at the time of his conversion. His election as bishop after only two years as a Christian came because of his considerable popularity with the people of Carthage, but it also won him the hostility of several older men who had been passed over in the choice. They became an active, and sometimes subversive, opposition to him until his martyrdom ten years later in 258.

Soon after his elevation the savage Decian persecution broke out in 250. At the urging of many friends he went into hiding in order not to leave the church without leadership through an untimely death. He wrote secret letters to the churches urging them to be faithful, but his church opposition made the most of his seeming cowardice and took matters into their own hands in his absence. Believers who had yielded to the demands of the state to burn incense to Caesar were received back into the churches without discipline or reproof. In reply Cyprian wrote his treatise *On the Lapsed* and set about to enforce discipline to preserve the purity of the church. At the same time an even more rigorous group arose in Rome under the leadership of a schismatic bishop, Novatian, who excommunicated the lapsed for life. Was baptism by this "heretical" group valid, people asked? Cyprian said no, and proceeded with the writing of *On the Unity of the Church* in defense of his position.

When the Valerian persecution broke out in August 257, he decided not to go into hiding a second time. He was immediately arrested and exiled to Curubia on the coast. A year later a second edict ordered that bishops should be put to death. Cyprian was returned to Carthage and sentenced to death by beheading as a "traitor," an "enemy of the gods and of the laws of the Roman state," and as the "actual initiator of crimes into which others are also misled." This was on September 14, 258, and, according to the record, "under the emperors Valerian and Gallienus, but in the reign of our Lord Jesus Christ."

Of the Unity of the Church

For Cyprian the centrality of the office of the bishop originated in Christ's charge to Peter (Mt. 16:18). The church is founded upon Peter, who received "the keys." The apostle Peter first received this grant alone, but after His resurrection Christ gave like power to all apostles. The unifying source was, however, to be in Peter. Peter, according to Cyprian, was not thereby authorized to dominate over the other "bishops" but symbolized their unity by being "first among equals." Each prelate was to act by his own free will after consulting with other bishops and the laity. Unity and independence must both be preserved. He considered Rome to be a sister, not a mother, to the other churches in the empire. The universality of the church lay for him in the particular concreteness of each region and even each congregation. Yet he was far from being a forerunner of congregationalism.

The church was for Cyprian both a social and a spiritual reality. The bishop leads by example, through preaching and teaching and discipline. There can be no church without bishops. Most problems in the church arise from disobedience to the bishop, whose reliability is affirmed by his apostolic succession. "So the office of the episcopate and the system of the church has been handed down, so that the church is founded on the bishops and every act of the church is directed by these ..." (Ep. 33:1). The authority of the office is safeguarded by Cyprian through a strong sacramentalism, even to the point where the bishop can forgive sin (Ep. 73:16). There is a sharp separation between clergy and laity.

It is not difficult to see how Cyprian was led to this position. From the beginning there had been offices in the church. The apostles had appointed officials or confirmed their election (Acts 6:1-6), had trained ministers (1 Tim. 1:2), and regulated church life. These soon increased in number, and with the growth of the church came a redefining of their functions. Yet during this early time bishop and presbyter meant one and the same thing and each local congregation had a number of men who were so designated (Titus 1:5, 7; 1 Tim. 3:1; 4:14). The *Didache* (mid-second-century document) speaks of only two classes of officers who were elected by the congregation at that time, bishops and deacons (cf. Phil. 1:1). The work of these bishops was originally the oversight of the congregation, while the prophets or *pneumatics* carried on the teaching ministry. However, because it was the duty of the bishops not only to preserve order but also sound doctrine (Acts 20:28-31), and because they were obliged to take the place of a prophet in his absence, the bishops-presbyters gradually began to assume responsibility for teaching also, and in time became the exclusive authorities for both faith and conduct. This became particularly crucial in times of persecution or the threat of heresy. Thus Cyprian wrote, "It is the duty of those placed over the believers to instruct them, that those who ought to be shepherds of the sheep may not become their butchers" (Ep. 9:2). With the increased burden of responsibility in trying times came increased prestige and authority.

In his emphasis on hierarchy Cyprian followed both Ignatius (d. 117) and Irenaeus (d. 202), but his chief mentor was Tertullian (d. 220/30). Tertullian's legalistic thought patterns led to a very juridical interpretation of the church, but it was softened by a strong reliance on the power of the Holy Spirit. As a lay Christian Tertullian also placed less emphasis upon sacramental unity. Cyprian went beyond this emphasis to a sacral, juridical, and political definition of the nature of the church. In many ways Augustine's later doctrine of the church, which was the theological equivalent of Constantinianism, was simply an elaboration of these early Cyprianic motifs.

Modern Free Church imagery prefers to liken the church to a

lighthouse in a dark world rather than to an ark of Noah, outside of which no one can be saved (*On the Unity*, 6). It prefers to describe the church as the covenanting people of God rather than as a ship with the bishop as pilot (Ep. 59:6). It rejects vigorously the imagery Cyprian used most of all, the church as the mother who joins together all the children of God into one great, happy family (*On the Unity*, 23). But Cyprian, the venerable martyr, is also a part of the history of the Free Churches. His emphasis upon purity and discipline in the church, his concern for regional independence, his resistance to the demands of the state even to the point of martyrdom, identify him as part of that history. Perhaps even his emphasis upon the church as an ark, as a ship with the bishop as pilot, and as the loving mother of the faithful has meanings which may be significant for the Free Church in the twentieth century.

For Further Reading

For his complete works see *The Ante-Nicene Fathers*, Volume V. Some of his writings, together with a fresh introduction, are found in S. L. Greenslade, *Early Latin Theology*, Vol. 5, of the Library of Christian Classics. Philadelphia: Westminster Press, 1956. A scholarly treatment by a Roman Catholic may be found in Johannes Quasten, *Patrology*, Volume II, Westminster, Md., The Newman Press, 1958. A most readable, brief chapter on Cyprian may be found in Erik Routley, *The Wisdom of the Fathers*, Philadelphia: The Westminster Press, 1957.

> "I cannot myself believe it possible for anyone to be saved who never works for the salvation of his neighbor."

5

John Chrysostom

Erland Waltner

John Chrysostom (ca. AD 345-407), the greatly loved "golden-mouthed" preacher of Antioch, who later became the patriarch of Constantinople, was born at Antioch in Syria around 345. He was the son of an army officer, who died soon after the child's birth, and Anthusa, a Christian woman of deep piety and considerable courage. He was baptized at the age of eighteen, and three years later was made a "reader" in the church of Antioch. He studied rhetoric, law, and literature under the great pagan orator Libanius in Antioch, and theology under Diodore of Tarsus, leader of the Antiochene School of biblical interpretation.

Though he early felt a strong call to monastic life, he postponed becoming a monk because of the appeal and need of his widowed mother. Later he entered a rigorous hermit life under the Pachomian Rule from 374 to 380, enduring austerities which affected his health adversely.

On his return to Antioch he was ordained by the Bishop Flavian, first as a deacon in 381, and then as a priest in 386, with special responsibilities for preaching. Between 386 and 398, he devoted himself diligently to the systematic exposition of the Bible. He has left homilies on Genesis, Psalms, Matthew, John, Acts, and all of the other New Testament writings except Mark, Luke, the General Epistles, and Revelation.

In 398 he was called to become the patriarch of Constantinople, a position he had not coveted but accepted dutifully. Conscientiously, though perhaps not altogether tactfully, he began to seek the reformation of both church and community in Constantinople. His own dedication to simple living was seen to be in sharp contrast to what

---

Erland Waltner was for many years President of Mennonite Biblical Seminary. He is author of the book *Learning to Understand the Mission of the Church*. He is also a Mennonite minister, and has served as President of his denomination. He received the AB from Bethel College, the STB from the Biblical Seminary in New York, and the ThM and ThD from Eastern Baptist Theological Seminary. For an entire decade he was President of Mennonite World Conference.

had prevailed in the palace of the patriarch in earlier days. He sought to bring about change in the lives of the clergy as well as of the laity. His deep concern was to lead his hearers forward into holy Christian living. He yearned that daily in his word and deed the life of Christ might be reproduced in the people. His preaching began to offend many citizens, including the Empress Eudoxia. A rival patriarch, Theopholis of Alexandria, hated him and looked for an opportunity to destroy him. In 401 Theopholis held a synod "at the Oak" near Constantinople, bringing many charges against Chrysostom, including "treason" because he had used "words offensive to the empress." The assembled bishops declared Chrysostom guilty on sixty-four items and deposed him from his position. The people of Constantinople, however, considered this an outrage and when an earthquake frightened the superstitious Empress Eudoxia, she rescinded the sentence against him.

Soon, however, there was trouble again and in 402 Chrysostom was banished from the city by Emperor Arcadius. He went into exile in Armenia. Except for the loneliness and the rigorous climate, his condition was tolerable, but by 407 his enemies insisted that he must be moved to Pithyus on the Black Sea. Without due regard for his age and ailing health, he was forced to march on foot. Exposed to heat and rain and without adequate rest on the way, he became exhausted and died with the words, "Glory be to God for everything. Amen."

The greatness of Chrysostom is hardly to be found in his theology but rather in his preaching, not in his churchmanship but in his pastoral sensitivities and relationships. He is remembered as a preacher of great eloquence, insight, and power. He has been called the greatest of Christian expositors. H. von Campenhausen has said, "As a theological thinker, Chrysostom was neither deep nor original. He was a typical representative of his school, his church, and of its ecclesiastical and spiritual ideals." But of his sermons he says, "The homilies of Chrysostom are perhaps the only sermons out of the whole legacy of the ancient Greek church which can still be read as Christian sermons today. They reflect something of the true life of the New Testament, just because they are so moral, so simple, and so sober."[1]

One of the dimensions of his strength certainly was his ability to use words effectively in public address. Having been trained in rhetoric and being gifted in the use of words, he attracted large crowds, in part, because people loved to hear him speak. In a day when rhetoric and oratory were valued highly, John Chrysostom stood well above his contemporaries. While he was apparently well prepared when he came to the pulpit, he was also able to respond dynamically to the mood of his audience. He engaged in a kind of dialogue with them, causing them to sense that they were personally addressed. Often crowds would applaud his sermons, a practice which Chrysostom tried to stop.

Another dimension of his greatness, however, was his dedication to biblical preaching and his skill as an exegete. Over six hundred of his homilies have been preserved. Ninety of these, for example, are based on the Gospel of Matthew. His exegetical pattern is to work through each book systematically. H. B. Riddle, in an introductory essay on St. Chrysostom as an exegete, notes both his strengths and weaknesses. Chrysostom did not know Hebrew and so his exegesis of the Old Testament is faulty in many points. Likewise, issues of textual criticism and of historical background are inadequately handled. But Riddle notes, "Where the exegesis deals with the human heart, its motives, its weakness, or with the grace and love of Jesus Christ, there Chrysostom rises and remains 'the master of Israel.' "[2]

Chrysostom does not define precisely his understanding of the inspiration of the Bible, yet it is evident that he recognized its divine-human character. He observed a progression in the Bible, while holding, however, to the essential unity of Scripture. He saw value in each and every part of the Old and New Testaments. He rejected the position of Valentinus and Marcion who would have eliminated the Old Testament, but he also rejected the view of the Jews who, he says, "hold it in such reverence that they obstinately try to observe it all, contrary to God's will.... The church of God, avoiding both extremes, steers a middle course, and neither lets herself be subjected to its yoke, nor permits man to disparage it...."[3]

In treating eschatological passages, Chrysostom is remarkably free of chiliastic extravagances. In the tradition of the Antiochene School, he generally avoids allegorical interpretations. In dealing with the epistles of the New Testament, he sees each as "a connected whole" and seeks to help his hearers recall the steps by which he has moved from the beginning of the epistle to the particular passage under consideration. Knowledge of the entire Bible and a love for it are everywhere in evidence.

Chrysostom's skill as an exegete, however, is matched by his ability to relate biblical truths to some contemporary situation, giving it immediate practical application. This in turn means that John Chrysostom was also a skilled interpreter of human needs, both individually and corporately. When people flocked to hear him preach, they sensed that it was their highest welfare which was his central concern.

One example of his ability to respond to a civic crisis is to be found in his sermons on the statues. In 387 Emperor Theodosius, needing more money, increased the already burdensome taxes. The citizens of Antioch broke out into open revolt, stormed into the hall of justice, and threw stones at the pictures of the emperor and of his family. Then they attacked and insulted the statues of the emperor, taking down the principal one and dragging it around in the streets. This was a very serious offense and reprisals were certain to come. Chrysostom responded to this by preaching a series of twenty-one sermons, "On the Statues," designed to calm the people, to help them face the critical situation in their city, to stir them to penitence for their rioting, and thus to help restore peace and order again. An almost certain bloody massacre of the city was averted, partly through the deliberate and effective preaching of Chrysostom, and partly through the humble emotional appeals of Bishop Flavian that the city be forgiven its grave offense and be spared. In these sermons, as well as in his expositions of passages in Matthew 5 and Romans 12, for example, it is evident that John Chrysostom was dedicated to "a ministry of reconciliation," though he was not a pacifist in the modern sense.

Another significant dimension of the writings of John Chrysostom is his contribution to the concept of the priesthood. He devoted considerable attention to the significance of the priesthood, and to the duties, the temptations, the problems, and the responsibilities of priests in the total life and work of the church. At the center of his concern is his emphasis on loving pastoral relationships. While it may seem strange to the modern reader to note how he pleads that even deception may be practiced as an expression of true love, he anticipates in some ways the contemporary emphasis on the centrality of love in ethics. The real issue in any Christian relationship, he insists, is expressed by Christ who said, "Greater love hath no man than this, that a man lay down his life for his friends." Of this standard, Chrysostom was himself an incarnation. As Stephen Neill observes, the people "knew that the preacher loved them, and cared for them personally. His words were the expression of a deep spiritual and pastoral concern."[4]

Footnotes

1. H. von Campenhausen, *Griechische Kirchenväter* (1956), p. 152.
2. M. B. Riddle, "St. Chrysostom as an Exegete," in Philip Schaff, ed., *Nicene and Post-Nicene Fathers* (1888), Vol. X, p. xxii.
3. Graham Neville, *Saint John Chrysostom, Six Books on the Priesthood* (1964), p. 117.
4. Stephen Neill, *Chrysostom and His Message* (1962), pp. 13-14.

"Thou awakest us to delight in Thy praise; for Thou madest us for Thyself, and our heart is restless until it repose in Thee."

6
Augustine

Linden M. Wenger

Augustine, bishop of Hippo (354-430), was born in Tagaste, North Africa. His father was a pagan, his mother, Monica, was apparently a devout Christian, deeply concerned for the welfare of her son.

The family was not wealthy, but found means to educate the young Augustine who early showed himself to be possessed of a brilliant mind. First at the local schools of Madaura, then at Carthage, and finally at Rome, he absorbed the learning of his day and became a teacher of rhetoric.

Augustine early became obsessed with a sense of his own sin and an overwhelming desire to arrive at some certainty of truth. His search led him first to become a Manichean because Manicheism offered the promise of rational certainty and, second, it provided an explanation of his own sinfulness by saying that all matter (including the human body) is evil. But the conclusions of his head did not quiet the restlessness of his heart. In Rome he studied the writings of the Neo-Platonists, and attempted in their philosophy to find the answers he so greatly desired. In Neo-Platonism he found the notion of deity as a creative force or energy, and the concept that if the world, including man, is the product of divine creativity, then nothing can be really evil, only incomplete or deficient. By this time he had once more come under Christian influence through Ambrose, bishop of Milan, but strangely, the allegorical method of biblical hermeneutics learned from Ambrose seemed to allow him to square Neo-Platonic concepts with Scripture.

Still, his sense of sin remained. Being driven almost to desperation, he was one day meditating and weeping in the garden of a friend

---

Linden M. Wenger has served as Assistant to the President and Assistant Professor of Philosophy, Eastern Mennonite College. He is a bishop in the Northern District of the Virginia Mennonite Conference. He received the AB and ThB from Eastern Mennonite College, and the BD and MTh from Union Theological Seminary (Richmond). He also participated in the 1966 Land of the Bible Workshop, New York University. He was for many years on the faculty of Eastern Mennonite Seminary.

in Milan when he heard a child's voice repeatedly saying, "Take up and read." He hurriedly turned to the Scriptures and read the first passage on which his eyes fell, Romans 13:13, 14. Augustine took the passage for himself, believed, and immediately received the peace and assurance he had so long sought, an assurance that remained with him for the rest of his life. The year was 386 and Augustine had reached the age of 32. He was baptized on Easter eve, 387.

The remainder of his life (44 years) was spent in the service of the church. Two years after his conversion he returned to Africa, intending to live a life of quiet reflection and study; but very soon (391) on the occasion of a visit to Hippo he was prevailed upon by the aging bishop and the urging of the people to take up the duties of the priesthood. In 395 Augustine was made bishop of Hippo, and gave the remainder of his life to the duties of church administration, and to the articulation and defense of Christian doctrine against all the assaults of heresy which threatened his day—against Manicheism which he once embraced, and against Donatism, Pelagianism, and Arianism. When he died in 430 the old Roman Empire was breaking up, and the Vandals were even then laying siege to the city of Hippo.

Augustine was a versatile and prolific writer. His works reflect his expanding and maturing thought, so that between his early and late writings there are certain incongruities, even contradictions. Some items he seems to hold in suspense, and some are simply unresolved. In his later life he wrote an extensive volume of *Retractions* in which he attempted to correct what seemed to him to be mistakes in his earlier writings. It must be observed that Augustine perhaps never entirely shed off the influence of his earlier affinity for Manicheism and Neo-Platonism. There were two anchor points, however, which served to delimit the scope within which Augustine operated; one was the immediacy of his own personal Christian experience, the other, his concept of the sovereignty of God and the authority of His Word.

It can be said that Augustine fashioned the first philosophical exposition of Christianity, and that he did more than any man outside the New Testament to shape the course of Christian theology for all time. But scholars have been far from agreement in their attempts to interpret his writings and to determine the central thrust of his philosophical and theological formulations. Most scholars agree that his emphasis on the sovereignty of God, and on the nature of man and of salvation, make him unquestionably the ultimate father of Calvinism and of the whole Reformed theology. Others have said that the primacy of his principle of inwardness has made him the precursor of present-day existential philosophy and its companion, Neo-Orthodox theology. Besides these a host of other writers have sought to find in Augustine the validation of the several concepts which they set forth.

The wonder of personal Christian experience is reflected in Augustine's *Confessions*, in which he captures both the natural depravity and the hopelessness of man, as well as the sweetness and confidence of a personal relationship with Christ. His preoccupation with describing his own personal acts of sin would seem almost morbid to us; but he was keenly aware of what so many religious writers of our time have forgotten—man's proneness to evil and his absolute dependence upon the work of God for redemption. No other writer has so successfully attempted to articulate the praise of God in human language.

Augustine's writings concerning the nature of God are among his most profound. God is immutable, eternal, creative, true, and good. His concern to establish the absolute sovereignty of God led him into several conflicts which he never completely resolved. One was the question of freedom and determinism. If God is completely sovereign, then man cannot be truly free nor can he really frustrate God's purposes. Augustine concluded for predestination. Some men are elected to salvation, while others are left to damnation. Still he felt that God must be vindicated and man somehow shown to be responsible. Of this dilemma Augustine gives no satisfactory resolution.

On the question of the relation of faith and reason Augustine is at his best. He comes out clearly in his defense of revelation and the absolute dependability of the Word of Scripture. The same is true of his confidence in the work of Christ as God's provision for man's salvation through faith. As a means to knowledge, faith is superior to reason. Augustine's conclusion was, "I believe in order that I may know."

Apparently the concept of creation by fiat was a difficult one for Augustine. Where the older philosophers had struggled with the problem of appearance and reality, Augustine from his Christian perspective puzzled over the relation of the Creator and the created. His hermeneutical use of the Book of Genesis may not satisfy us, but his confidence in it led him to the conclusion that creation is a mystery which the human mind cannot fathom but must receive on faith.

Augustine's concept of the nature of the church and his philosophy of history are elaborated in his monumental *City of God*. He sees history as linear and purposeful; yet perhaps more tightly bound by a divine determinism than we would wish to describe it.

The church unquestionably was God's institution on earth. The state was something of a necessary accommodation to the sinful condition of man but was clearly inferior to the church and subservient to its purposes. Augustine was again somewhat torn by his warm personal experience of salvation, with its mystical relation to the divine, and the necessary demands of an institutionalized church which could fulfill the functions envisioned in the *City of God*. Yielding to the demands of institutionalism he concluded that the only hope, the only way of salvation, lay in the sacraments administered by the regularly ordained priests of the church. Augustine himself never subscribed to the unique authority of the bishop of Rome. He did not believe that any one man was infallible; but he did accept the finality of the decisions of a group, such as a council made up of duly elected bishops, through whom the Spirit of God worked. In keeping with his concept of the church he did not hesitate to call upon the secular government to aid and promote the purposes of the church. The *City of God* definitely laid the foundation upon which the Catholic hierarchy later was built, and provided the apology by which the Holy Roman Empire attempted the spiritual and secular dominion of mankind.

In the area of ethics Augustine was a stern opponent of sin, emphasizing what man ought not to do, and stressing love for God as the basic motive of the good life. For him any good that man enjoyed was a gracious gift from God. He may not have adequately come to grips with the social problems of his day, perhaps because he looked upon life from a too deterministic point of view and considered the sufferings of man a purposive attempt on the part of God to make man aware of his miserable and hopeless condition. The most constructive point of Augustine's ethics was his emphasis on the importance of Christian love as one's motive.

For Augustine the life of man was primarily a life of misery and the divine purpose of that misery was to prepare man for the gift of God in Christ. For the Christian who had received that gift there was unspeakable joy in loving God truly. To love God for his own sake, and his neighbor for God's sake—this was the fulfillment and end of all Scripture. In Augustine we meet a sinner saved by grace, a man so richly endowed of God, and so devoted to His cause, that he became the most influential churchman between the Apostle Paul and Luther.

Bibliography

Selected Writings of Augustine: *The Confessions; The City of God; On Christian Doctrine* (4 books); *Retractions;* many treatises against pagan philosophies and Christian heresies.

About Augustine: Portalie, Translated by R. J. Bastian, *A Guide to the Thought of Saint Augustine;* M. C. D'Arcy, *A Monument to St. Augustine;* Henri Marrou, *St. Augustine and His Influence;* S. J. Grabowski, *The Church: An Introduction to the Writings of St. Augustine.*

> "*[The Bible] is, as it were, a kind of river, if I may so liken it, which is both shallow and deep, wherein both the lamb may find a footing and the elephant float at large.*"

7

Gregory the Great

Gerald C. Studer

Gregory was born in Rome of the aristocratic family Anicia about AD 540. Nothing is known of his early education but his marked ability, and his patrician birth, obtained for him the position of magistrate of Rome at the age of 30. His mother was Silvia, who is commemorated in Roman Catholicism as a saint on November 3. Perhaps not more than a year after entering his civil office, he resigned in order to enter upon a religious life. He devoted the family fortune which he inherited to the founding of monasteries. He established six monasteries in Sicily and one in Rome and in this, the famous monastery of St. Andrew, became a monk. He was especially interested in missionary activity and would certainly have pursued this calling had not Pope Benedict I forbidden his leaving Rome.

Pope Pelagius II succeeded Pope Benedict I in 578 and ordered Gregory to leave the monastic life, and ordained him as a deacon in Rome, and commissioned him in 579 as resident ambassador at the imperial court in Constantinople. Seven years later Gregory was made abbot (head) of his monastery at Rome. While functioning in this capacity, he achieved a great reputation with the general public, completed his exposition of Job, and delivered lectures on the five books of Moses, Joshua, Judges, Kings, the Prophets, Proverbs, and the Song of Songs.

The incident concerning Gregory recorded by the English monk/historian, the Venerable Bede, occurred during these years of his service in Rome. Passing one day through the Forum, Gregory saw some handsome slaves offered for sale and asked what nation they

---

Gerald C. Studer is pastor of the Plains Mennonite Church, Lansdale, Pa., and author of the definitive biography, *Christopher Dock, Colonial Schoolmaster*. He received the BA from Goshen College, and the ThB and BD from Goshen Biblical Seminary. He has made a huge collection of Bibles from many lands and in various languages. These Bibles may be seen at the Associated Mennonite Biblical Seminaries.

were from. "Angles," was the reply. "Good," said the abbot, "they have the faces of angels, and should be coheirs with the angels of heaven. From what province do they come?" "From Deira," was the reply. "Deira. Yes, verily, they shall be saved from God's *ira* [wrath] and called to the mercy of Christ. How is the king of that country named?" "Aella," Gregory was told. "Then must Alleluia be sung in Aella's land."

Gregory determined personally to undertake the conversion of Britain and with the pope's consent actually set out upon the mission, but he was overtaken by messengers after only three day's journey and commanded to return to Rome. It has been said that in this way the populace of Rome blocked his path when he desired to go to Britain—so great was his popularity among them.

In 590 Pope Pelagius II died of the plague and the clergy and the people unanimously chose Gregory as his successor despite his strenuous effort to refuse the papal crown. Gregory was bodily carried by the citizens to the Basilica of St. Peter's and there consecrated pope, in which office he served until 604. He served with such distinction that he came to be called "the Great," "Father of the Medieval Church," "Father of Europe," and "Consul of God." The title he assigned to himself and one still used by his successors to the papal throne was "servant of God's servants."

Gregory's reign as pope was characterized by his clear-sightedness, his realism, his cool assessment of any situation facing him, and his ability to adjust himself to facts which were beyond his capacity to change. He immediately set about righting abuses. He made the papal states the source of seemingly unlimited charities in his effort to alleviate the sufferings caused by the ravaging Lombards, a northern European Teutonic tribe that invaded Italy in 568. He ousted the court loafers and chose efficient clerics for his administrative body. He boldly resisted the imperial demands of Constantinople, and openly fought against the Lombards to protect his people and their properties.

As pope, Gregory I surrounded himself with priests and monks with whom he lived as though he were still in a monastery. In spite of constant ill health, he ministered unceasingly to the physical and spiritual needs of his people. One has said that his principal fault as a man of business was that he was too lavish with his revenues.

Gregory had learned during his official residence in Constantinople how firmly entrenched was the imperial ideology which considered the emperor to be divinity on earth. Although Gregory bowed to the unalterable facts in the East and never provoked the wrath of the Eastern Emperor, he believed deeply that the papacy should have political primacy as well as spiritual. Western Europe was not subject to imperial rule and this coupled with Gregory's missionary passion prompted him to relentlessly strive to extend the gospel and his papal rule by the "Romanization" of Western Europe. This Gregorian policy of bifurcation—one kind of policy toward Constantinople, another toward the West—bore fruit. It was from the farthest corner of Europe, the British Isles, that the impetus for the conversion of the north of Europe came in the establishment of Irish and Anglo-Saxon missions. The ties between England and the Roman

Church were well forged. Next to this historic reconversion of the English, Gregory's missions to the Lombards are equally noteworthy. They too were converted, although they were the military conquerors of Italy and the enemies of the Roman Empire. Through Gregory's scattered and extensive efforts in both the political and the spiritual spheres, for the first time in history the pope appeared as a political power.

In his spiritual and ecclesiastical rulership, he wisely tolerated local deviations from Roman usage, but he took pains to enforce the celibacy of the clergy, the trials of clergymen only in ecclesiastical courts, the removal of clergymen who lapsed into scandalous offenses, and the division of the revenues of each church into equal parts to be assigned to the bishop, the clergy, the poor, and the repair of the church building. Clearly realizing the value of liturgy as an external means to bind people together, he was greatly instrumental in reforming and refining liturgical practices. The exact details and extent of his influence in connection with the liturgy and church music (Gregorian chant is named after this Gregory) is a matter of doubtful tradition.

Gregory was a strong supporter of monasticism and he tried to enforce a strict observance of the Rule of St. Benedict. He forbade monks to minister in parish churches, specifying that any monk who was promoted to such an ecclesiastical responsibility should lose all rights in his monastery and should no longer reside there. He acted with leniency toward the Jews, protecting them from persecution, and securing for them the enjoyment of their legal privileges. He repeatedly attacked the "simoniacal heresy," that is, the crime of buying or selling ecclesiastical privilege, as well as the practice prevalent in Gaul (present-day France) of promoting laymen to bishoprics.

Gregory has been described as the last of the great Latin Fathers and the first representative of medieval Catholicism. Although counted among the doctors of the church, his claim to this position is not overwhelming. Although there is relatively little originality in his numerous writings, they were superbly attuned to the contemporary intellectual level and they exercised an enormous influence throughout the Middle Ages. The importance of his teaching lies mainly in its simple summarization of the doctrine of Augustine, and in its detailed exposition of contemporary religious conceptions which had not before been defined (for example, the views on angelology and demonology, on purgatory, on the Eucharist, and on the efficacy of relics). Until Anselm (1033-1109) no teacher of equal eminence arose in the church.

Gregory died on March 12, 604, and was buried in the portico of the Basilica of St. Peter. His remains were disinterred and reburied in the 9th, 15th and 17th centuries and now rest beneath the altar of the chapel of Clement VIII (pope 1592-1605).

In closing, hear several noteworthy statements from the writings of Pope Gregory: "The pastors are to be fervidly zealous about the inner wants of their subjects, without neglecting the care of their outer wants." "The priest must preach the law of the gospel; but for that preaching to be effective, the most persuasive argument, is to see the actual practice of the law in him who preaches it."

Bibliography

The best source of information about Gregory is of course his own writings, especially the 850 letters which have been preserved. See also the two-volume work of F. H. Dudden, *Gregory the Great*; also the biography by P. Battifol (French, 1928; English, 1929). See also the *Nicene and Post-Nicene Fathers*, Second Series, Vol. XIII.

> "To quote the Apostle, all is conflict without and anxiety within; but in my case, there are also conflicts within and anxiety without."[1]

8

Boniface
(Winfrith of Crediton)

S. F. Pannabecker

Commonly referred to as Saint Boniface (ca. 680-754), he was originally named Winfrith (Winfrid) and born in England. Ordained at the age of thirty, he undertook his first missionary trip to Frisia under Willibrord in 718 and thereafter until death was devoted to the expansion and building up of the church, becoming, as Latourette says, "one of the most remarkable missionaries in the entire history of the expansion of Christianity."[2] His service was mainly among the Germanic tribes.

At the time of Boniface in the eighth century the church-state relations and the religious-cultural relations of all parties were in a flux. The contribution of Boniface as a missionary administrator and as a missionary theologian was in the area of stabilizing and organizing, as well as expanding, a growing church which but superficially formed was also disrupted and disunified. That in his lifetime he was able to forge a type of organization which was accepted and became the basis of further development is the warrant for the statement that he was the "shaper of the mighty German West."[3]

Of the man himself there are many interesting features. He was deeply religious from youth, loved to hear stories of the saints, and received a biblical and classical education in monastery schools at Exeter and later at Nursling. Boniface was offered ecclesiastical posts of importance but rejected them all in favor of his life work of evangelism and organization.

His violent death epitomized much of his life. After thirty years of strenuous effort he returned to the field of his first love, Frisia, hoping

---

S. F. Pannabecker (1896-1977) served many years as missionary to China. He received the AB from Bluffton College, the AM from Witmarsum Theological Seminary, was a student in the College of Chinese Studies, Peking, received the BD at Garrett Biblical Institute, and the PhD from Yale University. Bethel College conferred on him the DD. He served as President Emeritus & Professor of Missions in Mennonite Biblical Seminary. His history of the Central District Conference of Mennonites is entitled *Faith in Ferment*, and that of the General Conference Mennonite Church, *Open Doors*.

for a few more years of evangelistic effort rather than quiet retirement. Here beside a stream, awaiting the arrival of a group of neophytes coming for baptism, his party was suddenly set upon by a crowd of angry pagans. Some resorted to arms to protect themselves against the enemy. These he rebuked:

> Sons, cease fighting. Lay down your arms, for we are told in Scripture not to render evil for evil but to overcome evil by good.[4]

He urged them to take comfort in the Lord and fear not them who kill the body, for the Lord will reward with eternal bliss and abode in heaven above. Thus he encouraged them as the mob attacked and left some thirty bloody bodies on the field.

Withal, Boniface was yet a man of his age. God and Christ were living, powerful, beneficent, at hand to help in all things. Miracles were expected and often accompanied symbols of the faith. The cross was efficacious and relics were used against the hosts of spirits and devils. His little bag of relics accompanied Boniface on all his travels. The saints also were vivid in mind, and prayer to them could bring assistance.

Thinking of Boniface as a theologian one must recognize first of all that he was not interested in theology from any speculative point of view. He was not bothered with any systematic organization of his belief. He was concerned about practical questions and on these he took positions which did have theological implications.

The Unity of the Church

Apart from the heathen idol-worshiping tribes, there were partly Christianized groups and many once-Christians who had practically reverted to heathenism. Irish missionaries had been working among these, especially in the Frankish lands, since the sixth century. The best known was Colomban who preached and founded monasteries. Bishops were appointed but belonged to no particular diocese and wandered indiscriminantly. The situation was somewhat similar to that of England before the arrival of Roman missionaries under Augustine. There the situation had been cleared by adopting the Roman diocesan pattern. To Boniface this was the answer to the problem which he faced on the continent. Unity was therefore found in the unity of one church under the pope at Rome.

In his oath of allegiance to the pope when consecrated in 722, Boniface stresses this unity of the church:

> I will uphold the faith and purity of holy Catholic teaching and will persevere in the unity of the same faith.... I will not agree to anything which is opposed to the unity of the Universal Church....[5]

Catholic standards thus became for him the unifying factor in a disordered church and in the churches yet to be founded. The pope similarly was the true center of organization and the judge in questions of practice. To Boniface this was the obvious and true answer to church unity, for the pope wore the sacred cloak of St. Peter.

The Nature of the Church

Conversion of the tribes was not a purely religious operation. Cultural and political motives were involved and conversions were often *en masse* even when not forced. Mass conversion did little to reform the thinking and living of those involved, and even when trained in Christian ways many reverted in life to the old heathen customs and remained Christian in name only. In Hesse and Thuringia Boniface found Christians, either secretly or openly, offering sacrifices to old nature deities, revering trees, stones, or springs, or practicing divination and magic. Bible texts were used as amulets and some converts assumed that meat offered to idols could be purified for eating by making the sign of the cross over it. Marriages were irregular and concubinage not uncommon. This was the church with which he had to deal.

If the first step toward purifying the church was unity with the papacy, the second step was support of the prince. The pope's commission of 719 to Boniface was accompanied with commendation to leaders in Thuringia and a special commendation to Charles Martel, Frankish prince and nominal Christian. The letter notes Boniface's assignment to work east of the Rhine and asks Charles to grant "constant protection against any who may stand in his way."[6] This was in accord with the desires of Boniface, for he had found earlier in Thuringia that he could make no progress without the support of civil authority.

With papal authorization and state support Boniface proceeded to his work, which was the reproving and correcting the heathen, baptizing and instructing inquirers, ordaining leaders to office, admonishing and disciplining unworthy priests, and particularly interpreting Christian mores as against heathen practices. Thorny questions were referred to the pope for advice, while the prince assisted with moral and physical support.

Carloman, the religious-minded son of Charles Martel, went further in assistance and proposed a synod for his part of the kingdom. Boniface wrote the pope for authorization and, with his approval, it came to pass in 742. The purpose was the regulation of church affairs. Carloman presided, and the synod came to be held annually. With these steps the association of church and state was well under way. Yet for Boniface it hardly nullified the independence of the church or weakened its spiritual nature. That the German churches would eventually be territorial churches and the Holy Father's authority entangled with that of the emperor he hardly foresaw.

Missionary Methods

Boniface seems to have proceeded in a few simple steps. First, convince people of error and win their consent to conversion; second, baptize them; third, teach, train, and discipline them into a regulated Christian life. His missionary methods might therefore be summarized in four words: evangelize, teach, discipline, organize.

Evangelizing began with preaching the gospel in which the

Scriptures were freely used. Directed first toward the upper class, with their approval, the common people responded more easily. "Conversion" was indicated by the recognition of error and a readiness to turn from the old ways and to accept the new. With this accomplished, baptism was in order and the evangelizing process completed. Baptism usually occurred at stated times and often involved large numbers. Boniface is reported to have brought one hundred thousand into the fold. Cleansed by the holy water of baptism, converts were then ready for training in the Christian life.

Teaching was essential, for the new Christians in name must become Christians indeed. Their old customs must be judged in the light of the gospel and either rejected or transformed. Multitudes of questions ranging over all aspects of life came to attention and Boniface must instruct converts on matters from eating of wild horse meat to marrying the widow of an uncle. Such supervision demanded more than one man, and for this Boniface called in helpers from all available sources, especially his own homeland. To facilitate their work, monasteries were established and became training centers for a growing Christian population. Especially interesting is the number of women whom Boniface attracted to this service and installed as heads of houses for women. The work of these institutions covered not only Christian teaching but work in language and literature and arts, as well as handicrafts and agriculture. They were civilizing, cultural centers.

Discipline had both positive and negative aspects. Positively, it was an extension of the teaching process in which desired traits were in practice inculcated into life. To stimulate right living a vivid sense of rewards and punishments was held forth. The great reward was eternal life and eternal bliss; wealth and success were rewards also and might be more immediately appealing. While it was hardly crassly stated that the favor of God could be earned, yet it was understood that His favor was granted to those who worked aggressively at their tasks. Negatively, discipline was a corrective process in which those in error were punished. Penance was imposed for misconduct and excommunication or anathema in flagrant cases. Church leaders, including bishops and deacons who violated their vows, were judged strictly.

Organization of church areas into dioceses and the appointment of bishops over them was the means whereby uniform standards of faith and conduct could be assured. The priests in each diocese were subject to careful scrutiny and trained in the service of God. With this organization came also the establishing of synods with their annual assembly whereby concerted action and understanding were assured.

In reviewing the life and work of Boniface it becomes apparent that he faced the common problems met in any age by those who would introduce the gospel to non-Christians. What really is the gospel? How is it communicated? What is demanded for a new believer? What in his former faith may be helpful or harmful? What is the relation of rebirth and cultivation? How far can the missionary depend on civil support or protection? When does the church emerge and what form should it take? Who shall direct the process and how?

Boniface had his answers. With some of them we may agree and from others we may learn. Surely his commitment and zeal, his self-sacrifice and loyalty, and his attempt at intelligent analysis we may well emulate.

Suggested References

Cambridge Medieval History, Vol. II, Macmillan, New York, 1913. See index for many references but particularly pp. 536-542, 697-699.

Duckett, Eleanor Shipley, *Anglo-Saxon Saints and Scholars,* Archon Books, Hamden, Conn., 1967. Chapter IV, pp. 339-455 is on Boniface with extended treatment of his life and work.

Latourette, Kenneth Scott, *A History of the Expansion of Christianity,* Vol. II, Harper and Brothers, New York, 1938. See particularly pp. 85-106.

Lortz, Joseph, *Bonifatius und die Grundlegung des Abendlandes,* Franz Steiner Verlag, Wiesbaden, 1954. Interpretation of Boniface's place in the political and religious development of western Europe.

Schieffer, Theodor, *Winfrid-Bonifatius und die Christliche Grundlegung Europas,* Verlag Herder, Freiburg, 1954.

Talbot, C. H., *The Anglo-Saxon Missionaries in Germany,* Sheed and Ward, New York, 1954. Contains the life of Saint Boniface by a contemporary but later priest (pp. 25-62) and correspondence to and by Boniface (pp. 65-149).

Footnotes

1. Talbot, ed., *Anglo-Saxon Missionaries in Germany,* p. 116.
2. Latourette, *History of the Expansion of Christianity,* II, p. 86.
3. *Cambridge Medieval History,* II, p. 542.
4. Talbot, *op. cit.,* p. 56 ff.
5. Talbot, *op. cit.,* p. 70.
6. Talbot, *op. cit.,* p. 74.

> "Solitude is the mother of
> prayer, as prayer is the
> manifestation of divine glory."

9
John of Damascus

Paul Peachey

John of Damascus—monk, preacher, theologian—died and was buried in a monastery near Jerusalem in December 749. The surname "Damascene" refers to his birthplace, Damascus, where his grandfather and father before him held ministerial posts in the government of the caliphs. The family was Christian, and due to the high position held by his father, John received both a Greek and an Arab education. Characteristically, the name "John" represents his Christian career rather than the actual family name. The date of his birth is unknown, possibly as early as 674.

John of Damascus flourished during that remarkable century, the beginning of which can be marked by the death of Muhammad in 632, and the defeat of the Arab forces near Tours in France in 732. During that century, the faith of Islam had swept from Western Asia across North Africa and on across the Mediterranean into Spain, reaching its crest at Tours. Wars within and between the Persian and Roman empires left many areas exhausted. Already the Arab peoples were on the move, and the spread of Islam increased their dynamism. But the hard walls which later separated Christians and Muslims were not yet fully in place. Scenes shifted, and in some times and places Christians continued their life and worship under Arab rule.

In the Western (Roman) church, John became known as the principal witness of Greek theology. His most important work, *Fount* (or *Source*) *of Knowledge*, is sometimes called the first compendium *(Summa)* of Christian theology. The author states that his purpose is to assemble from the decrees of the various church councils (Nicea, Chalcedon, etc.) a résumé of the orthodox faith. He undertook this work at the request of a former fellow monk who became a bishop.

Paul Peachey is a Professor of Sociology in the Catholic University of America. His 1954 doctoral dissertation at the University of Zurich in Switzerland was entitled *Die soziale Herkunft der schweizer Taeufer in der Reformationszeit*, and appeared in book form the same year. He has also written many learned articles, as well as a brief treatise, *Your Church and Your Nation*. He is a Mennonite scholar. He edited the volume *Biblical Realism Confronts the Nation*.

Thus John is a "compiler" or "encyclopedist" rather than a creative theologian. Scholars emphasize, nonetheless, that in the combination which he made there were traces of his own originality. The original version of the *Fount of Knowledge*, however, does not exist today. The present form is the product of revisions.

John of Damascus is clearly Greek in his training and thought. This treatise begins with a long résumé of Greek philosophical thought. This part of the compendium has been called the first philosophical manual devised as an aid to theology. A second major section briefly characterizes one hundred and one heresies. Only in the third major section does he finally set forth his formulation of Christian dogma. The purpose of this arrangement is to contrast truth with falsehood. In this third major part of the work, he deals with God as one and triune, with the human condition, and finally with virtues and vices. Basically the work reflects the great debates of the early councils on the Trinity and the person of Christ.

John, however, produced a considerable body of other writings. There are homilies (sermons), liturgical collections, and hymns. He wrote a great deal on heresies, and addressed himself polemically to Islam. But his role in the iconoclastic controversy was likely the most dramatic part of his career. In the East considerable concern had developed over the dangers of the use of images in Christian worship. This concern was nurtured in part by Jews and Muslims with their sharp repudication of idolatry. Eventually (726) the Emperor Leo (Isaurus), who came to the throne in Constantinople in 717, issued a decree against the use of icons. John boldly denounced this decree, and became in effect the spokesman for the opposition. A struggle ensued which continued well into the next century. At one point, shortly after his death, a council (Constantinople) condemned his writings, but eventually he was vindicated (Nicea II, 787).

The iconoclastic controversy is instructive, remote as it may seem to many modern Christians. Pope Gregory the Great had stated the argument for images succinctly: "What those who can read learn by means of writings, that do the ignorant learn by looking at a picture." John of Damascus, following the same line of reasoning, linked the icons to the incarnation. On the one hand he rejected, as do the Scriptures, the notion that God could be portrayed in any way. On the other hand, he viewed the incarnation as God's way of making His truth vivid to man's feeble grasp. Not all know letters nor possess the leisure to read, John reasons. Thus "it certainly happens frequently that at times when we do not have the Lord's passion in mind we may still see the image of his crucifixion and, being thus reminded of his saving passion, fall down and adore."

The same logic was evident in the use of the "saints." These were elevated as models for particular virtues. But in both instances, the medium of communication became, to so many (and to echo a contemporary slogan) the message itself. It is doubtful that these arguments for images and saints can be upheld. But the modern believer, particularly when he is a child of the radical Reformation or of Puritanism, must recognize where he stands when he judges. For his own position is very much the product of the printing press and of traditions of abstract thought which would have been alien to the unlettered laity a millennium ago. An age as ours so powerfully drawn by images on the screen, for example, should be able to understand the urges of past centuries to make of cathedrals, "Bibles" of stone.

By today's standards, John's scholarship, for all his influence and productivity, leaves something to be desired. This can be illustrated in his writings against Islam, for which he used the term "Ishmaelite." Already the term "Saracen" had come into use, a name of one of the Arab tribes. While the origin of the terms seems a bit uncertain, lexicographers trace it to an Aramaic word for eastern or the rising sun. John, however, links the word "Saracen" through Ishmael to "Sara," wife of Abraham!

John of Damascus, however, may also be esteemed in the more practical respects of faith and piety. He belongs in that company of Christian leaders across the centuries who left lives of wealth or power for the life of Christian witness. He and his family attract attention because they stood as Christians in high government service, eventually under an Arab ruler as earlier under one who represented "Christian" Byzantium. Few details are known, and so conclusions are hard to be drawn. John himself resigned from office and retired to a monastery under a Muslim, Caliph Abdul Melek (685-705), about the year 700. This caliph was becoming increasingly hostile to Christians. Was John's resignation a "flight" from responsibility? Did he run away from "life"? Did he conclude that his career was incompatible with his faith?

Perhaps these questions cannot be answered. But the quotation at the beginning of this sketch illustrates the fact that in any case he was deeply committed to monastic piety, to the cultivation of the life of faith. His theology may be of little more than historic interest. He lived at a time when Christians in great parts of the Mediterranean world were on the defensive. Many were increasingly isolated and surrounded by other forces. These facts were reflected in mounting theological stagnation. John of Damascus (as the writer and reader of today) was a child of his time. What abides and enriches is the testimony of his faith.

Bibliography

"St. John Damascene," *The New Catholic Encyclopedia*, Vol. VII, New York: McGraw Hill, 1967; J. H. Lupton, *St. John of Damascus*, London: SPCK, 1882; R. J. Deferrari, ed., *The Fathers of the Church: St. John of Damascus—Writings*, New York, 1958; *St. John Damascene on Holy Images, Followed by Three Sermons on the Assumption*, tr. by Mary H. Allies, London: Thomas Baker, 1898. See also standard works on church history and history of Christian thought.

"For by doubting we come to inquiry, by inquiry we discover the truth."

10

Peter Abelard

Ed. G. Kaufman

In the history of theology the conflict between Abelard (1079-1142) and Bernard typified the two conflicting viewpoints of the twelfth century: the importance of reason as over against the unquestioning acceptance of dogmatic truths on mere authority. Bernard represented the traditional, ascetic, and dogmatic spirit, while Abelard (or Abailard) stressed the importance of logical thinking and rational investigation of church dogmas, as indicated by the above quotation.[1]

Abelard was born near Nantes. His ancestors were warriors and his father was a feudal lord. As a young man, full of intellectual enthusiasm, he left his patrimony to his younger brothers to devote himself to study. Having no interest in the fighting of feudal lords, he "gave up the lure of Mars to be educated in the lap of Minerva." The father encouraged his son to pursue a scholarly career and at about age fifteen, Abelard left home to pursue higher education. As a wandering scholar he availed himself of the best teachers in different centers. He had a stormy and checkered career.

For a time he studied under Roscellinus, a famous dialectician who leaned toward nominalism and maintained that universals have no reality apart from particulars. From him Abelard learned the fundamentals of logic and the importance of reason. Later he went to Paris where he studied under the formidable philosopher William of Champeaux, a pillar of orthodoxy, who contrary to Roscellinus, held that universals exist independently from any material substance and outside of the mind conceiving them. He was a brilliant and popular teacher and attracted many students. The controversy between nominalists and realists aroused much attention and became the outstanding problem of the twelfth century.[2]

Ed. G. Kaufman (1891-1980) was Emeritus Professor of Philosophy and Religion, and President Emeritus of Bethel College, from which he received his AB degree. He earned his AM at Witmarsum Seminary, the BD at Garrett Theological Seminary, and the PhD at the University of Chicago. Bluffton College conferred on him the LLD, and Bethel College the DD. Among his books are: *The Chinese Student Movement, Mennonite Missionary Interest, Mission of the Mennonite Church, The Story of Bethel College, Kaufman Family Record, Living Creatively,* and *General Conference Pioneers.*

Abelard was neither a nominalist nor a realist; for him, universals were neither things nor names but simply concepts, predicated upon particulars. With youthful arrogance and debating brilliance he disagreed with his master to the great delight of the students and deep chagrin of the teacher. In his twenty-second year Abelard left Paris for a teaching position at Melun, where he attracted a multitude of students. From here he went to Corbeil and then back to Paris, challenging all and sundry to various controversies and by wit and brilliance defeated his opponents.

However, he was restless, and left to study theology, "the queen of the sciences," under the outstanding theologian of his day, Anselm of Laon. Here also he could not agree with the conservative master and after two years, he arrogantly left to resume his teaching. Notre Dame in Paris now offered him the position vacated by his former teacher, now retired, William of Champeaux. From all over Europe students flocked to hear Master Abelard. Here he reached the zenith of his career. He was both admired and persecuted. The scholarly disputes he promoted awakened medieval Europe.

But events soon took a different turn. At this time a young lady of seventeen, Heloise by name, beautiful and brilliant, resided close to Notre Dame with her uncle, Canon Fulbert. He placed her under the tutorship of Abelard. They fell in love with each other and Abelard forgot his duty, his lectures, and his fame. He took her to Brittany, where she was delivered of a son, who died early. Now they were married, and to keep it secret she was placed in the convent of Argenteuil. All this so enraged Fulbert that he hired ruffians who attacked Abelard and emasculated him.[3] The shame of this terrible act was the turning point for Abelard. Now he entered the monastary of St. Denis and Heloise took the veil at Argenteuil. After his grief had somewhat moderated he resumed his teaching.

Continued persecutions obliged him to leave St. Denis. Near Nogent-sur-Seine he built a rude hut in which he planned to live a hermit's life. But even here students flocked to him in such numbers that many could not be fed or housed. His students built him an oratory which he dedicated to the Holy Spirit and named Paraclete. Being subsequently appointed abbot of St. Gildas de Ruys in Brittany, he invited Heloise and her sisterhood, on the dissolution of their monastery at Argenteuil, to reside at the above oratory, where he received them.

In spite of persecution, Abelard and Heloise continued their devotion to, and love for, each other, which they carried on by voluminous correspondence. This, in later years turned to more religious themes, such as hymns, prayers, and topics of salvation. These letters have repeatedly been published in the original and in translations.[4]

Abelard became distinguished as grammarian, orator, logician, poet, musician, mathematician, philosopher, and theologian. Some of his more important works in theology are: *Introduction to Theology; Christian Theology; The Unity of Divine Trinity; Dialectics; Yes and No; Dialogue Between a Philosopher, a Jew and a Christian; My Story of Calamities*. His works were all written in Latin and later translated into other languages.[5]

Abelard withstood Platonic realism and more nearly followed Aristotle. This enabled him to emphasize the transcendence as well as the immanence of God and avoid the pantheistic tendency allied with extreme Platonism. He brought ethics into the domain of theology and held that "intention" determined the moral value and character of a person's action. His ideal Christianity was positive moral law rather than mere prohibitions and ceremonies. Faith needs to obey the laws of rationality even as nature does. Communion with God constitutes heaven, while hell is separation from God. Often he contrasted the simple lives of pagan philosophers with the immorality of the clergy of his day. For him, reasoning was a most noble activity in which man became more like and most worthy of his Creator. The odium to which he was subjected during his lifetime was partly due to the atmosphere of his day. This evaluation of him was later materially modified.

In Abelard the balance was lost between devotional and logical elements of the faith. In him the inquisitive spirit and the dialectic passion were given priority. He surpassed all his contemporaries as a dialectician. He had confidence that reason could and should probe the foundations of religious truth and aim to comprehend the gospel from center to circumference. Face-to-face knowledge is the reward expected in the future life but rational understanding is possible and necessary here.

In his *Yes and No—Sic et Non*—he listed clashing opinions of the Fathers on 158 points of theology. His aim was to show that to rest on authority alone, as was the fashion, is to lean upon a broken reed. Regarding the inspiration of the Bible, he held that even the prophets were not always under the influence of the Holy Spirit and sometimes uttered errors. Peter and Paul differed sharply and corrected each other. But if prophets and apostles could err, how much more the church fathers! The orthodox position on original sin he did not share. For how is it possible for infants to be guilty and deserve perdition?[6]

Abelard may be considered the founder of what is known as the moral view of reconciliation of man to God through Christ. He rejected the traditional view of the death of Christ being a payment to Satan to release mankind. He also scouts the idea that God should be placated by the slaying of His innocent Son. To Abelard the work of Christ, including His suffering and death, is a manifestation of divine love for the unworthy. This is to kindle gratitude in their hearts and so win them back to God. Christ's death, Abelard taught, was not meant to change the attitude of Satan or God toward man, but rather to change man's attitude toward God.

Abelard combatted what he thought were the heresies of his day, such as: the use of crucifixes, celebrating the mass, and especially the idea that ignorance in matters of faith was blessed and could be compensated for by the use of "Amens" as a sign of religious devotion. He was a bitter enemy of the growing materialism in the church, and also opposed the crusades that Bernard promoted.

His chief offense, however, lay in his view of the Trinity. Three persons in one meant tritheism and leads to polytheism. God is *one*, but manifested Himself as Creator and Father, Son and Redeemer, and Holy Spirit and Comforter. He used the illustration of a seal, the figure carved on it, and the impression of its stamp. For this view he was charged with Modalism, and in 1121 was condemned by the Council of Soissons to cast his writings on the Trinity into the fire with his own hands. In 1141, at the instigation of his archenemy, Bernard, Abelard's teachings were officially condemned by the Council of Sens. This verdict was sanctioned by Pope Innocent II, who adjudged him to perpetual confinement in a cloister. On his way to Rome to appeal to the pope in person, he fell sick, and was received by Peter, abbot of Cluny. Here he died in 1142.

Heloise asked for his body and had it buried at the Paraclete, of which she was abbess at the time, with a view of reposing at his side in death. She died in 1164. In 1800 the ashes of both were carried to the Museum of French Monuments at Paris, and in 1817 they were deposited under a chapel in the precincts of the church of Monamy. The small marble chapel, in which the figures of the ill-fated pair are seen reposing side by side, is today one of the most famous monuments in the Parisian cemetery of Piere la Chaise. Abelard's literary works, his love, and his misfortunes have secured his name from oblivion.[7]

For General Reference

Poole, *Illustrations of Medieval Thought*, ch. v.; Webb, *Studies in the History of Natural Religion*, Part iii, no. 3.

Footnotes

1. Quoted by Fredrick Mayer, *Ancient and Medieval Philosophy*, American Book Co., p. 411. For Abelard's career, beliefs, and ideals, see pp. 404-412.
2. Frank Thilly, *A History of Philosophy*, Henry Holt & Co., New York, pp. 172-175.
3. Fredrick Mayer, *op. cit.*, p. 408.
4. See *The Encyclopedia Americana*, Vol. I., 35-36, for good review of Abelard and Heloise relations. Also *Biographical History of Philosophy*, G. H. Lewis, Appelton, pp. 346-361.
5. M. De Wulf, *History of Medieval Philosophy*, Longmans & Co., p. 191.
6. G. P. Fisher, *History of Christian Doctrine*, Scribners, pp. 221-224. See also A. C. McGiffert, *A History of Christian Thought*, Scribners, pp. 201-221.
7. *The Encyclopedia Americana*, Vol. I., p. 36.

> "Man, therefore, has been able to look on the invisible things of God with the understanding of the mind, or rather he has looked upon them through the things which have been made."[1]

11
Peter Lombard

Daniel Hertzler

Peter the Lombard was born near Novara in Lombardy, Italy, about 1100. He studied at Bologna and Rheims, in the school of St. Victor, and may have been a pupil of Abelard. Beginning in 1140 he taught in the Paris cathedral school and became the bishop of Paris in 1159, but died a short time later, possibly as early as 1160.

About 1140 he wrote commentaries on the Psalms which were well received. His method of commentary was principally quotations from the Scriptures and the fathers, and he used this method later in his major work, the four *Books of the Sentences*, finished about 1150. The topics treated in these four volumes were: (1) God; (2) the Creation; (3) the Incarnation and Redemption; (4) the Sacraments, with some comments on Eschatology.

Though they make tedious reading today, Peter Lombard's sentences became a major textbook for study in succeeding centuries. "From the thirteenth to the sixteenth century," says McKeon, "perhaps no single book exercised an influence in the development of philosophical and theological sciences comparable to that of the *Four Books of Sentences* of Peter Lombard."[2] They became so influential that Roger Bacon listed a preference for the *Sentences* over the Bible as one of the theology student's seven sins! And Leff in describing an eight-year course for the master of theology in the University of Paris says that the first two years were given to Peter Lombard's *Sentences*, followed by two years with the Bible and four years of teaching and disputation.[3]

This distinction was not achieved by any originality of the thinking in the statements, since the bulk of the work was made up of

---

Daniel Hertzler is a Mennonite minister, and editor of the *Gospel Herald*, Scottdale, Pa. He received the AB from Eastern Mennonite College, the BD from Goshen Biblical Seminary, and the M Ed and PhD degrees from the University of Pittsburgh. He contributed chapters to the books, Paul Erb, *From the Mennonite Pulpit*, and Lawrence C. Little, *Measuring the Effectiveness of Theological Communication*.

quotations from Augustine. It was apparently the form which appealed to the mind of successive centuries. "His method," says Knowles, "was to propose a doctrinal thesis or question, to bring forward authorities for and against this thesis from Scripture, the Councils, the Canons and the Fathers, and then give judgment on the issue."[4] Not even this form was original, but Lombard provided a happy combination of form and subject matter which was to serve as a theological textbook in the developing universities and which dominated theology until the work of Aquinas finally superseded it.

According to Schaff, Peter perpetuated from Augustine a statement about the creation of man and woman which has been falsely credited to Matthew Henry: "that the woman was not taken from Adam's head, as if she were to rule over him or from his feet as if she were to be his slave, but from his side that she might be his consort."[5]

Other features of the Lombard's compiled theology included a belief in predestination, in original sin passed on through the body, denial of a theory common in the period before him that the death of Christ was a payment to the devil, and acceptance of immersion as the correct mode of baptism to remove the guilt of original sin. The method used in the *Sentences* combined two tendencies of the period, says de Ghellinck, the tendency toward speculation on the one hand, and on the other a dependence on authority.[6]

The fact that some of his questions were not fully reconciled appeared to stimulate scholars, and hundreds of commentaries were written on his work. In spite of their seeming orthodoxy, the *Sentences* were attacked on a number of occasions, but their opponents were never successful in banning them.

The only copy of the *Sentences* available to the writer was in Latin, which was unfortunately off limits. However McKeon provides an excerpt which gives a sample of the style. From this the following quotation is taken.

Concerning the image and likeness of the Trinity in the human soul

" 'Now, however, let us proceed to the consideration of where in the human mind, which knows God or can know him, we find the image of the Trinity.'[7]

"For as Augustine says in the XIVth book *On the Trinity*[8]: 'Although the human mind is not of the same nature as God, nevertheless the image of him than whom nothing is better, must be sought and found in that, than which our nature has nothing better, that is, in the mind. For in the mind itself even before it is a partaker of God, his image is found; for, even when the mind is deformed, when it has lost the participation of God, the image of God still remains. Indeed, the mind is the image of God in that by which it is capable of him and by which it can be partaker of him. Therefore, let us seek in it now the Trinity which is God. The mind, then remembers itself, understands itself, loves itself; if we are aware of this, we are aware of a Trinity, not yet God to be sure, but an image of God.' A certain Trinity appears here of memory, understanding, and love. 'These three, therefore, we shall treat principally—memory, understanding, will.'[9]

"... In what sense that which has been stated above should be taken, must be considered very earnestly here, namely, that these three, memory, understanding, and will are one, one mind, one essence. Certainly this does not seem to be true according to the proper meaning of the words. For mind, that is, rational spirit, is a spiritual and corporeal essence. But, these three natural properties are powers of the mind itself and differ from each other, because memory is not understanding or will, nor is understanding will or love."[10]

One can see how commentators might have a four-century field day!

For Further Reading

Brady, Ignatius, "Peter Lombard" in Paul Edward (Ed.), *The Encyclopedia of Philosophy*, New York: The Macmillan Company and The Free Press, 1967, Vol. 6, 124, 125. de Ghellinck, J. "Peter Lombard" in *The Catholic Encyclopedia*, New York: Robert Appleton Company, 1911, Vol. XI, 768-769. Knowles, David, *The Evolution of Medieval Thought*, Baltimore: Helicon Press, 1967. Though only pp. 179-184 are specifically devoted to Peter Lombard, the book places him in the context of his antecedents and followers. Leff, Gordon, *Medieval Thought. St. Augustine to Ockham*, London: The Merlin Press, 1959. The sentences are discussed on pp. 128-130; their influence is documented on p. 180. McKeon, Richard, *Selections from Medieval Philosophers I, Augustine to Albert the Great*, pp. 185-201, New York: Charles Scribner's Sons, 1929, includes an evaluation of and a selection from Peter's writings. Schaff, David, "Peter the Lombard and the Summists" in Philip Schaff (Ed.), *History of the Christian Church*, Grand Rapids: William B. Eerdmans, 1949, Vol. V, 631-636.

Footnotes

1. Peter Lombard as quoted by Richard McKeon, *Selections From Philosophers I, Augustine to Albert the Great* (New York, Charles Scribner's Sons, 1929), p. 89.
2. *Ibid.*, p. 185.
3. Gordon Leff, *Medieval Thought. St. Augustine to Ockham* (London: The Merlin Press, 1959), p. 180.
4. David Knowles, *The Evolution of Medieval Thought* (Baltimore: Helicon Press, 1962), p. 180.
5. David Schaff, "Peter the Lombard and the Summists" in Philip Schaff (Ed.) History of the Christian Church, Vol. V (Grand Rapids: William B. Eerdmans, 1949), pp. 631, 632.
6. J. de Ghellinck, "Peter Lombard" in *The Catholic Encyclopedia*, Vol. XI (New York: Robert Appleton Company, 1911), p. 769.
7. Augustinus, *De Trinit.*, lib. XIV, cap 8, n. 11.
8. *Ibid.*
9. Augustinus, o.c. lib. X, cap 11, n. 17.
10. McKeon, *op. cit.*, pp. 193, 194, 196.

> *"Jesus, Thou joy of loving hearts! Thou fount of life! Thou light of men! From the best bliss that earth imparts, We turn unfilled to Thee again."*[1]

12

Bernard of Clairvaux

Willard M. Swartley

Pure, devoted, mystical contemplation of Jesus was the goal and power that inspired Bernard of Clairvaux (1090/1-1153) to become the church's most outstanding monk of the early twelfth century. Aspiring to escape the world in his early career, Bernard later found the world at his wilderness doorstep, begging him to settle church disputes, choose the Pope, work miracles of all kinds, preserve the orthodoxy of the church, and lead Christendom in a Holy War against the "pagan" East.

In 1174 Bernard was canonized by Alexander III and in 1953 on the eighth centenary of Bernard's death, Pope Pius XII issued the *Doctor Mellifluous* encyclical which esteems Bernard and his teaching as an honored example for us to follow. The term *Doctor Mellifluous* means "the doctor whose teaching is as sweet as honey."[2] More than any other person, Bernard embodies the piety and devotion to Jesus which continues to inspire the Cistercian-Trappist orders of Catholic monasticism.

The Course of His Life

The course of Bernard's life can be outlined by three stages of development in his life pilgrimage. These are:

1. Fontaines lès Dijon to Citeaux

Born into a family of Burgundian nobility in 1090 or 1091 at Fontaines lès Dijon in Mideastern France, Bernard with a keen mind and an excellent basic education exhibited promising potential for political or ecclesiastical fame. To the surprise and consternation of his family and friends, however, Bernard chose at the age of 22 to enter the newly founded Cistercian monastery at Citeaux. This monastery, begun in quest of monastic reform, soon set for itself the reputation of

---

Willard M. Swartley is a Mennonite minister and an instructor in New Testament in Goshen Biblical Seminary, and 1979-81 Acting Dean of the Associated Mennonite Biblical Seminaries. He received the BD from Goshen Biblical Seminary and the Doctorate in Theology from Princeton Theological Seminary. He is the author of *Mark, the Way for All Nations*.

extreme austerity, self-renunciation, and a hard rule of discipline which, for example, allowed only one meal per day in winter and two meals in summer.

Since Citeaux experienced slow growth in its first years the arrival of Bernard and his thirty companions in 1113 was indeed a cloudburst of heavenly blessing. Though Bernard had decided to enter Citeaux six months earlier, he spent these months winning his "enemies" to his side. One by one those who opposed his Citeaux decision were suddenly overwhelmed by the rightness of the action not only for him but for themselves. When Bernard entered, almost all his relatives accompanied him.

2. Citeaux—Clairvaux—Étampes

Two features characterized Bernard's growing reputation as a monk: (1) his intense devotion to meditation which renounced all comforts and bodily needs (not wants!) and (2) his ability to persuade others to take up the monastic vows. Though outwardly Bernard appeared emaciated, yet his unique spiritual power attracted growing numbers to enter monastic life.

In 1115 Citeaux decided to spawn a second monastery with Bernard as abbot of the new house founded 60 miles north in the valley of Absinthe. The monks renamed the place Clairvaux, meaning "Valley of Light." From this time onward Bernard and Clairvaux synonymously denoted a source of radiance which penetrated wider and wider circles of the world.

The next fifteen years of Bernard's life unfold his rise to fame. Four significant developments of this period are: (1) his near death in the early 1120s when he learned that the body's basic needs cannot be continuously ignored; (2) his increased number of journeys in the 1120s to participate in the wider monastic movement; (3) a growing circle of friendship with other important abbots, including William of St. Thierry, who later became Bernard's first biographer; and (4) Bernard's own writings of this period. These are "On the Degrees of Humility" (1119), "On the Love of God," "On Free Will and Grace," and *Apologia*, all three from 1126-28.

All this sets the stage for Bernard's next major assignment in 1130, deciding at the Council of Étampes which of two rival popes is the true pope of Rome.

3. Étampes—Sens—Veselay

A papal schism in 1130 threatened to divide Christendom. Both Innocent II and Anacletus II claimed papal authority. Countries took sides according to personal attachment and ecclesiastical interests. Finally King Louis VI of France called a Council at Étampes to decide which "pope" on the basis of personal merit must be acknowledged as the true pope. Bernard, who was now known for his unique ability to still human tempests by an awing authority of love, was drafted against his wish to lead the assembly. In an assembly deeply divided, Bernard successfully led the assembly to perceive the superior spiritual qualities of Innocent II and thus to accept him as pope.

Ten years later in 1140 Bernard was again called upon to do for the church what no one else could do but many felt must be done. This was to challenge and to correct the teaching of the famous scholar, Abelard. Abelard brooked no rival in his ability to think, write, and teach theology. His critical, rational approach, however, threatened the predominant method in theological thought; namely, accepting the statements of the Fathers and popes as authoritatively final. Abelard's success in swaying students and even members of the Roman curia into a rational analysis of belief alarmed many. Bernard criticized Abelard for never being willing to "look through a glass darkly."

Consequently the tension mounted and climaxed in the Council of Sens in which Bernard by selecting the agenda for debate apparently disarmed Abelard who is said to have "gone blank," or for prudence' sake, declined to debate. The effect was a victory for Bernard and the primacy of faith in theology.

The next major moment in Bernard's life came when he in 1146 at the bid of both king and pope preached the Second Crusade to great throngs of people converging at Vezelay before departure to Palestine. Neither Bernard nor the people of the Constantinian order felt any contradiction between Bernard's piety and the bloody horror of war which they now promoted. They saw the Crusade as God's conquest of the pagans.

The Crusade's result of tragic defeat did, however, present problems. Many blamed Bernard. His response was that he would gladly take "the blows of slander and poisoned darts of blasphemy so that they do not reach God. I consent to be lost to honor, provided his glory is left untouched."[3]

The most important of Bernard's writings from 1130 to his death in 1153 are "Against the Errors of Abelard" (1140), *On Meditation*, and his sermons on the Canticles, both done in the last six years of his life.

The Sweetness of Bernard's Teaching

Bernard's work on the Canticles is considered to be his most significant contribution because it brims with Bernard's unique emphases: contemplation of the mystery of Christ and his mystical presence in his church.[4] The hymns by which we remember Bernard convey well his genius in contemplative adoration of Jesus. These hymns are "Jesus, the Very Thought of Thee," "Jesus, Thou Joy of Loving Hearts," and "The Passion Chorale" ("O Sacred Head Now Wounded"). Two lines which Bernard often repeated portray his never sentimental, but solid sort of sweetness: "Let us rest in the hearts of those we love as those we love rest in our hearts."[5]

"Truly I must love Him perfectly, in whom I have being, my life, and my knowledge...."[6]

Other emphases in Bernard's writings include the nature of freedom in his treatise, "On Free Will and Grace"; the limitless sacrifice of monastic charity in *Apologia*; and an exposition of orthodox viewpoint on the Trinity, original sin, and the atonement in "Against the Errors of Abelard." His work "On Meditation" stresses the primacy of the interior life of prayer, meditation, and reflection over external action. Consistently, Bernard supported the monastic piety and orthodoxy of the church so that with devotion he is remembered within Catholicism "as a man of the church," "the last of the Fathers,"[7] and *the saint*, whose sweetness and light generated the late-medieval monastic revival.

Sources

Helpful resources for the study of Bernard are:

St. Bernard of Clairvaux, by his contemporaries, William of St. Thierry, Arnold of Bonneveaux, Geoffrey of Clairvaux, et al., A. R. Mowbray, London, 1960. The basic account, heavy on his miracles.

Daniel-Rops, Henri, *Bernard of Clairvaux*, Hawthorn, New York, 1964. A well-written biography with a helpful survey of the history of the Cistercian-Trappist movement up until the 1960's.

James, Bruno S., *Saint Bernard of Clairvaux*, Hodder & Stoughton, London, 1957. A detailed, critical analysis of Bernard's life and contribution.

Merton, Thomas, *The Last of the Fathers*, Harcourt, Brace, & Co., New York, 1954. Exciting reading on Bernard's life and writings. It includes the encyclical *Doctor Mellifluous*.

Murray, A. Victor, *Abelard and St. Bernard*, Barnes & Noble, Inc., New York, 1967. Scholarly analysis of the Sens' debate.

Footnotes

1. *The Church Hymnal*, Herald Press, 1957, p. 86.
2. Merton, Thomas, *The Last of the Fathers*, Harcourt, 1954, p. 11.
3. Daniel-Rops, Henri, *Bernard of Clairvaux*, Hawthorn, 1964, p. 99.
4. Merton, *op. cit.*, p. 64.
5. Daniel-Rops, *op. cit.*, p. 48.
6. Merton, *op. cit.*, p. 62.
7. *Ibid.*, p. 67, and the title of the book.

> "If thou wilt be perfect, go and sell that thou hast, and give to the poor . . . and come and follow me."

13

Waldo

Leonard Verduin

Waldo was a man who lived in Lyons, in France, born around the year 1140. By buying and selling and by the practice of usury (the lending of money at cruelly high rate to people in distress), he had become very rich.

In April or May of what is known as "the year of famine," 1176, when he was about 36 years old, he underwent a great religious crisis, one which led him to get rid of all his wealth and assume a life of voluntary poverty. Leaving some real estate for the support of his wife and paying the way for his two daughters to enter a nunnery, he gave the rest of his wealth to the relief of the poor. A year later we find him begging "an alms for the sake of Christ."

The cause of Waldo's conversion is variously reported. One of the oldest accounts is that it came about when Waldo had been listening to a *jongleur* (a roving minstrel—these *jongleurs* entertained the rich and the nobles by singing for them the life story of some hero), who recounted the life of St. Alexis, a fourth-century saint who had been a great help to the poor.

Another ancient reference informs us that Waldo's conversion was brought about by the sudden death of one of the well-to-do persons of the city, who seems to have fallen dead while attending a meeting. A third report has it that it was Jesus' words to the young man, recorded in Matthew 19:21, that burned into Waldo's soul and made him seek to follow them to the letter.

It does not seem necessary to choose among these reports concerning the motivation for the rich young man's conversion. Probably all three united in making him critical of his own way of life hitherto and made him desirous for a life more in keeping with the gospel.

Leonard Verduin is a Christian Reformed minister, and was long the pastor to the student congregation at Ann Arbor, Mich. He received the BA from Calvin College, the ThB from Calvin Seminary, and the AM in History from the University of Michigan. He translated all the writings of Menno Simons from Dutch and from Latin into English for his *Complete Writings* (fourth printing, 1978). He wrote *The Reformers and Their Stepchildren*, a monograph on the Anabaptists and their forerunners.

At once Waldo had portions of the sacred Scriptures turned into the local dialect—also some of the writings of the earliest of the church Fathers. With these in hand he started to preach in the streets, to rich and poor alike.

Needless to say, this caused the leaders of the prevailing church to sit up and take notice. The medieval church—like any other totalitarian system—exercised rigid thought control. To it preaching by unordained persons posed a great threat. Matters were made worse by the fact that quite at once a company of followers had gathered around Waldo. Their group was known as "The Poor Men of Lyons" and all of them preached—for it was an integral part of Waldo's conviction that the prevailing distinction of clergy and laity was false and that anyone who believed could also preach.

The archbishop of Lyons, Guichard by name, could not wink at such goings-on. He ordered Waldo and his followers to stop the preaching—upon which these recited for his benefit the words recorded in Acts 4:19, words uttered by Peter in a strikingly similar situation, words to the effect that one must obey God rather than man in such matters.

However, Waldo and his followers were manifestly peace-loving people, persons who had no desire to break with the church. They tried to reach over the archbishop's head and hoped to get permission from those higher up, a vain hope indeed. The request was turned down at Rome, under Pope Alexander III. Nevertheless, they kept on preaching, no doubt in an even more critical vein. The "Poor Men of Lyons" were offically declared to be heretics and schismatics, and placed under the church's ban, an action that was finalized at the Council of Verona, which sat in 1184. Two years earlier already, in 1182, Guichard had expelled from his realm all the "Vaudois" as the followers of Waldo were being called. (The name is generally taken to be from the word "Waldo," via French dialects—although some very ancient sources derive it from "Val," meaning *valley*.)

From this point on, as is the case commonly with persons thus banished, the course of Waldo's life becomes altogether sketchy if not wholly unknown. He had to go underground, no doubt active and influential still, but out of sight by and large. Some say he fled to Metz; others say he went to Lombardy; still others say he fled to Bohemia; there is even an old report that he went to Flanders. All of these are probably conjectures, based on the fact that each and all of these areas soon became centers of Waldenses—as the *Vaudois* were called. (As usual in the case of people on whom the church had turned, many other names were invented, to spite the rebels who had dared to protest against the existing order. One of the most common was *Sabotiers*, a word derived from the French *sabot* meaning sandal or wooden shoe. The latter is the more likely, since the Waldensians were referred to as *Kloefers* or *Klompendragers* in medieval Flanders.)

It is assumed that Waldo (the surname *Peter* does not appear in the record until centuries later; it has been suggested that this name was appropriated in order to compete with the Catholic Church, doting as it does on its *Peter*) died in the year 1218, he being referred to in the past tense in a document dated the following year.

Peter Waldo left no known writings. His importance must be sought in the fact that he became a sort of rallying point for all who were alarmed at the secularizing and leveling process that had resulted from the fusion of the empire and the church in the days of Constantine.

Like all men whom history has made famous, Waldo had the good fortune to be born at the right time, when men were looking for someone to lead them in the direction they were already facing. Waldo *found* followers before he *made* any.

This goes far to explain the fact that at once there were Waldensians everywhere. In 1211 they were already so plentiful in the Strasburg area that eighty of them were put to death there in that year. Earlier than that, in 1192, they were a problem in Toulouse, where orders were given to imprison any and all who gave comfort to a Waldensian. In 1199 they posed a similar problem in Metz; in 1203, in Lüttich. In the 80s of the twelfth century they were very active in Languedoc; in 1194, in Aragon. In 1194 an Edict of Banishment was published in Spain, under Alphonse II, aimed at the Waldensians. His successor, Pedro II, imposed the penalty of death by fire (the first recorded instance, it seems, of the application of that devil-inspired way of silencing the "heretic"). In 1199 Innocent III was ordering all copies of the Waldensian Bibles to be burned. Colloquies staged by the church to reconvert Waldensians were held in 1191 and again in 1206. When one considers that all this occurred while Waldo was still alive, and that as early as 1230, only a decade or so after his death, there were reported to be 80,000 Waldensians in Austria alone, then we realize how true it is that Waldo met an already existing need.

Waldo's quarrel with the church was not primarily *doctrinal;* it was about *behavior*—as his own conversion indicates. Waldo felt that Christianity had lost its conduct-changing dimension. He read that a man who "names the name of Christ" must "depart from iniquity" (2 Timothy 2:19), and he felt called to restore this dimension to Christians.

For this reason the Waldensians loved the epistle of James—the very book which Luther disliked so vehemently. For this reason they could not accept the one-sided emphasis on *pardon,* and the correspondingly light emphasis on *renewal,* that characterized the German Reformation. It was somewhat different in the French-speaking areas and the somewhat different situation there. In these areas a great many of the Waldensians found it possible to adjust themselves to the theology of the Reformation—although not without much anguish of heart and manifest reservations—and move into its ranks.

For Further Reading

Consult religious encyclopedias and the works cited.

"Now the question arises..."

14

Duns Scotus

Paul M. Lederach

John Duns Scotus was one of the more famous Franciscan theologians of the Middle Ages. He was born in a family named Duns in the village of Duns, Scotland, around 1265 or 1266. That he was a Scot led to the addition of Scotus ("the Scot") to his name.

In his early or middle teens Duns Scotus joined the Franciscan order. He studied at Oxford and later taught there. Then he moved on to Paris. He taught four years in Paris and returned again to Oxford. In 1302 he returned to Paris as a lecturer. The next year Scotus was banned from France by Philip the Fair for failing to support the king in a quarrel with Pope Boniface VIII over taxation of the clergy. Two years later Duns Scotus came back to Paris (1305) and received a doctorate in theology. He was transferred to Cologne in 1307, and died there November 8, 1308, at about 43 years of age.

It is interesting to note that in the sixteenth century those who followed the teaching of Scotus were called "Dunsmen." Dunsmen were attacked by humanists like Erasmus for their distinctions without difference. As a result the word "Duns" became our word "dunce," meaning a stupid person, unable to learn. This, however, was not a description of the real Duns Scotus. Scotus was called the "subtle doctor" because with his first-rate mind he was able to make fine but meaningful distinctions such as the distinction between divine attributes and the divine essence, the necessity of interaction between divine intellect and will, with will limited only by the distinction between God's absolute power and His ordained power.

To understand Duns Scotus, it is necessary to know something about the time in which he lived. Duns Scotus lived at the point in medieval history when Scholasticism reached its peak. Scholasticism is a term used to describe the intellectual climate in which Catholic

---

Paul M. Lederach is a Mennonite minister and educational leader, having long served as Director of the Congregational Literature Division of Mennonite Publishing House. He has also served as President of the Mennonite Board of Education. He received the BA from Goshen College, the ThB from Goshen Biblical Seminary, the MRE from Eastern Baptist Seminary, and the DRE from Southwestern Baptist Theological Seminary. His writings include the books *Learning to Teach, Reshaping the Teaching Ministry,* and *A Third Way.*

teachers and writers worked during the Middle Ages. The word is derived first from "schola," the Latin word for school, and then from "Scholasticus," the Latin name for the master in charge of the schools the church then had. At the heart of Scholasticism was an attempt to bring together faith and reason. Among the early schoolmen were Peter Abelard (1079-1142), Bernard of Clairvaux (1090/1-1153), and Peter Lombard (1100-1160).

The "golden age" of Scholasticism was the thirteenth century. The outstanding intellectual giants were Albertus Magnus (1206-1280), Bonaventura (1221-1274), and Thomas Aquinas (1224-1274). The fourteenth century witnessed the decline of the Scholastic enterprise. In fact, Duns Scotus came into prominence because his thought led ultimately to the undoing of the synthesis of faith and reason which reached its height in Thomas Aquinas.

It should be noted that Thomas Aquinas was a Dominican, and Duns Scotus a Franciscan. Between these two great orders there was intense competition. Therefore, it was to be expected that Duns Scotus would turn his great abilities to a critical analysis of the work of Thomas Aquinas, the outstanding Dominican theologian.

Scotus attacked the work of Aquinas with the utmost acumen. Scotus' work appears in *Opus Oxoniensis*, his major work, which was based on his teaching at Oxford. Scotus' students were responsible for a second work, a report of his lectures at Paris, *Reportata Parisiensia*.

Wherein did Scotus attack Aquinas? At the risk of oversimplification, Aquinas felt that there was no real disagreement between theology and philosophy. Scotus admitted that some of the church doctrines were beyond the grasp of human intelligence. He asserted that absurdity did not lessen but rather added to their value. Scotus felt that theology is philosophically improbable, yet it is to be accepted on the authority of the church.

Aquinas, on one hand, taught that the very essence of God is being. He felt that God did what He saw to be right. Aquinas taught that God acts in accordance with reason. Therefore, God is bound by reason in that He does not act in a way not consistent with reason. Since human reason is derived from God, nothing God is or does is really out of accord with man's reason. Thus, through reason man can know much about God, and even though some of God's acts cannot be discovered through reason, they are not contrary to reason. Aquinas felt the incarnation and crucifixion were in very truth the wisest way to achieve man's salvation.

Scotus, on the other hand, taught that the essence of God is arbitrary will, and that what God wills is right. He taught that God is completely free and not bound by reason. God is not under any necessity to conform to reason. His acts, in fact, may even be contrary to reason, though this does not mean that God is capricious or chaotic. It was God's will not His reason that brought the world into being. Scotus did not hold that the incarnation and crucifixion were the wisest, because this would limit God's freedom. All Scotus would say was that this was the way God chose to do it.

Because of his emphasis upon the will of God, Scotus also regarded man as having more freedom of the will than did Aquinas.

Scotus believed, as did Aquinas, in original sin. But he held that because of it man has not lost the power of free decision. In this connection, it is interesting to note that Aquinas taught that the Virgin Mary shared in the original sin of the race. Scotus, however, held that she was free from it. He taught the doctrine of the Immaculate Conception [of Mary in her mother's body], which was declared to be a dogma of the church by Pope Pius IX in 1854.

Aquinas and Scotus also differed in how forgiveness was received. Aquinas maintained that sorrow for sin because of one's fear of punishment for sinful acts (attrition) was not the true repentance which leads to forgiveness. Rather, true repentance is sorrow because of love for God and for having slighted God's love. But Scotus held that sorrow because of fear of punishment (attrition) was a sufficient starting point toward forgiveness, not because man deserves forgiveness, but because God wills it.

Scotus has been called the keenest critic of all the schoolmen who attacked the work of Aquinas. Aquinas represented the apex of Scholasticism. He attempted to show that Christian beliefs were at least not inconsistent with reason, and that some could be established through reason. Scotus, however, took a path which led to the denial that the major Christian convictions could be demonstrated by reason or were even consistent with it. For Scotus they were to be believed simply on the authority of the church or the Scriptures.

Scotus' student, William of Occam (or Ockham), pushed the thought of Scotus to its logical end, a divorce between philosophy and theology. Occam (died 1349), known as the Invincible Doctor, taught that none of the Christian beliefs could be proved through reason or by the logic of the schoolmen. Even the existence of God could not be demonstrated. Occam found very inconclusive the arguments of Aquinas to demonstrate God's existence. Occam declared that one must accept the doctrines of Christianity, including the existence of God and the immortality of the soul, because the church teaches them and they are contained in the Bible. He gave up the hope of reconciling the wisdom of men with the wisdom of God. Scotus is important, therefore, because he set in motion the view that reason could not be used in undivided support of faith. "I believe in order that I may understand" (credo ut intelligam) was changed to "I believe because it is absurd" (credo quia absurdum)! By separating faith and knowledge the way was paved for empirical, secular sciences.

Duns Scotus used the "problem method" in teaching, then called the "question method," because every topic was approached in the form of a question, "Now the question arises whether...." This method aimed at formulating a conclusion after other possible answers had been examined and evaluated. The purpose was not only to develop as accurate a conclusion as possible but also to give guidance to students in thinking, evaluating, and deciding. Questions were discussed in four ways: (1) considerations in support of an affirmative answer, (2) arguments negating the answer, (3) the merits and demerits of each side, and finally (4) the teacher explained his own view and amplified the arguments in support of his view and answered those which opposed his view. Later this method was used not to deal with central issues as did Aquinas and Scotus; rather, the method was used to defend Aquinas from the disciples of Scotus, or to defend Scotus from the disciples of Aquinas. Rivalries between the followers of Aquinas (Thomists) and the followers of Duns Scotus (Scotists) raged until the Reformation. In fact, the issues they dealt with are still debated today.

For us the importance of Scotus rests in his separating faith and knowledge, in his emphasis upon the will, and in his view that man has not lost the power of free and responsible decision.

Bibliography

Latourette, Kenneth Scott, *A History of Christianity*, New York: Harper 1953, p. 514; Maurer, Armand, "Duns Scotus, John," *Collier's Encyclopedia* (1964), Vol. 8, p. 428; Qualben, Lars P., *A History of the Christian Church*, New York: Thomas Nelson, 1942; Sharp, Dorothea, "Duns Scotus, John," *Encyclopedia Britannica* (1946), Vol. 7, p. 744-45; Walker, Williston, *A History of the Christian Church*, Scribners, 1959.

> *"For though we walk in the flesh, we do not war after the flesh: (for the weapons of our warfare are not carnal, but mighty through God . . .)" (2 Cor. 10:3, 4).*

15
Peter Chelčický

Přemysl Pitter

Peter Chelčický might best be labeled A Prophet at the Beginning of a New Era. Comparatively little is known about his life. In the article "Czech Language and Literature" in the *Encyclopaedia Britannica*, Arne Novak of the University of Brno, and Robert Auty of the University of Cambridge, propose his life span as 1390-1460. Five years after the martyrdom of Jan Hus at Constance, the Hussite wars erupted and raged for fourteen years. The struggle was between the Union of Bohemian Cities and Emperor Sigismund, who began his crusade against the Bohemian "heretics" in 1420. The powerful nobleman, one-eyed Jan Žižka who had heard Hus preach, repulsed the forces of the emperor. After the untimely death of Žižka, the Hussite "Fighters for God" were joined by some rough elements who were bent on plunder, and this plundering herd actually penetrated deep into Germany.

In the midst of all this violence there was one clear voice which called for the end of all warring, that of *Peter of Chelčic*, in Czech, Peter Chelčický, the man said to be the greatest writer who employed the Czech tongue. That his works were long unknown even to his Czech countrymen indicates only how thorough the Catholic Counter Reformation was in Bohemia in the seventeenth century. Until the

---

The late Přemysl Pitter was born in Prague, Czechoslovakia, June 21, 1895. Deeply moved by his experience as a soldier during World War I, he became increasingly devoted to the welfare of his fellowmen, especially those in need. His first step was to establish a children's home. He became well known, not only among his Czech compatriots, but also among Sudeten Germans, as well as Jews. The latter he tried to help during World War II. For ten years he served among refugees in Germany, as a spiritual adviser and social worker. Later he lived in Switzerland, laboring with his pen for the spiritual deepening of his Czech friends, and issuing his *Hovory s pisateli* (Dialog with Correspondents).

Pitter died in Switzerland on February 12, 1976. Shortly before his death the University of Zurich conferred on him the honorary Doctor of Theology degree.

63

year 1946 no one was entirely sure who this Peter von Chelčický was, but the mystery was cleared up by the Czech historian František M. Bartoš. Chelčický was known originally as Peter Záhorka, a minor nobleman who lived in the vicinity of the village of Chelčic. This Záhorka lost his father in early childhood, after which he seems to have stayed with his uncle, a priest, who provided him with a splendid education. This Uncle Hostislav started the manuscript collection which later became the Rosenberg Library. Young Peter was fortunate enough to come into the possession of a Czech Bible, revised by Hus himself. Until his twenty-fifth year, young Záhorka's name occurs often in the records of that period, indicating something of his standing and prestige. But he gradually matured into a new man under the influence of such men as the author, Thomas von Štítné; the professor, Matthias of Janov; Jan Hus; and Jakobellus von Mies. It is also possible that he had become acquainted with the Waldenses who had reached Southern Bohemia, and were calling for the church to renounce its wealth and to return to the New Testament. An ardent Hussite convert, the former Roman priest Vojtěch of Chelčic, also seems to have made a deep impact on Peter Záhorka. The result of all these "heretic" influences was that Záhorka, the nobleman, did renounce his status and became simply a Christian brother, Peter Chelčický.

We first meet the new Peter Chelčický in 1419 when the professors in Prague gave as their ethical judgment that one might fight with arms in self-defense. Chelčický was alone in his position of absolute nonresistance. There are no circumstances ever, he held, when Christians may violate the commandment, "Thou shalt not kill." When the armies of the Crusaders were defeated by the Hussites at the very gates of Prague, there was of course great jubilation. But there was one lone prophet who raised his voice once more against violence and killing: Chelčický. He held that such measures stood in direct contradiction to the gospel of Christ. No one listened, so he returned to Southern Bohemia, only to find the tragic results of plundering and ravaging. The pastor, Vojtěch, had been burned for giving the communion cup to the laity. It was Chelčický himself who undertook to give guidance by his writings to the pastorless flock. He took up his facile pen to minister to the Hussites. And although his writings had to be copied by hand, they circulated widely. Both men and women studied the Word, so that Cardinal Piccolomini (later Pope Pius II), admitted in writing that many Hussite women knew the Scriptures better than many an Italian priest.

Chelčický's first major treatise, *Of Spiritual Conflict*, laid the foundation for his later works. Our conflict as Christians is not a physical struggle with human enemies, but a spiritual struggle with the demonic forces set in array against us. He rejected the doctrine of the threefold division of the population: priests, lords, and laborers. Rather, the church is to be one united body, with all men laboring for the common good. Chelčický went beyond Wycliffe and Hus, and also far beyond Luther, for his model was the apostolic church with its communities of peace and love. One can never, he held, defend Christianity with arms; arms can but betray the cause of Christ. Even when the Hussite "warriors of God" returned victorious from four campaigns, Chelčický was not impressed. They will yet fail, he warned. In 1433, to be sure, the Council of Basel seemed to grant a major concession to the Hussites, granting them communion in both kinds (the cup as well as the wafer). But this was more a tactical concession than anything else, and soon the whole movement came under the heel of Rome. The Hussite revolt was crushed, and only the compromising but widespread Utraquist Church was left.

When no one seemed willing to listen to this prophet in the wilderness, Chelčický retired to his village, where his disciples gathered around him, the "Brothers of Chelčický." After the death of their master they became a part of the stream which five centuries ago resulted in the *Unitas Fratrum*, the Union of Bohemian Brethren. The two greatest works of Chelčický were his *Postille*, a collection of sermons and devotional materials, and *The Net of True Faith*—both of which were preserved and published in the sixteenth century. The latter was translated from Old Czech into German by the German-Bohemian theologian, Carl Vogl, who also wrote a Chelčický monograph. "Why cannot the church 'catch' more converts in its net?" asked Chelčický. Because, said he, the net has been badly torn by two evil forces: the pope (ecclesiasticism) and the emperor (the state). "The abomination of Desolation of the Holy Place" really began when the Roman bishop Sylvester allied himself with the Emperor Constantine and heathen laws were imposed by force on the people. All sorts of "gangs" arose to exploit the people: noblemen, monks, scholars, priests. They persecuted and burned the true Christians, led the simple folk into a false external religion of forms, and constituted the church of Antichrist!

Chelčický was against the whole Constantinian "synthesis," and defied the entire Medieval system, regardless of who had defended it. He held that Romans 13 cannot be honestly appealed to as a basis for Christians to bear the sword. Paul was speaking of the state, the jurisdiction of which relates to non-Christians. The state, he said, necessarily uses force to restrain non-Christians. But Christians are to follow the Sermon on the Mount. They use only love in human relations. Therefore no Christian can bear arms; indeed, he cannot serve even as a judge.

Faith was for Chelčický "the light in man's spirit that gives knowledge." The Redeemer is born in "Bethlehem," that is, the hearts in which God's Word dwells richly are the true "House of Bread" (*Bethlehem* in Hebrew). But it was not granted to Chelčický to see many hearts of that type. He became a rejected and ignored old man. Just one ray of light came to him. One of his most devoted disciples, a Brother Gregory of Prague, had read his writings, and came to the village of Chelčický to seek him out. What a meeting of kindred men of God it must have been! And Gregory in turn became the chief founder of the Union of Bohemian Brethren. Apart from the work of Chelčický, there would have been no such church.

Carl Vogl is right when he speaks of Chelčický as a prophet at the turn of an era. Like one of the ancient prophets of Israel he stood up for God and denounced the sin, the violence, and the corruption of his era, both among the common people and among the priests and nobles. Chelčický did not live for popularity, and among the Czech people today his name is largely forgotten. Only the Marxists single him out—as a forerunner of communism!

But Chelčický's rejection of force and violence was not an isolated tenet of his; it was, rather, the other side of the coin—of his *faith*. Nonresistance was not a clever means for him; it was, rather, the expression of his faith in a living God and the power of His love as revealed in Jesus. Without this spiritual foundation, his doctrine of nonviolence lacks effective power in life.

Chelčický recognized that force must necessarily be used by the state in the maintenance of law and order, but in the divine kingdom there is no place for anything but love to induce men to come into the order of Christ. Chelčický's strategy was not withdrawal from the world, but summoning Christians to really be Christian, to have done with the weaponry and the means of control of an ungodly world. He tried to point them to true community, community as it exists in Christ through the work of His Spirit. Christians are to realize here and now the joy and the peace and the community of the kingdom of God. There are those who will regard this as irresponsible recklessness. But today the alternative seems to be the utter destruction of human society through a military holocaust which is beyond description.

Bibliographical Note

A fuller account of the life, work, and ideology of Chelčický is found in my German work, *Geistige Revolution im Herzen Europas* (Zürich und Stuttgart: Rotapfel Verlag, 1968, Seiten 49-63). This chapter was translated into English by Elizabeth Horsch Bender, and slightly condensed by the editor of this volume. Used by permission.

16
Thomas a Kempis

> *"Everywhere have I sought for peace, but nowhere have I found it save in a quiet corner with a little book."*

Delbert Grätz

Thomas Hammerken was born about 1380 in the village of Kempen, near Düsseldorf, Germany. When he was twelve he attended the school at Deventer in West Friesland, which was under the direction of the Brothers of the Common Life. In the manner of the time he was given a school name, Thomas from Kempen, or in Latin, Thomas a Kempis. This name has become known to all of Christendom, particularly because it is commonly thought that he was the author of the devotional classic, *The Imitation of Christ.*

The school at Deventer had been made famous by its founder, Geert Groote (1340-1384), who had been attracted to the monastic life by John Ruusbroec (1293-1381), a mystic from Flanders. Deventer was known for its mystic theology and practical Christianity. This was the home of and the era of the rise of *Devotio Moderna,* which had its influence on the rise of Humanism and the Reformation. Even though Groote and his early disciples were Thomas' ideal, he did not become a reformer of education as they had. After he pursued his studies at Deventer for seven years, Thomas joined the Augustinian order and went to the new convent of Mount St. Agnes at Zwolle. He was received there in 1399. He became a priest in 1413 and a sub-prior in 1425. For seventy years he lived and worked at St. Agnes. He died here in 1471 at the age of 91.

Thomas was a copyist. In this way he earned money to help support the convent. He copied books of devotion, missals, and a Bible. He also authored many original writings. These include a number of biographies, a chronicle of the monastery, sermons, and hymns. He also wrote a number of short works relating to the monastic life. Most scholars agree that the famous *Imitation of Christ* was composed by him, or at least was revised and added to by Thomas. Regardless, this work has been connected with his name and has brought his name to us today.

Delbert Grätz is Librarian, Mennonite Historical Library, Bluffton College. He received the BA from Bluffton College, the MA from Ohio State University, and the PhD from the Berner Universität. He earned the AMLS at the University of Michigan. He is the author of a monograph entitled *The Bernese Anabaptists.* He has engaged in research in many libraries and archives in Europe.

On a few occasions his monastic duties called Thomas away on brief trips, but most of his seventy years at Mount St. Agnes were spent in the day in and day out routine of the monastery. This was the regular alternation of prayer, study, and work. No spectacular or sensational events seem to have ever been a part of his experience. His élan was his monastery; his life of work and devotion, his cell. Only a Thomas a Kempis could write, "The cell, constantly dwelt in, groweth sweet . . . a dear friend and a most pleasant comfort."

Thomas a Kempis was also a teacher. He taught young members of his cloister. In his writings some of his teaching methods can be ascertained. He was able to arouse the enthusiasm of his students. He loved books and was able to engender this fondness in those who studied with him. His favorite motto, quoted above, is the joy of librarian and teacher alike.

His contemporaries, in writing of their beloved brother, give a picture of Thomas as a person of medium height, somewhat inclined to obesity. His large face and large features revealed his Flemish parentage. His robust health was expressed in his ruddy cheeks. His large, bright eyes were spoken of by the chronicler as "the windows through which shone the beauty of a great and noble soul."

The authorship of *The Imitation of Christ* has been the source of considerable scholarly research and speculation. Although many persons have been put forth as the real author by students of this era, the two others besides Thomas who have been given the most serious attention in this matter are Geert Groote, Thomas' teacher, and Giovanni Gersen, thought to have been the abbot of Santo Stefano in Vercelli, North Italy. Regardless of whether Thomas a Kempis was actual author or editor, or merely the copyist of this classic gem of devotional life, we have him to thank for its existence today, and it is through this book that we remember his name. Only the Bible itself has submitted more frequently to the hand of the translator. It is one of the few works that withstood the critical minds of the church Reformers of the century that followed.

All four books of the *Imitation of Christ* were written for the monastics of the contemplative life. Monastic virtues found among the Brothers of the Common Life are given in the first book. These include: prudence, humility, obedience, diligence, and mutual aid to each other. The author tells us the methods that can help in accomplishing these virtues. These include reading the holy writings, meditation on the life and Passion of Christ, not to delight in vanities, to speak only as necessary, and to bear with others' faults. "Let our chief study be to meditate upon the life of Jesus Christ."

The second book centers on inner devotion and the love of Christ. The friendship of Christ and the love of His cross are central themes. He begins this book with the central assumption, "Blessed is he that understandeth what it is to love Jesus and to despise himself for Jesus' sake." "The love of things created is deceitful and inconstant; the love of Jesus is faithful and enduring." The reality of practical discipleship is made clear by such statements as: "Jesus has now many lovers of His heavenly kingdom, but few bearers of His cross." "Many follow Jesus unto the breaking of bread, but few to the drinking of the cup of his passion." "O how powerful is the pure love of Jesus, which is mixed with no self-interest or self-love."

The third book, according to Thomas' autograph, but fourth in many texts, concerns communion in particular, as well as the sacraments in general. The faithful disciple must prepare himself well for holy communion. He will desire communion because of the union with Christ that it brings and the blessings which result. But again he warns not to search too deeply into this sacrament but to humbly imitate Christ by submission to Him. Faith must always predominate. "O most sweet and most bountiful Jesus, how great reverence and thanksgiving, together with perpetual praise, are due unto thee for the receiving of thy sacred body, whose dignity no man is able to express!" "What better and more profitable can I do than utterly humble myself before thee and to exalt thine infinite goodness?" "Blessed is that simplicity which leaveth the difficult ways of questions and disputings, and goeth forward in the plain and sure path of God's commandments. Many have lost devotion while they sought to search into high things. Faith is required of thee, and a sincere life; not the heights of understanding nor deep delving into the mysteries of God. Submit thyself to God and the light of knowledge shall be given to you in such a degree as shall be profitable and necessary for you."

The consolation of the inner man is brought out in many ways in the fourth book which, as noted above, is sometimes considered the third book. The world must be despised and one should have contempt for himself. Learning is less desired than knowledge of self and contempt for the world. God's Word must be listened to in all humility. Typical of the reflections given here are: "Blessed are those ears which listen not to the voice sounding without, but to the truth teaching within." "Let go all transitory things and seek those that are eternal." "Learn, O dust, to obey; learn to humble thyself, earth and clay, and to bow thyself down under the feet of all men." "Choose always to have less than more." "My son, be not curious nor trouble thyself with idle cares. Be not careful for the shadow of a great name or for the familiar friendship of many or for the particular affection of men, for these things distract and darken the heart." "Grant me prudence to avoid him that flattereth me, to endure patiently him that contradicteth me." "Never read the word of God in order to appear more learned or more wise. Be studious for the mortification of thy sins, for this will profit thee more than the knowledge of many difficult questions." In closing he utters this prayer in the spirit of the entire book: "Protect and keep the soul of thy poor servant amidst the many dangers of this corruptible life; and by thy grace accompanying, direct me along the way of peace to the land of everlasting light. Amen."

It is impossible to evaluate the great influence through the ages of this simple and pious monk of the Brethren of the Common Life. But it is not difficult to predict that many Christians in time to come will find aid in their search for Christian truth in the fifteenth-century writings of Thomas a Kempis.

Bibliographical Note

There are some six thousand editions of *The Imitation of Christ*.

"Born to die, to save the church...."

17
Savonarola

LeRoy Kennel

Born in 1452, Girolamo Savonarola died only forty-six years later, nineteen years before Martin Luther posted his *95 Theses* at Wittenberg. It is incorrect to say, however, that he died nineteen years before the Reformation since he himself was one of the greatest medieval preachers and reformers in the Catholic Church, particularly in Italy. Perhaps "born to die" for the church, to save the church from her own distortions was his life mission. Unafraid, unsatisfied, unhappy with the status quo, Savonarola repeatedly challenged the mother church's idolatry. Out of devotion to her he was compelled to speak his convictions—even though this prophetic word conflicted with the practices of the church authorities. Accordingly, Michael De La Bedoyere wrote a book about the deep conflict between two public leaders who never met in person, moral leader Dominican Girolamo Savonarola and immoral leader Spanish Pope Alexander VI, entitled *The Meddlesome Friar and the Wayward Pope*. The following etching concerns consecration, convictions, and contributions.

Consecration

Hus's dedication and commitment in the first half of the fifteenth century is matched with Savonarola's in the second half. Although it was planned by his parents that he enter the medical profession, he left home secretly to enter a Dominican monastery in Bologna at the age of twenty-three. His commissioning as an itinerant preacher came seven years later. Although not a successful preacher at first, he was invited to Florence in 1490 by Lorenzo Medici. By 1495 he held a leadership role of a "dictator." Only three years later he was hanged and burned for sedition and heresy by order of Pope Alexander VI. Characteristically, he maintained a firm belief that he was a chosen channel for communicating God's message.

Being severely moralistic, he engaged in a most rigorous attempt to purify the church. He considered himself, as did Joan of Arc, set aside and called by God. He knew that he had heard God's voice charging him to announce to the people and to the priests, and particularly

---

LeRoy Kennel is a Mennonite minister and Professor of Communication in Bethany Theological Seminary. He received his BA from Goshen College, the MA from the University of Iowa, the BD from Goshen Biblical Seminary, and the PhD from Michigan State University. Among his writings is *Mennonites: Who and Why*.

to Alexander VI, the judgment of God. During his period as a successful preacher, his message to Florence was: "Repent, forsake your images of evil." The effect was the destruction of works of art and artifacts of frivolity. Florence became, as a result of his preaching and later administration, "the city ruled by Jesus Christ." His speaking so aroused Alexander VI to opposition that he commanded him to stop preaching. When Savonarola resumed his prophetic speech during the 1497 Lent, excommunication followed. Nevertheless, in 1498 he again preached against the carnivals. Commercial interests also applied pressure, and the pope threatened Florence with an interdict. Savonarola's pleas to the sovereigns were unanswered. Consequently, he and two disciples were tortured, hanged, and burned for sedition and heresy on May 23, 1498, in the great piazza of Florence. He who had three years earlier been so praised was now so punished.

Convictions

A primary description of Savonarola's beliefs is that of iconoclasm. He so prophesied against the confusion of image with reality that he displayed a radical rejection of images. In addition to the rejection of the symbolism of images, he was convinced that card playing was evil. Therefore, his preaching aroused vested-interest groups—much as did Paul's preaching among the Ephesian silversmiths—with the result that Ameaux, a playing-card manufacturer, rallied a party of opposition. Under Savonarola, the people destroyed in the bonfires their musical instruments, playing cards, gaudy clothes, and works of art.

Savonarola believed moreover in a Christian Humanism, the result of which was his being a creative prophet. As a reforming prophet he spoke truth plainly and not oratorically as did Fra Mariano da Genazzano, a monk of the Augustinian Order, about whom the followers were "all ears" to his musical voice, chosen words, grand sentences, and harmonious cadence. In contrast Savonarola's friends told him that although his doctrine was true, useful, and necessary, that nevertheless his manner of delivery lacked grace. Savonarola is supposed to have replied, "These verbal elegancies and ornaments will have to give way to sound doctrine simply preached."

Anabaptists must empathize with Savonarola's conception of the church which puts limits on the authority of a church leader or institution. His high regard for the church as that which takes precedence over any man-made decrees is illustrated by his reply to the "sentence" at his execution. When told that he was no longer a member of the church militant or the church triumphant, he declared that the latter could not be so. Moreover, it must be noted that both charges of heresy and sedition were but disobedience to the pope.

Savonarola, who was also a "politician," believed that this avenue also was to be an instrument for serving God. Carrying out his role as Florence's ruler, he also sought to be more a prophet of the state rather than an administrator. Theologically, Savonarola was Old Testament oriented, with the Hebrew history's series of transgressions and punishments furnishing him with numerous arguments that universal corruption of the church does indeed draw down God's wrath upon it. Savonarola himself declared that he would have preferred to pronounce that the church will be scourged, as well as speedily regenerated in the immediate future, as a "revelation from heaven," but chose rather to support his preaching only upon reason and Bible authority.

Philosophically, he viewed life seriously, and with more integration of world view than others. One of the prevailing schools of thought was Platonist which became merged in a transcendental idealism of Giordano Bruno. Another school was Aristotelian, promoting the experimental method which gave impetus to physical science illustrated in Galileo Galilei. These two schools evolved in a third initiated by Bernardino Telesio and further established by Tommaso Companella, which was eclectic in that experimental philosophy and Neo-Platonist idealism were combined with Aquinas' theology but not with fusion or system. What distinguished Savonarola was his moral ideal, which being clear, precise, and powerful, provided cogency and unity to his life and thought.

Savonarola's thought would be incompletely described if his stress on the love of Jesus Christ was omitted. From a number of different pamphlets, it is clear that for Savonarola the love of Jesus Christ constituted the inspiration for Christians to bring the soul into a unity with Christ, to live the life of the Lord, not by external imitation, but by inward and divine inspiration. For Him, the Christian seeks that Christ's doctrine be a living thing in Him, desires even to suffer martyrdom, and mystically hang with Him on the same cross. This disposition results from love attained by the operation of grace since it raises man above himself, uniting the finite creature with the infinite Creator. Savonarola emphasized in his treatises of 1492 that man continually rises from humanity to divinity when animated by this love "which is the sweetest of all affections, inasmuch as it penetrates the soul, masters the body, and causes the faithful to walk the earth floating in ecstasy." Operationally, this grace is infused into man and consequently generates charity to others. Since this love joined finite creature to the infinite Creation, it contained both human free will and divine omnipotence. This Christological theological stance is reflected partly in the hymn which appears in *The Mennonite Hymnary:*

> Jesus, Refuge of the weary, Object of the spirit's love,/Fountain in life's desert dreary, Savior from the world above:/O how oft Thine eyes offended, Gaze upon the sinner's fall;/Yet upon the Cross extended, Thou didst bear the pain of all..../Jesus, may our hearts be burning With more fervent love for Thee,/May our eyes be ever turning to Thy Cross of agony;/Till in glory, parted never From the blessed Savior's side,/Graven in our hearts forever, dwell the Cross, the Crucified.

Contributions

If one asks who won, the meddlesome friar or the wayward pope, the obvious answer is the pope, of course. Savonarola fell, Alexander VI was seemingly triumphant. Few cared on that May day in 1498 when Savonarola was executed. The sovereigns did not answer his pleas for help and commercial interests had their day. He who had preached so boldly three years earlier was now quiet. Nevertheless, there was a faithful minority who remembered. Moreover, in the next few decades, the life and love of Savonarola were to reecho in other Reformers and Counter-Reformers. Although in this period Reformation thinking was in the air at many places, and although any definite causal relationship is difficult to trace, it still needs to be asked to what extent Savonarola influenced Luther's view that it was hopeless to hope for the purification of Rome, Zwingli's humanist-activism and iconoclastic tendency, Calvin's condemnation of "unholiness," his challenge of disparity between ideal and reality, and his sensitizing of the conscience and the calling of men to an ideal impossible to attain, and the Anabaptists' insistence that neither church nor civil councils could dictate practice and principle. Still others see the results of Savonarola as that of Counter Reformers centering in the Roman oratory of divine love, founded in 1517 for dedication to prayer, devotion, and service. Some would conjecture as to what degree his preaching caused the revolutionary challenge in the paintings of Michelangelo, who delighted in hearing him. Some would ask how his politics affected his successor Macheville to take a contrasting view of freedom of speech.

A summary contribution, in addition to influencing specific men and movements, is that of "freedom to conflict," the precedent of challenging the teaching of the church, particularly its "unholiness." Then and since, in every institution there is a tendency to place man above God. Savonarola desired to reverse this and to place God above man. The result was a man of "strife and contention," a great prophet and man, and his contributions. Savonarola's unique methodology for his time was his reliance upon, and practice of, the preached Word. It can only be conjectured as to how much more his contribution would have been had he exercised more carefulness in preaching adaptation.

Bibliography

Bainton, Roland. *The Horizon History of Christianity.* New York: Avon Books, 1966 (pp. 215-291);

De La Bedoyere, Michael. *The Meddlesome Friar and the Wayward Pope.* Garden City: Hanover House, 1957;

Gobineau, Arthur (Edited by Oscar Levy). *The Renaissance.* New York: G. P. Putnam's Sons (pp. 1-90);

_____. *The Golden Flower.* New York: G. P. Putnam's Sons, 1924 (pp. 1-121);

Latourette, Kenneth Scott. *A History of Christianity.* New York: Harper and Brothers, 1953 (pp. 624-683);

Marty, Martin E. *A Short History of Christianity.* New York: Meridian Books, Inc., 1959 (pp. 181-250);

Oliphant, Mrs. *The Makers of Florence.* New York: A. L. Burt (pp. 250-368).

Qualben, Lars P. *A History of the Christian Church.* New York: Thomas Nelson and Sons, 1942 (pp. 186-217);

Roder, Ralph. *The Man of the Renaissance.* New York: The Viking Press, 1935 (pp. 1-130);

Ridolfi, Roberio. *The Life of Girolamo Savonarola.* New York: Alfred A. Knopf, 1959;

Villari, Pasquale. *Life and Times of Savonarola.* New York: Charles Scribner's Sons, 1888.

> "People say to me: How can scholarly knowledge facilitate the understanding of Holy Scripture? My answer is: How does ignorance contribute to it?"

18
Erasmus

David Ewert

I. His Early Life

Erasmus was born in Rotterdam, Holland, ca. October 27, 1469. The fact that he was an illegitimate child is one cause for some of the obscurity that surrounds his earliest years. In his earlier schooling the Brethren of the Common Life left a deep impression on the lad. About 1487 he was persuaded to enter the monastery at Steyn. Although this gave him some opportunity to cultivate his literary interests, he was not entirely happy with monastic life, and looked for an opportunity to be released from it. Through the influence of a bishop, who looked for a secretary, Erasmus got a dispensation from the monastery. Eventually he got permission to go to Paris to study theology. He did not find the theological education of the Schoolmen particularly to his liking. Moreover, he had as yet no sense of vocation. By cultivating the friendship of prominent literary figures, among them Italian Humanists, he found his lot somewhat more bearable. Also, he greatly perfected his literary style while at Paris.

Through contacts with wealthy Englishmen, he was momentarily relieved from serious financial problems, and was able to go to England in 1499. At Oxford he met John Colet, who was almost of the same age as he. Also he became acquainted with Thomas More and other representatives of the New Learning. Colet made a deep impression upon him. In him Erasmus found that combination of Christian devotion, a first-rate mind, and scholarly tastes, which he admired. He sympathized deeply with Colet's desire to combat obscurantism and scholastic arrogance, but he felt that he himself lacked

---

David Ewert is a minister in the Mennonite Brethren Church. He served as Dean and Professor of New Testament Language and Interpretation in the Mennonite Brethren Bible College in Winnipeg. He received the BA from the University of British Columbia, the BD from Central Baptist Seminary, the MA from Wheaton College, the M Th from Luther Theological Seminary, and the PhD from McGill University. He has taught at Union Biblical Seminary, Yeotmal, India, and at Eastern Mennonite Seminary, Harrisonburg, Va. He is now Professor of New Testament at Mennonite Brethren Biblical Seminary, Fresno, Calif.

the courage and the equipment to join hands with Colet.

Erasmus had an unrivaled grasp of the Latin language, the *lingua franca* of the age, and upon leaving England, he was determined to perfect himself also in Greek. He saw how imperative it was for a biblical scholar to have a knowledge of the original text. Gradually he was finding his calling. He would apply the best Humanistic scholarship of his day to the documents of the Christian faith. In this way he hoped to cleanse and purify the Christian faith. This goal he pursued to the end of his life.

II. His Career

Upon his return from England, in 1500, he published the first edition of his *Adages*. It was the first work to bring him to the notice of the public. The book was a collection of classical proverbs with explanations, and represented a kind of digest of classical literature. Later, a larger edition was published. He moved about considerably in the years following 1500, residing for shorter or longer periods of time in various countries and cities. In 1509, he made his third visit to England. He attended the coronation of Henry VIII, and lectured at Cambridge.

Meanwhile his *Enchiridion militis christiani* had been published at Antwerp, in 1503. This treatise is a kind of manual for the humble believer, who must fight his spiritual battles. It reflects a blend of piety and learning on the part of the author. The message of the *Enchiridion* was presented in a very different form in the *Praise of Folly*, published in 1509, and dedicated to Thomas More. It is a kind of satire on many aspects of society, ecclesiastical and lay. What in the eyes of the world is the greatest folly, namely Christianity, turns out to be the highest wisdom.

In 1514 Erasmus made his way to Basel, where with the help of the printer Froben, he published the first printed Greek New Testament with a parallel fresh Latin translation. The title of the diglot work was *Novum Instrumentum* and it appeared in 1516. Although it was based on a limited number of late manuscripts, some not too carefully consulted, the publication was epoch-making. Three years later (1519), the first authorized edition of his *Colloquies* appeared. Through the medium of dialogue between his characters he was able to take up the great issues of his generation and bring his rhetorical art of persuasion to bear on them, besides concealing himself behind his characters. He had a special interest in the writings of the ancient Fathers and some of his more important patristic publications are *Jerome* (1516), *Augustine* (1529), *Chrysostom* (1530), and *Origen* (1536). The years 1516 to 1518 were in a sense the culmination of his career, in that his fame now spread to all the countries of Europe.

III. The Reformation

Erasmus' relations to the Reformation are somewhat ambiguous. Like the Reformers after him, he criticized severely the abuses of the church. Like them he called for a more genuine piety which drew its strength from the Scriptures. Luther read his works with profit and tried to win Erasmus for the cause of the Reformation, as did other Reformers. But Erasmus hesitated to side with Luther, and when Luther's treatises were condemned (1520) Erasmus' situation became most uncomfortable, for friends from both sides urged him to clarify his position. Roman Catholics suspected him of being a friend of Luther, and to escape their wrath he left Louvain and settled in Basel (1521), where the Reformation had been endorsed. In 1524 he published his treatise on the freedom of the will to define his position against that of Luther. Luther replied with his *De servo arbitrio* (The Bondage of the Will) in which he disdainfully repudiated the arguments of Erasmus. Luther felt that Erasmus did not really understand sin and grace. Now Erasmus had to defend himself not only against Luther, but also against the Roman Church. Whereas Erasmus was concerned with *ignorance*, Luther was concerned with *sin*. At first Luther accepted the scholar in Erasmus, not the Christian, but later he rejected him almost completely. Erasmus found it hard to accept the Reformers' radical break with Rome, and during his last years he published his work: *For the Reestablishment of Concord in the Church.* In spite of controversy, he concluded his life in his literary and scholarly activities. Soon after completing his treatise on preaching, *Ecclesiastes,* in 1536, in the midst of planning a move to the Low Countries, he died at Basel in 1536, and was buried in the cathedral which had been converted into a Protestant church.

IV. His Significance

As is the case with all great men, Erasmus is not easy to assess. He was defended and condemned by both Catholic and Protestants in his day, and that situation has not greatly changed to the present. He stands, as it were, between the Renaissance and the Reformation; he felt their common spirit, but also their contrasts. He combined in his person a deep piety with a high respect for learning, scholarship, and sheer intellectual grasp. One could hardly call him a philosopher or a theologian in the strict sense of these words; rather, he was a "literary historian." With the best critical and linguistic methods he hoped to combat ignorance and superstition and so to purify the church. Although he had a high respect for erudition, he realized that scholarship must not be an end in itself. For this reason he spent his life writing and publishing in order to enlighten as many as possible.

Erasmus was probably the greatest scholar of his age. He has been hailed as the outstanding Christian Humanist, as well as the spiritual father of Anabaptism (one has serious reservations about the latter). Although he helped to prepare the way for the Reformation, he was repudiated by it. Although offered a cardinal's hat, his works were put on the *Index* by the Council of Trent. And although often accused of compromise and cowardice, he consistently maintained his ideals to the end. His strength lay in his power to grasp important truths and to present them with irresistible eloquence. His greatness can be seen in a combination of brilliant intellectual gifts with sincerity and enduring purpose.

For Further Reading

P. S. Allen, *The Age of Erasmus* (Oxford: At the Clarendon Press, 1914); L. Bouyer, *Erasmus and His Times* (Westminster: The Newmann Press, 1959); M. P. Gilmore, "Erasmus," in *New Catholic Encyclopedia*, Vol. V, 508-511 (New York: McGraw-Hill Book Co., 1967); E. B. Harbison, "Erasmus," in *The Christian Scholar* (New York: Charles Scribner's Sons, 1956); J. Huizinga, *Erasmus* (New York: Charles Scribner's Sons, 1924); P. Smith, *Erasmus* (New York: Harper and Brothers, 1923).

> "Through faith in Christ, therefore, Christ's righteousness becomes our righteousness, and all that he has becomes ours; rather he himself becomes ours."

19
Martin Luther

Peter J. Klassen

Seldom in the history of the church has one man exerted so profound an influence or demonstrated so passionate a concern for an understanding of the essence of the Christian faith as this dynamic scion of stout German peasant stock. Born in Eisleben on November 10, 1483, he was educated at schools in Mansfeld, Magdeburg, and Eisenach before going to the University of Erfurt. His preparation for the practice of law was cut short when, in keeping with a vow made during a thunderstorm, he entered the Augustinian monastery at Erfurt in 1505. Luther had always been deeply religious; now he devoted himself to an intensive analysis of the divine-human relationship. He received the AB in 1502, and the MA in 1505.

In 1507 he was ordained a priest, and shortly thereafter he began teaching moral philosophy at the newly founded University of Wittenberg. After a brief return to study at Erfurt, and a disappointing visit to Rome, he completed his doctorate in theology in 1512, and became professor of theology at Wittenberg. As he lectured and studied, he increasingly rejected Scholasticism in favor of a biblical humanism. Early in 1514 his outlook was revolutionized by the discovery of the Pauline doctrine of "righteousness by faith." When he became convinced that justification by faith was the basis of salvation, a confrontation with the traditional theology became inevitable.

The battle was joined in 1517 when Luther challenged the validity of indulgences, then being vigorously championed by the Dominican John Tetzel, who was selling them on behalf of Archbishop Albert of Mainz. On October 31, at Wittenberg, Luther posted his famous ninety-five theses relating to indulgences. The Latin statements, quickly translated into German and printed in quantity and widely distributed, made Luther a household name and a popular hero. Efforts to silence the young monk by archbishop, cardinal, and pope all

---

Peter J. Klassen is Associate Professor of History and Chairman of the Department, Fresno State College. He received the BA from the University of British Columbia, and the AM and the PhD from the University of Southern California. Among his writings may be mentioned his monograph, *The Economics of Anabaptism, 1525-1560*.

failed, largely because Elector Frederick of Saxony protected the now-famous Reformer. Finally, in 1520, Pope Leo X issued the bull *Exsurge domine* (Arise, O Lord), threatening excommunication unless Luther would recant. The Reformer's response was to burn the document in a public bonfire. In 1521 Luther appeared before the Imperial Diet at Worms. Here, in the presence of Emperor Charles V, he dramatically refused to recant, and insisted that his conscience was bound by Scripture. Subsequently, in the Edict of Worms the emperor proclaimed Luther an outlaw.

Following the appearance at Worms, Luther was secretly taken to the castle of the Wartburg for safekeeping. Here he remained for almost a year, writing and translating the Bible. The New Testament was published in 1522; the Old Testament (including Apocrypha) would appear twelve years later. During his confinement, Luther learned that radical elements were pushing for sweeping reforms in Wittenberg. Afraid that his program of gradual and peaceful reform might be jeopardized, he returned to the city and, in a series of remarkably persuasive sermons, restored order. As Luther's ideas spread, the oppressed masses began to look to him for leadership. Since he had successfully challenged the religious hierarchy, why not also the princes who held a large part of the population in poverty and serfdom? At first he was sympathetic with the demands of the peasants. Luther encouraged the princes to alleviate the conditions of the poor, but with little success. Then, in 1524-1525, Germany was convulsed in the Peasants' War. Catholic and Lutheran princes, now encouraged by Luther, drowned the revolt in a sea of blood. Luther had flatly rejected violent revolution as a satisfactory means of correcting social ills.

But the religious Reformation, stimulated by Luther's voluminous writings and his stirring hymns, continued to spread. A program of visitation was carried on throughout Luther's state, electoral Saxony. Luther, or other like-minded churchmen, accompanied by officials of the government, visited the different parishes to make sure that the new faith was being taught in all the churches. The close collaboration of religious and civil leaders would continue to characterize the Lutheran Reformation. Indeed, when Luther died at Eisleben in 1546, he had just helped to settle a dispute between two counts.

Luther was a staunch champion of building strong family ties. In 1525 he married the former nun, Katherina von Bora. Six children were born into the home, and the busy Reformer found time to play with his children and tell them stories, while his generous hospitality often threatened to exceed the family income.

Central to the theology which Luther gradually forged in his intense searching was the concept of justification by grace through faith. Luther broke with the medieval tradition of seeking divine approbation by means of sacraments and works; instead, he confidently asserted that the Christian finds his joy and freedom in recognizing his complete dependence upon God's boundless grace, not man's feeble efforts.

For Luther, faith was no mere assertion of belief in the existence of God or participation in the sacraments; rather, it was a lively relationship with Him—a continuous encounter that reflected itself in trust and service. Luther believed that such a faith was usually gained through the written or spoken word. But even a positive response to the proclaimed word was possible only because of God's grace, for the "bondage of the will" made it impossible for man to overcome estrangement from God. This belief, which Luther expressed in Augustine's predestinarian terms, was for him a source of comfort and confidence, for it was an affirmation of trust in the all-sufficiency and mercy of God, and not a dependence upon human frailty.

Another distinguishing characteristic of Luther's theology was his emphasis upon "Scripture alone" as the source of authoritative guidance, the means whereby God confronted man. Scripture was of supreme importance because through it Christ was revealed; accordingly, Luther did not regard all books of the Bible as of equal significance. Even the New Testament books differed in the clarity with which they taught righteousness by faith!

Scripture could best be understood in the context of the church, the community of believers in whom the living Spirit interpreted God's Word to man. The marks of the true church were faithfully preaching the Word and observing the New Testament's two sacraments. Luther held that incorporation into the Christian community was through baptism, and that this sacrament should be given to infants. He maintained the doctrine of Christ's "real presence" in the Lord's Supper, asserting that the believer partakes of the body and blood of Christ which are "in, with, and under" the elements. Luther's rejection of the view that Christ was only spiritually present in the elements prevented a union with some other Reformers, notably the Swiss leader Zwingli.

Luther believed that in the church, clergy and laity together constituted the priesthood of believers. Ministers were not to be regarded as a special, essential class of mediators between God and man; all believers were priests, to each other and for each other, directly related to each other and to God. Such a view did not negate the necessity of having a trained ministry that could faithfully proclaim the Word, but it did abolish the medieval view of higher and lower callings. In the freedom and confidence given through faith, all believers, whatever their station in life, could equally serve God.

Brief Bibliography

Bainton, Roland. *Here I Stand: A Life of Martin Luther* (Mentor Books). A vivid, gripping portrait of a man of genius.

Boehmer, Heinrich. *Martin Luther: Road to Reformation* (Meridian Books, 1967). A sympathetic study of Luther up to his stay at the Wartburg.

Erikson, Erik. *Young Man Luther* (Norton, 1962). A highly controversial psychoanalytic biography of Luther's formative years.

Forell, George W. *Faith Active in Love* (Augsburg, 1954). Convincing proof that Luther was profoundly concerned about social issues.

Lau, Franz. *Luther* (Westminster, 1963). An indispensable account.

Lilje, Hans. *Luther and the Reformation* (Fortress, 1967). The famed Lutheran churchman examines the basic problems confronting the Reformer.

Prenter, Regin. *Spiritus Creator*, tr. John Jensen (Muhlenberg, 1953). The author sees Luther's concept of the Holy Spirit as a cardinal part of his theology.

Rupp, Gordon. *Luther's Progress to the Diet of Worms* (Torchbooks).

———. *The Righteousness of God* (Allenson, 1953). An analysis of Luther's theology.

Schwieberg, E. G. *Luther and His Times* (Concordia, 1950). Luther's impact upon his world, especially Wittenberg University.

Thulin, Oskar, ed. *Life of Luther*, tr. M. O. Dietrich (Fortress, 1966). A superbly illustrated re-creation of the highlights in Luther's career.

Watson, Philip. *Let God Be God* (Fortress, 1947). A penetrating interpretation of Luther's theological emphasis.

> "Master Philip comes along
> softly and gently...."
> —Luther

20
Philip Melanchthon

John S. Oyer

Philip Melanchthon was born on February 16, 1497, at Bretten in Southwestern Germany. His family had sufficient means to send the promising lad to study, privately and then to various schools, even though his father, an armorer, died when the boy was only ten. His maternal great-uncle, the humanist Reuchlin, took an active interest in his education. It was Reuchlin who devised a Greek form of his family name, calling him Melanchthon instead of Schwartzerd [black soil]. He matriculated at Heidelberg in 1509, and at Tübingen in 1512. By 1514 he had earned his master's degree and had begun to lecture at Tübingen. Here he went beyond the rather pedantic study of Latin into full-blown humanism. Melanchthon found the study of Latin, Greek, and Hebrew a source of delight. Already at Heidelberg, a traditional scholastic haven, he had earned a reputation for his mastery of Greek, a mastery superior to that of some of the professors.

In 1518 the Saxon Elector invited Melanchthon to come to his new university at Wittenberg to lecture on Greek. His arrival caused no stir among either professors or students. Some of the former had openly favored a more mature scholar, such as Peter Mosellanus of Leipzig. A few days after his arrival he delivered his Inaugural Address in which he proposed that all branches of learning, including theology, be grounded in the study of language. But all learning in turn, he said, must be brought under the kingdom of God. Among the professors Luther was especially favorably impressed. Eventually Melanchthon surpassed even Luther in the advocacy of Scripture as the sole authority in matters of faith, by which Melanchthon meant, of course, the Scriptures in their earliest available form. For this reason one should study Greek and Hebrew. Melanchthon also lectured on the Bible, and even took a degree in theology in 1519 at Wittenberg.

If Melanchthon changed Wittenberg, Wittenberg also had its effect upon Melanchthon. He became completely engrossed in the new evangelical cause. By 1521 he produced the first systematic theological

---

John S. Oyer is Professor of History at Goshen College, and editor of the *Mennonite Quarterly Review*. He is also on the editorial board of *Studies in Anabaptist and Mennonite History*. He received the BA from Goshen College, the AM from Harvard University, and the PhD from the University of Chicago. He is the author of *Lutheran Reformers Against the Anabaptists*.

statement for the evangelicals, *Loci communes rerum theologicarum.* He also participated in some of the earliest church visitations in Saxony; these visitations were designed to establish the new faith in the parishes themselves, and to discover what work needed to be done by Wittenberg in order to spread the faith. The burning issues of his time caught Melanchthon and would not let him remain a mere humanist. One suspects that his personal piety, derived in part from his father, also enhanced his interest in the religious issues of his day.

Melanchthon's theology is best discussed in relation to that of Luther *(q.v.).* No systematic treatment of his theological views will be presented here. Rather, one should begin with Luther and delineate Melanchthon's significant deviations from the former's views.

Luther espoused a rigorous determinism. Man is hopelessly bound by sin. As a humanist Melanchthon was inclined to give some weight to man's ability to exercise his own will to some extent, at least in matters of faith and morality. Melanchthon was unhappy with the dispute between Erasmus and Luther on the freedom of the will in the mid-1520s, though he tended to side with Luther. In his revised *Loci* of 1535 Melanchthon declared that original sin had not taken from man the ability to exercise his will in making correct decisions when he was under the influence of grace. Man's will is able to assent to truth when it is revealed through the power of the Spirit. To Luther's Word and Spirit working in man to bring about his justification, and even his faith, Melanchthon added the partially active will of man, which had to struggle against its own weakness and error but which was not totally devoid of power to choose the good. In the same vein, Melanchthon tended to emphasize the value of teaching the law as a means of inciting men to live morally. He once declared that good works, along with justification, were necessary for eternal life, and on this occasion he did not add that justification by its nature produced good works. Melanchthon never fully resolved the relation between faith and works. Luther and Melanchthon never broke on this issue. Indeed, it came to the surface as a challenge to Luther's thought primarily after Luther's death in 1546. Melanchthon and his subsequent followers called Philippists were charged with the error of synergism by the rigidly orthodox Lutherans, men such as Matthias Flacius Illyricus (1520-75). In point of fact Melanchthon was much more Lutheran on faith, justification, and good works than his enemies within the orthodox Lutheran camp were willing to admit. But his humanist passion for ethics made it difficult for him to fully agree with Luther on the latter's unfree will and his seeming relegation of ethics to a minor role.

Melanchthon provided a systematic treatment of Luther's theological ideas, with his own characteristic touch, in the numerous editions of the *Loci,* the Augsburg Confession of 1530, and in other writings. Both his mind and writing style were clear and admirably suited to the task. Most of the evangelicals' position papers were drawn up by him. But his work was larger. He was stung by Erasmus' quip that wherever Lutheranism gained, learning lost. More than any person in the Lutheran camp he promoted learning by fusing good letters with the faith. He was indefatigable in his efforts at school reform, as well as education and training for clergy out in the parishes. He revised curricula for Latin grammar schools in several cities, and he set the curricular pattern for the German universities as well. The University of Wittenberg was reorganized under his influence, and the University of Greifswald chose his pattern, and even his textbooks, in 1545. He helped found the universities of Königsberg, Jena, and Marburg, and he revised the curricula of Cologne, Tübingen, Leipzig, and Heidelberg. Ever since his 1518 Inaugural he sought to infuse the schools with two burning concerns: a return to the sources and a knowledge of Christ. He brought the best of humanism into the church. The mixture was uniquely his own, although both Erasmus and Luther served as sources of inspiration for him.

The last fourteen years of Melanchthon's life were marred by bitter controversy. After Luther's death the Protestant cause in Central Germany appeared gravely threatened and even doomed when Emperor Charles V, finally freed from dynastic and Turkish wars, advanced to settle the religious question by force of arms. The cause appeared to be lost when Protestant Duke Maurice turned traitor for political gain. Maurice was awarded Electoral Saxony for his support of Charles, and then declared he wanted Wittenberg to regather its teaching corps and remain the center of Protestant teaching. The strictly orthodox would make no peace with Maurice; Melanchthon did. For his pains he received a torrent of abuse from the self-appointed "Lutherans." Melanchthon was determined to salvage what he could from the disaster. The emperor pressed for doctrinal statements designed to heal, or paper over, the breach between Wittenberg and Rome. To some of these attempts Melanchthon gave his blessing, less than wholehearted, to be sure. He was willing to relegate some issues—the unimportant ones, the *adiaphora*—to a minor role. Which issues? A return to seven sacraments? But Melanchthon would regard most of them as rites with no sacramental value. The necessity of good works to salvation? But Melanchthon had never quite renounced these, nor would he give good works a Roman interpretation. His enemies thought he conceded on justification itself, and on the dominion of the pope.

Melanchthon was irenic by nature; he hated bitter controversy. He had always been foremost among the Lutherans in trying to find the means for reconciling the differences between Wittenberg and Rome. For the sake of peace and the gospel he was willing to compromise, and sometimes went beyond his deepest convictions and had to retract later his statements of assent. His enemies thought him weak-willed rather than irenic. Luther knew better. He once wrote:

> I am rough, boisterous, stormy, and altogether warlike. I am born to fight against innumerable monsters and devils. I must remove stumps and stones, cut away thistles, and thorns, and clear the wild forests; but Master Philipp comes along softly and gently sowing and watering with joy, according to the gifts which God has abundantly bestowed upon him.

Melanchthon simply believed that no one had gained a complete understanding of truth, nor could he, on this side of eternity. Therefore all human efforts should be expended to reveal the truth. He was ecumenical, although he could not tolerate either the Anabaptists or Zwingli.

Worn out by interminable wrangling and strife, Melanchthon died in 1560 at the age of 63, and was buried beside Luther in the Castle Church in Wittenberg. He had turned Luther's ideas and work into teachable form. He brought the best of humanist thought into the church, and reformed the schools. He was indeed the *Preceptor Germaniae*, the teacher of Germany.

Literature

Most of the literature on Melanchthon is written in German. A large number of articles appeared on the quadricentennial of his death, in 1960. The best work in English is Clyde L. Manschreck, *Melanchthon, the Quiet Reformer* (New York: Abingdon Press, 1958), who follows the style of Roland H. Bainton, *Here I Stand* (New York: Abingdon Press, 1950), and the data of James Richard, *Philip Melanchthon, the Protestant Preceptor of Germany* (New York: Putnam, 1898), but provides his own interpretation. Melanchthon's own writings were published in the *Corpus Reformatorum*, Vols. I to XXVIII, edited by Bretschneider and Bindseil (Halle, 1834-1860). Selected works of Melanchthon have been edited more recently by R. Stupperich, *Melanchthons Werke in Auswahl*, 6 vols. (Gütersloh, 1951 ff.).

"The Word of God is so sure and strong that if God wills all things are done the moment that He speaks His Word."

21

Ulrich (Huldrych) Zwingli

Robert Holland

Zwingli is important for four good reasons: (1) He was one of the first major scholars and preachers of the developing Reformation with a thorough humanistic education. He used this asset vigorously in his writing and pastoral work, and he was an important figure in the circle of Erasmus, Oecolampad, and numerous other humanistic scholars and preachers of his day. (2) He was *the* theologian of German-speaking Switzerland and his ideas and works are felt there and in Protestantism even today. (3) He exercised a decisive influence on the character and expansion of Swiss, Austrian, and South German Anabaptism. Its development into what George Williams calls the "radical wing" of the Reformation (*The Radical Reformation*, 1962) is much more important than is generally realized for the understanding of the American church in its non-Reformed denominations. (4) His concept of the church contributed to the preservation of the "state church" in Switzerland and Europe and promoted Anabaptist reaction.

Zwingli was born in 1484 in the northeastern part of Switzerland at Wildhaus, canton St. Gallen. If the region in which one is born has any effect on personality, it is demonstrated in Zwingli, for he showed all the best traits of the Swiss: sturdy independence, strong patriotism, zeal for religion, and a deep appreciation for scholarship.[1] One might add also a deep love for music.

An account of his education reads like a list of noted humanist scholars from Bern to Vienna. His uncle Bartholomew Zwingli oversaw initially the development of his intellectual abilities, then he was sent to the Latin School of St. Theodore in Klein Basel. After this, he studied music with Heinrich Wölflin, the well-known humanist musician in Bern. Because of his passion for music, he nearly entered the Dominican monastery there. From 1500 to 1502 he was at the

---

Robert Holland is a Presbyterian minister who has served in Fresno Pacific College in Fresno, Calif., as Associate Professor of Biblical Studies. He received the BA from Texas A & M, the BD from Princeton Theological Seminary, and the D Theol from the University of Basel. His doctoral dissertation was entitled *The Hermeneutics of Peter Riedeman*.

University of Vienna, where his friends and fellow students included Joachim von Watt (Vadian), Heinrich Loriti (Glarean), Johann Heigerlin (Faber), and John Meyer of Eck, later the most notable of Luther's opponents. Returning to his homeland he attended the University of Basel, which had recently moved into the humanistic atmosphere. There he earned the BA in 1504 and the MA in 1506. Thomas Wyttenbach deeply influenced him at Basel with the new methods of biblical study in his lectures on the *Sentences of Peter Lombard.*

After ordination (probably at Constance) he became parish priest at Glarus (1506-1516) and continued studying on his own, teaching himself Greek. It was while he was priest at Einsiedeln (1516-1518), that he became an enthusiastic follower of Erasmus. The year 1518 saw him elected cathedral preacher at Zurich. Here he would spend the remaining twelve years of his life, 1519-1531. This gave him the opportunity to start reforms for which he had seen the necessity at Einsiedeln. The next six years he attacked purgatory, prayers to saints, monasticism, papal control, fasting, and clerical celibacy.

The Colloquy of Marburg in 1529 brought events resulting in the decline of the influence of Zwingli's movement. His difference of opinion over the Eucharist with Luther was so serious that it prevented any possibility of union between the Protestant forces. The cantons of Basel, Schaffhausen, St. Gallen, and Zurich were united against the five Catholic forest cantons of Lucerne, Zug, Schwyz, Uri, and Unterwalden. The religious and economic pressure put on them by Zurich mounted until in 1531 the forest cantons attacked the poorly prepared Zurichers. Zwingli as chaplain carried the flag and was killed at the battle of Kappel, October 11, 1531. As a result of the defeat, the spread of the Reformation in German-speaking Switzerland was permanently halted and the situation has remained geographically much the same since the sixteenth century.

The keys to Zwingli's theology, of course, are his humanistic background and the Scriptures. When we compare him to Luther, there are some sharp differences: in general we can say Luther's involvement in the Reformation grew out of his existential concern to be justified before God, for this was the burning question of the sixteenth century. Zwingli's involvement and concern were much more along intellectual lines. His humanist pursuits had led him to the conviction of the supremacy of Scripture. The natural distaste of the Swiss for foreign interference, whether political or ecclesiastical, tied in well with Zwingli's proclamation that only the Scripture was binding on man.

Luther's efforts at practical reform fell considerably short of Zwingli's, for Zwingli excelled at this. In Luther's central emphasis on justification, and his lack of success at implementing it in a practical program, he was a less complete theologian than either Zwingli or Calvin.

It is important to see that the practical outworking of Zwingli's theology was tied in with his commitment to the sovereignty of God and his understanding that ultimate earthly authority was the civil government acting in obedience to and in accord with the Scriptures.

He assumed that this was possible in Zurich. His reforms, both spiritual and political, were simply an extension of his understanding of Scripture and a logical result of his preaching.

While Zwingli was "his own man" theologically, he was closer to Calvin than to Luther because of their similar educational background. Luther retained more of his Roman Catholic ideas than he realized. Though Zwingli was a pungent writer and a fine critical scholar, Calvin excelled him as a thinker and as an interpreter of the Scriptures because he had a greater unity and consistency than Zwingli. It would be safe to say that Zwingli was a rational supernaturalist. Calvin resembled him in this, but Calvin had a deeper insight into the spiritual meaning of the Scripture.

Both Calvin and Zwingli were firmly committed to the principle of educating the laity for reform, and not pushing the reform on the laity until there was a broad base of support to carry it. It was this commitment that caused the break between Zwingli and the Swiss Brethren. It was inevitable that the impatience of Conrad Grebel and the unyielding firmness of Zwingli would produce an explosive situation. Zwingli unintentionally contributed to the spread of Anabaptism into Southern Germany, Austria, and Moravia by his relentless persecution of the Anabaptists.

Zwinglian liturgy in Switzerland is noticeably bare even today. The dislike of liturgy among non-Reformed denominations in America today is a direct result of the influence of Zwingli on the Anabaptist movement before it broke off from him, and ultimately upon American Protestantism. A reason for this is Zwingli's idea of the supremacy of Scripture over all else. His theology, like many groups in America, is a theology of the Word, to the exclusion of a well-developed liturgy.

Bibliography

Bromiley, G. W., *Zwingli & Bullinger*, Library of Christian Classics, Westminster, Philadelphia, 1953.
Courvoisier, *Zwingli, Soldat de Dieu*, Geneva, 1957 (tr. into Eng.)
Farner, Oskar, *Zwingli the Reformer*, New York, tr. D. G. Sear, 1952
Garside, Charles, *Zwingli and the Arts*, New Haven, Yale Univ. Press, 1966
Jackson, S. M., *Huldreich Zwingli*, New York, Putnam, 1903
Rilliet, Jean, *Zwingli, Third Man of the Reformation*, 1964
Walton, *Zwingli's Theocracy*

Footnote

1. Bromiley, G., *Zwingli and Bullinger*, 1953, LCC, p. 13.

"I believe the Word of God simply by grace, and not from learning."

22

Conrad Grebel

J. C. Wenger

Scion of one of Zurich's old and illustrious patrician families, Conrad Grebel was born about the year 1498 to Jacob Grebel and his wife, Dorothea (Fries) Grebel, third child and first son in a family of six children. His parents gave him every advantage which money could provide. From eight to sixteen he studied in a Latin school in Zurich called the Carolina, named for the ruler whom the Germans know as Carl the Great (Charlemagne in English). The fall of 1514 he enrolled in the University of Basel, where he remained for one academic year. The next autumn his father succeeded in securing for him a royal scholarship from the ruler of Austria to attend the University of Vienna, where he remained, 1515-18. So far as we know, all through his university days, Grebel became more and more a humanist, dedicated to the great classics, especially in Latin, and basically indifferent to the voices for Reformation which were coming from Wittenberg and Zurich, from 1517 and 1519 respectively. The fall of 1518 Grebel went to the University of Paris, aided by a scholarship, which his father wangled from the king of France. (Incidentally, the father kept a large share of the scholarship money, and great tension developed between son and father.) Later Grebel secured a papal scholarship to study at the University of Pisa, but this plan fell through—partly because of Grebel's poor health (perhaps brought on by loose living), and partly through the joy Grebel found in the learned circle of scholars which gathered around Zwingli to study Greek.

A new epoch began in the life of young Grebel in 1521 when he utterly lost his heart to a girl whom we know only as Barbara. She evidently came from a poor and humble family, and may not have been

---

J. C. Wenger, the editor of this volume, is a Mennonite minister and bishop, and served as vice-president for North America of the Presidium of Mennonite World Conference. He is Professor of Historical Theology in the Associated Mennonite Biblical Seminaries, and author of various books on Anabaptist-Mennonite history and doctrine, as well as *God's Word Written* and *Introduction to Theology*. His BA is from Goshen College, his MA from the University of Michigan, and his ThD from the University of Zurich. He has also taught at Eastern Mennonite Seminary and at Union Biblical Seminary in India.

particularly earnest in moral endeavor. But nothing mattered to Grebel except to claim her as his bride. Grebel's parents were sure of only one thing: Never would he marry below his station, especially Barbara. But on February 6, 1522, on a day when his father was out of the city (Zurich was then a city of about 8,000), Grebel and his *holokosme* ("all the world") slipped into the home of a Zurich priest and were duly married. The father raged, and the mother seemed on the verge of total collapse, but Grebel had his bride. Barbara bore him three children: Theophilus, 1522; Joshua, 1523; and Rachel, 1525. All of Grebel's living descendants come through the second son, Joshua. (For many years now, the pastor of the Great Minster in Zurich, Zwingli's church, has been Hans Rudolf von Grebel, a lineal descendant from Conrad Grebel, of the thirteenth generation.)

Zwingli began his glorious ministry of the Word of God in the Great Minster, the leading Zurich cathedral, on New Year's Day, 1519. Increasingly, God blessed his ministry with success, and a glorious renewal of New Testament Christianity began to emerge. In 1522, sometime after his marriage, this gospel ministry reached the heart and life of Conrad Grebel, and the young disciple turned from humanism to Christ. He was thoroughly converted, and became an earnest and faithful disciple of Christ. He had long been Zwingli's friend, and now he also looked to him as his spiritual mentor. Grebel forgot about his health troubles in his newly found joy in Christ. He was particularly thrilled at the prospects for a soundly evangelical Bible church which he saw Zwingli about to establish.

Zwingli in turn, although increasingly frowned upon by the bishop of Constance (to whose diocese Zurich belonged), was also supremely happy and confident about the work of renewal which Christ by His Spirit and Word was bringing to Zurich. Zwingli called for "Disputations" with his Catholic opponents, and it was soon evident that in a general way the major governing body of Zurich, the Council of the Two Hundred, was firmly (for the most part) behind him in his reform work. By the fall of 1523, however, it became evident that Zwingli was perhaps moving a bit too rapidly to secure the approval of many of these two hundred senators. On the other hand, Zwingli shocked some of the young men who had been his most ardent supporters by agreeing to allow the Council of the Two Hundred to determine the tempo of the Reformation. He would not (Zwingli declared) make any changes without the approval of his "lords." Men such as Conrad Grebel and Simon Stumpf objected to this attitude of submission to the state in matters of faith.

Thus the Disputation (October 1523), which was intended to mark another step forward in overcoming Catholicism, actually marked the real beginning of disunity in the Zwingli camp. During 1524 the tension between Zwingli and his continuing supporters, and Grebel and his more radical colleagues, grew more intense. On September 5, 1524, Grebel wrote a long letter, in two installments totaling 345 lines, to a radical Reformer in Germany, Thomas Müntzer. Grebel knew but little of the man, his only acquaintance being through two tracts which had reached him. But in these 345 lines we obtain a clear and sharply focused portrait of the biblical church which Grebel hoped to see established. This letter has been published (Herald Press, 1970) in both facsimile and in translation.

In December, and again in January 1525, Zwingli made valiant efforts to re-win Grebel for his program. On Tuesday, January 17, 1525, Zwingli and Grebel engaged in a formal disputation before the Council of the Two Hundred, the issue centering on infant baptism and its significance for a New Testament Church. Zwingli, who had taught as recently as 1523 the desirability of baptizing catechumens like the fourth-century church did, now argued for infant baptism, while Grebel and his colleagues, Mantz and Reublin, upheld believer's baptism. The Council declared Zwingli the victor. Not only that, on the following day the Council ordered all parents to have their infants baptized on pain of exile for non-compliance. And on Saturday, January 21, 1525, the Council issued an order that Conrad Grebel and Felix Mantz dared no longer hold Bible study meetings. The Grebel party, consisting of possibly fifteen persons, met that night to discuss their plight. No one dreamed what would there occur.

The meeting was held, it is believed, in the home of the mother of Mantz in Zurich. The group felt fearful and anxious, and knelt in prayer for divine help and guidance. Following the prayer, a converted priest, now known to us as George Blaurock, knelt before Grebel and asked for baptism! Grebel complied. The others then requested George to baptize them, and he did so. This solemn hour therefore marked the formal organization of the first modern Free Church. Since they called each other "brother," in time they were nicknamed the Swiss Brethren, but commonly they were called *Täufer* or Anabaptists in derision. (A decade later a Frisian priest named Menno Simons was converted, and united with a similar Dutch group. Eventually all these Free Churchmen were designated as Mennists—Mennonites in English—in America as well as in Europe.) In a matter of days the Grebel group began to observe the Lord's Supper. They also evangelized in various towns and Swiss countrysides with remarkable success. By Easter of 1525 the congregation of the Brethren at St. Gall is said to have numbered 500.

Soon the canton and city of Zurich were firmly resolved to crush the new church by force. The leaders and members were usually only a jump or two ahead of the catchpoles who were seeking them. A goodly number, including Grebel, spent the winter of 1525-26 in prison, but made their escape—probably through the connivance of Jacob Grebel, one of the senators—in the spring of 1526. The summer of 1526 Grebel was at Maienfeld in the canton known in English as the Grisons (Graubuenden in German), where one of his sisters lived. There he died of the plague in July or August, 1526. He thereby escaped official execution which became the lot of many of his colleagues.

Grebel held warmly to the great doctrines of the Christian faith: a personal God, His incarnation in Jesus Christ, the blessed ministry of the Holy Spirit, the full inspiration and authority of the Word of God, man's need of repentance and the new birth, the possibility through the sanctifying work of the Holy Spirit of living a life of holiness and of victory over sin, the adequacy of divine grace for our human shortcomings, the church as a holy brotherhood of regenerated disciples, baptism and Lord's Supper as holy and joyful covenant celebrations, and the personal hope of Christ's return. He further believed that the Christian life involves cross-bearing and unjust suffering, that disciples of Christ must always accept such suffering in meekness and love, and must never under any circumstances resort to violence and killing. He believed that prior to the age of accountability children are in the kingdom of God, and stand in no need of any ceremony. The most basic commission of the church is evangelism.

Grebel's early death—just a year and a half after he founded the church—was a great loss to his brotherhood. His wise and capable leadership was sorely needed in the trying days of persecution which were already upon them. Mantz was spared until the authorities executed him by drowning in the Limmat River on January 5, 1527. Another promising leader, a South German named Michael Sattler, was tortured and burned at the stake in Rottenburg in Germany on May 21, 1527. George Blaurock escaped the fate of Mantz in 1527 because he was not a citizen of Zurich, but was captured in the Tirol and after torture burned at the stake on September 6, 1529. It seems like a miracle that the little band of nonresistant Brethren survived at all.

Lit. The definitive biography, *Conrad Grebel, ca. 1498-1526, The Founder of the Swiss Brethren* . . . by Harold S. Bender, published in 1950 and reprinted in 1971 (Scottdale, Pa.: Herald Press, 1971). More recently J. C. Wenger edited *Conrad Grebel's Programmatic Letters of 1524* (Scottdale, Pennsylvania: Herald Press, 1970). *The Mennonite Encyclopedia* also contains an excellent summary of Grebel's life and work by Harold S. Bender. Irvin B. Horst has discovered that Rome put all of Grebel's writings on the famous Tridentine Index (*Auctors librorum prohibitorum*) as early as 1564, and continued to so list them as late as 1726 (*Mennonite Quarterly Review,* Oct., 1970, pp. 389 f.). Other writers in the "first class" (*Auctors primae classis),* that is, all their writings were under the ban, included Luther, Zwingli, and Menno Simons. John L. Ruth has authored a splendid volume, *Conrad Grebel of Zurich.* And Leland Harder is currently preparing a massive work which may be entitled *Grebeliana.*

> "The poor needy people are now so badly deceived that no tongue can tell it adequately. With all words and actions they fix it so that the poor man can't read because of the struggle for existence. And they preach without shame that the poor man shall let himself be cheated and pushed around. When will he then learn to read the Bible?"[1]

23
Thomas Müntzer

Franklin H. Littell

Thomas Müntzer (ca. 1490-1525) was a radical of the sixteenth century whose dramatic role during the Peasants' War in Thuringia, culminating in his capture, torture, and death, has inspired the most varied treatment by churchmen and historians. Because of his contact with the "Zwickau prophets," Martin Luther—to whom critics of the establishment were all the same—damned him as an "Anabaptist." Because he came from Luther's camp at Wittenberg, the Roman Catholics used him as an illustration of the bad results of Lutheran "individualism."

The first appreciative treatment of Müntzer came after the French Revolution when several historians (Strobel, Seideman, Förstemann) portrayed him as a fighter for social justice. With the rise of Marxism, a number of writers have seen in him the authentic champion of the people's cause in contrast to Luther, who is said to have betrayed the peasants (Engels, Kautsky, Bernstein, Bax, Meusel, Smirin). Since World War II Müntzer has been the hero of plays and movies in East Germany, in which he comes through as a "proletarian" hero contrasted with the "bourgeois" Luther.

In point of fact, Müntzer was alienated from Luther, was condemned by the Anabaptists, and was not a "leader" of the peasants but at most an agitator who fanned the fires of their resentment of oppression. Furthermore, he was more of a "bourgeois" than Luther, since he early fell heir to a legacy that provided him a living. Nevertheless, in a time when the subject of "Christianity and Revolution" is

---

Dr. Littell is Professor of Religion at Temple University and a well-known writer on radical religion, from the Left Wing of the Reformation to contemporary conflicts between church and state. Among his degrees: BA (Cornell), BD (Union), PhD (Yale), Dr. Theol. (Marburg), and Lit D (Thiel).

widely discussed, Müntzer's worldview and message are not without interest and significance.

Like almost all of the radical Reformers, Müntzer was a primitivist. That is, he believed that the early church was normative, that the church had "fallen" when it became prosperous and powerful after Constantine, and that a restitution of true religion was at hand.

> "I have read often and much the history of the old Fathers. I find the Church of Christ spotless and a virgin up to the death of the disciples of the Apostles."[2]

The true church was spoiled by the avarice and commerce of the priests. Müntzer's vision of the early church was, however, confused with his dream of the lost Eden. In both, communism of goods had prevailed, and the "fall" was tied to the introduction of private property. Moreover, his view of the restitution confused the restoration of the true church with the final restoration of all things. The impending climax of history meant for Müntzer the coming of the kingdom; the church reform was simply the first step toward that consummation.

Müntzer's ideas of radical church reform carried a heavy load of general social and economic critique, and his hopes for the future encompassed the world as well as the church. When the lords ignored his plea that they, with the daybreak of the Reformation, give up their power and property and share with the poor, he became a preacher of political rebellion. In his sermons he drew heavily from the Old Testament prophets of social justice, and he condemned the robbers and exploiters of the common man in their spirit: woe unto them that lay house to house and field to field, that grind the faces of the poor!

> "Look, our lords and princes are the basic stock of covetousness, of thievery and robbery. They take all creatures as property—the fish in the water, the birds in the air, the fruit of the earth, everything must be theirs. And then they let the word of God's commandment out among the poor and say, God has commanded, thou shalt not steal. But they don't apply this commandment to themselves."[3]

The godless now dominate and rejoice in their position, but they shall be overthrown.[4]

Finally he proclaimed an unrestrained message of the slaying of the godless to usher in the kingdom of righteousness.

> "For the godless have no right to live, but only what the elect will permit them...."[5]

His seal and banner (April, 1525) were explained as follows:

> "The banner is the sign of the new covenant, in which God—as once in the apostolic time, again speaks directly with his elect through visions and dreams. The red cross and the naked sword are to indicate that the elect have the right and the duty to wipe out the godless by force."[6]

Calling himself a "knight of God against the godless," armed "with the sword of Gideon," he urged the peasants to be of good cheer and brave in heart—"for God promises often in the Bible that he will help the poor, the pious, and destroy the godless."[7] The tyrannical and unjust lords will be destroyed as Israel of old slew the Canaanites. The peasants therefore went into battle singing hymns, expecting divine intervention on their behalf, but were slaughtered in great numbers.

In spite of his scandalous end, and the use both Roman Catholics and Lutherans made of it, Müntzer's influence on church matters reached further than might be expected. He published a handbook with materials for use in Christian holiday services. Several of his hymns were popular and continued in use for many years after his death. His church order was used in Braunschweig as late as the early eighteenth century.

While at Alstedt, Müntzer rejected infant baptism, though he never introduced believer's baptism. He also wrote profusely to express the common people's disappointment that Luther did not press forward and introduce the expected age of equality and brotherhood. In 1523 Müntzer put out no less than 18 anti-Lutheran tracts on an underground press.

Andreas Bodenstein von Karlstadt too had broken with Luther and was leading a radical reorganization of the church at Orlamünde. There he led the service dressed in peasant's clothing and administered communion to the people in both kinds. But when Müntzer wrote him to enlist his support for revolution, Karlstadt rejected the appeal and published a refutation of rebellion against the appointed authorities.

Although he was not a very good organizer, in two respects Müntzer anticipated the revolutionary methods that became standard in the twentieth century. First, he believed that a gifted leader would be sent to give the people the direction they needed in their radical change.

> "In order that the holy church shall be made new by the harsh truth, a servant of God filled with grace must come forward in the spirit of Elijah, Matth. 17:3, Kings 18, Revelation 11. And he must bring all things into the right offensive."[8]

Second, he founded the kind of revolutionary band that by its discipline and secret understanding of the course of history wields much greater influence than its numbers warrant. This he did at Alstedt, after leaving Wittenberg. Membership was about 300. A new community of "saints," bound together in a secret covenant, was formed. Within this Gideon's band, which thought of itself as carrying history through a drastic reversal of social classes, a communism of sharing was introduced.

Müntzer had a vivid sense of human history's rapid rush toward the day of judgment.

> "I tell you one must pay keen attention to the new movement of the world today. The old guidelines are totally useless any more...."[9]

In certain other ideas and expressions he also showed a combination of religious and revolutionary imagery which appeared from time to time thereafter. He identified his times as the "Fifth Age" of earth, the age of iron and iron men. His model man was a revolutionary type, an "absolute man" of action, not counting the cost. He believed that the most appalling odds could be equalized by the power of the Spirit: the gift of the Spirit was in fact the power to accomplish the impossible.

He was a forerunner, then, of the idea that convulsive and confused times of historical transition can be directed and managed by disciplined men of resolute courage and adequate ruthlessness. The records would indicate that he did not himself qualify, being primarily a verbalizer. But there have been numerous "iron men" since Müntzer, whose fore-shortened view of history and tough practice of the "politics of the deed" put them in his track.

Sources

1. TM: *Ausgetrückte emplössung* . . . 1524 (Jordan edition, p. 6)
2. *Intimatio Thomae Muntzeri manu propria scripta et affixa Pragae a.1521 contra Papistas* (Strobel edition, p. 35)
3. Quoted in Bloch, Ernst, *Thomas Münzer als Theologe der Revolution* (Munich: Kurt Wolff Verlag, 1921), p. 60.
4. *Hochverursachte Schutzrede* . . . 1524 (Enders edition, p. 22)
5. *Auslegung Danielis* (Strobel edition, p. 161)
6. Böhmer, Heinrich, *Studien zu Thomas Müntzer*, p. 17
7. *Müntzers Rede an das Volk vor der Schlacht bey Frankenhausen* (Strobel edition, p. 110)
8. *Ausgetrückte emplössung* . . . 1524 (Jordan edition, p. 17)
9. Quoted in Bloch, Ernst, *op. cit.*, p. 33

"Faith in Christ Jesus reconciles us to the Father and gives us access to Him."

24
Michael Sattler

Myron S. Augsburger

The Reformation of the sixteenth century stands as a watershed in the history of Christian theology. Among historians it is debated as to whether the Reformation or the Enlightenment is the more crucial turning point into the modern period. There is little doubt that the rediscovery of *sola gratia* and the universal priesthood of the believer gave rise to the development of an individualism that is characteristic of Western thought. Some interpret the Reformation as the rediscovery of Augustine's doctrine of grace which had been eclipsed by his doctrine of the church. For most, the key to understanding Reformation theology is Luther's concept of justification by faith.

But there was more to the Reformation than the Catholic and the Protestant dimensions. In the past several decades scholars have been speaking of a third wing, the "radical Reformation," the "Anabaptist movement," and more recently the "Free Church Movement." The latter designation is the most expressive term to describe this third wing of the Reformation. This movement confessed that the true church is free from the powers, that it operates under the mandate of the lordship of Christ. Such a separation of church and state was a radical one, because it saw the church as operating under a higher authority than the state, that of Christ the Lord who makes the believers members of the kingdom of heaven.

While the movements of both Luther and Zwingli centered more in ecclesiastical and educational circles, the Free Church was more a people's movement. It spread rapidly across Europe from its origin in Zurich, Switzerland, in 1525, until within a few years it had not only

---

Myron S. Augsburger is a well-known evangelist, and served many years as President of Eastern Mennonite College and Seminary. He received the AB and ThB from Eastern Mennonite College, the BD from Goshen Biblical Seminary, and the ThM and ThD from Union Theological Seminary (Richmond). Additional graduate work: George Washington University and the University of Michigan. He is President of Inter-Church Evangelism, and is active in the National Association of Evangelicals. He has conducted many evangelistic crusades and preaching missions in North America, Europe, and Asia. Among his many books are *Called to Maturity, Quench Not the Spirit, Plus Living, Invitation to Discipleship, Faith for a Secular World, Pilgrim Aflame* (historical story of Sattler), and *The Broken Chalice*.

permeated the whole of Europe but had converted so many to its cause that both Lutherans and Catholics were afraid that all Europe would become Anabaptist!

This movement was basically existentialist; it insisted on a personal experience with the risen Christ, upon a conversion which was expressed in a transformed life. It regarded the church as a fellowship of believers whose witness to their conversion was supported by their associates and who practiced together the mutual discipline that made the congregation a covenant community. They held that the Holy Spirit was present in the life of the believer in a special way, inspiring and enabling him to understand and interpret the Scripture, and empowering him for victorious living as a new man in Christ. They believed so strongly in the priority of the kingdom of heaven that they rejected participation in the magistracy and forbade their members the use of the sword or the swearing of an oath of allegiance to any earthly power. They saw themselves as members of the kingdom of God whose mission was the extension of that kingdom through witness and evangelistic outreach. They were the evangelistic wing of the Reformation. They called synods to discuss, plan, and expedite evangelistic ventures for the spread of the church. At the same time they continued in dialogue with members of other church groups, both Catholic and Protestant, as is evidenced by the record of many disputations. This demonstrated an ecumenicity which would meet anyone anywhere on the basis of holy Scripture. Martyred by the hundreds, by both major religious groups, new leaders were called from the group. The contribution of the gifted early leaders was cut off, and lay leadership was elected to fill the vacancy. As a result, the contribution of the early leaders of the Anabaptist movement was limited, especially in terms of the creative writing of theological works.

One of the most significant leaders of the early days of the movement was Michael Sattler. He joined the movement as early as March 1525, in Zurich, Switzerland, within two months of its founding. His creative service was rendered to the Free Church Movement in the first two years of its existence. While his service was brief, his contribution was major. He labored with other well-known leaders of the movement such as Conrad Grebel, Felix Mantz, George Blaurock, Wilhelm Reublin, and others. He was arrested, and examined by Ulrich Zwingli in Zurich, in the spring of 1525. He shared in conversation and theological interchange with the Reformers in Strasbourg and later in South Germany where he built a strong congregation in the community of Horb.

Sattler has left a legacy of eleven writings, six of them definitely his, and the other five carrying supporting evidence as well as an internal character which appears to identify them as Sattler products. These eleven writings, coming from the first two years of the Anabaptist movement, are quite significant in understanding the thought of the early days of that movement. As the persecution against the Anabaptists increased, the finality of the hostility was expressed in the martyrdom of Felix Mantz in Zurich, Switzerland, January 5, 1527. The Anabaptist answer to this blow was to call a synod. This was the first free synod in the Christian Church for approximately a thousand years, a meeting of church leaders apart from the magistracy. The synod was held at Schleitheim in Schaffhausen on February 24, 1527. Michael served as leader of this synod and drafted the Schleitheim Articles which is the earliest confession of faith in the Free Church tradition. Incomplete as a confession, the articles spelled out only those areas where there was need for unity of thought on issues that divided them. The uniqueness of the Schleitheim Synod is that this meeting probably determined the fate of the Anabaptist movement, whether it would live or whether it would die. It was therefore certainly one of Sattler's greater contributions. This service, as well as his work in general, leads to our designating him a major unifying theologian in the Swiss Brethren movement.

Shortly after his return from the Schleitheim Synod, he was arrested and charged with heresy. An additional factor in his condemnation was his having on his person an outline for evangelistic ventures by which the Anabaptist movement would permeate new areas of Europe. He was kept in prison at Binsdorf for thirteen weeks with his wife and other Anabaptists. Brought to trial at Rottenburg on the Neckar, May 17, 1527, he answered nine charges against him. Condemned to death by his 24 judges, his sentence was one of the most barbarous: "Michael Sattler shall be delivered to the executioner who shall lead him to the place of execution and cut out his tongue, then forge him fast to a wagon and thereon with red-hot tongs twice tear pieces from his body, and after he has been brought outside the gate, he shall be plied five times more in the same manner...." After this had been done in the manner prescribed, he was burned to ashes as a heretic. The date of Sattler's martyrdom was May 21, 1527. His wife was drowned several days later. Professor Koehler said, "In Sattler's death there passed from the Anabaptist circle one of the noblest and most pious personalities, yes, from the evangelical-minded circle in general."

Evidence of the significance of Sattler's contribution is seen in that both Zwingli and Calvin wrote at length to refute the Schleitheim articles of faith. Zwingli said the articles were so popular among the Anabaptists that practically everyone carried a handwritten copy. Among Anabaptists a devotional booklet was printed entitled "The Acts of Michael Sattler," including the account of his trial and various of his writings. In the Netherlands, far to the North, copies of his trial and his acts were also circulated, and in addition the Dutch composed a lengthy song in tribute to Michael Sattler. They praised his faith and commitment to Christ and sang the story in the "Mennist" churches across the Netherlands. Thus the influence of the Swiss and South German Anabaptists reached the Netherlands early. It became one of the contributing factors to the conversion of Menno Simons, another official from the Roman Church who later became a strong leader in the movement and left it the name Mennist or Mennonite. Sattler himself had been a prominent man in the Roman church. Having been well educated, with the ability to debate in whatever language the opponent should choose, he had served as prior of the St. Peter's Monastery near Freiburg, South Germany. Sattler's conversion, and his leaving the monastery, were stimulated by hearing the evangelical preachers of the Reformation movement in South Germany and by his own study of the Scripture.

Sattler's theological premises may be discerned by a careful study of his writings and his defense. Basic is the view of Scripture and his system of hermeneutics. Sattler believed the whole of Scripture to be the written Word of God, but he also believed that there is a spirit of Scripture and not just a letter. This is to say that in addition to his conviction that one needs the illumination of the Holy Spirit for interpretation, one seeks to discern the spirit of Scripture itself. His method of interpretation could be called a Christocentric hermeneutic, beginning with Christ and the "new creation" and interpreting the Christian life and the message of God's Word from this perspective. This Christocentric hermeneutic elevates the New Testament above the Old as the culmination of God's self-disclosure and the fullness of His revelation. Most important in this respect is the application of the New Testament to the orders of the common life. This accounts for his strong insistence on an existential experience with the risen Christ, on a believers' church as the result of personal commitment to discipleship, and on the way of holiness and peace as members of the kingdom of heaven.

Second, Sattler's theology emphasized the absolute necessity of personal conversion for membership in the church of believers. The believers' church and consequent believers' baptism were issues which grew out of the deep conviction that an individual's life is to be converted through the work of the Holy Spirit whereby he becomes part of the people of God. The relation of conversion and church is one of cause and effect. From Sattler's perspective baptism into the believers' church was administered upon the confession of sharing in the resurrection life in Christ. His strong emphasis on a life of holiness, however, was neither a "works righteousness" nor perfectionism. The tract, "Two Kinds of Obedience," is one of the finest treatises against legalism or "works righteousness" in the history of Christian thought. In numerous of his writings he distinguishes between works of merit which he condemns, and works of faith which are expressions of the grace of God at work in one's life. He insisted strongly on separation unto Christ, the sanctification of the Spirit, and the transformation of the whole life in obedience to the will of God.

A third emphasis is his perspective on Christian ethics, his emphasis on Christian discipleship. It is significant that Sattler, with other Anabaptists, related ethics to Christology in the same way that general Christendom relates soteriology to Christology. For Sattler the relationship with Christ was one of sharing in His righteousness. Rather than to regard the "righteousness of Christ" merely as an imputed righteousnes, Sattler saw the righteousness of Christ as an experience of reconciliation through Christ, a relation in which a person is brought into right standing with God. The Anabaptists called for a discipleship of obedience, a faith that identifies with Christ in pledging to live by His will. Regarding the church, both Catholic and Protestant, as a "fallen church," they sought to rediscover Christianity as a continuum of first-century experience. They condemned both Catholicism and Protestantism for the failure to take Christian discipleship with utmost seriousness, thereby denying the lordship of Jesus Christ in life. (There is a remarkable relationship between this emphasis and Dietrich Bonhoeffer's analysis of "cheap grace" in twentieth-century Christendom.) Sattler emphasized separation from serving earthly kingdoms in a superior loyalty to the kingdom of heaven. This is the theological basis for his rejection of the sword, of participation in war and violence. This should also be seen in relationship to the Anabaptist sense of an evangelistic mission for the spread of the kingdom. Such disciples were even expendable in martyrdom for the sake of bringing the kingdom into the consciousness of men. Such commitment to the kingdom was necessary for its ultimate fulfillment. It has been said that the Free Church movement was out of step with its time, that it was two hundred years ahead of its time. But the Free Church movement has been of great significance in promoting God's program in history.

Sattler's life and thought have made an abiding contribution to Christian theology. Insisting on the supreme authority of the Scripture, he yet held the illumination of the Spirit to be necessary for its interpretation. Holding firmly to justification by faith, he insisted that there are works of faith even though faith rejects any idea of works of merit. Confessing the universal priesthood of the believer, Sattler held to the necessity of each individual experiencing a spiritual birth which meant participating in both forgiving grace and transforming grace. His interpretation of the sanctity of life called for a radical discipleship, interpreting ethics from a Christological perspective. His concept of the church, as a voluntary church of believers, was interpreted to mean a disciplined body giving and receiving correction to the extent of using the ban for unrepentant sinners in the group. The extent to which he carried this matter of discipleship is seen in a twofold emphasis on the Christian as an agent of reconciliation; first, in evangelistic witness to unbelievers; and second, in expressing only love rather than retaliation to one's enemies. Perhaps his greater contribution is his emphasis on wholeness of life, or holiness of life, possible through the Holy Spirit's work of inner transformation. This dimension of his theology cannot be copied, it can only be witnessed to, for it must be experienced in the lives of believers in personal relationship with the risen Christ.

Brief Bibliography

For those interested in further study of Michael Sattler's work and thought, they should see the following:

(1) "Michael Sattler, d. 1527, Theologian of the Swiss Brethren Movement," unpublished doctoral dissertation, Union Theological Seminary, Richmond, Virginia, by Myron Augsburger, May 1964.

(2) *Pilgrim Aflame*, a novel of fictionized history of the life of Michael Sattler by Myron Augsburger, published by Herald Press, Scottdale, Pa., 1967.

(3) *The Mennonite Encyclopedia*, article on Sattler, volume 4, pp. 427-434, Harold S. Bender, Editor, Scottdale, Pa., Mennonite Publishing House, 1959.

(4) Articles in issues of *Mennonite Quarterly Review*, Oct. 1945, Oct. 1946, Jan. 1947, April 1947, Oct. 1947, Jan. 1968.

(5) John H. Yoder, *The Sattler Legacy*, Scottdale, Pa.: Herald Press, 1973.

> *"The Lord makes His presence known in your gathering; God is with you within your community; therefore remain steadfast and fear not."*

25
Peter Riedemann

Leonard Gross

I

What course would Anabaptism have taken, had a Grebel or a Mantz lived on beyond those first two or three years of uncertain beginnings? Such a question of course remains without answer. Yet it is a matter of history that almost without exception the Anabaptist leaders of the 1520s died before the end of the decade—generally a martyr's death.

One of those rare first-generation leaders who did manage to live well beyond the earliest years of the movement was the Silesian shoemaker, Peter Riedemann. In this capacity he furnishes us with a clue as to the "whither" of classical Anabaptism. Indeed, the adventures of this remarkable leader spanned three decades of activity. A fearless shepherd, he encouraged his congregations to continue within the best traditions of the first short-lived generation of Zurich and South German leaders.

To understand the significance of Riedemann, one must first come to understand the Anabaptist milieu of the late 1520s and 1530s. Such figures as Grebel, Mantz, Denk, and Sattler were taken from this world through death by 1527, some two years after the birth of the movement. Blaurock was granted two extra years of life, time first spent within Switzerland, where ever increasing hardship ultimately forced him to take refuge in Austria. Here he shepherded Anabaptist congregations in the Tirol.

After Blaurock's martyrdom in 1529 at the Tirolean village of Klausen, Jacob Hutter became his successor within the general region. When persecution intensified, many Anabaptists removed to the more tolerant lands of Moravia, settling in the small village of Auspitz. Hut-

---

Leonard Gross is Archivist of the Archives of the Mennonite Church, editor of the *Mennonite Historical Bulletin*, and executive secretary of the Historical Committee of the Mennonite Church. He received the BA from Goshen College, the BD from Goshen Biblical Seminary, and the PhD from the University of Basel, where he was a Fullbright scholar. His doctoral dissertation was on *The Golden Years of the Hutterites ... 1565-1578*; it was published in 1980 by Herald Press.

ter not only organized this mass emigration, he also cemented the small Anabaptist brotherhood at Auspitz together in unity and mutual concern. Soon other less well-coordinated groups looked to Auspitz for guidance and fellowship.

This first period of consolidation and growth abruptly ended in 1535. Rumors had been spreading about the Münster tragedy of Westphalia, where revolutionary "Anabaptists" had become the symbol of rebellion and sedition. Dissident groups throughout Europe became suspect. This included the non-revolutionary peaceful Anabaptists of Moravia, where the lords of the land, complying with the demands and threats of the Hapsburg government, ousted the populous Hutterites and other sectarians. The various communities dispersed, Hutter took the opportunity to visit scattered remnants of Anabaptist fellowships still in Tirol. There he died at the stake in 1536. His successor, Hans Amon, led in the slow process of community rebuilding, once the persecution stopped. Upon Amon's death Peter Riedemann enters the scene. Before continuing with the Moravian Anabaptist story, however, we should note Riedemann's known activities before this juncture.

Peter Riedemann was born in 1506 in Hirschberg, a village within the Duchy of Silesia. As others in the shoemaking vocation, Riedemann traveled about, finding his way into Upper Austria during the 1520s. By the late 1520s he was already an Anabaptist. Our first definite knowledge of the man begins with the year 1529, when he was suffering what would prove to be a three-year imprisonment in Gmunden, Upper Austria. After gaining his freedom he journeyed to Moravia, joined with the Auspitz Anabaptists in 1532, and wholeheartedly accepted the communal life idea being established so firmly during these very years by Hutter. Riedemann married, demonstrating a deep love and loyalty to his Catherine, whom he affectionately called "Treindle."

On one of his many journeys as missioner, Riedemann was once again apprehended, spending the years 1533-1537 in the city tower prison of Nuremberg. Another journey took him to Hesse in 1539. This time he returned safely. Later that same year Riedemann traveled to Upper Austria, visiting an Anabaptist group called the Philippites. Then he pushed on to Bavaria, to Lauingen in the Duchy of Neuburg, to Heilbronn, and ultimately to Hesse, where his work as missioner proved highly rewarding. In early 1540 he had gathered one hundred converts whom he sent on to Moravia, most of them reaching the Hutterite communities safely. However, Riedemann himself was apprehended, chained in a dark cell in the Hundsturm (the "dog's dungeon") in Marburg.

At this point we return to the year 1542, the year that Hans Amon, the leader of the total complex of Hutterite communities, died. Leonhard Lanzenstiel became the new leader. The brotherhood profited greatly from his economic and practical know-how. But who could lead the community in spiritual matters? The imprisoned Peter Riedemann was to be contacted. Should he be able to regain his freedom without harm to his conscience, the plea read, he was to do so. Riedemann found his freedom, probably as a result of his having promised the authorities never again to return to Hesse as a missioner. He now became truly the spiritual leader of the Hutterites to the time of his death in 1556.

The years 1542-1556 were filled with hardships and persecution brought on by the Schmalkaldic War and other political turmoil of the age. That the brotherhood withstood the test of dispersal, of pangs of hunger months on end, was due in large part to the constant vigilance and comforting exhortations of "der grosse Peter."

II

Not without reason was Riedemann called the "second founder of the Hutterites." True, Jacob Hutter established the communities upon a solid footing before he was martyred (1536)—he welded a small group of Tiroleans into a spiritual and economic monolith, strong enough to attract hundreds and even thousands into the ever-expanding sixteenth-century Hutterite brotherhood. Yet such a continuing unity of purpose and doctrine again was in large part due to Peter Riedemann, thanks to his special, written contribution to the brotherhood, the Hutterian confession of faith. This programmatic work came to be acknowledged by the total community as the finest expression of what Christianity is all about. Such group assent made possible community growth and longevity, granting exceptional brotherhood endurance and viability, strong enough to weather the next four centuries of Hutterite history. Compare this unity of purpose and doctrine still to be seen today to the disunities within the short-lived Gabrielite community or the Philippites (other Anabaptist groups), and we begin to understand the importance of Riedemann's work.

Indeed, the years Riedemann had spent in prison were not lost years. During his first imprisonment, 1529-1532, he wrote what is known as his first "Rechenschaft" or "Account" of his religion. The author, in this edifying tract on Christian love, betrays some affinity to the spirit and message of a Hans Denck or a Wolfgang Brandhuber— Anabaptists who also approached Christianity from the standpoint of Christian charity.

Yet Riedemann's *magnum opus* remains in the form of his already mentioned work conceived and written during 1540 and 1541 while in prison in Hesse, his second or "great *Rechenschaft,*" entitled in the English translation: *Account of our Religion, Doctrine and Faith.* Within months after the document found its way into the hands of the brotherhood, it was accepted by the Hutterites as the definitive statement on practically the whole spectrum of Hutterian-Anabaptist thought. By 1545 the work was printed as the community's official interpretation of faith. Sent to magistrates, it served as an apology, depicting the movement for what it was, neither seditious nor politically revolutionary in character. The small, leather-bound, metal-clasped volume also traveled in missioners' pockets, a quiet but thorough message which convinced many seekers about the validity of the Hutterian way of life. When the first edition became exhausted, a second printing was issued in 1565, again showing the special acclaim the volume enjoyed throughout the century and beyond. For Riedemann's volume remained the only Hutterian work published in the sixteenth century.

Peter Riedemann composed at least forty-six hymns. Thirty-six of his letters are still extant, as is also his first "Rechenschaft." Yet his great contribution lies in his own towering spiritual personality which he allowed God to use to His glory. Without such a yieldedness to his Creator and Lord, Riedemann would not have been called out of prison by his fellow brethren to lead "God's people." Nor would even a most beautiful and inspiring volume on the nature of Christianity have been accepted, had it been written by anyone else than just such an authentic man of faith, seeking only God's truth. One song writer reminisces about "the great Peter, a highly gifted man." The Hutterite chronicler extols: "He was rich in the mysteries of God. The gift of the Word of the spirit flowed from his mouth like a well of fresh water. And all souls who heard him rejoiced."

Bibliography

No book-length monographs have been written on Riedemann. The definitive work is Robert Friedmann's perceptive interpretation: "Peter Riedemann: Early Anabaptist Leader," *MQR*, January 1970. I herewith want to record my thanks to the late Professor Friedmann (1891-1970) for granting me prepublication access to his manuscript, elements of which have found their way into this article. Reference is also made to Friedmann's articles on "Riedemann" in the *ME* and *ML*, where additional bibliographical materials may be found. Finally, mention should be made of Riedemann's main work: *Account of our Religion, Doctrine and Faith, given by Peter Rideman of the Brothers whom men call Hutterians*, Suffolk, England, 1950; Rifton, N.Y., 1970.

"Love is the total content of Scripture."

26
Menno Simons

Cornelius Krahn

Menno Simons was born in the little village of Witmarsum in the Dutch province of Friesland. It is assumed that he was born in 1495 or 1496 and that he died in 1561. Although little is known about his background, youth, and parental home, his parents must have been dairy farmers. He became a priest at the age of twenty-eight, which was likely in 1524, and he withdrew from the Catholic Church in 1536 in order to become a leader to the "sheep without a shepherd." He could have obtained his education in one of the nearby monasteries. First he served as an assistant priest in the parish of Pingjum near Witmarsum, 1524-31. Already during the first year doubts entered his mind whether the bread and wine used in the mass were actually being changed into the flesh and blood of Christ as he had been taught in Catholic theology and practice. These doubts were widespread in the Low Country and caused a movement which led to the beginning of both Anabaptism and the Reformed Church. Cornelis Hoen advocated the spiritual meaning of the Lord's Supper and renounced the belief in transubstantiation. (Later Zwingli followed Hoen.)

Menno was tormented by these doubts for about two years. Finally he turned to the Bible. He "did not get very far in it" before he saw that he "had been deceived." He accepted the spiritual concept of the Lord's Supper and became a Bible reading evangelical preacher.

One day in 1531 he heard that someone [Sicke Snijder] had been put to death in the capital city of the province of Friesland because he had received "a second baptism." He now investigated the matter of infant baptism in the Bible and the writings of the Reformers. Soon he was thoroughly convinced that believer's baptism was scriptural. Yet in 1531 he accepted a call to become the pastor of his Roman Catholic home church at Witmarsum. This was the time that Melchior Hof-

---

Cornelius Krahn served long as Professor of Church History and German in Bethel College and as Director of the Mennonite Historical Library on that campus. He received the MA from the University of Wisconsin and the ThD from the University of Heidelberg. He wrote an important monograph in German, *Menno Simons*, and a most significant volume, *Dutch Anabaptism*, in English. He revised the volume of C. Henry Smith, *The Story of the Mennonites*, and served as Associate Editor of the four-volume *The Mennonite Encyclopedia*.

mann spread the Anabaptist movement from Strasbourg to the Low Countries. After Hofmann's imprisonment in Strasbourg (1533), the Anabaptist movement of the Netherlands lacked sound and able leadership. Very severe persecution set in right from the beginning. The expectation of the coming Lord and His kingdom drove some to expect his coming at definite places where the evangelical faith had been accepted. One of these places was the city of Münster in Westphalia. "Apostles" were sent out by some radical "Melchiorites" to invite the persecuted believers to come to the place of refuge or the city of God. Menno had some debates with these agents whom he did not trust. During an insurrection (1535) of such radicals in the nearby *Olde Klooster*, he lost some members of his parish, even his blood brother. He now stated that "the blood of these people, although misled, fell so hot upon my heart that I could not stand it, nor find rest in my soul.... Pondering these things my conscience tormented me so that I could no longer endure it." Menno "prayed to God with sighs and tears that He would give" him, "a sorrowing sinner, the gift of His grace" so that he "might preach His exalted adorable name and holy Word in purity, and make known His truth to His glory." Menno was soundly converted.

Menno preached and wrote against Jan van Leyden, the "second David" of the "New Jerusalem" at Münster. After nine months of evangelical preaching, teaching, and writing, he found his life endangered, renounced all "worldly reputation, name, and fame," and "willingly submitted to the stress and poverty of the heavy cross of Christ" by leaving the community and parish, and starting a life "underground." This was in late January 1536.

For a while Menno found shelter in the neighboring province of Groningen. He "sought out the pious" and found "some who were zealous and maintained the truth" and even reclaimed some of the erring from the "snares of damnation and gained them for Christ." Menno spent much time in reading and writing. In 1540 his guidelines for the believers, *The Foundations Book*, appeared. The motto on all of his writings was "For other foundation can no man lay than that is laid, which is Jesus Christ" (1 Cor. 3:11).

At the request of some "pious souls," among whom were Obbe and Dirk Philips of the quiet, non-political "Melchiorites," Menno became the leader of the Anabaptists, who soon became known as "Mennonites." His major tasks were to travel, preach, baptize, and strengthen those in need of help. Menno married Gertrude and must have had at least one son and two daughters who shared the life of hunted refugees with him.

This is a brief outline. In 1544 after a theological discussion with John a Lasco, the leader of the Reformed Church of East Friesland, he was active in preaching and baptizing in the Lower Rhine region near Cologne. In the fall of the same year, he had discussions with the followers of his former co-worker David Joris. During the following years he was in Emden, the Lower Rhine, the Low Countries, and even in the Danzig area where he visited and strengthened "the children of God" to whom he later wrote one of his finest letters. In 1553-54 he was in the Hanseatic city of Wismar, where he had a discussion with his Reformed opponent Martin Micron about basic theological concepts. It was here that the Wismar articles dealing with the view of the church and disciplined Christian living were accepted (1554). From Wismar Menno proceeded to a place of refuge called Wüstenfelde near Lübeck, where he found a protector in Bartholomeus von Ahlefeldt, also a congregation of refugees, and a printing shop. The building in which the printing shop was located and a big linden tree now constitute a monument to his lifework.

The basic concern of Menno was the restitution of the true brotherhood of believers based only on the Scriptures. He experienced many hardships and disappointments in his effort to build the true church. Severe persecution of those who challenged the established churches was unavoidable. Controversies within the brotherhood in regard to the nature and the maintenance of a truly disciplined brotherhood followed. He had to make numerous trips which always endangered his life. He made his last trip as an ambassador of peace, unity, and discipleship when he went to Harlingen via Emden and Franeker in 1557. Many hearts and minds were disturbed by a somewhat legalistic application of the ban and shunning. Dirk Philips and Leenaert Bouwens, Menno's co-workers, were rather rigid. Others wanted a more lenient and loving practice of discipline and discipleship. The matter was not settled during Menno's lifetime.

After this last visit to his home country, Menno wrote to a friend, "If the omnipotent God had not preserved me last year as well as now, I would already have gone mad. For there is nothing upon earth which my heart loves more than it does the church, and yet I must live to see this sad affliction upon her" (*Complete Writings*, 1055). Menno died soon after, but the foundation on which he aimed to build the church of Christ remained. His death date was January 31, 1561.

Literature

Menno Simons. *The Complete Writings*. Leonard Verduin, Trans., J. C. Wenger, Ed. Scottdale, 1956, 1966, 1974, 1978. (A biography of Menno Simons written by H. S. Bender is included.)

"Menno Simons," by Cornelius Krahn. *The Mennonite Encyclopedia*. Vol. III: 577-583.

William E. Keeney. *The Development of Dutch Anabaptist Thought and Practice 1539-1564*. Nieuwkoop, 1968.

Cornelius Krahn. *Dutch Anabaptism. Origin, Spread, Life, and Thought 1450-1600*. The Hague, 1968. Pp. 150-53; 169-82; 187-96; 222-26; 237-44.

"Mastered by a Sovereign God."

27
John Calvin

J. C. Wenger

If Luther was the father of the sixteenth-century Reformation, it is also true that Calvin was easily the outstanding theologian of the movement. Born in 1509 at Noyon in Picardy, sixty miles northeast of Paris, young "Jean" was sent to the University of Paris in 1523 to prepare for the service of the Roman Church as a priest. In 1528 he transferred to the University of Orleans, and still later to the University of Bourges. By the grace of God he experienced a "sudden conversion" in the year 1533, was twice imprisoned for being a Protestant "heretic," and for a time even his life was in danger. Eventually he wound up in Basel, Switzerland, where in March 1536, his *magnum opus* was published, the *Institutes of the Christian Religion.* This was a Latin treatise on the Christian faith as understood by the new evangelicals (Protestants), and was based on the Apostles' Creed. It contained six chapters. Calvin wrote it in Latin so it could be read by scholars in all countries, but it was immediately translated into "all the languages of Europe." Calvin himself authored a French version of the *Institutes.* All through his life he kept enlarging the work, adding greater fullness and clarity to what was already a classic of Protestantism. His last revision in Latin (1559) had 104 chapters—not through radical reorganization, but simply by writing with greater breadth and fullness, and spelling out more fully that which had been expressed briefly in 1536. Many editions of the English *Institutes* have appeared, the latest and best being that translated by F. L. Battles and edited by John T. McNeill (SCM Press, London, 1961). Calvin also wrote a huge list of Bible commentaries, and many other works, so that his collected *Opera* total fifty-nine volumes, and also include 4,271 letters.

In July 1536, four months after the publication of the *Institutes,* Calvin spent a night in Geneva, Switzerland, in the course of making a journey—but by the violent insistence of the Reformer William Farel was almost compelled to remain and to assist in the great task of reforming the church of Geneva. And so, instead of staying one night he remained there the rest of his life—except for a period of over two

---

J. C. Wenger is Professor of Historical Theology in the Associated Mennonite Biblical Seminaries, Elkhart, Ind., and the author of various books on church history and theology.

years when he was driven out of Geneva by the enemies of his radical Reformation, and lived in Strasbourg in Alsace, the Reformation city of Capito and Bucer, 1538-41.

A small, frail, thin man, Calvin was a tremendous intellectual, a scholar's scholar. Romance was not for him. His concern was the defense of the gospel against Romanism, and the actualization of a New Testament church. His friends, however, thought it would be a help to him if he had a suitable life companion. Calvin informed Farel that the only "beauty" he cared about was that his wife should be "modest, obliging, not arrogant, thrifty, patient, and careful for my health." And that was exactly the kind of companion which God provided for him. The lucky girl was a former Anabaptist, and now a widow, Idelette de Bure, whose former husband, Jean Stordeur, Calvin had converted from Anabaptism to the Reformed faith. They were married early in August 1540, and had eight happy years together. Their little son, Jacque, was born July 28, 1542, but died as an infant of less than two weeks. Idelette passed away on March 29, 1549, one of the hardest blows of Calvin's life. After her death Calvin praised her fidelity and courage, indicating that she would have been ready to face exile and poverty, even death with him. She was, he said, his "faithful helper in the ministry." Idelette left a son and daughter from her first marriage in the tender care and custody of Calvin.

Except then for the short sojourn of a few years in Strasbourg, Calvin did his lifework in Geneva from 1536 until 1564. And the life and work of Calvin made Geneva a sort of Protestant "Rome." He carried on a lively correspondence with the Reformers of many other lands, and was a source of inspiration and guidance to them all. He greatly elevated the sanitary standards of the city, promoted trade and lifted the economic life of the city, and founded the university there, the first college being opened on July 5, 1559, and which attracted 900 students from all over Europe the first year. (When a Catholic opponent reproached Calvin, pointing out that God punished him by not allowing him to have a son, Calvin replied that he had "sons" all over Europe—and in very truth students did flock to his feet from everywhere.)

Calvin literally sought to create the kingdom of God on earth; he tried to make Geneva into a little beachhead of heaven. No sin was to be tolerated in the city: no crime, no immorality, no drunkenness, no dancing, no idle games, no gambling. The magistrates were charged to enforce a strict Christian way of life on all citizens—in a way which few adherents of the Calvinist tradition (Reformed and Presbyterian) would defend today. Visitors marveled at the success of the little Frenchman in making Geneva a Christian city. Little by little Calvin won out over those more worldly men and women who tried to withstand the high disciplinary standards which Calvin led the city fathers to adopt. Heresy was suppressed by force, even by death in some instances, the most tragic execution being the burning of Michael Servetus on October 27, 1553, for not holding a sound view of the holy Trinity. Calvin had urged that the "heretic" be beheaded, but the zealous city fathers decided on the stake. Three and a half centuries later, on October 27, 1903, the Reformed churches of Geneva and

France erected a monument to Servetus with this inscription: "Respectful and grateful sons of Calvin, our great Reformer, but condemning an error which belonged to his century, and firm believers in the freedom of conscience according to the true principles of the Reformation and the gospel, we have raised this expiatory monument, October 27, 1903."

Less well remembered, but far more happy, was Calvin's sincere but vain attempt in 1555 to establish a mission in Brazil. The whole project actually began when a strange character named Nicholas Durand de Villegagnon decided to establish a Reformed colony in Brazil, but felt compelled to solicit Calvin's help. Calvin in turn commissioned thirteen Reformed missionaries to locate in Brazil with the Reformed colony—the first Protestant missionaries to the Americas. The leaders were Pierre Richer and Guillaume Chartier. But there was severe disagreement, discord, and even executions in the colony, and in a short time the whole project came to a tragic end.

Theologically, Calvin followed in some respects the great Bishop of Hippo, Aurelius Augustine, although Calvin always appealed directly to the Word of God. Calvin was overwhelmed by the sovereign love and grace of God, as illustrated by His choice of Isaac from Abraham's sons, and of Jacob from Isaac's sons (Rom. 9). To Calvin (as well as to Luther and Zwingli) the doctrines of predestination and election in grace should melt the human heart in penitence and gratitude. Calvin made much of the Christian doctrine of surrender to God. "I offer my heart," he said, "to God as a sacrifice." "We are not our own," he wrote, "we belong to the Lord.... Let our reasons and our wills then never predominate in our thinking and in our acting." Man needs to recognize, he insisted, "that he is not his own." He must take "the lordship and rule of himself" away from his own mind, and hand it "over to God."

Calvin assigned to the church great authority, for he saw it as the body of Christ on earth which needs to be kept pure by discipline. (Unfortunately, he encouraged the civil authorities to force what he considered a New Testament style of life on the citizens of Geneva.) Calvin did not share Luther's pessimism about the impossibility of Christianizing the structures of society. Calvin also subscribed to Augustine's theory of a "just war" being legitimate for the children of God. Perhaps the very center of Calvin's theology was his emphasis on a faith union of the Christian with the Lord Jesus Christ, effected in the power of the Holy Spirit. In his doctrine of the Lord's Supper Calvin was something of a mediator between Luther's doctrine of the "real presence" of Christ, and Zwingli's view of the emblems as symbols. Calvin was perhaps closer to Zwingli than to Luther, but he also stressed the value of the bread and the cup in making Christ real to us; the emblems, he held, should strengthen our faith and build us up spiritually. In any case, it is said that when Luther read Calvin's wise words on the Eucharist he remarked that if Oecolampad and Zwingli had dealt with the subject as Calvin did "the dispute would have been shorter and less bitter." It should also be mentioned that Calvin deeply venerated the father of the Reformation: "... we consider Luther a great apostle of Christ, through whose mission and work the gospel has, in our time, been brought back to almost its original purity."

Calvin did not take second place to any of the Reformers in sharp words against his opponents, even condemning men, such as Menno Simons, whom he did not know personally. Perhaps he was irked by the way the Anabaptists kept insisting on the universal love of God, on separation of church and state, on Christian toleration and on freedom of conscience, on nonviolence and nonresistance, and on believer's baptism. Calvin attempted a refutation of the Anabaptist Schleitheim *Confession of Faith,* adopted in 1527 in Switzerland. Calvin passed away at 54 on May 27, 1564, and was buried in Geneva—at his request in an unmarked grave.

Bibliography

Any good library has numerous books and encyclopedia articles on Calvin, as well as monographs by Calvin himself. His commentaries are especially significant. His most influential work was undoubtedly his *Institutes of the Christian Religion.*

> *"If we are true children of Abraham, then we can have confidence that God wills to be the God of our children."*

28

Martin Bucer

John H. Yoder

Alsatian by birth, Dominican, an early disciple of Erasmus and then (1518) of Luther, Martin Bucer, 1491-1551, served as Strasbourg's Reformer 1523-49, hand in hand with Wolfgang Capito.

Next to Zurich, Strasbourg was the major center of the non-Lutheran Reformation in the earliest years. The *Grund und Ursach* ("Grounds and Cause") which he wrote with his colleagues in late 1524, to explain the transformation of the mass and other ecclesiastical practices they had begun to introduce, was foundational for the spread of the Reformation elsewhere. In addition to his service at Strasbourg, Bucer was often called upon by other local governments as a consultant in how to implement a Reformation (Ulm 1531, Augsburg 1534ff, Hesse 1538-9, Bonn and Cologne 1542-3). Strasbourg's own Reformation was finally consolidated in the Synod of 1533.

In his theological work Bucer was respectful of Zwingli, yet freely differed from him with regard to the significance and independence of church organization and discipline. Whereas for Zwingli the outward organization of the church is the business of the magistracy, acting in the name of the total civil-Christian community, for Bucer there should be a distinct ecclesiastical organization with its governing elders, teachers, and deacons, and its own discipline. Both in this respect and in numerous other theological issues Bucer is the father of many of the ideas of John Calvin, who spent 1538-41 in Strasbourg at Bucer's side. In liturgy, hymnology, theology, and church structure,

---

John H. Yoder has served as President of Goshen Biblical Seminary and Professor of Theology. He received the BA from Goshen College, and the Dr. Theol. from the University of Basel. He is an associate at The Center for Reformation and Free Church Studies, Chicago Theological Seminary, and a Professor at Notre Dame Graduate School of Theology. Among his books are *Karl Barth and the Problem of War*, *The Ecumenical Movement and the Faithful Church*, *Peace Without Eschatology?*, *Reinhold Niebuhr and Christian Pacifism*, *As You Go*, *Taeufertum im Gespraech*, *Taeufertum und Reformation in der Schweiz*, *The Politics of Jesus*, *The Christian Witness to the State*, *The Christian and Capital Punishment*, *Nevertheless*, and *The Original Revolution*.

what Calvin solidified at Geneva and propagated from there into the Netherlands, Hungary, and Scotland was largely what he had learned from Bucer.

Bucer's serious concern for the faithful, visible church was also linked to his relationship to Anabaptists, for whom Strasbourg, the most tolerant city of the time, was often a haven. He debated and conversed with Hans Denck, with Michael Sattler (whom he especially respected), with Ludwig Hätzer and Jacob Kautz and Pilgram Marpeck. A major portion of the agenda in the 1533 Strasbourg Synod which finally settled the legal basis of the Reformation, was the testimony of the numerous Anabaptist, Melchiorite, and spiritualist dissenters. In 1538, in the service of Philip of Hesse, Bucer spoke so convincingly with a few Anabaptists at Marburg (see F. Littell item in bibliography) that they agreed to return to the state church, on the condition that the state church would introduce a serious disciplinary practice so that unbelief would be reproved and persistent unbelievers expelled. This Butzer did in the Ziegenhain Hessian church order (1538-9), in which confirmation was introduced as a sort of functional equivalent of believer's baptism, so that all adult members of the church would have knowingly committed themselves to her discipline. Thus the Reformed practice of confirmation owes its origin to a concession Bucer made to Anabaptism. His concern for church discipline continued to be an offense in his relationship to the Strasbourg authorities.

The most extensive dealing with Anabaptism was the exchange of views with Pilgram Marpeck in 1532-3 (see Bibliography, Krebs-Rott). Bucer's entire argument was based on the permanence of the divine covenant with Abraham. "If we are true children of Abraham, then we can have confidence that God wills to be the God of our children."

Within the politics of the magisterial reformation, the major significance of Bucer is as a mediator between the Lutheran and Reformed streams. Serving as adviser to Philip of Hesse, who pursued on political grounds the same kind of moderation as Bucer sought on doctrinal grounds, he sought to bridge the controversies, especially concerning the Lord's Supper, with mediating formulations. This mediation finally failed as Strasbourg chose the Lutheran side and for the sake of the peace of the empire discharged Bucer, who went to England for his remaining years (1549-51) as guest of Archbishop Cranmer and professor in Cambridge. His growing seriousness of concern for a process of church discipline which would be viewed as essential to the church was also a contributing cause for his expulsion. His mediating concern was carried on nonetheless by his spiritual successor Calvin, who sought to avoid both the extreme symbolism of the Zwinglian view of sacraments and the extreme substantialism of the Lutheran view.

In England Bucer finished writing his major work, *Two Books on the Reign of Christ*, an optimistic plan for the religious and social renewal of England by the young King Edward to whom it is dedicated. Bucer's theocratic vision is a synthesis of materials from the Bible and from the Christian imperial heritage of Theodosius and Justinian. At the center of his vision on the reign of Christ is his joyfully affirmative evaluation of the age of Christendom.

"Thus such princes [i.e., all Christian princes since Constantine] devote and surrender themselves to the public ministers and pastors of the churches, as well as to the churches, to the maintenance and strengthening of which they devote great care, to accomplish the word of Isaiah, 'Kings shall be your foster fathers and the princesses, their wives, shall be your nursing mothers. With their faces to the ground they shall bow down to you and lick the dust of your feet (Is. 49:23).' "

Bibliography

Martin Bucers Deutsche Schriften, ed. Robert Stupperich, Gütersloh/Paris, 1960 ff.; Franklin Littell, "New Light on Butzer's Significance," in F. Littell, ed., *Reformation Studies*, John Knox, 1962; Elsass I: Vol. VII in *Quellen zur Geschichte der Täufer*, eds. M. Krebs and H. G. Rott, Gütersloh, 1959.

"... things written with my hand, contrary to the truth which I have in my heart."

29

Thomas Cranmer

Walter Klaassen

At the south end of St. Giles Street in Oxford stands a stone memorial to three men who were burned to death there during the reign of Queen Mary. Nicholas Ridley and High Latimer died in October 1555, and Thomas Cranmer in March 1556. That Cranmer was not burned together with his fellow bishops was due to his office as Archbishop of Canterbury. It was also symbolic of his reluctance to change his mind and of the dilemma into which his convictions led him.

He was born into a well-to-do British family in the year 1489. At the age of fourteen, he was sent to Cambridge University where, evidently a gifted student, he became a fellow of Jesus College by 1510. After the death of his young wife, he devoted himself to studies for the priesthood, was ordained in 1523, and soon thereafter took his doctorate in divinity.

Cambridge University even then had a reputation for dissent, for Cranmer and others used to gather at the White Horse Inn to discuss Lutheran theology. He lectured at Jesus College in divinity, and as an examiner in theology, insisted that students for degrees have a thorough knowledge of the Bible.

In 1529 Cranmer, by accident, came to the attention of King Henry VIII, who was at that time contemplating a divorce from Catherine of Aragon. Cranmer had suggested that the English ecclesiastical courts could handle the matter without appeal to the pope. In 1533 Cranmer was appointed Archbishop of Canterbury and one of his first acts in that office was to guide Henry's suit for divorce successfully through the church courts and at his consecration as archbishop he was required to take two oaths of loyalty, one to the

---

Walter Klaassen is Associate Professor of Religious Studies at Conrad Grebel College, the University of Waterloo. He received the BA from McMaster University, the BD from McMaster Divinity College, and the D. Phil. from the University of Oxford. He is a recognized authority on the Reformation of the sixteenth century, particularly on the Anabaptists. One of his monographs is entitled *Anabaptism: Neither Catholic nor Protestant.*

pope and the other to the sovereign. But Cranmer stood for the supremacy of the sovereign in matters relating to the church, and he made a special point of insisting that he swore allegiance to the pope only insofar as that was consistent with his allegiance to the king as supreme. He remained unwavering in his loyalty to Henry VIII and Edward VI, whose church policies he carried out faithfully.

Cranmer is associated more than any other man with the Reformation in England. In keeping with his insistence on the importance of biblical knowledge, he provided for the availability of the Bible in the vernacular as early as 1538. He did, however, not move to a fully evangelical position until 1546 when he denied transubstantiation and affirmed the Lutheran doctrine of justification by faith.

It was during the reign of Edward VI that reformation began in earnest. Cranmer was not a strong leader but major changes in English church life took place under his patronage and under the vigorous leadership of the other bishops. To Cranmer himself goes the credit for the Book of Common Prayer, which was a radical and yet a conservative recasting of the liturgy, and the Forty-Two Articles (later reduced to thirty-nine), which became the basis of Anglican faith and order.

Cranmer was not an original theologian and can therefore not be said to have made any major contribution. Doctrinally, he began as a Lutheran and ended as Zwinglian or Calvinist, his chief mentor being Martin Bucer. But in terms of church order and authority he was Lutheran, as also in his view of the relation of church and state, which was that the sovereign is head of the church.

This doctrine plunged him into a dilemma when Mary Tudor, a devout and determined Catholic, became queen. Her object was to restore Catholicism and she immediately arrested a number of reforming bishops including Ridley, Latimer, and Cranmer. She revived the heresy laws which spelled death for the imprisoned bishops. While Ridley and Latimer calmly faced the flames, Cranmer was signing recantations which avowed the truth of Catholic faith and of the supremacy of the pope, and even agreeing that Protestant views were heretical. (He said later he had signed because he was afraid of the fire. There was also another reason, his extreme belief that the sovereign determines the faith of the subjects and that one has no right to private judgment. When therefore the sovereign was Catholic he felt compelled, by his doctrine, to obey.)

When he was ordered to make these recantations public in St. Mary's Church in Oxford, it having already been determined that he should burn, he surprised the whole assembly by declaring that his recantations had troubled him more than anything he had ever done, that they were contrary to what he believed in his heart, and that he now renounced them all! The offending hand that had signed would, he said, be the first to burn.

And so it was. He died serenely in the flames, March 21, 1556. While he was a man afflicted with weakness and hesitation, he nevertheless demonstrated at the end that he was both an honest and brave man. In death he affirmed that ultimately God called men to make their own decisions.

Bibliography

Owen Chadwick, *The Reformation*, Vol. 3, of the *Pelican History of the Church*, Chapter 4, a brief general treatment of the English Reformation.

John Foxe, *Acts and Monuments*, 1563. This volume, usually called *Book of Martyrs*, contains the description of the events in St. Mary's Church and Cranmer's martyrdom.

F. E. Hutchinson, *Cranmer and the English Reformation*, 1951. This book deals with both his life and thought.

> "Hookers's *Lawes of Ecclesiastical Politie* gave the Church of England a voice and a character."

30

Richard Hooker

Dwight Y. King

Richard Hooker, a leading Anglican theologian, was born in 1554, attended Oxford, and served as tutor and fellow at Corpus Christi College. Ordained in 1581, he became noted as an antagonist of Calvin and an opponent of the Puritan Party. He represented the established church in a famous theological controversy with Walter Travers, a Calvinist, and later gave the Church of England and the "Elizabethan Settlement" a theological foundation in his eight-volume work, *Lawes of Ecclesiastical Politie*. Hooker died near Canterbury on November 2, 1600.

The English Reformation can be divided into two distinct historic movements. The political movement of King Henry VIII (1509-47), who severed the church from Rome *before* any basic doctrinal reform had taken place and simultaneously subjugated it to the Crown in Parliament, marks the initial stage. This was the Thomas Cranmer era. Upon the death of Henry, the Reformation was accelerated under Edward VI (1547-53) and then forcefully retracted in favor of a restoration of the medieval church under papal authority during the reign of Mary (1553-58). When Elizabeth ascended the throne in 1558, England was in a chaotic state of affairs. Externally, she was threatened by France, Spain, and the pope at Rome; internally, the country was divided into three main factions: 1) a vigorous minority group of Catholics who supported Mary's purge and rejected the whole concept of a Protestant Reformation, 2) those who favored an ecclesiastical establishment on the pattern of Calvin's Geneva, and 3) those who constituted a middle party that wanted neither subserviance to Geneva nor Rome, but a Church of England purged of the abuses of the Middle Ages. Elizabeth's reign (1558-1603) marks the second stage of the English Reformation. The so-called "Elizabethan Settlement" was an attempt to harmonize Roman Catholicism, Protestantism, and English nationalism by legislating uniform religious services according to the *Book of Common Prayer* (1559) and uniform doctrinal belief according to the "Thirty-nine Articles" (1563).

Dwight Y. King received the BA from Goshen College, the BD from Harvard University, the MA from Johns Hopkins University, and the PhD from the University of Chicago. He teaches at Northern Illinois University at DeKalb.

Doctrinal leadership for Elizabeth's mediating policy was forthcoming from Richard Hooker. Hooker believed England to be a Christian commonwealth and sought to justify a unification of civil and ecclesiastical authority in the Crown. This of course utilized what historically has been the bastion of prestige and authority in England, namely the monarchy, and acknowledged the economic practicality of a state church. Hooker's key presuppositions in undertaking his work were that Christian society is taught both by the natural light of reason and by the supernatural light of Scripture. He realized, quite correctly, that the relationship between the institutions for guiding human conduct (church and state) depend ultimately on the kind of relation believed to exist between natural principles knowable by reason and by divine revelation. Scripture, in his view, provided the whole truth necessary to salvation, but not exclusive and sufficient instructions for the government of Christian Society. At no time in history had the foundation of governments, families, and corporations been based on Scripture. Rather, they had been based on universal principles of human nature which manifest themselves in customs and through reason. His controversy with Calvin was not whether Scripture was the ultimate source of authority, but whether it was a complete body of positive law governing every aspect of the life of the church.

Hooker found the Bible often ambiguous or silent (e.g., in matters of church organization or worship); he insisted that patristic tradition must then be consulted, and if no help could be found in either of these, the common understanding of reasonable men should be relied upon. When conclusions were reached through this process, he required no explicit scriptural authority, providing the results were not contrary to the Bible. In like manner, he justified episcopacy—which, incidentally, Elizabeth held necessary for the safety of kings—and the *Book of Common Prayer* as both reasonable and congruous with Scripture. Reason is grounded in God Himself and therefore is the major source of all knowledge. Following Thomas Aquinas and the Scholastics, he held that we obtain analogous knowledge about God through the study of occurrences in the created world—via reason—since all secondary causes point, at least in one sense to the First Cause. All things are ordered by God, and God works in accordance with His laws, which Hooker saw as "operative in nature, as regulating each man's character and actions, as seen in the formation of societie and governments." Thus the supernatural law of the Scripture is only part of God's law and requires knowledge of the natural law to be understood.

Reason being axiomatic, it is the foundation for both church and state. All men are endowed with reason, free will, and the inherent capacity for goodness; no one has authority over another except it be granted by the consent of the governed. The law of reason—ultimately derived from God—leads men to the realization that society must be ordered. Thus Hooker sought harmony between the two sources that give rise to the state: (1) God's divine law and (2) the social contract. If a dissenting minority should arise, they should defer to the higher right to judge (i.e., the consent of the majority), the possessor of power.

The visible church arises, just as the state, out of the "natural inclination which all men have unto sociable life and consent to some certain bond of association." But it is distinguished from other societies by the exercise of the Christian religion. Theoretically, the church has a juridical autonomy to determine her rites and customs, but not complete autonomy. Hooker grants that in other lands where the true religion is not believed in there may be a real distinction between church and state. In England, belief in the true church (religion) obliterates this distinction. Membership in the Church of England did not substitute nor displace membership in the church universal according to Hooker. Just as all organizations of civil society are qualified by time, place, etc., so also the visible Church of England, although necessarily a branch, yet maintained both complete catholicity and apostolicity. Perhaps mindful of biblical precedents like David and Melchizedek, Hooker united the church and state as divinely ordered aspects of one society in an unstable equilibrium; the monarch, as head of the state, was also the temporal head of the church.

Richard Hooker emphatically rejected the Machiavellian moral duality, in vogue in his day, of a moral church and an amoral state. Yet his opting for a theocratic society with a national clergy and sacrosanct monarch coincided with a petrification in the church's ability to respond to intense social change. Nevertheless, with the restoration of the episcopacy after the Civil Wars, his work came quickly into eminence. He is credited with determining the Anglican "middle way" between Calvin and Rome and giving the cosmic orientation to Anglican theology.

Furthermore, his discussion of natural and civil law, of the role of reason in determining justice, of government by the consent of the governed, and the advantages of gradual change over sudden revolution eventually came to regulate the political progress in England and gradually modified its constitution. And it was from Hooker that Locke drew support for many of his views on political theory. From Hooker on, theology and revelation were no longer viewed as necessary prerequisites for understanding natural law.

Brief Bibliography

A. G. Dickens, *The English Reformation*, N. Y.: Schocken, 1964; C. F. Dirksen, *A Critical Analysis of Richard Hooker's Theory of the Relation of Church and State*, Notre Dame, 1947; G. Hillerdal, *Reason and Revelation in Richard Hooker*, Lund: CWK Gleerup, 1962; R. Hooker, *Of the Laws of Ecclesiastical Polity*, Vols. I and II, London: J. M. Oent, 1954; J. T. McNeill, *Books of Faith and Power*, New York: Harper, 1947.

"The heart has its reasons that reason cannot know."

31
Blaise Pascal

Owen H. Alderfer

Pascal, Blaise, 1623-1662, was a French scientist and man of letters who contributed significantly in mathematics, physics, philosophy, and theology. He was born at Clermont-Ferrand, June 19, the son of a minor noble, Etienne Pascal, a scientifically minded government official who undertook personally the education of his children. Pascal's natural inclinations and opportunities early led him toward scientific and mathematical interests. A precocious child, he published a major mathematical work on conic sections at age 16, and produced a computor before he was 20. A brilliant scientific future lay before him; however, events were to change the nature of Pascal's major contributions.

The Pascal home was pious in the ways of contemporary Catholicism, but not ardently religious. An accidental fall and injury to the father in 1646 brought the family into contact with the Jansenist movement. Through this influence Blaise experienced his "first conversion" in 1646. For a time his interests were torn among his scientific interests, the enjoyments of Paris social life, and religious concerns through continuing contacts with the Jansenists.

Shortly after his father died in 1651, Pascal's younger sister Jacqueline entered the Jansenist convent at Port-Royal. With these and other events in his life he found in himself an intense longing for God, and gave himself to spiritual quest, turning to the Scriptures as his guide. On the night of November 23, 1654, Pascal had a profound religious experience—his "definitive conversion." He recorded his dis-

---

Owen H. Alderfer is a minister in the Brethren in Christ Church (the Christian body in which President Eisenhower's grandfather was a minister). Dr. Alderfer served for many years (1965-80) as Professor of Church History at Ashland Theological Seminary. He received the AB from Upland College, the BD from Asbury Theological Seminary, and the PhD from Claremont Graduate School. Since 1980 Dr. Alderfer has occupied the C. N. Hostetter Chair of Theology at Messiah College.

covery and sewed the account in the lining of his coat. In part it declared in staccato fashion:

> From about half past ten in the evening until about half past twelve FIRE
> God of Abraham, God of Isaac, God of Jacob, not of the philosophers and scholars.
> Certitude. Certitude. Feeling. Joy. Peace.
> God of Jesus Christ.
> My God and thy God . . .
> I will not forget Thy word. Amen.

From this time Pascal devoted his life to spiritual concerns and religious activities until his early death in 1662.

The Theological Work of Pascal

Pascal left numbers of learned mathematical and scientific treatises; however, the main concern here is his religious thought. After his conversion Pascal purposed to prepare as his *magnum opus* an apology for the Christian religion. From 1654 to the end of his life he made notes and gathered materials for his work; however, other tasks demanded his time and attention, and death came before the work was completed. All that he developed of the apology was in the form of notes and loose papers, some as formulated ideas and others as disconnected notes. In spite of the shape of the material the content was of such interest and quality that friends collected and published it as *Pensées*—Pascal's *Thoughts*.

A great deal of Pascal's time and energy during the years after his conversion was devoted to a defense of the Port-Royal brotherhood against Roman Catholic views on works for salvation in general, and Jesuit rationalization and casuistry in particular. The Jansenists, whose leader Arnauld had been convicted of theological error, sought to have their case presented to the public and pressed Pascal to write in their interests. Part of the time using a pseudonym he produced a series of nineteen writings known as the *Provincial Letters* in which he embarrassed the Jesuits and gained the support of the public for the Jansenist cause with his clear emphasis upon moral consciousness and divine grace. The letters, in spite of their occasional nature, are literary masterpieces filled with keen insight and sparkling with satire and humor.

These *Thoughts* constitute Pascal's chief literary contribution in religion and philosophy. In spite of the fragmentary nature of the material, Pascal has left a statement of his reflection and faith which has challenged the thinking of many since his time. Though it is difficult to discover a plan in the work the central ideas seem to be summarized in his statements:

> *First part:* Misery of man without God.
> *Second part:* Happiness of man with God.
> Or, *First part:* That nature is corrupt. Proved by nature itself.
> *Second part:* That there is a Redeemer. Proved by Scripture.

Pensées reflects a scientific mind turned to religion. Here, in an era of scholastic reasoning and the multiplication of abstruse arguments, Pascal cut across doctrinal formulations and broke through to the heart of spiritual and moral issues in language that has spoken to men's hearts since. Though he appeals to reason, Pascal knows that "the heart has its reasons that reason cannot know." His appeal is to the whole man who, apart from God, is in a desperate plight.

Pascal, who may be regarded as an early religious existentialist, began with man: compared to other bodies and to infinity man is nothing. For man to see himself in his isolation is terrifying; this is the misery of man without God. But how can man know God? Certainly not by unaided reason and scientific methods; this was the error of scholastic theology. Life as we experience it is in three orders, body, mind, and spirit, and there is no crossing of lines among these orders. "From all bodies and minds, we cannot produce a feeling of true charity; this is ... of another supernatural order." As his own experience had proved, the supernatural must break through—the I-Thou relationship of personal encounter must take place. Faith, as a gift of God, precedes knowledge and gives meaning to all other experience.

Brief Bibliography

The two great religious-philosophical works of Blaise Pascal are the *Provincial Letters* and the *Pensées*, both of which are discussed above. His writings have been collected, the best edition being Pascal's *Oeuvres Complètes* edited by L. C. Brunschvicg. Modern English translations of *Pensées* include those of W. F. Trotter (1958) and Martin Turnell (1962); of *Provincial Letters*, that of Thomas McCrie (1941). Helpful studies of the life and thought of Pascal include:

Morris Bishop, *Pascal: The Life of Genius*, 1936, an intellectual biography.

Emile Cailliet, *The Clue to Pascal*, 1943, a study of the arrangement and thought of *Pensées*.

Jean Mesnard, *Pascal, l'homme et l'oeuvre*, translated by G. S. Fraser as *Pascal, His Life and Works*, 1952, a useful biography and introduction.

"Wherever I have seen the print of his shoe in the earth, there I have coveted to set my foot too . . ."

32
John Bunyan

Jacob J. Enz

The Pilgrim's Progress has as much to contribute to contemporary Christian theology as that theology has to contribute to an understanding of the book itself. Thus, R. M. Frye evaluates the work and the greatest book coming from the hand of John Bunyan (1628-1688).

Bunyan was born of poor parents in Elstow in Bedfordshire, England. His boyhood was made up of limited schooling, hard work, games, and church-going. He grew up in a village society which was then becoming conscious of its political powers, while Puritanism struggled with the established church. The education of Bunyan probably involved acquiring knowledge and mastery of the English language, mainly from reading the Bible. Like his father, John was a worker in brass. He was drafted into the parliamentary army at 16, and took part in the English Civil War, an experience probably reflected in his book entitled *The Holy War* (1682). He was married at 21 to a woman of piety. His interest in religious questions was awakened only after marriage. His first wife died around 1656 leaving him four children; he married again in 1659.

He was received into the church in 1653 at the age of 25, in an independent congregation at Bedford, and was formally recognized as a preacher in 1657. The inner struggles of this period called forth by the consciousness of sin and fear of perdition are portrayed in his work *Grace Abounding to the Chief of Sinners* (1666). Intensive study of the Bible and a Reformed approach to the understanding of the Bible guarded his feeling-oriented Christianity from moving into the direction of emotional sects. Suffering much from the repressive measures

---

Jacob J. Enz is an ordained minister and Professor of Old Testament and Hebrew in the Associated Mennonite Biblical Seminaries in Elkhart, Indiana. He received the AB from Bethel College, the STB from the Biblical Seminary in New York, and the PhD from Johns Hopkins University. He was a Fellow in the Summer Institute of Near Eastern Civilizations and a post-doctoral student in the Hebrew Union College Biblical and Archaeological School, Jerusalem. He was earlier Professor of Bible and Christian Education in Bethel College in Kansas. He is the author of *The Christian and Warfare: The Old Testament Roots of Pacifism.*

(e.g., laws against preaching without a license) of Royalists after the Restoration of 1660, he spent most of the time, 1660-1672 in the Bedford jail. He would make no promise to stop preaching the Nonconformist doctrine despite the fact that his wife needed help with his four small children, the oldest of whom was blind. After 1672 he worked among independents (Baptists) at Bedford and took part in evangelistic work in other parts of the country. His ministry in general was one of awakening, being one of many "mechanic preachers" who spread the gospel through the countryside. In later years he assumed the duty of the spokesman for those of his persuasion, and increasingly emphasized doctrines relating to the church.

Of his literary activity the chief and most famous is *The Pilgrim's Progress*, 1678 and 1684, which has been described as the most popular book ever written in English.

According to his *A Confession of My Faith* Bunyan embraced most of the essential doctrines of the faith held historically by the Christian church. Of the biblical writings Bunyan said that all the Holy Scriptures are the words of God. The Holy Scriptures are able, "without the addition of human invention," to make the man of God perfect in all things.

As for salvation, since God is holy and just as well as good and merciful, "none shall be saved without the means of a Redeemer." The purpose of the "clothing of himself with our flesh and blood was that he might be capable of obtaining that [which] before the world was intended for us." The completion of this salvation will be at his (second) coming when "his saints shall have a reward of grace for all their work and labor of love which they showed to his name in the world."

The manner of man's justification in order to stand before God in the day of judgment is through the "imputation of the righteousness of Jesus Christ ... an act of free grace" without man's deserving. The power of this imputation "resideth only in God by Christ.... The offer of this righteousness as tendered in the Gospel, is to be received by faith." Man in the very act of receiving it judges himself as sinner. Christ as propitiation of man's sin provides a sacrifice to appease the displeasure of God.

Bunyan made much of the doctrine of election. "Election is free and permanent, being founded in grace and the unchangeable will of God." This decree, God, "having all things present to him, in his wisdom," made before the world was. The decree has in it not only the persons but "the graces that accompany their salvation." Furthermore, neither election, grace, nor salvation may be considered apart from Jesus Christ. Nothing can hinder the conversion and eternal salvation of the elect of God. Man knows his election by his being called.

It is at the point of man's being called that the means God has appointed to bring man to him are necessary despite election. The call consists of (1) true awakening about the evil of sin, especially of unbelief, (2) awakening about the world to come and the glory of unseen things, and (3) sanctifying virtue. The call produces faith, hope, and repentance. Repentance is further described as "turning the heart to God in Christ," fear, zeal, love, and loathing sin. The objects of love (the fruit of repentance) are the name, word, and truth of God as well as the sincerity of grace, faith, and holiness in man. Love also has the faculty "of bearing and suffering afflictions, putting up with wrongs, overlooking the infirmities of the brethren, and in serving in all Christian offices the necessities of the saints ... it designeth a holy conversation [manner of life] in the world, that God, and Christ and the word of Christ may be glorified thereby."

Bunyan's *Confession of My Faith* regarded magistrates as appointed by God; it is a judgment of God to be without these who put wickedness to shame. "Many are the mercies we receive by a well-qualified magistrate; and if any (magistrate) shall at any time be otherwise inclined, let us show our Christianity in a patient suffering for well doing, what it shall please God to inflict by them."

A Reason of My Practice in Worship immediately follows Bunyan's *Confession of My Faith*. Communion is defined as "fellowship in the things of the kingdom of Christ." He does not regard it necessary to detach himself from non-Christians in honest civil affairs. He dares not have communion with the elect except as they are visible saints by calling. He is tolerant at the point of refusing to exclude the secret hypocrite if he be hid by visible sainthood.

Bunyan speaks of water baptism and the Supper of the Lord as "shadowish and figurative ordinances" which are of excellent use to the church in this world as representations of the death and resurrection of Christ. But he does not regard them as fundamentals. "Servants they are, and our mystical ministers to teach and instruct us." He regarded them with reverent esteem, refusing to remove them as did the Quakers, or with others to attach to them more than their primitive institution permitted. He practiced believer's baptism in his ministry, though he accepted those baptized as infants if they were godly professing Christians. He pleaded for baptism by immersion but he asked for "a bearing with our brother that cannot do it for want of light." He regarded the unity of all Christians as a major New Testament teaching.

Bunyan regarded prayer as an ordinance of God to be used publicly and privately in order to gain familiarity with God, to get great things for the person prayed for and for the person praying, and to be a means of opening the heart to God as to a friend, obtaining fresh testimony of God's friendship. "Prayer is a sincere sensible affectionate pouring out of the heart or soul to God through Christ in the strength and assistance of the Holy Spirit for such things as God hath promised or according to the word, for the good of the church, witness of mission in faith, to the will of God." The best prayers have often been more groans than words. But praying must also be with the understanding as well as through the Spirit.

Of self-denial Bunyan said, "It is for a man to forsake his all for the sake of Jesus Christ—meaning that we prefer Christ above all things this world affords or the heart can wish for, which the Christian may with good reason do. . . . It must be done in the spirit of faith, of love, and of a sound mind. . . . By self-denial the power and goodness of the truths of God are made manifest to the incredulous world. God does not require it as the means to obtain salvation but hath laid it down as a proof of the truth of a man's affections to God and Christ."

His doctrine regarding last things included belief in the world to come, a resurrection of the dead, both of the just and the unjust, with the just being equal to the angels and being the children of God and the resurrection. The impenitent shall be tormented with the devil and his angels.

His greatest impact undoubtedly was to make theology come alive in his own discipleship in a way that the reflection of that in his writing made it come alive for countless others. It is said he helped common unlettered men in later religious movements to see their value in the sight of God.

For Further Reading

All standard religions encyclopedias have articles on Bunyan, and indicate monographs on the man. But one ought to read Bunyan's own works, especially *The Pilgrim's Progress*.

"There is no place in God's Church for a Half-Way Covenant."

33
John Davenport

Howard J. Zehr

John Davenport (1597-1670) has been referred to as one of the great men of early New England days who united learning with piety, and knowledge of men with kindness of heart. He was cofounder and first minister of the New Haven Colony. He was born at Coventry, Warwickshire, England, in 1597. He died in Boston in March 1670.

Davenport graduated from the University of Oxford with a BA in 1615 and received the MA and BD in 1625. He was made chaplain at Hilton Castle northeast of Durham for about six months, 1615-1616. From there he went to London where he became curate of St. Lawrence Jewry in 1619, and vicar of St. Stephen's on Coleman Street in 1624. He won great regard by his faithfulness to duty in 1625 when the city was devastated by the plague. In 1626 he joined in a scheme to purchase impropriations (church property held by laymen) and use the profits to maintain ministers in various parts of the kingdom, and was one of twelve *feoffees* (trustees) entrusted with the care of the funds raised for this purpose. The plan was considered by Bishop William Laud and others as a movement in the interest of nonconformity. Suit was therefore brought against the *feoffees*, and in February 1633 the association was dissolved as illegal and the impropriations which had been purchased were confiscated.

In 1629 Davenport helped to obtain the charter for the Massachusetts Bay Colony, gave a sum toward the expenses, and his name was first on the committee to draw up instructions for the colonists. He took alarm when Bishop Laud, who had long been suspicious of him, was appointed archbishop in 1633. He therefore late in the year went to Holland where he became copastor with John Paget of the English church in Amsterdam.

Davenport did not approve of the baptism of children whose parents were not church members. Controversy, therefore, arose between the two pastors on this subject. In less than six months,

---

Howard J. Zehr (1916-1977) was a minister and bishop in the Mennonite Church and Executive Secretary of his denomination. He received the BA from Goshen College, the ThB from Goshen Biblical Seminary, and did additional study at Goshen Biblical Seminary and at Northern Baptist Theological Seminary.

Davenport gave up preaching in public. He returned to England sometime between 1635 and 1637. In 1637 he and a friend and member of his church, Theophilus Eaton, sailed with a band of colonists for New England through the advice of John Cotton. They landed in Boston June 26, 1637. Although well received there, in April 1638 he went to New Haven and served as minister of the new colony. He approved of the provision in its constitution, which was settled in June 1639, limiting the franchise and eligibility to civil office to church members, and was one of the seven pillars of the state who were charged with the government. In 1642 he declined an invitation to attend the Westminster Assembly, and in 1661 helped to shelter the regicides Whalley and Goffe. He was a leader of the opposition to the Half-Way Covenant, a controversy which was rending New England, and which caused a split in the Boston church to which he had been called in 1667, resulting in the formation of the Old South Church.

He was involved in all the general troubles of the day! As a minister he took part in the secular government as well as in the ecclesiastical. He was a thorough nonconformist. He opposed the baptism of children whose parents were not church members. He believed it to be the church's duty to take responsibility for secular government.

John Davenport did only a small amount of writing. Some of his publications were: *Instructions to the Elders of the English Church* (1634); *Report of Some Proceedings Against John Paget* (1634); *Allegations of Scripture Against the Baptizing of Some Kind of Infants* (1634); *Catechism Concerning the Chief Heads of the Christian Religion* London (1659); occasional sermons were also printed.

Brief Bibliography

The New Schaff-Herzog Encyclopedia of Religious Knowledge; The Oxford Dictionary of the Christian Church, edited by J. L. Cross; *Cyclopedia of Biblical, Theological, and Ecclesiastical Literature* by John McClintock, D. D. and James Strong, S.T.D.

"Where Christ Himself is King, there is found a constitution sublime above all others."

34
Comenius

Přemysl Pitter

Jan Amos Komensky (1592-1670), the great Czech theologian and educator, was born in Moravia. His name he Latinized as Comenius, and as such he is best known in the West today. As the gifted son of the Unitas Fratrum (the Hussite Bohemian Brethren) he gave masterly expression to the principles for which his people had in the past suffered and died. His invincible faith, his love, and his hope inspired his Brethren to perseverance in this faith. And his own road of suffering reflected that of his people in the seventeenth century. His father before him was a member of the Bohemian Brethren in Uhersky Brod, and the castle museum and library in that town is a worthy memorial to this great man.

Comenius lost his parents at an early age, and his relatives sent him to the schools conducted by the Brethren, where he received excellent training. Nevertheless, the educational methods of that era stood in sharp need of reform. The Brethren recognized the unusual talents of young Jan Amos, and decided to send him to the famous Reformed university at Herborn, and then to Heidelberg University in Germany, for his theological and philosophical education. The Brethren felt that the University of Prague was no longer a suitable school for their young men. The theology there was now Catholic, and there were immigrant Jesuits on the faculty. Although 90 percent of the Bohemian lands followed Jan Hus, the Catholics were seeking to win the people back to the faith of Rome. The Brethren press had to go underground. It located at Kralice, and its most celebrated product was the Kralice Bible.

The late Přemysl Pitter was born in Prague, Czechoslovakia, June 21, 1895. Following his distress as a soldier in World War I, he began to work unceasingly for the welfare of his fellowmen, especially those in need. First, he established a home for children. He became well known, not only among his Czech compatriots, but also among Sudeten Germans, as well as Jews. The latter he tried to help during World War II. For ten years he served refugees in Germany as a spiritual adviser and social worker. He resided in Switzerland, laboring with his pen for the deepening of the spiritual life of his Czech friends, issuing his *Hovory s pisateli* (Dialog with Correspondents.) Died Feb. 12, 1976.

When Comenius returned home on foot after three years of university study, Count Carl Žerotín put him in charge of the Latin school in Přeroo, the school of which he himself was a graduate. He set about at once to improve the pedagogical system there, and succeeded brilliantly. He was soon called to serve as preacher and leader of the Brethren school of the German congregation at Fulnek on the Silesian frontier. There he spent several happy years, the last carefree years of his life. There he also established his family and began to write.

But trouble came to the land when the Hapsburgs acquired the throne. The king of Bohemia repeatedly violated the religious freedom of the people. The result was that the Bohemian Estates chose the Elector Palatine as their ruler—an act of insurrection which brought on a religious war which in some areas lasted three decades. The worst suffering was in Bohemia and Moravia, and by 1620 with foreign help the Hapsburgs were victorious—a victory which led to a Counter Reformation (Catholic), and religious freedom was lost for three centuries. There were numerous executions of Protestant leaders. On June 21, 1621, twenty-seven outstanding men were put to death, including Vaclav Budovec and Dr. Jessenius, making that day as famous for the Czechs as July 6 (1415), when Jan Hus was martyred. They died for their faith, as well as for justice and religious freedom. All pulpits and church property then fell to the Catholics. The wife and child of Comenius took ill with the plague and died. In this national and personal distress Comenius fed richly on God's Word, declaring that "no food was ever so sweet." He wrote a masterpiece of Czech literature, *The Labyrinth of the World, and the Paradise of the Heart.* Comenius and his Brethren had to seek refuge in caves and forests to avoid the Jesuits. He then fled abroad, seeking help for the Brethren, especially a place to which they might flee. This refuge turned out to be Leszno, Poland. In 1627 Catholicism was declared to be the only religion permitted in his native land, and an estimated 30,000 families, one fourth of the population, resorted to emigration to escape the lot of those remaining in Bohemia. They settled mostly in Saxony, Lausitz, and Slovakia. Comenius helped the refugees who settled in Poland, and also wrote, while hiding in the mountains, a Czech treatise on education to guide his people spiritually and educationally, *Guidance in the Education of a Better Race.*

At Leszno (Lissa) in Poland Comenius became director of the Brethren secondary school. His spirits rose, when in the autumn of 1631 it appeared that by military action, led by King Gustavus Adolphus, the "Lion of the North," the Protestant refugees could once more return to Bohemia. But by May 1632 the new regime was crushed, and Catholicism again reigned in that land. Comenius continued on with his pioneering educational growth in Poland, writing various educational treatises, seeking to make schools less rigorous, and closer to "play." He called for the education of all children, both boys and girls, and became in reality the father of the modern school system. His *Janua linguarum,* a new approach to learning Latin, the universal language of scholarship in that era, was adopted in twelve European and four Asiatic areas. Comenius was invited to various European nations, including England. He settled in Swedish territory, Elbing in

East Prussia, where he labored for six years to advance educational theory and practice. He might have stayed longer, had he not been recalled to Poland to become bishop of the scattered Bohemian Brethren.

The year 1648 was bad for Comenius. His second wife, the mother of five children, died, and even worse, the Bohemian lands were ceded permanently to the Hapsburgs, marking the national end of that country. Comenius wrote a pathetic work, *Testament of the Dying Mother—the Unitas Fratrum* (his beloved Bohemian Brethren). He looked forward to the hour when the wrath of God for Czech sins would be appeased, and "the government of your cause will return into your hands, O my beloved people of Bohemia!" But before 1648 was over, Comenius was called to his innovative educational services in Hungary, and settled in Saros Patak. Here he produced a remarkable educational textbook, encyclopedic in character, *Orbis pictus*, a presentation of the universe. It was used in the schools for almost two centuries, and was printed in Nuremberg, Germany. Both Goethe and Herder used it.

In 1654, Comenius was back in Poland—only to suffer the loss of all his notes and writings when the city of Lissa was reduced to ashes during a war between Poland and Sweden. A man of 64, Bishop Comenius led his people to Frankfurt on the Oder, and personally went on to Amsterdam at the invitation of an old friend. Here he wrote a seven-volume work on "Human Improvement," with but two of the volumes being published, and the other five only discovered in Halle in 1936! Holding that there is a "spark of God" in every man, Comenius believed that there should be: (1) universal textbooks, (2) universal schools, (3) a universal college of teachers, and (4) a universal language. He hoped for a universal world unity, and a universal Christian unity—by the rejecting of undue theologizing and the completion of the (now unfinished) reformation of the church. The Sermon on the Mount, he held, must be applied to all human relationships. He told Descartes in person, "All human knowledge that is derived from mere sensory perception and logic is incomplete and fragmentary." A person needs to "turn himself and with him all things to God."

Comenius envisioned great world progress as part of the plan of God, and the outcome of our prayer, "Thy kingdom come." It is tragic, thought Comenius, that men attempt to bring in the divine kingdom by human effort, in human pride and in self-reliance, and worst of all, by armed force. In his works Comenius often has a radiating sun, and this Latin sentence inscribed around its border: "Omnia sponte fluant, absit violentia rebus" (Let all things happen voluntarily; let violence be kept far from these things). This was his life motto.

Although increasingly a world citizen, Comenius ever remained the dedicated and consecrated bishop of his beloved Bohemian Brethren. He was especially concerned for those in the "diaspora." He raised funds for them, and issued various editions both of the Bible and of his own devotional writings in the Polish and Czech languages. His last work was a confession of faith entitled *Unum necessarium* (the one thing needful). This sublime work has again and again touched people, even those theologically not in agreement with

Comenius. He concludes with these words: "My whole life has been a pilgrimage, an ever-changing place of shelter. Nowhere a fatherland! Now, however, the heavenly Fatherland is in sight, to whose threshold I have been led by my Guide, my Light, my Christ, who has gone on before to prepare a place for me in the Father's House where there are many mansions. And He will come and take me there, that where he is, there I may be, also. This is therefore the One Thing Needful: that I forget the things which are behind, and run for the prize of God's final call." When Comenius died in 1670 he was interred in the church cemetery of the Walloon exiles in Naarden in the Netherlands.

In the centuries since the Comenius era the Bohemian people have had a rough time. Compelled to be Catholic outwardly, they often read secretly their hidden Bibles, as well as forbidden sermons by the fifteenth-century Peter Chelčický. All too many people of Bohemia have indeed lived by quiet acquiescence, but hypocritical yielding is surely not the answer. The future lies only with brave men of the Spirit like Jan Hus and Jan Amos Komensky.

For Further Reading

See also in German the fuller account of the life and work of Comenius, "John Amos Comenius, Lehrer der Nationen," in my book, *Geistige Revolution im Herzen Europas* (Zürich and Stuttgart: Rotapfel Verlag, 1968, Seiten 75-80). Translated into English for this volume by Elizabeth Horsch Bender, and slightly condensed by the editor. Used by permission.

> "And so the saints, the church that are in this new covenant, and come to Jesus, the mediator of it, betwixt them and God, they see him walk in the midst of his churches, his general assembly, exercising his offices ... as a prophet to open to them, who, they do hear, and as a priest that offered up himself for them; and offers them up to God without spot or wrinkle, and as a king to rule in their hearts by faith."

35

George Fox—The First Quaker

Lewis Benson

George Fox (1624-1691) was born in Leicestershire, the son of a weaver. He had little formal education, but it was said of him that he could have reproduced the Bible from memory.

When he was nineteen Fox experienced an inner crisis. It seemed to him that the power of evil in himself was greater than his spiritual and moral resources. He was brought to the brink of despair and of doing away with himself. He left home "at the command of God" and became a wanderer, seeking counsel from religious leaders, but none could speak to his condition. When he had lost all hope of help from any human source, he heard a voice which said, "There is one, even Christ Jesus, that can speak to thy condition." It was then revealed to him why there was none upon earth that could speak to his condition; namely that "Jesus Christ might have the preeminence, who enlightens, and gives grace, faith and power." It was Christ who gave him the power to resist evil, and by this power he was brought through

---

Lewis Benson studied Quaker history and theology at Pendle Hill and Woodbrooke, and has also been a guest lecturer at both these Quaker study centers. He was a Research Fellow at Woodbrook in 1954-55, exploring the unpublished writings of George Fox. He is the author of the recently republished *Catholic Quakerism*, and several pamphlets including *Prophetic Quakerism* and *The Religionless Christianity of George Fox*. His articles on "George Fox's Conception of the Church" (*Friends' Quarterly*) and "The Early Quaker Vision of the Church" (*Quaker Religious Thought*) have stimulated Quaker thinking on the nature of the church.

his personal crisis. He then saw that it was by this same power that God had been preparing, fitting, and furnishing him for "the service he had appointed me to."

A Unique Mission

He believed he had been called to a unique mission, and he says, "when the Lord God and his Son, Jesus Christ, did send me forth into the world to preach his everlasting gospel and kingdom ... I was to bring people off from all their own ways to Christ, the new and living way, and from the churches that men had made and gathered, to the church in God...." His task was to proclaim that "Christ has come to teach his people himself," and to gather a Christian community of a different order from any of the existing churches. This task absorbed all his energies for the remainder of his life. Before he died one in every hundred Englishmen had been gathered into this new model church. In 1650 these new communities were nicknamed *Quakers*. Since 1787 they have been known as *The Society of Friends*.

Fox was not a reformer in the sense of having a program for improving the existing churches. He was attempting to rebuild the new covenant church from the foundations. He rejected the church of his parents and during his seeking years, he says, "I was never joined in profession of religion with any." His mission was not to any one denomination, but to them all. The first Quaker communities were composed of former members of nearly all the denominations.

The story of Fox's life is a tale of high spiritual adventure. He has been remembered as a doer rather than as a thinker. Yet he left behind a mass of writing, published and unpublished, that deals with the theological position that underlies all his work. He never attempted to produce a systematic summary of his theology. His ideas are scattered through 420 pastoral epistles, a multitude of short doctrinal papers, and polemical writings. But when these scattered fragments of his thought are studied as a whole, it is possible to discern a well-rounded theological structure which is marked by a high degree of consistency.

The Problem of Religion

According to Fox, the central thrust of the Bible's message is the call of God for an obedient people, who will live under His rule. The prophets declare that God is seeking to gather a people to Himself, who will witness to His power and authority by obedience to His Word. Obedience and religiousness are not the same thing, and the prophets deplore the way man's religious interests and activities can overshadow, and even eclipse, the main task. They look forward to a time when God will resolve the tension between preoccupation with the cultic aspects of religion, and the weightier matter of obedience in righteousness. They foretold that God would end this tension by giving men a new way to himself through a new covenant. Fox maintains that this new way and new covenant are Christ. Through Christ there can be a truly obedient people, the kingdom of God, without the machinery of institutional religion, and there can be true obedience in righteousness without legalistic moralism.

The Light of Christ

How does God bring this about by sending Christ into the world? Fox's teaching about Christ focuses on *the presence in the midst.* This is the new fact which is constitutive of the new covenant. The new covenant is not a new cultus in the place of old cultus, but a person, Jesus Christ, risen and present in the midst of those who gather in his name. The most significant aspect of Fox's thought is what he says about the *activity* of Christ as He is present in the midst of God's new covenant people. It is what Christ *does* in the midst of His people that creates a new community and a new righteousness. As the eternal prophet "like Moses," He teaches the principles of God's righteousness to God's people, and gives them power to obey; as the eternal priest "after the power of an endless life," He intercedes for God's people in the place of a human priesthood; He is the King of God's people, and a scepter of righteousness is the scepter of His kingdom. These "offices of Christ" (what He does when He is present in the midst) constitute the central meaning and power of the new covenant.

Most summaries of Fox's teachings refer to his so-called *doctrine of the inner light.* Fox seldom, if ever, uses the term "inner light." "Light," the term he used most frequently, applies to *Christ.* For Fox, the Light is this Prophet-Priest-King, who is the Teacher of righteousness, and Ruler and Orderer of God's people in the new covenant. There is no other "light" in Fox's theology. "The light," he says, "is Christ, the covenant of God."

The Church

The new covenant community is not an anarchy. Its order and government come directly from the Prophet-Priest-King in its midst. He calls and qualifies pastors, ministers, teachers, evangelists, and He has a service for the least member. These services do not confer rank upon those called. This church is a disciple church—a fellowship in hearing and obeying the Master. It is also a church of the cross because, where there is hearing and obeying, there will also be fellowship with Christ in His sufferings. It is not a collection of religious individualists. When it gathers in the name of Christ, it waits to be shown the right way for all. It is not a sacral society. It does not meet in holy places at holy times to perform holy acts and read holy books. Fox called the internal order of this community *gospel order,* which signifies a community in which Christ orders and teaches His people as He is present in their midst.

The Nature of Man

Fox understood the statement, "man was made in the image of God," to signify the *relation* that man bears to God. Man is a creature to whom God speaks, demanding an obedient response. When man obeys God, he bears the "image of God." When he is disobedient, he loses God's image. Fox taught that Christ came to restore the image of God, by which he meant that the coming of the eternal prophet, who is to be heard and obeyed in all things, restores the relationship to God that was lost through disobedience. To "receive Christ" means to receive him as Prophet, Priest, and King, and to listen to His voice, and be obedient to His Word. To be a man, means to live by the word of the Creator. In turning a deaf ear to God's counsel, man has forfeited his manhood. Christ restores this lost manhood. "The gospel," says Fox, "brings a man to be a man."

Eschatology

Fox's view of history is the linear conception found in the Bible. History had a beginning, and will have an end. The Creator is active in history, and He will have the last word in history. The gospel is not good news about what God will do at the end of the world, but about His action in sending Christ, which is His supreme redemptive act which will not be superseded. Eschatology means "last times." The one whom God promised in the "last times" has come, and we are living in these "last times." Therefore the church of Christ is not a community which has inherited from the Jews the role of waiting for God's supreme redemptive act at the end of history. Nor is the church a society of those who await the kingdom of God. For Fox, the church does not have a life and destiny distinct from that of the kingdom.

The Rejected Stone

The cornerstone of Fox's theology is Christ, who is present in the midst of His church in all His offices. This is the stone that the builders of man-made religion have rejected. Fox was a revolutionist, storming the walled city of man-made religion, and gathering a people whose task is to "show the new way to them that be in the old."

Brief Bibliography

Fox, George, *The Great Mystery*, London, 1659.

_____, *The Journal of*, London, 1694. (The preface, by William Penn, contains a brief history of the Quaker movement and a valuable character sketch of Fox. This preface has been reprinted many times under the title: *The Rise and Progress of the People Called Quakers.*)

_____, *A Collection of Epistles*, London, 1689.

_____, *A Collection of Doctrinal Books*, London, 1706. (The *Journal, Epistles,* and *Doctrinals* compose the first edition of Fox's collected works.)

_____, *The Works of*, Phila. and New York, 1831. (8 volumes, which include *The Great Mystery, Journal, Epistles,* and *Doctrinals.*)

_____, *The Journal of*, Norman Penney, ed., Cambridge, 1911 (verbatim et literatum).

_____, *The Short and Itinerary Journals*, Norman Penney, ed., Cambridge, 1925 (verbatim et literatum).

_____, *The Journal of*, John L. Nickalls, ed., Cambridge, 1952.

No detailed full-length study of Fox's theology is available.

"For though God doth principally and chiefly lead us by his Spirit, yet he sometimes conveys his comfort and consolation to us through his children...."

36

Robert Barclay

D. Elton Trueblood

The fact that Quakerism survived the stormy days of the seventeenth century to be a force even in the twentieth century is amazing. It is amazing because other movements, with apparent similarities, promptly died. Some did not even go on after the turbulent days of the English Civil War, during which they were spawned. But the people called Quakers *did* go on and even became important factors in the growth of the English colonies of North America. Why was the Quaker story so different from that of many now-forgotten sects?

The full answer to this important historical question is complex, and may not be fully known, but one part which is known is that of the intellectual leadership of Robert Barclay (1648-1690). Barclay is generally recognized as the one great theologian of Quakerism. He joined the Quaker movement in 1667, as an extremely precocious youth, and moved quickly into his chosen vocation as a Christian thinker. When he was only twenty-six years of age he wrote, in Latin, the still acknowledged standard exposition of Quaker thinking, the famous *Apology for the True Christian Divinity*. The book appeared in Latin in 1676 and in Barclay's own English translation two years later. Subsequently, it has appeared in many other languages and in numerous English editions. It has been the most widely read and distributed of all Quaker books.

What Barclay did was to provide the Quaker Movement with what it needed sorely, a reasoned account of the Christian faith. Without

---

D. Elton Trueblood is one of the major voices of Christendom, an eighth-generation Quaker. When he wrote this essay, his mother was still living, aged 100. He received the AB from William Penn College, the STB from Harvard University, and the PhD from Johns Hopkins University. He is the recipient of nine honorary degrees and the author of over two dozen books, including *Robert Barclay, The Predicament of Modern Man, Confronting Christ, The Company of the Committed*, and *The Incendiary Fellowship*. He has been designated "Professor-at-Large" at Earlham College and President of the Yokefellow Associates.

this, the enthusiasm engendered by the charismatic George Fox (1624-1691) might have gone on a little longer, but it certainly would not have survived the creative period of 1650-1690. In order to win widespread public respect it was necessary that the truths which the unlettered Fox felt so vividly should be recast in a form able to attract and to convince the minds of thoughtful outsiders. This task was partly performed by the gifted William Penn, who was an able writer as well as a colonizer, but the major responsibility was carried by Barclay. So successful was his effort that he won the respect of a wide variety of readers, including Voltaire.

Robert Barclay was born in Scotland, at the famous house of Gordonstoun, because his mother was a Gordon. Through his mother Barclay was a distant cousin of the reigning Stuarts, Charles II and James II. He developed a deep friendship with the latter, a friendship undeterred by the fact that the king was a Roman Catholic. The two men were brought closely together by their joint opposition to laws which prohibited worship other than that in accordance with the Established Church of England.

Robert Barclay studied in Paris as a boy and there received a strong dose of indoctrination in Catholicism. His mother died while he was in Paris and, soon afterward, he returned to Scotland in accordance with her dying wish. Soon after this he settled with his father, Colonel David Barclay, at the beautiful estate of Ury, sixteen miles south of Aberdeen. From that time until his death, when a little less than forty-two years of age, Ury was his home. It was at Ury that he wrote all of his works except those which were composed in Aberdeen Prison. His father became a Quaker before Robert made the step, the elder Barclay being strongly influenced by a fellow prisoner in Edinburgh Castle.

The young scholar of Ury was largely self-taught, but in this enterprise he was greatly aided by the fact that, in Paris, he had learned to employ Latin as easily as he employed English. He had a good library, some volumes of which are still extant and bear his signature. We now know that he kept a notebook for several of his early years. Part of the notebook was filled with pages of a shorthand radically different from any shorthand in use today. The shorthand resisted all efforts to decipher it in the nineteenth century, but has now been deciphered by a remarkable combination of circumstances. We owe the solution of the problem to Douglas Lister, who first attempted the deciphering while a resident of Ethiopia. The notebook is helpful to the contemporary scholar because it presents several early formulations of ideas which were later developed in a mature fashion in the *Apology*.

In 1967 another important discovery was made in Barclay scholarship when Barclay's diaries were brought unexpectedly to light. There are two diaries, one covering the period of 1678-1685, and the other dealing with events from 1685 to 1690. Great quantities of Barclay manuscripts have been identified and are now available in Friends House Library, London. Among the manuscripts are valuable letters from William Penn and from Princess Elizabeth, the well-known friend of Descartes and granddaughter of James I.

Part of the present interest in Robert Barclay arises from the fact that, while he was an able thinker, he was also a man involved in public life. His most important public responsibility was that of being the nonresident governor of the colony of East Jersey. In 1682 the Proprietors of East Jersey, seeking a man who could give moral prestige to their experiment in government, met in London and appointed Robert Barclay governor for life. As governor he helped religious prisoners to be set free and to become colonists. Also he equipped ships and aided prospective colonists financially. Always his major concern in this connection was religious liberty.

Barclay's imprisonments were caused by his attending religious meetings which contravened the law against holding of conventicles. The most severe of his imprisonments occurred during the winter of 1676-1677, when he and many other Quakers were crowded into the Tolbooth at Aberdeen. In spite of the crowding, as well as the lack of adequate light, air, and heat, Barclay wrote that winter one of his most moving books, *Universal Love Considered*. Also he carried on a voluminous correspondence while in prison, including several letters to Princess Elizabeth, whom he visited, along with Penn, the following summer.

Barclay, in his published theology, did not suppose that he was writing in a sectarian fashion. Instead he thought of himself as presenting basic Christianity in the simplest and clearest form which he could imagine. The pattern which he followed was roughly similar to that followed by John Calvin in his *Institutes*, more than a century earlier. Barclay first published in Latin a set of "Theses" and then, in his major work, defended these. The "Theses" were really the "Table of Contents" of the *Apology*.

The crucial points of Barclay's theology are four in number, Experience, The Light of Christ, the Ministry, and Worship. He sees the basic experience of the divine-human encounter as being more primary than the Scripture, because the credibility of the Scriptures depends, ultimately, upon the reliability of the religious experience of the Scripture writers. While honoring the Bible, Barclay never termed it the primary rule of faith and life. He directed his readers to what he called the fountain rather than the cistern. Like his mentor, George Fox, Barclay sought to lead men to an experience as significant as that of the men who wrote the books of the Bible.

By the universal light of Christ, Barclay meant the incarnation and *more*. Is it conceivable, he asked, that God would limit salvation to men who have had the good fortune to know of the historic Christ? His answer was negative, because in that case God would, he believed, be unloving and therefore not like Christ. Barclay agreed that Christ is the only "way," but saw no reason to suppose that His saving revelation is limited to His few years on earth. Instead, Barclay followed the lead of John 1:9, stressing, as did other Quakers, the conviction that the light of Christ is independent of both time and geography. Unless this is true, there is no chance for such a man as Socrates. Thus Barclay provides a lead for modern man by presenting an alternative both to indifferentism and exclusiveness. Herein lies part of Barclay's contemporary significance and striking relevance.

Brief Bibliography

Barclay's works were collected and published with the general title *Truth Triumphant*, in 1692. The *Apology* is usually published as a separate volume. *Barclay's Apology in Modern English*, translated by Dean Freiday, was published in 1967. This and other Barclay works are available at Friends Book Store, 302 Arch Street, Philadelphia.

Robert Barclay, by D. Elton Trueblood, a study of Barclay's life and thought, was published by Harper & Row in 1968.

> *"One should therefore emphasize that the divine means of Word and sacrament are concerned with the inner man. Hence it is not enough that we hear the Word with our outward ear, but we must let it penetrate to our heart, so that we may hear the Holy Spirit speak there, that is, with vibrant emotion and comfort feel the sealing of the Spirit and the power of the Word."*

37

Philipp Jacob Spener

Orlando H. Wiebe

Philipp Jacob Spener was born in Alsace in 1635, the son of a steward in the service of a duke of Rappoltstein. He was especially indebted to his mother for his early religious influences, but it is also known that the Countess Agathe of Rappoltstein, one of the sponsors at his baptism, exerted a formative influence on him in his boyhood. His early manifest interest in things "pious, earnest and quiet"[1] was nurtured by his pastor, Joachim Stoll, who was to him catechist, preacher, and counselor.

Attracted to the books in his father's library, young Philipp selected for his devotional reading several English books which he found in German translation—Emanuel Sontham's *Golden Treasure of the Children of God*, Lewis Bayly's *The Practice of Piety*,[2] and Johann Arndt's *Wahres Christenthum* which became, next to the Bible, his favorite book.[3] The criticism of conventional Christianity by the English Puritan writers and the serious tones of Arndt's work combined to instill in Spener a fear of becoming involved in the revelry and vulgarity of his day, and a strong desire for a genuine religious life.

In 1651, at the age of sixteen, Spener completed his preparatory studies and entered the University of Strassburg. After a two-year period of study of philosophy, history, and languages, he was granted the

---

Orlando H. Wiebe has served as Director of Field Education and Associate Professor of Pastoral Theology in the Mennonite Brethren Biblical Seminary, and as a minister in his denomination. He received his AB from Tabor College, the BD from Fuller Theological Seminary, and the PhD from the State University of Iowa.

master's degree which qualified him to lecture as a *Privat-Docent* (instructor). Although the faculty at Strassburg was steeped in Lutheran orthodoxy, the spirit was not that of Scholasticism. The zeal for pure doctrine was matched by the concern for practical Christianity and the revival of vital piety. The professor of theology who influenced Spener most was John Conrad Dannhauer, who induced Spener to read Luther's works, and taught him to think of salvation as a present experience of God's grace.[4] Dannhauer, who reportedly devoted an hour a day to prayer, insisted that all study of theology must lead to the practice of piety.

Following his master's degree, Spener spent several years in travel. This brought him to Basel, Geneva, Lyons, and Tübingen. It was at Geneva that he heard the French Reformed preacher, Jean de Labadie, on a number of occasions, and was probably influenced by his concept of house gatherings. Spener then returned to Strassburg, where he pursued his doctorate in theology, completing it in 1665 at the age of twenty-six. During this time of study he had a pastoral responsibility which required of him nothing more than a sermon every few weeks. When an invitation came to him to enter a larger parish in Frankfurt, now that he had finished his theological preparation, he protested that he did not have the experience to match the responsibilities of the position.[5] However, upon the advice of the councils of the cities of Strasbourg and Frankfurt, Spener decided to accept the call, believing that his new opportunity carried within it the possibility of wider advancement for the kingdom of God. Thus in 1666 Spener began a twenty-year ministry which placed him at the head of a movement of ultimate worldwide significance.

During the first three years of the new work nothing out of the ordinary took place in his ministry, although his sermons had a decided appeal as indicated by the increasing number of hearers in his services. His chief obligation as minister was to preach the Sunday morning sermon, and to this task he devoted himself with the earnest, specific purpose of urging upon the people the necessity of inner holiness and godliness.[6]

The ground thus appeared to be prepared for the first clear innovation in Spener's ministry which resulted from his famous sermon on the sixth Sunday after Trinity, 1669, on the text Matthew 5:20.[7] Spener pointedly exposed the gross error of the church member who thinks he has done enough when he has attached himself to a congregation, attends its services regularly, feels himself in harmony with its doctrine, and conducts himself according to accepted standards of propriety. This false righteousness in which such a man rejoices is nothing more than a pharisaical facade by which no man can be saved. Even further, he stands under the "woe" of Christ's condemnation.

The sermon shocked the congregation, but a small group ventured to ally itself with the pastor in a pursuit of true Christianity.[8] Thus there developed the small-group meeting for mutual sharing and Bible discussion—the *collegia pietatis*. In the beginning these groups, under Spener's direction, not only read and discussed the Scriptures but interacted with the main points of the sermon of the preceding Sunday. This was supplemented by the reading of such devotional literature as Arndt's *Wahres Christenthum* and Bayly, *The Practice of Piety*.

In 1675, Johann David Zunner, a publisher of that city, was planning a new edition of Johann Arndt's *Postille*.[9] More than fifty years had elapsed since Arndt's death and a number of editions of the *Postille* had been published during that time, but Zunner felt the need of issuing a new comprehensive edition.

In order to recommend this edition to the Christian readers, Zunner turned to Spener, the senior of the Frankfurt ministerium, for an appropriate preface. Having been concerned for some time about the need for a revival of practical Christianity, Spener gladly assumed the responsibility, seeing it offered to him "the opportunity to sum up in a programmatic manner that which displeased him in the life of the Church of his time, and wherein he saw the possibility of remedying the damages."[10]

Although Spener's activities as a leader of house gatherings had aroused some criticism, it was the appearance of this preface to Arndt's *Postille*[11] that created an immediate sensation. Within the next few months the author had it published separately under the title *Pia Desideria*.[12] Having portrayed the religious indifference of the day, the prevailing immorality in all levels of society, and the absorption in scholastic theology, Spener proposed a six-point reform program. This called for more intensive Bible study by all classes, increased lay participation in the church, greater consistency of Christian practice, dealing with unbelievers and heretics in the spirit of love, stress on genuine piety as well as theological learning, and a revival of preaching pointed toward spiritual edification.

Within a few years Spener received numerous responses expressing favorable comment on his analysis of religious conditions and the proposals for reform. Spener followed up his own writing with specific efforts to implement that which he believed to constitute a remedy for the ills of the church.

After twenty years in Frankfurt he was offered the position of court chaplain to the electoral prince of Saxony, Johann Georg III, at Dresden. He assumed this position in 1668 and served for a period of five years. With his encouragement, two young university lecturers, August Hermann Francke and Paul Anton, began the *Collegium philobiblicum*, a society for the exegetical study of the Bible, in the University of Leipzig, after the pattern of Spener's conventicles in Frankfurt. Spener's ministry in Dresden was not without difficulty, however, since his sympathizers, called "Pietists," had become involved in a controversy over prevalent worldly practices.[13]

In the summer of 1691 Spener left Dresden for Berlin where his position was that of "visitor" of the churches, and preacher in the Church of St. Nicholas. Consistent with his previous ministry, he began with a series of sixty-six sermons on *Wiedergeburt*.[14] His personal pastoral ministry became so well known that he was compelled to carry on a voluminous correspondence much of it later compiled in *Theologisches Bedencken*. In 1704, on a trip to Saxony he dedicated for the advancement of the kingdom of God, his godson, the young Zinzendorf.

During the last three years of his ministry Spener preached a series of sermons on the texts and selected concepts from the first three books of Arndt's *Wahres Christenthum.* These were published in 1711, six years after his death.

In evaluating Spener and his work, it becomes evident that his central concern was the renewal of Christian life. The specific directives for reforms which he set down in his *Pia Desideria* and carried out in his own ministry with a good measure of success were not entirely new, however, for most of the ideas and proposals had been presented periodically before his time. "Yet nobody but Spener was capable of putting them together in the way in which we find them in the *Pia Desideria.*"[15]

Sources Cited

1. Jakob Schmitt, *Die Gnade Bricht Durch* (Giessen: Brunnen-Verlag, 1958), p. 61.
2. Lewis Bayly's book, *Practice of Piety,* was first published about 1610; the exact date is not known.
3. Werner Marholz, *Der Deutsche Pietismus* (Berlin: Furche-Verlag, 1921), p. 100.
4. Philipp Jacob Spener, *Pia Desideria,* ed. Theodore G. Tappert (Philadelphia: Fortress Press, 1964), p. 10. Further references to this work will be Spener, *PD.*
5. Spener, *TB,* I, 3-4.
6. Schmitt, p. 61.
7. "For I say unto you, That except your righteousness shall exceed the righteousness of the scribes and Pharisees, ye shall in no case enter into the kingdom of heaven."
8. Spener, *Erbauliche Evangelisch-und Epistolische Sonntags-Andachten* (Frankfurt, 1716), p. 638, quoted in Spener *PD,* p. 13.
9. A collection of sermons on the appointed gospels of the church year, originally published in 1615.
10. Kurt Aland, *Spener Studien* (Berlin: W. De Gruyter, 1943), p. 527.
11. See Philipp Jacob Spener, *Pia Desideria,* Herausgegeben vem Kurt Aland. (Berlin: Verlag von Walter De Gruyter & Co., 1940), III.
12. The title page reads in part: "PIA DESIDERIA oder Hertzliches Verlangen nach Gottgefälliger Besserung der wahren Evangelischen Kirchen." See Aland, *Pia Desideria,* title page. Tappert's translation reads: "Pia Desideria or Heartfelt Desire for a God-pleasing Reform of the true Evangelical Church, together with several simple Christian Proposals looking toward this End." Spender, *PD,* p. 29.
13. *Ibid.,* p. 22.
14. See Spener, *Von Der Wiedergeburt,* Aus seiner Berliner Bibelarbeit herausgegeben von Hans-Georg Feller (Stuttgart: J. F. Steinkopf, 1963).
15. Aland, *Spener-Studien,* pp. 57-58. Quoted in Spener, *PD,* p. 18.

> "Those who call others heretics
> are the heretics proper, and
> those called heretics are the
> real Godfearing people."

38
Gottfried Arnold

Donald F. Durnbaugh

Gottfried Arnold (1666-1714) was a church historian and mystical theologian of German Lutheran background, whose life and thought were of high significance for Christianity. Born in Saxony, the son of a high school teacher, he was half-orphaned early in life and from the age of thirteen on had to earn his way through school by tutoring. His academic ability is indicated by the earning of a master's degree at the University of Wittenberg at the age of twenty. Classical studies, history, and theology were his major subjects of study, although he was not impressed by the stiff orthodoxy of his Lutheran professors. He later remarked that he was glad that his thirst for learning during his university stay had preserved him from the usual excesses of student life.

The young graduate found a position as tutor in the home of a noble family in Dresden, where he was attracted to and deeply influenced by the leader of German Pietism, Philip Jacob Spener (1635-1705). Arnold's pietistic convictions cost him his position when he dared to criticize the worldly lives of his young charges and their parents. In 1692 he moved to Quedlinburg, a center of pietist and enthusiast activity, once again as a tutor for a wealthy family. Here he plunged into massive historical studies, resulting in the publication in 1696 of his important work *Die Erste Liebe*, a detailed and loving description of the early church. He was concerned to show that reform in church life could come only by taking early Christianity as the model.

The well-received volume (six editions before 1780) earned him the prestigious post as professor of history at the University of Giessen in the state of Hesse. After not quite a year's tenure, Arnold resigned

---

Donald F. Durnbaugh is Professor of Church History in Bethany Theological Seminary. He received his BA from Manchester College, his MA from the University of Michigan, and his PhD from the University of Pennsylvania. Among his books are: *European Origins of the Brethren*, *The Brethren in Colonial America*, and *The Believers' Church*. He is a minister in the Church of the Brethren, earlier known as German Baptists, and an outstanding historian in the Free Church tradition.

his post—an unheard of step. He explained his resignation in a widely circulated tract, asserting that he had hoped that a career in teaching would prove to be more conducive to a life of Christian piety than would other professions, only to find that university life was corrupting and distracting. For the sake of his soul, he was forced to retire from the academic arena.

Back in Quedlinburg, he put the finishing touches on his master work, the *Impartial History of the Church and Heretics (Unpartheiische Kirchen-und Ketzer Historie)*, first released in 1699-1700. The four-volume work was reprinted in 1729 and once again in 1740-1742, this time with another volume of additions and corrections and responses to criticisms. (Arnold's history has recently been reissued in Germany, an indication of its continuing importance.) Probably no other book on church history, before or since, has created as much controversy as followed its publication. It was alternately praised as second in value only after the Bible, or condemned as the most wicked and pernicious book ever written.

The storm was caused by Arnold's methods and aims. He set out to seek true Christianity in every century of Christian life, undeterred by previous judgments of "heresy" or "orthodoxy" by the official church. To do this he tried to go to the original writings of all Christian movements and not depend on the slanted assessments of later writers. The result of his original and impressive research in the sources was the finding that, more often than not, the "heretics" represented vital Christian faith, instead of the church of councils and consistories, of prelates and princes. He has been accused of turning church history upside down, that is, of making the heretics into the true church, and orthodoxy into heresy. This is not quite true, but it is the case that he was little concerned with creed and official dogma but looked rather at the evidences of Christian life and piety. This he often found in the camp of the dissenting movements.

After the publication of the *History*, Arnold wrote many other books on mystical and historical subjects, more than fifty by the time of his death. After 1702, he moderated his criticism of the church and accepted a pastorate. His reason for this action was that he felt he was selfish in wishing to continue a life of solitude and scholarship. He thought that the chafing burdens of pastoral duties would benefit his soul exactly because he had little desire to engage himself in them. In 1707 he was made pastor and inspector in Perleburg in Brandenburg, where he remained until his death in 1714. He had been weakened in 1713 by a siege of scorbutic fever (of scurvy), but continued his duties. While he was conducting a communion service on Pentecost Day, 1714, Prussian recruiters invaded the sanctuary to seize bodily some of his young parishioners for military duty. Arnold was so shocked by this outrage that he died after an illness of ten days.

Arnold's Thought

Gottfried Arnold was deeply influenced by the mystical theology or theosophy of Jacob Boehme (1574-1624), whose emphasis was upon a mystical relationship with God. Ordinary church life, to Boehme and his followers, was a matter of shadows, not reality. Many of the Boehmists became separatists from organized church life, for they saw no possibility of salvation in a tainted institution. During the radical separatist period of Arnold's life he composed a "Dirge for Babylon," attacking in bitter language the shortcomings which he noted in the churches—their compromising with the world, their tired theological controversies, their lack of true piety.

Men of this frame of mind placed high importance on personal purity. They believed that this should include celibacy, that the marital state was a fallen state. In this they approached the spirit of Roman Catholic monasticism, from whose ranks they found many writers of spiritual insight. They believed that the truly spiritual person seeks a mystical unity with a heavenly bride or bridegroom, not a mortal one. In many of Arnold's writings he praises the "heavenly Sophia" or divine wisdom who alone is to be courted. He used quite sensual terms in describing the bliss which can come from this spiritual unity. Much to the disappointment of Arnold's friends, he seemingly changed his views on this by taking a Pietist wife in 1701 and then raising a family.

An important part of Arnold's thought was his conviction about the fall of the church. He saw church history as a saga of the decline and fall of Christianity. In this he was close to Sebastian Franck and others in the Radical Reformation who were convinced that church institutions as such represented a fall from the primitive purity of Jesus' teachings. Since then, what is seen is a process of decay or degeneration. Arnold's writings persuaded many of his contemporaries that the only possible church life was that which imitated early Christianity and tried to restore its forms and practices. Later rationalists, such as Goethe, used Arnold as witness that the church was so bankrupt that it should be dropped.

More positive aspects of Arnold's thought included his emphasis in all of his writings on reform in congregational life, his passionate concern for individual conversion, and his warm devotional interest. His emotion-laden hymns are still being sung in German-speaking lands. Probably the most important contribution he made was the rehabilitation of many of the dissenting Christian movements of the past. After Arnold's books, it was impossible to write them off simply as heretics. Their witness had to be taken seriously. For this reason, some have called Arnold the father of modern church history.

Brief Bibliography

Almost all of the important work on Arnold has been done in Germany. Among the more recent studies are: W. von Schröder, *Gottfried Arnold* (1917), Erich Seeberg, *Gottfried Arnold: Die Wissenschaft und Mystik seiner Zeit* (1923), Walter Nigg, *Das Buch der Ketzer* (1949), and Herman Dörries, *Geist and Geschichte bei Gottfried Arnold* (1963). Robert Friedmann discusses Arnold's significance for the Anabaptists/Mennonites in *The Mennonite Encyclopedia*, I:164-165. There is a good discussion of Arnold and his background in C. David Ensign, "Radical German Pietism (ca. 1675-ca. 1760)" (unpub. PhD dissertation, Boston University, 1955)

"The devout man ... lives no longer to his own will ... but to the sole will of God."

39

William Law

John R. Mumaw

During the early seventeenth century William Law (1686-1761) demonstrated again the dignity of faith in choosing an unpopular career. He courageously refused to damage his conscience by a voluntary religious compliance with secular state demands. The radical decision was made at a time when he had a bright prospect for a lifetime income from the state. To him the question centered in the state-church issue. He was well-trained for the pulpit. The Church of England offered him an attractive position. He had all the qualifications needed. But at that point he had to choose between a cherished career and dismissal from the Anglican priesthood. The issue was whether or not the state has authority over the church. Law saw how the church was being made a tool of political advantage. He saw the state more concerned about the political position of the bishops than it was about their spiritual fitness. The parish priest had become the puppet of the state. Law could not conscientiously sign up under these conditions.

Another factor that helped to determine Law's future stood in the life of the church. He observed a generally shallow profession of faith. He was keenly disappointed in the anemic witness of the church. He was therefore deeply moved with the need for religious renewal. He saw the church as a "valley of dry bones." He saw church membership as a nominal profession of Christianity. He grieved over the apathy and indifference that prevailed. Congregations were made up of "decent people" but without the vitality of an authentic message. This was the inevitable result of the paralyzing effect of church statism and formalism. The young preacher therefore refused not only to condone the adulterous church-state relationship but he also decried internal corruptions and hypocrisy. He lost his job. The door was closed to preaching, but he found the way to a fruitful literary career.

John R. Mumaw is President Emeritus of Eastern Mennonite College, and a former moderator of his denomination, the Mennonite Church. He is also Emeritus Professor of Christian Education of Eastern Mennonite College. He is a director of the Mennonite Mental Health Services Board. He received the BA from Elizabethtown College, also the D Sc in Ped, and from the American Theological Seminary, the MRE. Among his books are *Assurance of Salvation* and *The Resurrected Life*.

William Law became an author in his own right. He is listed today among the great writers of classic devotional literature. To him the answer to meaninglessness is in finding reality in personal experience with God. He had learned through his own habits of devotion that God is real. Out of great depths of conviction about this issue he wrote a powerful message, *A Serious Call to a Devout and Holy Life*. This book stands high on the list of devotional classics and carries a universal message. It is not an elaboration of Christian doctrine but a sharp delineation of the moral and spiritual implications of being Christian. It is experience-centered and presses for a return to a depth and fervor of Christian experience like that of the early church.

The writings of William Law represent an early, although unconscious attempt to formulate a theology of Christian experience. While they are somewhat hortatory in form they are testimonial in spirit. Law is primarily concerned about the increase of virtue in the believer's life. He points to the exercise of devotion as a means of achieving Christian reality. By devotion he means "a life given or devoted to God." Then he goes on to say, "He, therefore, is the devout man, who lives no longer to his own will, or the way and spirit of the world, but to the sole will of God; who considers God in everything, who serves God in everything, who makes all the parts of his common life parts of piety, by doing everything in the name of God, and under such rules as are conformable to His glory."[1]

In relation to the concept of "devotion" and "holiness," Law makes frequent reference to the function of prayer. We pray to God for reasons other than self-advancement. We pray because living wholly unto God involves a constant turning of our human actions into acts of piety and obedience to Him. We pray because in this exercise of grace there are ways of expressing our dependence on God, and our obedience and devotion to Him. It becomes a matter of glorifying Him in all the acts of our common life as inspired by this repeated primary contact with God. Law makes it clear, however, that prayer as such is "a very small thing" as compared to that devotion which is to be expressed in every other circumstance of life. He says, "There is no reason for our prayers to be according to the will of God but that our lives should be of the same nature, full of the same wisdom, holiness, and heavenly temper, that we may live unto God in the same spirit that we pray to Him."[2]

In his repeated emphasis on prayer Law urged spontaneous expression. Although he did not reject the use of a prayer book he stressed the need for a worshiping heart at all times and in all places quite independently of external forms. He says, "The way to be a man of prayer and be governed by its spirit is not to get a book full of prayers; but the best help you can have from a book is to read one full of truths ... that God is your all and that all is misery but a heart and life devoted to Him. This is the best outward prayer-book you can have, as it will turn you to an inward book and spirit of prayer in your heart, which is a continual longing desire of the heart after God, His divine life and Holy Spirit."[3]

The general tone of Law's writing has a strong emphasis upon morality. To him upright living is a primary element of Christian faith.

He calls for a pronounced obedience to the teachings of Christ. He sees in His commands an absolute authority which tolerates no opposition. One's life is to be conformed to the will of God in every aspect of human relations. Law believes the Christian must face even the "hard sayings" of Christ and apply them to personal living. The nominal Christian of his day was in need of being stabbed awake with the kind of truth that allows no complacency, no halfhearted performance. He called for an untainted loyalty that held the will of God supreme in every area of life. "We can not be said to live unto God unless we live unto Him in all the ordinary actions of our life, unless He be the rule and measure of all our ways."[4] He goes on to say, "There can not anything be imagined more absurd in itself than wise and sublime and heavenly prayers added to a life of vanity and folly where neither labor nor diversions, neither time nor money, are under the direction of the wisdom and heavenly tempers of our prayers."[5]

Law keeps referring to the "spirit of prayer" and "spirit of love" as essential elements of a normal Christian experience. The emphasis, in all of this, is on the need for the Holy Spirit and for the "baptism of fire." His position on this reflects the influence of both mysticism and Quakerism. John Wesley felt he went too far in promoting "inner light" and in teaching the "spiritual observance" of baptism and communion. Wesley confessed to having been "offended" by many parts of the *Serious Call* and *Christian Perfection* but he also expressed gratitude for having been convinced by them more than ever before "of the exceeding height and breadth and depth of the law of God."[6] However, he felt that Law gave too much attention to the incarnation of Christ and not enough emphasis upon the saving merit of His blood. In addition to the error in regard to the doctrine of atonement and of faith and justification, Wesley felt in Law's writings a neglect in teaching about the justice and mercy of God. He also accuses Law of encouraging the "total neglect of the ordinances."

Law wrote various tracts on controversial issues. In these he used a convincing logic and returned again and again to his recurring theme of holiness. He stood in defense of experiential belief. He was indeed a moral philosopher, as well as a theologian. He promoted high standards of ethics and a high regard for Scripture. Doddridge says, "His writings have a severity seldom to be found; his language is generally just and beautiful and very nervous; but he is too ready to affect points of wit and strokes of satire."[7] Yet he employed these literary forms with unusual skill.

As an author, Law disapproved of critical attacks upon devotional literature. He wanted his readers to open their hearts to receive impressions beyond that of a purely "head" knowledge. To him it was a miscarriage of purpose to read with a critical spirit. Rather, if one is to receive benefit from a spiritual message he must read in the spirit of prayer and love. Literature devoted to an expression of sacred and intimate realities about Christ should be regarded with deep respect.

The devotional fire of Law's writings, especially his *Call to a Devout and Holy Life*, is derived mainly from his deep sense of the claims of Christ. He powerfully urged Christians to live entirely consecrated to Him as a living Lord and to walk in obedience to His teachings. He is constantly reminding his readers that being Christian involves a daily application of the gospel in all areas of life. "He is the religious man who ... worships God in every place by a purity of behaviour ... who is as wise and heavenly at home or in the field as in the house of God."[8]

Footnotes

1. Law, William, *A Serious Call to a Devout and Holy Life* (Westminster Press, 1948), p. 1.
2. *Ibid.*, p. 2.
3. Law, quoted by Stephen Hobhouse in his book *William Law and Eighteenth Century Quakerism* (Geo. Allen & Unwin, Ltd., 1927), p. 290.
4. Law, *op. cit.*, p. 3.
5. Hobhouse, *op. cit.*, p. 290.
6. *Ibid.*, p. 312.
7. Quoted in Allibone's *Dictionary of English Literature and British and American Authors* (Lippincott, 1870, Volume II), p. 1066.
8. Law, *op. cit.*, p. 85.

"There is an absolute and universal dependence of the redeemed on God. The nature and contrivance of our redemption is such, that the redeemed are in every thing directly, immediately, and entirely dependent on God."

40

Jonathan Edwards

Keith L. Sprunger

Jonathan Edwards was a leading eighteenth-century American theologian, preacher, and revivalist of the Great Awakening. He stood in the Puritan tradition of New England although Puritanism as a movement had largely dissipated itself by his day. Born October 5, 1703, he was the son of the Reverend Timothy Edwards and the grandson of another famous preacher, Solomon Stoddard. He was a precocious lad and entered Yale in 1716, not yet thirteen, and graduated with an AB in 1720. Edwards entered the Congregational ministry and spent much of his life as minister at Northampton, Massachusetts. He was known as a powerful preacher and a profound writer.

His theology was Calvinist and orthodox Congregationalist; as such he was an utter enemy of Arminianism, of Anglicanism, and of every sort of worldliness. The Protestant church of his day was weak and ineffective through the influence of Deism and rationalism. The eighteenth century is commonly known as the Enlightenment or the Age of Reason because of its rationalistic, secular approach to life, but Edwards was hardly in tune with its basic spirit. For him the great need of the day was repentance, conversion, and orthodoxy. Like Wesley in England, his contemporary, Edwards saw the need for a fervent awakening. Under his preaching in 1733-35, Northampton experienced a great religious revival with hundreds of conversions and with scores added to the church. "Scarcely a single Person in the whole Town was Left unconcerned about the Great things of the Eternal World," wrote Edwards. The results were amazing, and Edwards reported that religion uplifted the whole community; "I never saw the Christian Spirit in Love to Enemies so Exemplified, in all my Life as I have seen it within this Half-year." The preaching of men like Edwards

---

Keith L. Sprunger is a Professor of History in Bethel College. He received the AB from Wheaton College, and the MA and PhD from the University of Illinois.

prepared the way for the Great Awakening, a widespread American revival movement reaching its climax in the early 1740s. George Whitefield (1714-1770), the English evangelist, was the primary preacher of the Awakening with Edwards also playing a considerable role.

Edwards was a prodigious scholar and tireless worker. He generally arose at 4:00 a.m. and spent at least thirteen hours a day in study. His life was austere and his convictions uncompromising. In his youth he had resolved, "Never to do anything, which, I should be afraid to do, if I expected it would not be above an hour, before I should hear the last trump."

Controversy in his Northampton parish led to his dismissal as minister in 1750. For the next several years he served as missionary to the Indians, but in 1757 he was called to Princeton College as president. He died a few months later on March 22, 1758, from a smallpox inoculation.

Theology

Edwards, above all, was a Calvinist, emphasizing the sovereignty of God and the complete dependence of man. He discarded the earlier Covenant or Federal theology of Puritanism to become the foremost American spokesman for pure Calvinism. Arminianism and free will, he feared, robbed God of His glory and full power; and so he preached divine sovereignty without exception. An early sermon, "God Glorified in Man's Dependence" (1731), is an unequivocal statement for predestination. According to Edwards, (1) God does everything in redemption, (2) man's desire for God is God-given, (3) whatever holiness man obtains comes from God dwelling in him, (4) God communicates his own beauty to the saints (Winslow, p. 146). Said Edwards, "God is glorified in the work of redemption in this, that there appears in it so absolute and universal a dependence of the redeemed on him."

At the same time, while preaching his stern orthodoxy, Edwards was aware of the newest currents of thought and took account of them. His preaching and theology were all the more powerful because of his keen sense of the time. Typical of the Enlightenment, Edwards showed an interest in science and wrote various scientific papers, including essays on rainbows and flying spiders. He accommodated Calvinist theology to the new theories of John Locke and Isaac Newton but in such a way as to stress the mighty power of God who had set the scientific laws in place. He used Locke's theory of knowledge to gain psychological insight into human nature.

Edwards was also one of the great evangelists of modern times. His most famous sermon, "Sinners in the Hands of an Angry God" (on the text "their foot shall slide in due time"), preached in 1741 during the Great Awakening, testifies to his power as a revivalist and to his psychological insight. The sermon pictures the frightful state of mankind: "The God that holds you over the pit of hell, much as one holds a spider, or some loathsome insect over the fire, abhors you, and is dreadfully provoked; his wrath towards you burns like fire; he looks upon you as worthy of nothing else, but to be cast into the fire...." And yet, "it is nothing but his hand that holds you from falling into the fire every moment." Edwards' preaching wrought such a convulsion that "there was a great moaning and crying out through ye whole House—What shall I do to be Saved—oh I am going to Hell—Oh what shall I do for Christ." Edwards' theology, although centered in the sovereignty of God, nevertheless powerfully called men to repentance through a fervent evangelicalism.

In spite of the emotional appeal in Edwards' preaching, he was not a fanatical, ranting preacher. He preached as much about practical piety as he did about eternal fire and brimstone. His manner was calm and unemotional (he would preach with his eyes on the bell-rope at the back of the church) even though his material often tended to evoke emotions. His theological writings are clear and reasoned.

Jonathan Edwards stands as one of the foremost American theologians. In an age of declining religion he preached an unswerving Calvinist-Puritan orthodoxy, and through his efforts helped to bring in the Great Awakening. He was a notable scholar and possessed one of the best minds of colonial America. Perry Miller called him "infinitely more than a theologian. He was one of America's five or six major artists, who happened to work with ideas instead of with poems or novels."

Brief Bibliography

The most valuable biographies of Edwards are Perry Miller, *Jonathan Edwards* (1949), which emphasizes intellectual development, and Ola Elizabeth Winslow, *Jonathan Edwards, 1703-1758* (1940), a full-scale study. A useful selection of his writings is found in Vergilius Ferm, *Puritan Sage* (1953).

> *"By perfection, I mean perfect love, or the loving God with all our heart, so as to rejoice evermore, to pray without ceasing, and in everything to give thanks."*

41
John Wesley

J. C. Wenger

As the eighteenth century broke upon England, God's people were in desperate need of renewal. It pleased God to bring the "Evangelical Revival" to the British nation through an unusual man—one of the most effective servants of Christ in all of church history—John Wesley, MA (as he wrote it). Christened John Benjamin Wesley, he was born at Epworth, England, on June 28, 1703 (June 17, Julian calendar). He lived to the advanced age of almost 88, dying in London on March 2, 1791. He was the son of an Anglican pastor, the Reverend Samuel Wesley, and his gifted and brilliant wife, Susanna Annesley. John was her fifteenth child (of nineteen)—and she in turn was a twenty-fourth child! She taught her children the subjects usually learned in elementary school, and much more, she inculcated in them a remarkable knowledge of God and His Word. She was especially effective as a disciplinarian, allowing no eating or drinking between meals, and insisting on a quiet household. The small children were taught even to cry softly.

The basic facts of Wesley's life can be stated briefly. Perhaps the most significant event of his entire childhood was his deliverance from the fire which devoured the Epworth rectory on February 9, 1709. It happened that forty years later Wesley was in a Watchnight Service in the West Street Chapel, London. He writes, "About eleven o'clock it came into my mind, that this was the very day and hour in which, forty years ago, I was taken out of the flames. I stopped, and gave a short account of that wonderful providence. The voice of praise and thanksgiving went up on high, and great was our rejoicing before the Lord."

At the age of ten he entered the Charterhouse school in London, where he remained six years. There he somewhat dropped the careful Christian way of life which he had been taught as a child. On June 24, 1720, he entered Christ Church College at Oxford from which he graduated (BA) in 1724. He then began to study theology, and was or-

---

J. C. Wenger is Professor of Historical Theology in the Associated Mennonite Biblical Seminaries. He received the BA degree from Goshen College, the MA in Philosophy from the University of Michigan, and the Doctor of Theology from the University of Zurich. Among his books are *They Met God.*

157

dained as an Anglican deacon in the Christ Church Cathedral on September 19, 1725, by Bishop Potter of Oxford; and Anglican priest in the same cathedral on September 22, 1728, again by Bishop Potter. He received his MA degree at Oxford, February 14, 1727. He assisted his father at Epworth, 1727-29, then returned to Oxford. He was a teaching Fellow at Lincoln College, Oxford, 1729-1736, lecturing on logic, Greek, and philosophy.

In 1765 Wesley entered a bit of his spiritual pilgrimage in his famous *Journal*. He reports that in 1725 he read Bishop Jeremy Taylor's *Rules of Holy Living and Dying*. He was deeply moved. The next year he got acquainted with Thomas a Kempis, whose *Imitation of Christ* made a deep impression on him. In 1727 he read William Law's *Serious Call*, and longed for a total consecration of himself to God. In 1730 he became *homo unius libri* (a man of one Book), and his lifelong devotion to the Bible is now well known. At Oxford he was the leader of a Bible study and prayer group which was variously ridiculed as the Holy Club, the Bible Moths, the Supererogation Men, and various other epithets. This little band of godly scholars met together each night to study the Greek New Testament, to pray, and to share. They also did prison visitation. In his own personal study, Wesley worked on the Greek and Latin classics, logic and ethics, Hebrew and Arabic, metaphysics and natural philosophy (physics), oratory and poetry. On Sundays he read theology. He also took up French.

A new chapter opened in his life in 1735 when on October 21 he sailed for America, to serve as a minister to the colonists in Savannah, Georgia, a town of some 500, and as a missionary to the American Indians. Although George Whitefield spoke in the highest terms of Wesley's good work in America, Wesley arrived back in England on February 1, 1738, feeling that he had been a flat failure. On this trip he came deeply under the influence of some Moravians, and felt that they had a peace and a calm and confident trust in Christ which he, in spite of all his hard labors for Christ, still lacked. So great was his confidence in the Moravians that he allowed them to break up his possible marriage to a girl whom he dearly loved. "The will of the Lord be done," he murmured.

Back in England, Wesley dragged himself to a small assembly on Aldersgate Street on the memorable date, May 24, 1738. He had had some conversations with a Moravian, Peter Boehler, who shook Wesley deeply, not only by pointing out to him from the Scriptures the possibility of genuine inner holiness and abiding peace, but also introduced him to several believers who were able to testify simply and sincerely that this was indeed their experience. At the Aldersgate meeting, about 8:45 p.m., as he sat listening to the reading of Luther's *Preface to Romans*, Wesley suddenly felt his heart "strangely warmed." He continues in his description: "I felt I did trust in Christ, Christ alone for salvation: and an assurance was given me that he had taken away *my* sins, even *mine*, and saved *me* from the law of sin and death." A similar inner witness was to come to him many years later (1760): "As soon as Mr. Fugill began to speak, I felt my soul was all love. I was so stayed on God as I never felt before, and knew that I loved him with all my heart.... I could only give thanks. And the witness that God had saved me from all my sins, grew clearer every hour." Wesley's *Journals* are replete with his comments and testimonies of what God did for him. In 1885 the Boston publishers, McDonald & Gill, published a marvelous collection of extracts from Wesley's writings, *Christian Perfection as Taught by John Wesley*, compiled by Rev. J. A. Wood. And an even fuller and more comprehensive collection of extracts was published in 1954 by the Abingdon Press, *A Compend of Wesley's Theology*, edited by Robert W. Burtner and Robert E. Chiles. The major topics here covered are: (1) Religious Knowledge and Authority, (2) God, (3) Jesus Christ, (4) Holy Spirit, (5) Man, (6) Salvation, (7) Moral Ideal, (8) Moral Standard, (9) Church, and (10) Eschatology.

Wesley, a small but well-built man, was most abstemious and amazingly full of energy. He ate sparingly, slept sparingly (rising each morning at 4:00), he wrote over 200 books, preached over 40,000 times, and traveled a quarter million miles, mostly on horseback. He crossed the Irish Channel forty-two times, and made twenty-two visits to Scotland. He had bright eyes, a clear complexion, a strong face, and he wore shoulder-length hair. He lived on a severely limited budget, and annually gave away as much as £1,400.

The most pathetic aspect of Wesley's life was his relations to women. He wanted to marry Sophia Hopkey in Georgia, and meekly allowed the Moravians to dissuade him. In 1749 his brother Charles in a most cruel manner broke up his engagement with a lovely widow named Grace Murray. On February 18, 1751, Wesley made the saddest mistake of his life when he married Mary Vazeille of London, also a widow. She was mean, selfish, and suspicious, and treated Wesley harshly, even dragging him around by his hair. (She seems to have been emotionally ill.) Some notion of what Wesley had to bear may be gained from his letter to "Molly" dated October 23, 1759. When she died in 1781 they had been separated much—by her wish—and Wesley learned of her death only after she was buried. Wesley had no children of his own.

In his work as an evangelist and field preacher—and especially as an organizer—Wesley is almost without peer in the history of the Christian church. Hated, opposed by mobs as well as by many of the clergy, Wesley continued on in his dauntless proclamation of the gospel, maintaining a strict discipline through his class meetings, membership cards, and lay preachers. In 1753 he thought he was about to die, and to prevent a eulogy, prepared his own tombstone epitaph: "Here lieth the body of JOHN WESLEY, a brand plucked out of the burning, Who died of consumption in the fifty-first year of his age, Not leaving, after his debts are paid, Ten pounds behind him, Praying, 'God be merciful to me, an unprofitable servant.' " While recovering from this illness he prepared a revision of the King James New Testament, with notes, entitled *Explanatory Notes Upon the New Testament*, by John Wesley, M. A. It is a remarkable revision, and a good, brief commentary. But God gave him almost four more decades to proclaim Christ!

By 1746 Wesley saw no essential difference between bishops and other clergy, so he felt qualified to select before his death an American superintendent (or bishop), Dr. Thomas Coke, 1747-1814, and ordained him in 1784. He also consecrated Alexander Mather to the same office in 1788, to take charge of the Methodists of the British Isles. At Wesley's death there were 71,668 Methodists in Great Britain, served by 294 preachers; and in the United States, 48,610 members, with 217 preachers. The mobs had not been able to stop the work of the Spirit of God, and neither had those clergymen who opposed Wesley. He preached his last sermon on February 23, 1791, wrote to Wilberforce on February 24 to continue with his crusade against the slave trade, and died March 2, 1791. He compared Wilberforce and his labors in the House of Commons to the fourth-century Athanasius *contra mundum* (against the world). As Wesley's strength was slipping away on his deathbed, he twice cried out, "The best of all, God is with us." After he expired, the friends around the bed united their voices in singing: "Waiting to receive thy spirit, Lo! the Savior stands above, Shows the purchase of His merit, Reaches out the crown of love." Wesley's last word was a simple "Farewell." Thus died a great man of God.

Bibliography

The body of writings left by Wesley was extensive, including his *Journals*, his *Sermons*, and other *Works*. During his lifetime he wrote 233 books of his own, and reissued or edited another 100. All major religious encyclopedias contain articles with bibliography, as well as *The Encyclopaedia Britannica*. One of the best biographies is that of John Telford, 1924.

> *"Two things fill the mind with ever new and increasing admiration and awe ... the starry heavens above and the moral law within."*

42

Immanuel Kant

Elmer A. Martens

Immanuel Kant was a German philosopher of the eighteenth century whose views, particularly on the place of reason, are so important that one present-day theologian holds that Kant "created the most original and influential system of modern times." His works represent a watershed in philosophy, as indicated by book titles such as *Protestant Thought Before Kant* and *An Outline of the History of Christian Thought Since Kant.*

Born on April 22, 1724, in the East Prussian town of Königsberg, Kant was the fourth child of parents said to be of Scottish origin. His father was a harness-maker; his mother, highly respected by Kant for her teaching and piety, died when Kant was thirteen. All his life Kant was dominated by a thirst for knowledge. His interest range included Greek and Roman classics, physics, philosophy, mathematics, and theology. After a period of tutoring he was appointed university lecturer in 1755, and in 1770 professor of logic and metaphysics at the University in Königsberg. Near the end of his life, because of views regarded as radical, Kant was forbidden by the government to speak or write on religion—an injunction to which he submitted. His health began to fail in 1798. He died in his eightieth year in 1804.

In appearance Kant was small, thin, and hollow-chested; he had a deformed right shoulder. Though frail and much concerned about his diet, he was basically healthy. He remained a bachelor and lived alone with a man servant for most of his life. He once said, "When I needed a wife, I could not support one." He took his meals in the company of his friends at hotels. He seldom attended church services. In his later years he was extremely disciplined in his schedule—so much so that neighbors could set their watches by his outdoor walks. He was a man of intellectual power and ethical seriousness. His broad knowledge of the world came from reading; only once did he travel outside East Prussia. Although he published as early as age 22, his major philo-

---

Elmer A. Martens is a Professor in the Mennonite Brethren Biblical Seminary. He received the BA from the University of Saskatchewan, the B Ed from the University of Manitoba, the BD from the Mennonite Brethren Seminary, and the PhD from the Claremont Graduate School.

161

sophical works began with *Critique of Pure Reason*, written when he was fifty-seven.

The intellectual climate of his time was characterized by the Enlightenment—a movement that appealed to reason rather than to intellectual or religious tradition. The epistemological skepticism of Locke and Hume awoke him, Kant said, from his slumbers. The church, often only a cog in the bureaucracy, focused on ceremony and orthodox belief. To such a situation there were two reactions: Pietism, which emphasized individualism; and deism, which occupied itself with a universal natural religion. Kant, who was raised in the tradition of the first, Pietism, gave his energies to the second, the examination of deism.

A philosopher must ask, said Kant, What can I know? What ought I to do? What can I hope for? Such was the progress of science in his day that men had wondered whether reason was not itself sufficient for the purpose of religion and whether revelation, prophecy, or miracle were not unnecessary accretions. Kant attempted to harmonize the world of Newtonian physics, particularly mechanistic causality, with the world of freedom. Could one be an adherent of both reason and faith? Could one profitably speculate about God, immortality, and freedom? His answers are found in his books, the most important of which are *Critique of Pure Reason*, *Critique of Practical Reason*, and *Critique of Judgment.*

Can one determine the reality of God, the soul, or immortality by theoloretical reason? Kant's radical answer: No! Theoretical knowledge, said Kant, depends on that which is supplied by experience plus the interpretation given by the understanding—an interpretation which is itself governed by laws derived from experience. "Experience" already embodies an "interpretation." Science and reason can deal with sense-experience—the material world; but they cannot establish the reality of the supersensible world. In the course of his argument against speculative metaphysics he dealt ruthlessly with the traditional, time-honored "proofs" for the existence of God, which argued theoretically from sense-experience; the proofs from causality, from design, and from ontology. So forceful are his arguments about the process of knowing that he is sometimes said to have initiated a Copernican revolution in epistemology.

Kant argues, however, for the reality and the existence of God, the soul, and immortality—not on the basis of theoretical reason, nor on the basis of revelation, which he rejected as a source of knowledge, but on the basis of man's moral experience, his feeling or awareness of obligation. Just as he distinguished between two worlds, the material and the supersensible, so he distinguished between two orders of reason, the pure theoretical and the pure practical. Since pure theoretical reason cannot determine metaphysical realities, the supersensible world must be approached from another direction. Practical reason—the joint operation of will, intelligence, and affection—is sensitive to duties, laws, and obligations. Awareness of this obligation is the highest quality in man. From this basic certainty of "ought," Kant inferred the existence of human freedom, for to be moral we must be free. More than that, man's experience of obligation necessitates a God who can ensure the success of right action and virtue. Then, from man's inability to perform the right continually in this life, Kant postulated an infinite life after death to permit continual growth toward moral perfection. God, freedom, and immortality are affirmed with vigor, but for new reasons. Essentially, Kant broke new ground for the establishment of the primary truths of religion. In so doing, he opened a world view in which science, morals, and religion could be harmonized.

To the second question: What ought I to do? Kant answered in what is known as the categorical imperative, "Act only on that maxim whereby thou canst at the same time will that it should become a universal law." Its corollary, sometimes spoken of as a philosopher's formulation of the Golden Rule, is, "So act as to treat humanity, whether in thine own person or in that of any other, in every case as an end withal, never as a means only." He argued that men should do right because it is right, not for the sake of reward or the fear of punishment. He limited reason, so he said, to make room for faith. This faith is grounded in ethics. Indeed, religion is nothing more than the recognition of all duties as divine commands.

For Kant, religion remains morality. Christianity is a preferred religion, for in Christ is disclosed the ideal example. Belief in Christ is striving after the ideal of a perfect man. He regarded the church as a school of moral education with Jesus as a model. Prayer focuses our moral idealism, but it is a crutch. The more man advances morally, the less he needs such crutches. To Kant salvation is character. He has no place in his system of thought for divine forgiveness or redemption. If man obeys the categorical imperative, he is pleasing to God and so is a son of God. The visible church should be a fellowship for mutual stimulus to that obedience.

The bearing of Kant's thought on Christian theology is considerable. He broke loose from the tutelage of the past. He denied revelation as a means of knowledge. He rejected all mystical elements in religion. Those following him have readily thought of man's reason (though newly defined) as autonomous and supreme. Such a position represents an anthropological approach and opens the door to humanism. Moreover, from Kant's time theology is forced, when employing reason, to do so more critically. Any apologetic for the rational belief in God must take into account Kant's critique of the traditional arguments. A few theologians, such as Ritschl in the nineteenth century, have tried to build theology on Kantian premises.

Further, Kant has influenced theologians and philosophers to think of two spheres: the material world in which science and reason operate, and the supersensible world with its moral, spiritual, and historical aspects. Whether this distinction is a presupposition of the Bible requires analysis: modern philosophy has moved in new directions.

Finally, Kant stressed that our life is a conflict between inclination and duty. He placed high valuation on moral duties and the dignity of man. He insisted on man's freedom in moral behavior and the consequent responsibility for his actions. His thought, however, leads in the direction of thinking in which pleasing God is not a matter of faith but of morality. The ethical emphases of later liberal theology are more easily understood in the light of Kant. One church historian notes that German idealism, of which Kant was a fountainhead, brought about the greatest revolution in Christian thought in modern history.

Brief Bibliography

Kant, Immanuel, *Religion Within the Limits of Reason Alone*. Translation and Introduction and Notes by Theodore M. Greene, H. H. Hudson, and John R. Silber. New York: Harper Torchbooks. Pb. edition, 1960, first published 1934. CLV-190. Deals with specifically theological material more than Kant's other writings. Includes a 78-page introduction to the life, writings, and philosophy of Kant plus an assessment of the ethical significance of this work.

Körner, Stephan, *Kant*. Harmondsworth, Penguin Books, 1955. 230 pp. A fine general introduction.

Blakney, Raymond (editor), *An Immanuel Kant Reader*. New York: Harper & Brothers, 1960. Brief selections on various subjects from Kant's major works together with a short editorial comment on each.

The Encyclopedia of Philosophy. Paul Edwards (editor), 8 volumes. New York: Macmillan, 1967. Technical, but helpful and good.

Barth, Karl, *Protestant Thought: From Rousseau to Ritschl*. New York: Harper & Row, 1959. Analyzes influence of Kant's thought on theology, pp. 150-196.

> "Every person has an inalienable right to act in all religious affairs according to the full persuasion of his own mind, where others are not injured thereby."

43
Isaac Backus

T. B. Maston

When viewed through the perspective of time, Isaac Backus (1724-1806) looms as the outstanding Baptist of his day and as one of the most important men in New England from the days of the Great Awakening to the opening of the nineteenth century. His contributions were particularly significant in the battle for freedom of worship and the separation of church and state in the founding days of our nation.

Backus was definitely a child of his age but also of the new age that was being born. He was nurtured in the principles of civil and religious liberty, and he became a fighter for liberty of conscience. He was converted at seventeen years of age, during the Great Awakening, and became an Awakening preacher. He lived in turbulent days, and he was a turbulent soul. His was an age of political and religious dissent; he became a leading dissenter.

He, along with his mother, were among the first to withdraw from the established church (1744) and to become a part of the Separatist movement. Later, feeling called to preach, he became pastor of a Separate church at Taticut, in Massachusetts. After several years of struggle, personal and as a group, he and five others withdrew and formed a Baptist church. He served as pastor of this group from the time of its founding in 1756 until his death in 1806.

Backus was prominent in the work of the Warren Association of Baptist churches from its beginning in 1767, when he was elected

---

T. B. Maston wrote this chapter as a retired Professor of Christian Ethics, Southwestern Baptist Theological Seminary (1922-1963). He received his AB from Carson-Newman College, an MRE and a DRE from Southwestern Baptist Theological Seminary, an MA from Texas Christian University, a PhD from Yale University, and an honorary LittD from Carson-Newman. His dissertation at Yale was on *The Ethical and Social Attitudes of Isaac Backus*, later abridged and published under the title *Isaac Backus: Pioneer of Religious Liberty*. Among his other books are: *Right or Wrong? God's Will and Your Life, The Bible and Race, Christianity and World Issues, Biblical Ethics, The Christian, The Church and Contemporary Problems*, and *Suffering: A Personal Perspective*.

165

clerk of its organizational conference. His greatest and most lasting work for the Association, for Baptists, and for America in general, was his activity on behalf of liberty of worship and of conscience. For ten years (1772-1782, when the office was abolished) he served as Agent of the Association. During those years he became the recognized champion of the religious dissenters of New England. One writer has suggested that no individual since Roger Williams stood out so prominently as a contender for religious liberty.

His influence was felt not only in New England, it reached all sections of the country. For example, in 1774, Backus was asked by the Warren Association to present the grievances of Baptists to the Continental Congress, meeting in Philadelphia. The memorial or appeal was not presented to the entire Congress but to the delegates from Massachusetts. Some years later (1789) at the request of the Warren Association, Backus made a rather extended trip to North Carolina and Virginia, presenting his convictions.

Backus' concern for religious liberty was not only a major factor in his activities but also in his writings. And it is possible that his writings, more than anything else, have continued to make Backus a man of major importance. In spite of his limited education, he was one of the most prolific writers of his period. No one thing has won him more lasting recognition than his *A History of New England, with Particular Reference to the Denomination of Christians Called Baptists*, which was originally published in three volumes (1777, 1784, 1796) but published later (1804) in a one-volume abridgment. He wrote the history with a conviction that it could be an important factor in settling the controversy with the "standing churches," which in turn would mean liberty of conscience not only for Baptists but for others as well.

As voluminous as his history, and doubtlessly more influential in his day, were numerous tracts or pamphlets. There were thirty-seven of these, ranging in length from seven to one hundred and fifty pages. Nine of them were written specifically in the interest of liberty of conscience, with seven of the nine written in a ten-year period (1770-1780), which was particularly significant from the perspective of the Colonies and the founding of our nation. In addition to the pamphlets, he wrote many newspaper articles, prepared or helped to prepare numerous memorials or petitions, maintained a diary, and carried on a far-ranging correspondence, much of it related directly to the struggle for liberty of worship and for the separation of church and state.

Although Backus had an aversion for active participation in political life, he as well as other ministers, because of their concern for freedom of worship and for the separation of church and state, became actively involved in political affairs. They hoped through their involvement to help achieve their goal of full religious liberty, which they believed could not be attained without the separation of church and state. When Middleborough met to choose four delegates to the State Convention, which was to consider the new federal Constitution, the first one chosen was Backus. When notified, he first thought he would refuse, but he later said, "As religious liberty is concerned in the affair, and many were earnest for my going, I consented." While most of the

Baptists of Massachusetts were opposed to the new Constitution, Backus, without any great enthusiasm, voted for ratification.

The achievements of Backus are the more remarkable not only when we consider his limited education but also the fact that he was pastor for fifty years of a comparatively small church, largely isolated from the main currents of life and thought. In spite of these limitations, he was a leader in the founding of Rhode Island College (Brown University), was a trustee from its founding in 1765 until he resigned because of age in 1799. He counted among his closest friends James Manning, the first president of Rhode Island College and a graduate of Princeton University; Hezekiah Smith, a classmate of Manning at Princeton; and Morgan Edwards, born and educated in Great Britain and a leader in the founding of Rhode Island College. He died at 82 in 1806.

Measured by his permanent contribution, particularly to religious liberty and the separation of church and state, Isaac Backus stands, after almost two centuries, as one of the most important Americans of his day.

Bibliographical Note

Note the entries under the author-introduction at the beginning of this essay. *Ed.*

> "Religion is 'immediate self-consciousness' or 'the feeling of absolute dependence' on God."

44
Schleiermacher

Marlin E. Miller

I. The life of Daniel Friedrich Ernst Schleiermacher (1768-1834) spanned one of the most rapidly moving periods in Prussian intellectual, cultural, religious, and, in part, political history. In the midst of these various currents, he developed his theological-philosophical system, seeking a conscious and total unity between thought and action.

After several years in a *Herrnhuter* boarding school and seminary, Schleiermacher left the seminary in 1787 to enroll as a theology student at the University of Halle. There he began serious study of Kant and Plato, who were to represent the major philosophical influences upon this thought. During his years as a Reformed chaplain in the Charité, a public hospital in Berlin (1796-1802), he was intimately associated with the circle of Romantic poets and writers led especially by Friedrich Schlegel. During this time he published the *On Religion: Speeches to its Cultured Despisers*, as well as the *Soloquies*, a half-poetic harbinger of his later ethics. From 1804 until Napoleon invaded Prussia and closed the university three years later, Schleiermacher was professor of theology in Halle. During this time he wrote the *Christmas Eve Celebration*, a dialogue prefiguring elements of his later Christology.

From 1808 until the end of his life, Schleiermacher lived in Berlin as theology professor at the Humboldt University, active member of the Berlin Academy of Sciences and regular preacher at the Dreifaltigkeit Church. Besides these positions, he engaged in the efforts of a group of Prussian patriots to instigate resistance against French sovereignty, participated in drills of the local militia with other university

---

Marlin E. Miller for a number of years served students from the so-called developing countries who come to Paris to continue their education. He assisted them with housing and food arrangements, and also sought to witness to them of Christ. He was under the direction of Mennonite Board of Missions. He received the BA from Goshen College, continued with his studies at Goshen Biblical Seminary, and received the ThD from the University of Heidelberg. His dissertation dealt with Schleiermacher. Since 1975 he has been president of Goshen Biblical Seminary, and has been teaching courses in theology in the Associated Mennonite Biblical Seminaries.

professors, and served several years in the governmental Department of Education. Nevertheless he continued to champion what he considered the strict separation between church and state, actively defending, at times even against the king, the right of the churches to determine their own polity, liturgical forms, and practices, as well as doctrinal teaching. He also worked energetically for the union of the Lutheran and Reformed churches and became the moderator of the first unified Berlin Synod.

As a professor in Berlin, Schleiermacher lectured on such widely varied subjects as *Dialectic, Teaching on the State, Psychology,* and *Aesthetics* as well as continuing the philosophical and theological lectures already begun at Halle. His lecture on *The Life of Jesus* was the first given at a German university. But his most frequent lectures throughout his career remained *An Outline on Theology, Christian Ethics,* and *The Christian Faith.* The latter, his major theological work, was first published in 1821-22 and again in 1830 with extensive formal, although not substantial revisions. The literary fruits of his prolific activity have been gathered into thirty volumes of collected works, about equally divided between sermons, theological lectures and writings, and philosophical materials. Most of his exegetical lectures as well as some other materials have never been published. The uniqueness of his synthesis, the scope of his interest, and the sophistication of his teaching have made Schleiermacher one of the most controversial figures in modern theological history: he has been lauded as "the reformer of protestant theology," and decried as the root of all that is heretical in modern Protestant thought.

II. Schleiermacher's mature theological and philosophical system maintained the position, taken already in the "Speeches on Religion," which distinguishes religion from speculative knowledge (metaphysics) on the one hand and human action (ethics) on the other. Religion is described in *The Christian Faith* as "immediate self-consciousness" or the "feeling of absolute dependence." This "feeling" *(Gefühl)* was not meant in a post-Freudian psychological or subjectivistic sense. Rather, it is to be understood as the underlying unity or existence of man as man, and the focal point for an ontology of history, whereby history is seen as the variety of dialectical interactions between human consciousness and the rest of reality. Even though this feeling of absolute dependence on that which is the origin and source of all being (God) cannot be conceptualized, religion became the center of Schleiermacher's total system and its description absorbed the traditional theological and speculative assumptions of Western thought.

Within the ontology of history, the prime theologically relevant questions became the source and goal of human history. In Schleiermacher's philosophical ethics this goal was characterized as the highest good, which would include the totality of human activity. Human activity in turn was understood in analogy to the productive and sustaining activity of God in bringing forth the world. This totality of human activity and the results of human action are described differently, depending on the type of historical movement taken as the perspective. From the standpoint of religion, it appears as the kingdom of heaven. But within the philosophical ethics, this totality can only be postulated and neither further characterized nor realized. Similarly, the need for a source and ground of history became apparent in the philosophical appropriation of reality, but could not be derived or described there. Thus philosophy is unable to describe Christ as the Founder, and God as the ground of the kingdom of God. In this manner, philosophy complements theology by remaining within its own boundaries, and theology simultaneously provides the supporting pillars of philosophy without infringing on its task.

Schleiermacher's theology then becomes a theology of the kingdom of God. In his lectures on the life of Jesus, he found the continuing relevance of Jesus in his action toward the founding of, and in his teaching on, the kingdom of God. In *The Christian Faith*, the task of theology in relation to its content is nothing other than the explication of Jesus' proclamation which is also the source for all Christian doctrine (##19 and 103). The latter part of *The Christian Faith* is in fact parallel in content and outline to Schleiermacher's reconstruction of Jesus' teaching on the kingdom. And it is this latter part of his dogmatics from which Schleiermacher theologically derives the propositions in the rest of his systematic theology. Although the term "kingdom of God" is frequently employed, it is often replaced by the concept "the new total unity of life" *(neues Gesamtleben)* which Schleiermacher considered synonymous to the kingdom of God, but more appropriate to the contemporary theological and linguistic situation. This new, all-embracing life unity was understood in the context of Schleiermacher's view of religion as the perfect and pervading consciousness of God, inaugurated by Jesus as the Redeemer and ultimately encompassing humanity, one with itself and one with God. From this centrality of the kingdom spring Schleiermacher's Christological concentration and his ecclesiological emphasis.

Schleiermacher's Christology in the broader sense includes not only the doctrines of the person and activity of Christ, but also those of the rebirth and sanctification of the believer. This unity between the traditional elements of Protestant Christology and the appropriation of Christ's redeeming activity is based upon the unity between Christ and the believers given in the new totality of life. The reality of this new life was originally in Christ, but resides now in the fellowship of believers. Ecclesiologically, this means that the "inner circle" of the Christian church becomes the locus of the kingdom of God in the world. This inner circle is, however, not identical with the visible church nor with a smaller group of the "faithful." Rather, it is the inner, spontaneous spirit of the church, so far as it is perfectly determined by the consciousness of God. Insofar as history is constituted by both spontaneous activity and the reception of that activity, the kingdom of God would not even be identical with the church if all men were Christians, but would remain the inner circle.

Schleiermacher's use of a consciousness dominated by God as the critical measure of dogmatic statements simply robbed many orthodox doctrines of their theological significance. For example, the doctrine of the Trinity was for all practical purposes assigned the status of an appendix, the resurrection of Christ was judged doctrinally irrelevant, and the statements traditionally gathered under the rubric of "the last things" were declared self-contradictory or of little merit for further describing the higher consciousness of God. Such consequences are, however, only symptomatic of the deeper questions underlying Schleiermacher's thought.

In a profound sense, he was a *volkskirchliche* theologian. Neither his experience among the *Herrnhuters*, nor as a theologian and preacher of the Reformed Church gave him a vision of the church which could carry out its mission without the state as its substratum, and without sublimating the Western intellectual tradition to the bridge between Jesus and contemporary Christendom. Thus, the separation of church and state for which he struggled, and which he taught, was informed perhaps more by the specter of secularization fed by the French Revolution, by a new philosophical orientation, and by an effort to account for all of human activity and reality in a harmonious whole, rather than beginning with a different kind of church. And his apparent rejection of the Western metaphysical theology amounted ultimately to its transposition into an ontology of history which was supported by a higher consciousness of God. Within the limits of his understanding of the theological task and of Protestant Christianity, Schleiermacher's theology stands as a monumental effort seldom surpassed and perhaps, within those limits, the best theological answer of his time. But Schleiermacher assumed those limits and did not make them an object of theological reflection. Perhaps that was his greatest weakness.

Brief Bibliography

For an exhaustive bibliography of Schleiermacher's writings and secondary literature until December 1964: Terrence N. Tice, *Schleiermacher Bibliography, with brief Introductions, Annotations and Index*, Princeton Pamphlets No. 12, Princeton Theological Seminary, 1966.

The major biography remains: Wilhelm Dilthey, *Leben Schleiermachers*, I. Band, Berlin, 1870; Zweite Auflage hg. v. Hermann Mulert, Berlin und Leipzig 1922; new edition by Martin Redeker in process. II. Band, *Schleiermachers System als Philosophie und Theologie*, hg. v. Martin Redeker, Berlin und Göttingen, 1966. An abbreviated biography: Wilhelm Dilthey, *Gesammelte Schriften*, IV. Band, SS. 354-402.

Selected newer literature:

Karl Barth, "Schleiermacher" in *From Rousseau to Ritschl*, London, SCM, 1959—"Schleiermacher" in *Die protestantische Theologie im 19. Jahrhundert*, 1947.

Marlin E. Miller, *Der Uebergang, Schleiermachers Theologie des Reiches Gottes*, Gütersloher Verlagshaus Gerd Mohn, 1970.

Richard R. Niebuhr, *Schleiermacher on Christ and Religion, A New Introduction*, Charles Schribner's Sons, New York, 1964.

Gerhard Spiegler, *The Eternal Covenant, Schleiermacher's Experiment in Cultural Theology*, Harper and Row, New York, 1967.

> "It is ... heresy to entertain doubt in a sermon...."

45

Søren Kierkegaard

Arthur M. Climenhaga

Søren Aabye Kierkegaard was born May 5, 1813, in Copenhagen, Denmark. Son of a retired wealthy wool merchant, Michael Pedersen Kierkegaard (d. 1838), and his second wife, a servant in the home when the first wife died, Søren was the seventh child of elderly parents. With the exception of short periods in Germany, he spent his whole life in Copenhagen, Denmark, and died November 11, 1855, at the age of 42.

Søren Kierkegaard's home did not offer many diversions and thus he early became accustomed to occupying himself alone with his own thoughts. His father seldom allowed him to go out, but instead in walks back and forth in the room would take him on imaginary tours of the country and abroad. Later the father permitted Søren to listen and then to engage in philosophical debate and discussion. All of this set a pattern of melancholia from which he never recovered. Whether this was hereditary or acquired is debatable, but it did set a pattern of life which caused some to characterize him as "mad."

Financially, Søren Kierkegaard inherited a substantial fortune which gave him time to think and to write, although during his later years his resources became a grave concern. On October 2, 1855, he fell unconscious on the street while returning home from the bank from which he had withdrawn what remained of his fortune. There was just enough to care for funeral expenses when he died.

Kierkegaard matriculated at the age of 17 in the University of Copenhagen, passing his examination *cum laude*. Approximately six months later, April 25, 1831, he passed his "Second Examination" and for the next seven years studied in history, literature, and philosophy, and a little theology. This period represents the enthronement of the

---

Arthur M. Climenhaga has served as Executive Secretary of the National Association of Evangelicals and as President of Messiah College. He is a bishop in the Brethren in Christ Church, and has served as Adjunct Professor in Missions and Comparative Theology in Ashland Theological Seminary. He received the BSL from Upland College, the AB from Pasadena College, the MA from Taylor University, the STD from the Los Angeles Baptist Theological Seminary, and the LL D from Houghton College. He is coauthor of the book *Draw Nigh unto God*, Rhodesia Christian Press, and author of various chapters in composite volumes. Dr. Climenhaga was Dean of Western Evangelical Seminary, Portland, Ore., for a number of years.

aesthetic in his thinking and writing. But it should be noted that he never slipped into treating religion as a "value," which would avoid any possible conflict between religion and philosophy. For Kierkegaard Christianity was either true or untrue, either absolute truth or not truth at all. At first he regarded religion as an unequal competitor of philosophy. But increasingly he became less confident of discovering absolute truth through philosophy, since he was dissatisfied with the Hegelian system—the philosophy then in vogue.

From a composite of several experiences came the prolific number of works embodying Kierkegaard's poetic flare and religious determination. The first was the melancholic disposition derived from his father. The second was an early escapade involving a drunken "affair" which so shocked his ethical sensibilities that Kierkegaard was never quite able to escape the inherent moral effects of it in his own emotional life. Thus in a sense the third flowed out of these two.

In 1837 he fell in love with a fourteen-year-old girl, Regine Olson, and was engaged to her on September 10, 1840. But the next day he was convinced he had made a mistake. He saw in her the fulfillment of life, yet feared that marriage to her was not in the divine will. She did not readily give him up but after a series of rebuffs and struggles between both of them, the engagement was formally broken in 1841. Very soon Regine was married to another, yet in reading Kierkegaard's works written under pseudonyms it is evident he never ceased loving her, and likely she him.

A fourth influence was Kierkegaard's testimony of experiencing a real conversion in 1838. As a result he returned to the study of theology and passed his examination with honors in 1840. Almost inexplicably he never allowed himself to be ordained in the Lutheran ministry even though at times he dallied with the thought of ordination and of taking a country charge. This was due largely to his increasing sense of dissatisfaction with, and finally revolt against, the established church of his day in Denmark—the state church, Lutheran in character. He did not openly attack the church until the death of the primate, Bishop J. P. Mynster, an old and respected friend of Kierkegaard's father. But following that he attacked the institution of the church in such a way as lead some erroneously to believe that he was attacking Christianity as well. Today we can see that his attack was against Christianity as decadent institutionalism, not as a religion of experience.

From this mood Kierkegaard has become known as the father of existentialism. But it must never be forgotten that he ever held a high view of the inspiration of Scripture, and he had also a warm personal understanding of conversion and living faith experience. Two quotations from his *Journals* give evidence of this: (1) "The category of my work is: to *make men aware* of Christianity, and consequently I always say: I am not an example, for otherwise all would be confusion." (2) "The moment I take Christianity as a doctrine and so indulge my cleverness or profundity or my eloquence or my imaginative powers in depicting it: people are very pleased; I am looked upon as a serious Christian. The moment I begin to express existentially what I say, and consequently to bring Christianity into reality: it is just as though I had exploded existence—the *scandal* is there at once."

In this Kierkegaard was sharply diverse from a modern theological existentialism and from a secular philosophical existentialism. Thus some scholars are inclined to feel that had he lived in a modern setting, with his insights and experience, he would most likely have been found in the "evangelical" framework of belief and life.

A fifth experience affecting Kierkegaard is known as the "Corsair" affair. As a result of an interchange between him and the editors of a weekly paper characterized by some as scandal-mongering and titled "The Corsair," he was personally ridiculed by the paper's editors and for a time became a public joke. This too influenced him to renounce a country pastorate so as to take up his pen with increasing vigor. Kierkegaard never ran away from the spirit of conflict.

The writings therefore that flowed from Kierkegaard's pen in the view of the writer of this essay comprised four distinct types: (1) The aesthetic-ethical works written under pseudonyms: (e.g., *Either-Or, Fear and Trembling,* et al.); (2) Devotional-Theological (e.g., *Purity of Heart—Is to Will One Thing,* et al.); (3) Personal (e.g., The *Journals* of Kierkegaard, et al.); (4) Polemical-Theological/Philosophical (e.g., *Attack Upon Christendom*).

From this brief review, what then can be said of Søren Kierkegaard, the man, religionist, theological thinker, and his influence? The circumstances of his early childhood and family left an unshakable imprint on his life. The severe upbringing, the religious experience, the broken engagement, the "Corsair" affair, were all currents in the composite of his life. These were the issues of life which produced the lonely man and the dedicated Christian. They made him stand apart from his age and criticize it. As a result he had some extreme views of the church, of suffering, of the individual, and of guilt. Yet in a timely way he brought thinking man into a sharp personal confrontation with these issues.

Professor Alden M. Long of Messiah College in an unpublished S.T.M. thesis succinctly evaluates it:

"In a time when modern theology seeks to reduce the difference between man and God, the life and authorship of Kierkegaard provide a corrective in calling men to supernatural, biblical, and dynamic faith which is like a cool breeze on a sultry afternoon. Discovering Kierkegaard is a great aid in discovering what it really means to be a Christian.

"Nevertheless, he must be read with discretion. He looked upon his own theology and emphases as a corrective to things as they existed in his own day.... Some think that Kierkegaard emphasized the transcendence of God at the expense of His immanence. This is partly true. His interpretation of Christianity as essentially a form of suffering, the emphasis upon the individual at the expense of Christian fellowship, and a kind of Christian asceticism are other exaggerated emphases....

"A further warning must be stated. Kierkegaard has been criticized for emphasizing subjective truth to the detriment of objective truth. It must be remembered that he also had a religious and intellectual development. And if one views an early concept as being representative of the whole, then distortion results. Therefore, if his emphasis upon subjectivity in *Postscript* is to be rightly understood, it must be tempered by his emphasis upon objective revelation which appears in his reply to Adler, which is one of the latest of his works. By this process then, one sees that 'subjectivity' in Kierkegaard is far different from subjectivity in Schleiermacher.

"Kierkegaard put forth his powers unreservedly in teaching the world that God, the Eternal and Unsearchable One, is not man. In graphic ways he presents the claims of this God upon the life of each man and calls men to decision. Who can say he has not succeeded?" (*The Christian Existentialism of Søren Kierkegaard and Its Influence Upon Rudolf Bultmann*, unpublished S.T.M. thesis, the Biblical Seminary in New York, 1958).

Two more quotations so aptly sumbolize the thinking of Kierkegaard:

"A Christian address deals to a certain extent with doubt—A Sermon operates absolutely and entirely through authority, that of Holy Writ and of Christ's apostles. It is therefore neither more nor less heresy to entertain doubt in a sermon, however well one might be able to handle it."

"The result of human progress is that everything becomes thinner and thinner—the result of divine providence is to make everything more inward."

Brief Bibliography

Arbaugh, George E. and George B., *Kierkegaard's Authorship*, Augustana, 1967.

Gates, John A., *The Life and Thought of Kierkegaard for Everyman*, Westminster, 1960.

Lowrie, Walter, *A Short Life of Kierkegaard*, Princeton University Press, 1942.

Numerous translations of Kierkegaard's works have been printed by Harper & Brothers, Oxford University Press, and Princeton University Press: *Attack Upon "Christendom", Christian Discourses, Concluding Unscientific Postscript, For Self-Examination and Judge for Yourselves, On Authority and Revelation, Purity of Heart, The Concept of Dread, The Journals of Kierkegaard, The Point of View, The Sickness unto Death*, and *Training in Christianity*.

"After filling him with the Spirit, God used Finney to bring conversion and renewal to a vast number of people."

46

Charles G. Finney

J. J. Toews

The flaming evangelist of the nineteenth century, Charles Grandison Finney, was born on the American frontier in Warren, Connecticut, to his pioneer and nonreligious parents, Mr. and Mrs. Sylvester Finney, August 29, 1792. His father had been a soldier of the Revolution at fifteen. While his mother's name is not mentioned, it is reported that one of his ancestors, seven generations back, came over on the *Mayflower*.

At the age of two the family moved into the midst of the Oneida Indians at Hanover, New York. There Charles attended the frontier school, spending two years in the Indian Institute. In 1808 the oxcart creaked westward again, this time to Henderson, Henderson Bay, at the eastern end of Lake Ontario. Conditions here were so primitive that the seventeen-year-old Charles seemed to be the best qualified to teach in the common school. After four years, he made his way to Warren Academy for two years of further study and then accepted the invitation to teach in New Jersey, while still continuing his studies privately. He declined the invitation of his teacher to go south with him, but returned to his parents in Henderson to be with his sick mother.

All the while, however, he had a growing interest to become a lawyer. So when he was twenty-six years of age, he entered the law office of Judge Benjamin Wright, at Adams in Jefferson County, New York. Here he read the legal works of Wm. Blackstone, who repeatedly quoted from the Pentateuch and other Scriptures as a basis for legal premises. This aroused an interest in the young lawyer to purchase

---

J. J. Toews has served as the Executive Secretary of the Office of Evangelism of the Canadian Conference of the Mennonite Brethren Churches of North America. He received the B Th from Western Baptist Theological Seminary, the BA from Willamette University, the MA from the University of Toronto, the BD from Waterloo Lutheran Seminary, and the M Th from Winona Lake School of Theology. He studied at a number of other institutions including Southwestern Baptist Theological Seminary. He received the doctorate in Missions from Dallas Theological Seminary. He is presently pastor of the Neuwied Mennonite Brethren Church in Germany, is teaching here and there for the M. B. Board of Missions, and is also working among the *Umsiedler* (those coming from Russia to settle in Germany). He was born in 1914.

and read his first Bible. Besides, his earlier musical training opened an opportunity to become the choirmaster in the local Presbyterian Church, where Rev. George W. Gale was pastor. Finney found these church services uninteresting and the reading of the sermons by Gale monotonous. He was particularly disturbed that so many projected principles lacked proof to satisfy an alert mind, but he noted the vitality of the sacred page of Scripture, and became convinced that "the Bible was the true Word of God."

Continual reading of the Scriptures gripped Finney's heart with conviction and he felt compelled to make a decision whether to accept Christ or pursue a worldly life. On October 10, 1821, his feet took him into the woods outside of Adams, instead of to his law office. Here he tarried in overwhelming conviction until the words of Jeremiah 29:13 flashed through his mind. "Ye shall seek me and find me, when ye shall search for me with all your heart." To this Finney responded with the cry, "Lord, I take Thee at Thy Word." All sense of sin and consciousness of guilt left him; he leaped for joy and hurried back to the village at noon. In the evening, as he meditated further on what had happened, the Holy Spirit descended on him as a surge of electricity, "like waves of liquid love." Immediately he felt compelled to give himself to the preaching of the gospel and his legal ambitions left him.

Judge Wright and others in Adams broke down under the impact of Finney's spiritual dynamics and also believed. During the next three years, he took theological studies under pastor George W. Gale. These studies resulted in many disagreements of Finney with the strong Calvinistic views of Gale, who held that man is entirely passive in repentance, conversion, and regeneration. Finney again contended that God's command for man to repent and believe implied man's ability to do so, otherwise God would not expect it of him. With considerable qualms the Presbytery agreed to license him to preach on December 30, 1823, and ordained him on July 11, 1824. After being commissioned by a women's society in Oneida County, his blazing revival trail began with his preaching in Evans Mills and Antwerp and throughout the surrounding areas of rural New York.

These Great Revivals burned on and mass evangelism continued for nine years (1824-1832). Wherever Finney went, people in great numbers were gripped by conviction and cried to God for forgiveness and salvation. But these labors ended in his "complete fatigue." His new theological emphasis, as well as methods, and possibly even his success, brought him severe opposition from other men of God. Among these opponents were Asahel Nettleton and Dr. Lyman Beecher of Boston.

In 1832, Finney accepted the call to the Second Free Presbyterian Church in New York City which had just bought and remodeled an old theater on Chatham Street. A group of men under his influence decided to build a tabernacle on Broadway, and invited Finney to be the pastor of what they planned to be a Congregational church. Finney, craving the elbow room of Congregational democracy, agreed. However, while he was cruising the Mediterranean for health reasons, the uncompleted tabernacle burned. And Finney returned to preach in the Chatham Street Theater until the tabernacle could be rebuilt.

Here, in one of Finney's most discouraging moments, his Revival Lectures were born. The immediate purpose for these lectures was to rejuvenate the life of the dying periodical, *The Evangelist.* But it accomplished more. Not only did these Revival Lectures draw capacity crowds to the theater each Friday night during the fall and winter of 1834-35, and bring in a flood of subscriptions for *The Evangelist,* but the lectures were published in book form and offered to a world audience. Thus these lectures became one of the most lasting contributions which Finney has made to the evangelical world.

For the next three years (1835-1839), Finney spent his summers in Oberlin, Ohio, "to build up a Department of Theology in the new frontier Collegiate Institute" and returned to the Broadway Tabernacle for the winter.

In 1837, he discontinued his pastorate in New York and assumed the pastorate of the First Congregational Church in Oberlin, where he labored until 1872 in a growing church and in world evangelism.

From 1851 to 1866, Finney served as President of Oberlin College, where thousands flocked to matriculate and be influenced by his theology. While at Oberlin, he made several visits to Boston and also to England and Scotland, lighting fires of revival wherever he went to present his logical and divinely empowered messages.

His last three years, after retiring from the pastorate, he spent in meaningful contacts with students, and continued his theological lectures until July 1875. His preaching ministry in the churches continued to be greatly desired until his death on August 16, 1875, when, after a few hours of pain, which had seized his heart, he left this world to go to his reward, just short of 83 years of age.

Finney cannot easily be categorized with any known theological system of his day. His successor at Oberlin, President Fairchild says, "Mr. Finney was taken from the world and not from the church. He was brought up with very slight associations with religious institutions or churchly influences. With a nature strongly impressible to religious truth ... he had still stood apart from the church in the attitude of a critic upon her doctrines and her life.... His natural independence of character led doubtless in the same direction. The training he had received in his pursuit of the law cooperated to the same result."

"He came to the study of the Bible and the doctrines of the gospel with the same freedom of judgment and of rational instinct, with which he had apprehended and embraced the principles of law, and looked for a similar self-evident truthfulness. Thus he turned away at once from the Old School dogmas of sin in the nature, of obligation beyond ability, of the literal transfer of the sinner's guilt and punishment to Christ, and of regeneration by a change of nature."[1]

Finney took strong issue with his teacher of theology, Rev. George W. Gale, a student of Princeton. Gale held to the theory of limited atonement, which Finney rejected, maintaining that the Bible clearly taught atonement for all men. When Gale admitted that the Bible required all who hear the Gospel to repent, believe, and be saved, Finney asked, "But how could they believe and accept a salvation which was not provided for them?"[2]

Gale insisted that Jesus literally paid the debt of the elect and fully satisfied exact justice. Finney recognized a great danger here, in that the universalist needed only to prove from Scripture that the atonement was made for all men (which would not be hard to do) to contend that all men would be saved. Finney contended that "Christ had only satisfied public justice by honoring the law, both in his obedience and death, thus rendering it safe for God to pardon sin.... Christ, in his atonement, merely did that which was necessary as a condition of the forgiveness of sin; and not that which cancelled sin, in the sense of literally paying the indebtedness of sinners."[3]

Gale again believed that the subject was entirely passive in repentance, faith, and conversion, because divine sovereignty did it all. Finney replied that the Bible appeals to the will of man to respond to salvation and thus makes it more dependent on human volition than divine sovereignty. He contended that for man to have a will meant that God had granted him self-determination and that obligation laid upon man cannot exceed the ability of man to respond. Thus Finney came to look upon regeneration and conversion as synonymous terms, descriptive of a coetaneous act, both of the Holy Ghost and of the human will.

Finney believed that by regeneration, men are brought into a state of continued holiness, increasing in volume, or into states of alternating from entire holiness to entire sinfulness, with the former state finally predominating and thus resulting in the preserving of everlasting life. In this latter view, he was in accord with Calvinism, even though he rejected unconditional election, limited atonement, total moral inability, and the irresistible efficaciousness of God's grace for the salvation of the elect. In all but the perseverance of the saints Finney rejected the Westminster Confession.

But the above areas of disagreement with Calvinism do not give us the liberty to place Finney into the Arminian Camp. Finney could not be associated with its doctrine of sanctification. In fact he says, "I had known somewhat of the view of sanctification entertained by our Methodist brethren; but as their idea of sanctification seemed to me to relate almost altogether to states of the sensibility, I could not receive their teaching."[4] For Finney, sanctification is something very practical. He says it may be entire in two senses: "(1) In the sense of the present and full obedience, or entire consecration to God; and (2) In the sense of continued, abiding consecration or obedience to God."[5] Thus, in sanctification, the whole concern is for the rectification of the will. This is unacceptable to the theology of the Holiness brethren. They lament, "Finney failed to connect the obtaining of sanctification with the baptism with the Holy Ghost."[6] It may not be easy to see how Finney can be entirely consistent when he first makes sanctification depend entirely upon the will, and on the other hand, says that it is not obtained by any works of law or works of any kind, nor even by any effort of man, but purely by faith alone.[7]

But in one thing Finney does agree with the Holiness Brethren, namely in his insistence on the baptism with the Holy Ghost for service. Speaking of his theology teacher, Mr. Gale, he writes, "If he had ever been converted to Christ, he had failed to receive that divine anointing of the Holy Ghost that would make him a power in the pulpit and in society, for the conversion of souls. He had fallen short of receiving the baptism of the Holy Ghost, which is indispensable to ministerial success."[8]

Even though Finney may not fit into either category, Calvinism nor Arminianism, Professor Wright says, "President Finney has, we believe, succeeded better than any other author with whose writings we are acquainted, in elaborating a system of theology which combines and harmonizes the truth of these contending parties."[9] To understand Finney's theology one must break through the inflexible limitations of any system and be open for new light from the insights of a man who was a persistent biblicist.

The uniqueness of Finney's theology is in his concept of moral law and moral obligation. In the preface to his *Systematic Theology*, he says that he had published it in one volume instead of three, because he owed it to the church and the world to speak only to the points in which he differed from other generally accepted systems of theology.[10] Moral law and moral obligation constitute the main subject in his 619-page publication. He shows that moral law is rooted not in the decrees of God, but in the very nature of God. The moral law differs from the physical law in that the latter requires involuntary compliance, while the first calls for a response of the will. This is the reason why God addresses Himself, in Scripture, to the will of man. To Finney it is unthinkable that God should make demands to His creatures without first endowing him with the ability to respond. With God, obligations never exceed ability. For Finney no revival nor evangelism can occur without a clear presentation of these basic concepts.

Footnotes

1. Hills, A. M., *Life of Charles G. Finney*, Office of "God's Revivalist," Cincinnati, Ohio, 1902.
2. *Ibid.*
3. *Ibid.*
4. Hills, *op. cit.*, p. 222.
5. Finney, C. G., *Lectures on Systematic Theology*, Colporter Kemp, South Gate, Calif., 1944, p. 405.
6. Hills, *op. cit.*, p. 226.
7. Finney, *op. cit.*, pp. 433-440.
8. Hills, *op. cit.*, p. 55.
9. *Ibid.*, p. 211.
10. Finney, *op. cit.*, p. XI of preface.

"The child is to grow up a Christian, and never know himself as being otherwise."

47
Horace Bushnell

George G. Konrad

Horace Bushnell (1802-1876), sometimes known as the "Father of American Religious Liberalism," was born April 14, 1802, in the village of Bantam, Connecticut, the eldest child of Ensign and Dotha Bushnell. In 1821 he "owned the covenant," entered Yale College two years later, and graduated in 1827. His plans had been to enter the ministry but his faith had deteriorated. Under the influence of Coleridge's "Aids to Reflection," he became convinced that the appeal and demonstration of religion is only to the heart and not to the intellect. Burdened with intellectual doubts, he entered short terms of teaching and journalism.

In 1829 he returned to Yale to study law. During the revival of 1831 he was the moral leader of a group of disenchanted students, but then also "took the principle of right." His doubts were dissolved and the joy and confidence of the kingdom of God became his possession. As a result he enrolled in Yale Divinity School completing his work in 1833. Upon graduation he assumed his only pastorate, the North Congregational Church in Hartford. Here he married Mary Apthorp. Ill health forced his resignation in 1859, but he remained in Hartford until the day of his death, February 17, 1876.

In Hartford he soon became known for his civic interests and as a great preacher. Wesleyan College conferred the Doctor of Divinity degree on him in 1842.

Bushnell's best-known work, *Christian Nurture*, first presented in 1846 and 1847 was rewritten and enlarged in 1861. Many other books came from his pen enlarging upon theological concepts that were often threatening to his contemporaries. From 1849 to 1854 heretic proceedings were initiated against him by the Fairfield West Association of Connecticut. He "barely escaped." His other books include: *God in Christ* (1849), *Sermons for the New Life* (1858), *Nature*

George G. Konrad is Dean and Professor of Christian Education in the Mennonite Brethren Biblical Seminary. He received the BRE from the Mennonite Brethren Bible College, the BA from the University of British Columbia, the MRE from Southwestern Baptist Theological Seminary, and the Doctor of Education, also from Southwestern.

and the Supernatural (1858), Christ and Salvation (1864), The Vicarious Sacrifice (1866), The Moral Uses of Dark Things (1868), and Forgiveness and Law (1874).

No denomination or theological system has been named after Horace Bushnell, yet the confluence of historical forces was such that his ideas and insights found wide acceptance. Several New England controversies set the stage for his distinctive role. These were being waged between the liberal and conservative factions of the Congregationalists, Calvinists, and Unitarians. The major issues were the Trinity, Christology, native depravity, and the atonement—the same that appeared in the writings of Bushnell. New Haven theology had become "orthodoxy"; God's sovereignty, the dogma of original sin, and total depravity had become normative belief. Bushnell represented a reaction against revivalism, creedalism, and sacramentalism.

Basic to Bushnell's theology was his theological method. Influenced by romantic idealism and Jonathan Edward's concept of the "sense of the heart," he concluded that religious knowledge is obtained intuitively by direct communication with God. As Christian experience this knowledge was unassailable and not dependent on language and discursive reflection.

Bushnell's theory of language dealt a severe blow to creedalism and propositional theology. Language, he said, has two levels—the first of sense or fact and the second of thought of truth. All language is based on the first level—on sensory phenomena. Meaning gained from the sense level is then metaphorically transferred to the thought level. Thought level language is always figurative and thus can never represent objective truth. Applied to theology this means that there can be no objective or scientific theology.

Since language cannot convey truth objectively, it follows that it only shows one side, and that in a figure. On this basis he developed the idea of Christian comprehensiveness. We must combine the insights of all parties and perspectives into one comprehensive truth.

Horace Bushnell protested the Unitarian doctrine of the essential goodness of man. He took seriously man's fallen nature in which he lost the principle of good. He believed deeply in a theocentric concept of progress, although man was not totally depraved, so that in his freedom he could still respond to the call of God in the gospel. Bushnell challenged the extreme individualism and arbitrary supernaturalism of New Haven theology. In *Christian Nurture* he reemphasized the covenantal doctrine that children of Christian parents were "federally holy." The church-like quality and redemptive role of the family as an organic unity was thus brought into focus.

The theology of Bushnell was Christocentric. To him Christ was "the Grand Chief Miracle of the world ... a Saviour come to bring salvation." However, he felt compelled to counteract the tendency of the traditional Trinitarians to deny that Jesus' divine nature had any direct part in His life and death, and so he rejected the standard two-nature formulation of the incarnation. He insisted on the complete unity of the person of Christ and questioned that Christ had a "human" soul. Certainly the human nature of Jesus did not have a distinct subsistence so as "to live, think, learn, worship, suffer, by itself."

His emphasis on the divine nature of Christ earned him the accusation of docetism.

Bushnell clearly taught that restoration of fallen man came from God through the atonement. From the subjective perspective the end of Christ's work was to renovate man's character and restore him to fellowship with God. He strongly emphasized God's love and forgiveness. For many years he had no room for the traditional notion that Christ's death was necessary to propitiate the Father, and thus render Him favorably disposed toward the believing sinner. However, in *Forgiveness and Law* (1874) he finally conceded that propitiation was necessary to release the forgiving nature of the Father, but he continued to renounce all punitive elements.

The original Trinitarian view of Bushnell was somewhat evasive. He sought for decades to avoid a definitive statement, specifically concerning the ontological basis of the Trinity in the Godhead. On the other hand, he did not hesitate to recognize the instrumental value of a Trinitarian interpretation. The Trinity must be understood in terms of Christian revelation, rather than as a doctrine about God as He is in Himself. It was more a summary of how one may know God in his own Christian experience. But again, later in life, he conceded to an eternal threeness in the very being of God.

Bushnell made a lasting contribution to American theology and church life and showed that a more liberal and less creedal theology could survive in the church.

Brief Bibliography

In addition to books by Bushnell listed earlier, the following are significant:

Cheney, Mary Bushnell, *Life and Letters of Horace Bushnell*. New York: Harper and Brothers, Publishers, 1880; this is the classic, comprehensive biography written by Bushnell's daughter.

Cross, Barbara M., *Horace Bushnell: Minister to a Changing America*. Chicago: The University of Chicago Press, 1958; a competent exploration of certain phases of intellectual history of Bushnell that casts him in a more orthodox role than is common.

Smith, H. Shelton, editor, *Horace Bushnell*. New York: Oxford University Press, 1965; a compilation of significant exerpts from Bushnell's major works together with interpretive editorial comments.

"Back to the New Testament, by way of the Reformation."

48
Albrecht Ritschl
(1822-1889)

G. Irvin Lehman

Ritschl's father was General Superintendent of the Lutheran Church of Pomerania. Young Ritschl's inquiring mind led him to study at Bonn, Halle, Heidelberg, and Tübingen. Later he taught at Bonn and Göttingen. While at Tübingen he accepted and promoted the position of Baur, his teacher. Baur taught that Gentile Christianty was the result of the fusion of two antithetical viewpoints, Petrinism and Paulinism, Baur's famous "double gospel." He held that first-century apostolic Christianity evolved into the third-century old Catholic Church by a logical process of historical development. But Baur's work, *Paul, the Apostle of Jesus Christ*, became a point of departure for Ritschl. *The Rise of the Old Catholic Church* by Ritschl shows his reaction against the teachings of his old professor. Ritschl claims, in opposition to Baur, that the old Catholic Church developed differently. He states that there was only one message which appeared in Christ and in the apostles in the apostolic church. Pressures, internal and external, so altered the original gospel that by the third century the resultant old Catholic Church was a separate and distinct institution.

Ritschl reacted not only to Baur but to the prominent schools of thought of his time, as Hegelianism, natural theology, metaphysics, and religious mysticism. He criticized philosophy for intruding into Christian theology. The problem was the theory of knowledge. How do we know God? Ritschl insisted that we can know God only in the way and to the degree that He makes Himself known to us. God is known then only through the person and work of Christ. Antagonistic to this clear-cut viewpoint was the previous theology of the church as influenced by foreign philosophy. For example, early Christianity was influenced by Platonism, that of the Middle Ages by Aristotelianism, and the Reformation by a new Scholasticism. The aim, then, of Ritschl was

---

G. Irvin Lehman served long as Professor of Old Testament Language and Literature in Eastern Mennonite Seminary. He received the BS from Elizabethtown College; BD, Eastern Baptist Seminary; STM, Hartford Theological Seminary; and the MA and PhD, New York University. He also studied at the American School of Oriental Research, Jerusalem, and the Government School of Modern Hebrew, Tiberias. He served the Mennonite Central Committee in Ethiopia, 1945-47. He is an ordained minister.

to extricate Christian theology from its relations to and dependence upon non-Christian influences and ideologies.

On the positive side Ritschl had something to offer, even though it has been greatly criticized. He sees religion as a practical affair and not theoretical. Man finds himself in a state of tension with the world about him. This problem is solved by religious faith. In fact, religious faith arose as a result of man's struggle for existence. The purpose of a loving God for man is moral perfection as found in Jesus. The uniting of men on the basis of moral values constitutes for Ritschl the kingdom of God. As with the Reformers, Ritschl greatly emphasized the doctrines of the atonement and justification. He accepted the Bible as the Word of God only to the extent that it emphasized Christ.

Ritschl's critics remind us that he denies the doctrine of original sin, and practically omits dealing with the doctrines of the Trinity, the virgin birth, and the resurrection. The men of the Ritschlian school differed widely in their theology, but shared in common an appreciation for Ritschl's method of approach. His influence spread widely, affecting the thinking of Harnack, Loofs, Herrmann, Troeltsch, Kaftan, and Kattenbusch.

In Ritschl's world, higher criticism was challenging traditional views of the Bible, natural science was opposing supernaturalism, and philosophy was attempting to answer ultimate problems. Such a climate helped to motivate Ritschl in his quest for certainty in religion. But certainty comes only to him who experiences God's revelation as manifested in Christ!

Selected Publications of Ritschl

The Christian Doctrine of Justification and Reconciliation (1870), *The Old Catholic Church* (1850), *Christian Perfection* (1874), *Theology and Metaphysics* (1881), and *History of Pietism* (1880-6).

Other Bibliography

Edghill, Ernest, A., *Faith and Fact—A study of Ritschlianism*, Macmillan and Company, London, 1910.

Garvie, Alfred E., *The Ritschlian Theology*, T. and T. Clark, 1902, Edinburgh.

Hefner, Philip, *Faith and the Vitalities of History*, 1966, Harper and Row.

Mackintosh, Hugh R., *Types of Modern Theology*, Nisbet and Company, 1954, London.

Orr, James, *Ritschlianism*, Hodder and Stoughton, 1903, London.

Encyclopaedia Britannica, Chicago, 1967.
Encyclopedia of Religion and Ethics, T. and T. Clark, 1918, Edinburgh.
New Catholic Encyclopedia, McGraw Hill, 1967, New York;
New Schaff-Herzog Encyclopedia of Religious Knowledge, Baker Book House, Grand Rapids, 1957.

> "Suppose we quietly agree that the seminary may die, but we'll die first."

49
John A. Broadus

W. R. Estep, Jr.

The above words were those of John A. Broadus (1827-1895). The occasion was a consultative meeting of the four faculty members of the Southern Baptist Theological Seminary, called to determine whether the seminary should remain closed as it had been during the Civil War or attempt to reopen with no promise of money or students. With the South impoverished and Baptists divided, the prospects of the fledgling instituion were bleak indeed. But the seminary did live, and John Albert Broadus' indomitable spirit was one of the reasons. Hence the life of Broadus and that of the seminary to which he gave his life were inseparable. Preeminently a preacher, Broadus found no complete fulfillment until becoming a professor in the institution he helped to establish. Thus, the pulpit and the classroom became the twin arenas in which he fought the battles of the Lord until death.

Born in Culpepper County, Virginia, on January 23, 1827, where James Ireland had spent six months in jail for preaching the gospel, Broadus was, conceivably, a part of the fruits of that first Baptist witness proclaimed in the person of Ireland and other imprisoned Baptist ministers. Subsequently, Culpepper County became a stronghold of the Baptists. It was into a devout Baptist home that John was born, the fourth child of Major Edmund Broadus and his wife, Nancy Sims.

Although surrounded by Christian influences in his own home and that of a maternal uncle, he succeeded in reaching sixteen years of age without becoming a Christian. It was in May 1843 at the Mt. Poney Church in Culpepper that John confessed his faith in Christ and shortly thereafter was baptized. A few months later while attending a service, the preacher exhorted the congregation to witness personally to those who might be present but were not Christians. John obeyed and won his first convert. He never lost the desire to make disciples the remainder of his life.

W. R. Estep, Jr., is Professor of Church History at Southwestern Baptist Theological Seminary. He received his BA degree from Berea College; his ThM degree from Southern Baptist Theological Seminary; and his ThD from Southwestern Baptist Theological Seminary. He has pursued postgraduate studies both in Europe and in America. He is the author of *The Anabaptist Story; La Fe de los Apostoles; Baptists and Christian Unity; Colombia: Land of Conflict and Promise; Anabaptist Beginnings, 1523-1533*; and numerous articles.

Within a short time, while teaching school a few miles from Culpepper, he became a teacher and later a superintendent of the local Sunday school. In the meantime, he maintained a rigorous schedule of disciplined self-study, and to a substantial knowledge of Latin and French, he added Greek and Hebrew. All the while he was trying desperately to decide upon his life's vocation. Finally, he chose medicine and with that in mind, prepared to enter the University of Virginia. However, before he actually embarked on his university career, he attended an associational meeting where S. M. Poindexter, representing Columbia College, was speaking on the work of the ministry. Poindexter laid great emphasis upon the necessity of consecrating one's all to the high calling of the gospel ministry. During the intermission, Broadus was so moved he sought out his pastor and with choking voice said, "Brother Grimsley, the question is decided; I must try to be a preacher."

In the fall young Broadus enrolled in the university where he spent four full years of diligent study, graduating in 1850 with the MA degree. Immediately afterward he embarked on the study of theology on his own, seeking advice and bibliography from every possible source. Before the year was up, he was ordained to the gospel ministry and married to Miss Maria Harrison, the daughter of one of his esteemed professors.

During the next eight years his reputation as an effective preacher of the gospel put a premium on his services. Insistent calls came constantly. He did accept the invitation from his alma mater to serve as tutor in Latin and Greek but resigned after one year to devote all of his time to his pastorate at Charlottesville. Later, the pastorate was interrupted for a two-year period of service as chaplain of the university.

By 1858, Southern Baptists were attempting to form their first theological seminary. Broadus, along with two other young minister-scholars, helped to shape the design of the institution, including its confession of faith and curriculum, but then refused the initial invitation to join its first faculty. But that decision just could not stand, and even Broadus sensed this as did his future colleagues. Therefore in 1859, he left his native state and his beloved pastorate to become Professor of New Testament Interpretation and Homiletics, which position he held the remainder of his life.

The next thirty-six years were to witness a phenomenal ministry and all of it in the face of the most difficult circumstances. After bearing him three children, Mrs. Broadus died quite suddenly when in her twenty-sixth year. Then on July 23, 1860, little Maria, his oldest daughter, died of diphtheria. To his colleague and lifelong friend, J. P. Boyce, he confided:

> As we came to Virginia on the cars, who, if told that two of the company would die in a few weeks, would have selected as the persons James Witt and that laughing little girl? Oh my daughter! but the will of the Lord be done. I have stood by the deathbed and the grave of father and mother and sister, of wife and child; I am confident they are all safe in heaven; God help those who are left to follow them there.

The infant institution to which Broadus had dedicated his life faced a seemingly impossible future. It lacked its own buildings and library and had virtually no financial backing. The original faculty of four carried on the entire work of the seminary, administrative and academic, in addition to the constant responsibility of raising sufficient funds for continued operation. Every teacher held a pastorate in order to stay with the seminary.

Then came the Civil War. Seminary students failed to gain exemption from the draft. Therefore the seminary was forced to close its doors in May 1862, not to reopen until more than three years later. The South lay prostrate and South Carolina was hopelessly impoverished. The seminary had no funds to operate. But under Broadus' prodding it did reopen with four professors and seven students. Broadus had only one student in homiletics and he was blind. During those trying days, he wrote to a close friend, "If only we had some students to teach." But in customary dedication Broadus gave that one student his best and from those lectures came his classic work, *Preparation and Delivery of Sermons*. It won immediate acclaim as the finest work of its kind in the English language. Printed in England, as well as America, it has seen a century of use in the classroom, going through numerous printings and revisions, incidentally giving its author and the seminary an international reputation for excellence in theological education.

Broadus' health was never good. He was frequently incapacitated. His colleagues were determined he should live so they made possible a year's travel and study abroad. England and Europe's greatest scholars and theologians became his personal acquaintances and some his lifelong friends. Knowledge gleaned through studious travels in the Holy Lands, Greece, and Italy provided him with additional insights that enhanced his work as an exegete and as a preacher. Doubtless his commentary on the Gospel of Matthew was the remarkable work it became due in part to this experience. Sought after by churches, universities, and seminaries, both North and South, Broadus remained a humble servant of the Lord with the single-minded purpose to serve his God through the education of students for the ministry. Yet, from the beginning to the end of his own ministry, Broadus considered himself first and above all a preacher of the gospel. The quality of his scholarship caused the universities of Chicago, Brown, Georgetown, Richmond, and Crozer Seminary to seek his services at one time or another and his abilities as a preacher made him the welcome guest in some of America's greatest pulpits. In 1889 he delivered the Lyman Beecher Lectures on Preaching at Yale University, becoming the first Southern Baptist accorded this honor.

Broadus lived in an era of great preachers, among whom he was widely acclaimed as one of the greatest, along with Charles Haddon Spurgeon. While he did not agree with all Spurgeon did and said, he did hold the London preacher in high esteem and shared his profound reverence for the Bible. Unlike Spurgeon, Broadus was an able critical biblical scholar, well acquainted with the scholars of Tübingen, whose books he read in the German. Nevertheless, he refused to accept their conclusions as his own, and steadfastly maintained the authority of "the blessed word of God" for his preaching and life. Broadus never used the pulpit for a display of knowledge. His sermons were the soul of simplicity. They were well thought out but never written down word for word. Even extensive notes prepared in the process were never carried into the pulpit. He looked directly into the faces of his congregation and preached for a verdict. His manner was earnest and personal. He did not shout but there was no doubting his concern nor the intensity of his appeal. Like Spurgeon, he enjoyed the greatest of freedom in delivery, carrying his audience along with him from thought to thought. Doubtless, he was a great preacher because he was a great man.

Wherein lay the greatness of this man? This is the question that invariably rises. The answer is multifold. He was a man of unquestionable integrity, examples of which are not hard to come by. His denunciation of the then popular Ku Klux Klan, of lynching, and of alcoholism are only partial indicators of the measure of the man. His steadfast devotion to what he conceived to be the will of God for his life in the service of his beloved seminary, rejecting every temptation to leave, regardless of the attractiveness of the offer, is a still better index. Thus, he remains an example of a man whose lifework was inseparably welded to an institution, the seminary. This relationship provided the perennial challenge of the classroom, and the sense of God's leadership in it, enhanced his pulpit ministry, and catapulted him into the first internationally known and recognized scholar among Southern Baptists. Whether in the classroom or the pulpit, or through the printed page, Broadus impresses one, even yet across the years, as a man of God. For that kind of man, there will always be a pulpit.

Bibliographical Note

His biography is summarized in various religious encyclopedias and reference works.

> "Medicine, physiology, psychology, philosophy, religion: what a life span of study!"

50
William James

H. R. Baerg

William James (1842-1910), the father of modern (American) psychology and one of the founders of pragmatism, was of Scottish-Irish descent and of Calvinist-Puritan tradition. His father, Henry James, was of wealthy parentage, pursued no regular profession, and later turned to the Swedenborgian faith. The family moved from the United States to Europe and back several times in the course of William's youth. The atmosphere of the home was one of total permissiveness and complete lack of spontaneous religion. Probably "transcendentalism" (deism) would best describe his religious background.

William was frail and sickly, and throughout his life suffered from neurasthenia. He suffered from periods of total exhaustion being almost completely invalid the last years of his life. At the age of eighteen he was very attached to his family, emotionally somewhat immature, and of very delicate nervous constitution.

In 1861 he enrolled in Harvard Medical School where he studied chemistry, biology, and physiology. With the Darwinion controversy raging at this time, James became enamored with philosophy. He also pursued, very energetically, studies in the areas of psychology, ethics, and metaphysics. His studies and research brought him into an inner darkness from which he emerged as a believer in the "free will of man." At Harvard, James completed his medical studies and then served a brief internship in a hospital; however, he had no intention to practice medicine.

In 1873 he became a professor at Harvard, a profession which he pursued for about 35 years with an occasional leave of absence. He was rated as a very inspiring teacher. At first he taught in the field of physiology, however, he soon entered the fields of psychology and

---

H. R. Baerg received the BA from Tabor College, the BD from Tabor Seminary, and the MA from Wichita University. Further studies at the University of North Dakota. Taught six years in the Mennonite Brethren Bible College, Winnipeg. Has been pastor of the Portage Avenue Mennonite Brethren Church, Winnipeg, and president and instructor in Winkler Bible Institute, Winkler, Man. He is currently pastoring a Mennonite Brethren Church in Salem, Ore.

philosophy, and also lectured in ethics and metaphysics. In 1876 James taught his first class in psychology. Two years later he contracted with a publisher to write his *Principles of Psychology* which, however, did not come off the press until twelve years later.

Although James had never taken any formal lectures in philosophy—he said the first lecture in philosophy which he heard was one he gave himself—he gradually moved into this department. In 1878 he began publishing articles resulting in a flow of productions, articles, essays, and books which lasted for thirty years.

In 1878 he married Alice H. Gibbens, a remarkable woman of beauty, humor, and stamina. They had five children—four boys and one girl. James died in August 1910, much before he had said everything he wanted to say. However, he raised many questions to which psychology, philosophy, and theology are still looking for answers.

James' philosophical thought was so detailed, complex, and rich; his personality so unusual, and his mind and heart so generous and free, that it is difficult to comprehend in one view or reduce to a system the vast body of ideas which he turned into the mainstream of American thought. He wandered into many fields of investigation and sowed many seeds of thought into the philosophical and psychological ground, many of which took root in diverse people and places. As to the question of priority, it is difficult to say whether his pragmatism, radical empiricism, pluralism, anti-intellectualism, or his moral and intellectual freedom deserve first place; however, it has been said that if James were to be identified with one tradition only, it would be pragmatism with which he would be associated.

He is still considered one of the most popular philosophers which America has produced. His first interest was toward the profession of art, but he soon gave this up for science, and later philosophy. He is the chief apostle and popularizer of pragmatism, the theory which holds that truth is tested by practical experience. To him, and to many others, this was a break with the wretchedness of borrowing only from tradition and living at secondhand. It was a deliberate attempt to bring change, instead of just waiting for it to occur. James coined the term pragmatism from "pragmatic" or practicalism. To him truth was discovered only from the practicality of ideas. James held that consciousness, belief in God, and thought have reality only in experience or the happenings of time. His doctrine of pure experience became the basis and foundation of his pragmatism.

He was empirical, a believer in freedom—personal freedom of faith—as opposed to deterministic monism. However, it was also a revolt against idealism and against much of speculative philosophy which had been so strong in Europe. His open mind took him to pluralism and to individualistic moralism as an answer to the determinists' God and a set standard of faith. He refused to accept the absolute authority of the Scriptures, he held to an optimistic view of human nature, and he affirmed the limits of the rational method, holding that experience is more real. His radical empiricism provided him with an affirmative answer that experience is as real as God.

His pragmatism is considered by some to be as epoch-making as the Protestant Reformation and supposedly displaced all rationalistic systems. Many passionately criticized him for his experience-centered views; others complained because of his ambiguity. Still others felt that he placed too much emphasis on the role of the intellect. His intellect demanded a concept of life which was natural and scientific, yet which extended beyond science into the metaphysical. In his epistemology, however, he is limited by his pragmatic view.

James sought not to undermine personal faith or religion but to strengthen them in a naturalistic way. He would say, "Be respectful of the beliefs of others as you are jealous of your own freedom of thought. Treasure your own experience of God but do not imagine that God cannot reveal himself to others in entirely different manners." James could in some respects be classified as a naturalist, for nowhere does he affirm faith in the Bible as God's revelation. On the other hand, he did not accept a pantheistic conception of God but looked upon him as the "higher presence," a God who is powerful, yet whom we can address intimately as "Thou," not distant, but one who appreciates our ideals and collaborates with us in their achievement.

The philosophers which James read were all naturalists and skeptics; it is then little wonder that James felt at home in the camp of liberalism. In his twenties he said, "If God is dead, or at least irrelevant, ditto to everything pertaining to the Beyond." Yet he classified himself as a "natural supernaturalist." So, to him, metaphysics seemed essential to gain insight into the physical world.

Although rationalists and positivists are in accord in condemning faith, James seeks to build it up by asserting that all of us rely on faith every day of our lives without affirming it by experiments. In his *Will to Believe,* he does not take the view of the skeptic or agnostic but allows the privilege to everyone to believe what he wishes. We really need faith. Faith to him is an assent to the reality of a divine power with whose moral ideals we are to cooperate in working both for our personal salvation and for the salvation of the world.

It is commonly asserted that pragmatists "have no ethics," and that they justify anything that is useful to the person involved. James stated that science teaches us what *is;* but what about the vast moral field of what *ought* to be? He felt that action should be judged by its results rather than whether it adheres to some doctrine. Morality becomes the basis of his religion rather than the reverse. However, he did believe that religion then transforms morality.

His hypothesis on human immortality is rather mystical in that he sets forth that human consciousness might ultimately be subsumed in the "mother-sea" of infinite consciousness; this is man's guarantee of survival.

James was interested in maintaining religious values and religious experiences, and the integrity of the believer's inner consciousness, but he was not interested in the social and institutional side of religion. He classified himself as a "Methodist without a Savior." Though he made distinctions, such as "once-born" and "twice born" men, he did this for purposes of classification, and did not attach evangelical meaning to them.

In 1870 he appears to have experienced some crisis in his life which dispelled his doubts and caused him to pursue moral and utilitarian ends. This crisis proved to be a turning point but not to a vital Christian faith. He never did satisfactorily solve the problem of evil to himself or others. His study of human nature was probably more from the psychopathic point of view. He considered religious experiences as physical visitations, and though "morbid" in origin, the religious life still is of significance to the individual.

Brief Annotated Bibliography

Principles of Psychology, New York, Henry Holt, 1890. This book was written over a period of 12 years (1878-1890), while James was teaching psychology. It is a summary of existing psychological knowledge set forth in principle and practical application instead of in theory and experiment. His interests went more along the functional than the structural lines.

The Will to Believe, and Other Essays in Popular Philosophy, New York, Longmans, Green & Co., 1897. This book was written in answer to moral problems rather than to the problem of theory. It presents a "saving gospel" apart from "saving grace." It is a series of articles and addresses touching upon knowledge, metaphysics, and ethics. He sets forth conviction and confidence, in contrast to skepticism and doubt which became quite popular in this period. His answer was belief with restraint, pluralism instead of an infinite God, and freedom instead of determinism.

Human Immortality: Two Supposed Objections to the Doctrine, Boston, Houghton-Mifflin, 1898. He held to supernormal knowledge and mediumistic-spiritist manifestation based on his belief in a continuum of cosmic consciousness. This book is based on the "Ingersoll Lectures on the Immortality of Man." Mind has only a functional dependence upon his body and so he can outlast it and outlive it: this was his contention in answer to the materialist. Mind is not a product of matter but is released through it. The dissolution of the brain merely meant to be subsumed in a cosmic consciousness as the raindrop is merged in the "mother-sea."

Varieties of Religious Experiences. A Study of Human Nature, New York, Longmans, Green & Co., 1902. The Gifford Lectures in 1901, 1902, which set forth his practical philosophy and a search for the meaning and value of the religion of his father. He set forth two kinds of faith in human experience, the fighting faith as set forth in the *Will to Believe* which battles its own way through, and the comforting faith which springs from human weakness and seeks refuge and security in God. It is a pragmatic approach to religion with examples of the virile type and the psychopathic type of experiences given. It is a valuable source for the study of conversion.

Pragmatism: A New Name for Some Old Ways of Thinking, New York, Longmans, Green & Co., 1907. He espouses an individualistic, practical philosophy to life, which provides the freedom to reject evil and choose the ideal. There is much more in the unseen than God; He is only the ideal part. He sets forth the value of the teleological and practicalism. In *Pragmatism* James gave a name, an emphasis, and a new formulation to a view which he had held over the years.

Essays in Radical Empiricism, New York, Longmans, Green & Co., 1912. This book subsumes his theory, knowledge, and views, and seeks to construct a world based upon "pure experience." It sets forth an ordered, self-styled universe not essentially theistic and which rejects the absolute. It is a pluralistic empiricism expressed radically. Man has constructed his own world, not chance.

"The Kingdom of God comes with a Christianized Social Order."

51

Walter Rauschenbusch

Clarence Hiebert

Walter Rauschenbusch (1861-1918) is historically associated with the "social gospel" emphasis prominent in America at the turn of this century. Walter, the son of the German immigrant minister, Augustus Rauschenbusch, was the seventh pastor in a direct line of ministers. Walter received his theological education in Germany and at the Rochester Theological Seminary (New York), where his father taught. In particular, his father carried responsibility for educating pastors to minister to German-speaking immigrants. His father, once a Lutheran, had converted to the Baptists.

Walter Rauschenbusch's first and only pastoral ministry (1886-1897) was in New York City's Second German Baptist Church, located in an oppressed region popularly known as "Hell's Kitchen." This experience, along with other influences through his reading and his background and the social situation of his times, led him to a reexamination of the Christian faith. The result of this rethinking was ultimately to dub him as the chief proponent and catalyst for the American social gospel movement of which he is considered to be the most important theologian of its early stages. Rauschenbusch was, in reality, a product of many merging influences and forces—his father's strong interest in radical Christianity as typified by the Anabaptists, German piety, doctrinal orthodoxy, and the social concerns of his times and setting in New York City.

Following his first distressing experiences and "rethinking" years in "Hell's Kitchen," he read widely the works of Tolstoi, Mazzini, Marx, Ruskin, Bellamy, and so on. In a year of study abroad in Germany and England he sharpened his thinking on the issues of economics and theology by observing the industrial conditions of England. The Fabian socialist movement, the Salvation Army, and the Consumers' Cooperatives intrigued him. The 1893 industrial depression in the U.S.A. added fuel to his ongoing theological reap-

---

Clarence Hiebert is Chairman of the Division of Biblical Studies and Philosophy at Tabor College. He received the AB from Tabor, the BD from the New York Theological Seminary, the MA from the Graduate Theological Seminary of Phillips University, and the PhD, Department of Religion, Case Western Reserve University. He is the author of *Brothers in Deed to Brothers in Need, The Holdeman People,* and other books.

praisal. What he had been taught, he would assert, "didn't fit" what he saw. "One could hear human virtue cracking and crumbling all around," he wrote. Emerging out of this ideological struggle, he became a proponent of the necessity for a "social gospel."

His platform, after his 1897 pastoral assignment, became the Rochester Seminary, where his father had taught, where he remained for the rest of his life. He was soon in wide demand as a speaker, frequently wrote for journals, and was deeply involved in social issues in Rochester—social and civic reform, public school issues, Sunday evening forums, etc. The most distinctive organization reflecting his emphasis was an association which he founded, which met annually (1893-1915), and which published a quarterly journal, *The Brotherhood of the Kingdom*. This gathering of individuals was bent on being serious about their Christian faith in order to make an impact on the existing social order.

Rauschenbusch was a dynamic person. His writings reveal a keen sense of historical perspective along with a critical analysis of the issues current in his times. What he said and wrote he did from a basic stance as an evangelical Christian. In this sense he was different from the social reformers who were his contemporaries. He insisted on being known as a "Christian socialist." In contrast to his contemporary social reformers, he stressed concepts such as original sin, a belief in the reality of Satan, and the necessity of the kingdom of God evolving out of one's relationship to Jesus Christ. Illustrative of this strong evangelical orientation is his involvement in the popularly used *Gospel Song* book of the German-speaking people in America for the first half of this century, the *Evangeliums-Lieder*, of which he was the editor and the translator of many of the gospel songs. In his *A Theology for the Social Gospel* (1917) he writes:

> The social gospel is the old message of salvation, but enlarged and intensified. The individualistic gospel has taught us to see the sinfulness of every human heart and has inspired us with faith in the willingness and power of God to save every soul that comes to him. But it has not given us an adequate understanding of the sinfulness of the social order and its share in the sins of all individuals within it. It has not evoked faith in the will and power of God to redeem the permanent institutions of human society from their inherited guilt of oppression and extortion. Both our sense of sin and our faith in salvation have fallen short of the realities under its teaching. The social gospel seeks to bring men under repentance for their collective sins and to create a more sensitive and more modern conscience. It calls on us for the faith of the old prophets who believed in the salvation of nations (p. 5 f.).

It is somewhat difficult to "classify" Rauschenbusch. Some of his own contemporaries considered him insignificant; others dubbed him as a "social reformer" along with all the others contemporary to his times. From his writings it is quite evident that he did not share the optimistic outlook which the social reformers generally carried, though from time to time there is some evidence of undue optimism in his evolving "kingdom of God" concepts. For him, reform was seen to be possible only through an evolving social order based on justice and righteousness—which was for him the kingdom of God. He saw the kingdom both as a present and a future reality. The basis for such a belief stemmed from his restudy of the Scriptures—a new understanding of the role of the Old Testament prophets and the meaning of apostolic Christianity.

Capitalism was viewed by him as the greatest enemy to the fulfillment of the kingdom of God. He believed that the social and political order had become corrupt because of man's selfishness. Private enterprise with its dominating emphasis on competitiveness "exalts selfishness to the dignity of a moral principle. It pits men against one another in a gladitorial game in which there is no mercy and in which 90 percent of the combatants finally strew the arena" (quoted from Olmstead, p. 492). To abolish the hatreds which result from this self-seeking economic competition was the mission to which Rauschenbusch set himself. Reform, he believed, could result from the impulse of Christian love, something that was possible only where men would live in cooperation with each other in such a pursuit.

The significance of Rauschenbusch can be viewed from several perspectives. He himself, surveying the situation in 1917, just a year prior to his death, optimistically stated:

> The social gospel ... is no longer a prophetic and occasional note. It is a novelty only in backward social or religious communities. The social gospel has become orthodox. It is not only preached. It has set new problems for local church work, and has turned the pastoral and organizing work of the ministry into new and constructive directions. It has imparted a wider vision and a more statesmanlike grasp to the foreign mission enterprise.... Conservative denominations have formally committed themselves to the fundamental ideas of the social gospel and their practical application. The plans of great interdenominational organizations are inspired by it. It has become a constructive force in American politics (*A Theology for the Social Gospel*, p. 2 f.).

Contemporary historians associate the catalytic work of Rauschenbusch with the establishment of interest on the part of many American seminaries in programs of Christian sociology and ethics. Another indication of the significance of his social emphasis may be seen in a new rash of social creeds that were issued by various denominations, agencies, and groups of congregations at that time. Some historians indicate that this interest also contributed to the formation of the Federal Council of Churches (1908) which ultimately became what is now known as the National Council of Churches, USA. The Social Creed (1908), which was the first strong rallying point of this association of North American denominations, called for "equal rights for all men, uniform divorce laws, child labor laws, laws against the liquor traffic, protection for workers in their places of employment, old-age benefits, labor arbitration, one day of rest weekly, reduction of working hours, safeguards for the rights of workers, guaranteed living wages, and 'the application of Christian principles to the acquisition and use of property'" (Olmstead, p. 494). Interests of this kind in the churches of North America are, in large part, attributed to the significant work of Rauschenbusch, through his teaching, preaching, and the seven books which came from his pen.

Brief Bibliography

Rauschenbusch Writings: Rauschenbusch, Walter, *Christianity and the Social Crisis* (New York, 1907); *For God and the People: Prayers of the Social Awakening* (Boston, 1910); *Christianizing the Social Order* (New York, 1912); *"Unto Me"* (Boston, 1912); *Dare We Be Christians?* (Boston, 1914); *The Social Principles of Jesus* (New York, 1916); *A Theology for the Social Gospel* (New York, 1917); *The Rochester Theological Seminary Bulletin* (Sixty-Ninth Year: November 1918)—a "Rauschenbusch Number," containing reports of the funeral and memorial services, various tributes, and some items by Rauschenbusch himself.

Other Writings: Handy, Robert T., ed., *The Social Gospel in America, 1870-1920,* Gladden, Ely, Rauschenbusch (Oxford University Press, 1966, New York); Bodein, Vernon Parker, *The Social Gospel of Walter Rauschenbusch and Its Relation to Religious Education* (New Haven, 1944). Vol. XVI, Yale Studies in Religious Education; Landis, Benson Y., ed., *A Rauschenbusch Reader: The Kingdom of God and the Social Gospel*—with an Interpretation of the Life and Work of Walter Rauschenbusch by Harry Emerson Fosdick (New York, 1957); Sharpe, Dores R., *Walter Rauschenbusch* (New York, 1942); Singer, Anna M., *Walter Rauschenbusch and His Contribution to Social Christianity* (Boston, 1927); Smucker, Donavan E., "The Origins of Walter Rauschenbusch's Social Ethics" (typed PhD thesis, University of Chicago, 1957); _____, "Multiple Motifs in the Thought of Rauschenbusch: A Study in the Origins of the Social Gospel," *Encounter,* XIX (1958), 14-20.

"Supernaturalism is the very breath of Christianity's nostrils."

52

Benjamin Breckenridge Warfield

C. Norman Kraus

B. B. Warfield (1851-1921), as he is usually referred to, was an ordained Presbyterian minister and seminary professor, first at Western Theological Seminary and later at Princeton Theological Seminary.

He was born and raised in Kentucky in the atmosphere of "Old School" Presbyterianism. He was trained at Princeton College and Seminary and at the University of Leipzig, where he studied New Testament. During his nine years at Western (1878-1887) he taught in the area of New Testament studies. Then in 1887 he became Professor of Didactic and Polemic Theology at Princeton, where he taught until his death.

Warfield was primarily a man of the study. He served one interim pastorate for a year, but his major work was done in the class room and as a writer and editor. He served as editor in chief for *The Presbyterian and Reformed Review* for the life of that journal (1890-1902). Most of his writing was in the form of learned articles for the theological journals of the day. These articles cover an astonishing variety of subjects, and many of them have been collected and published in book form since his death. He also was the author of fourteen essays of various length which were published as separate volumes.

Warfield was a thoroughly convinced Calvinist in the tradition of Charles Hodge (1797-1878), who formulated an American version of classic Calvinist theology, which had first been developed in seventeenth-and-eighteenth-century Europe. Warfield had the highest admiration for the *Westminster Confession*, which he referred to as "the final crystalization of the very essence of evangelical religion." His personal statement prefacing his inaugural address as Professor of

---

C. Norman Kraus served long as Professor of Religion at Goshen College. He received the BA from Goshen, the BD from Goshen Biblical Seminary, the ThM from Princeton Theological Seminary, and the PhD from Duke University. He has also taught at Eastern Mennonite College in Virginia and at Serampore Theological College in India. Among his writings are: *Dispensationalism in America: Its Rise and Development, Integration! Who's Prejudiced? Missions, Evangelism, and Church Growth*, and editor of *Evangelicalism and Anabaptism*. He is now a missionary in Japan, serving as a Bible teacher at the invitation of the Japanese Mennonite Church.

198

New Testament at Western gives a clear picture of his character and conviction.

> I wish ... to declare that I sign these standards not as a necessary form which must be submitted to, but gladly and willingly as the expression of a personal and cherished conviction; and, further, that the system taught in these symbols is the system which will be drawn out of the Scriptures in the prosecution of the teaching to which you have called me—not, indeed, because commencing with the system the Scriptures can be made to teach it, but because commencing with the Scriptures I cannot make them teach anything else.[1]

Warfield was primarily a teacher and a polemicist. For several reasons he did not attempt to write a systematic theology of his own, although he was a prolific author. Francis Patton, president of Princeton Seminary and colleague of Warfield, noted that he was by temperament a controversial rather than a systematic theologian. Further, he observed that he was entirely content to make Charles Hodge's system the basis of his own teaching.[2] This predilection suited his historical context. He wrote at a time when liberal theology from Europe was making its first major impact in America and more particularly in the Presbyterian Church. He was caught up in the battle against all forms of liberalism, and was determined to maintain and defend the traditional Calvinist synthesis as the final theological statement. For example, several of his major articles in biblical inspiration and revelation were written in the context of the controversy which led to the heresy trials of Charles A. Briggs (1895) and Henry Preserved Smith (1894).

Whether he was writing on theories of atonement, the virgin birth, inspiration of the Bible, or Christian perfectionism, Warfield's major concern was to enunciate and rationally vindicate a system of supernatural theism. Supernaturalism, he wrote, is "the very breath of Christianity's nostrils and an anti-supernaturalistic atmosphere is to it the deadliest miasma."[3] Along with his colleagues at Princeton, W. H. Green and Caspar W. Hodge, he insisted on not only a doctrine of God as supernatural Spirit but as the absolute, free, and self-determining Spirit who can and does act directly in history. A fully adequate understanding of supernaturalism requires also a supernatural mode of operation in history which is distinguishable from the natural process of cause and effect, that is, general providence.

Therefore in his *Counterfeit Miracles* he makes a clean distinction between answers to prayer which are mediated through natural means, no matter how unusual they may be and miracles which are the direct intervention of God superseding nature. Likewise in his concept of revelation, he contended that the theophany of the patriarchal era was the mode par excellence of revelation. In relation to theophany, he wrote:

> The objectivity of the mode of communication which is adopted is intense, and it is thrown up to observation with the greatest emphasis. Into the natural life of man God intrudes in a purely supernatural manner, bearing a purely supernatural communication. In these communications we are given accordingly just a series of "naked messages of God."[4]

In the two volumes of essays entitled *Perfectionism* he examines the various forms which the doctrine of Christian perfection has taken since the time of the early Quakers and John Wesley. He is critical of perfectionism because, he holds, it is based implicitly if not explicitly upon Pelagian assumptions, namely that man has some freedom and ability to strive toward his own sanctification. He is especially incensed with the Ritschlian conception of the perfectability of man, and labels Ritschl "the Rationalist." In these two volumes and in *The Plan of Salvation* he argues vigorously against granting man any freedom of the will or remnant of goodness that would make him capable of initiative or cooperative action in his salvation. Salvation must simply be understood as God's supernatural miracle. He observes caustically that Ritschl's doctrine of awakening faith and regeneration does not eliminate all mystery from the process, it only eliminates "all that is supernatural."[5]

The Scriptures as understood according to the definition of classic orthodoxy were the source and authority for Warfield's theology. He understood revelation to be a verbal transmission of information—a rational word—not merely an act or event, and he identified supernatural revelation with Scripture. According to his doctrine of verbal and plenary inspiration the written Scriptures are the "perfectly infallible" repository of revelation. Thus theology was for him inextricably tied to careful biblical exegesis.

A typical passage from his essay, "God Our Father and the Lord Jesus Christ," will illustrate this biblical orientation, as well as his method of argument and the pervasive polemical flavor of his work. After a detailed grammatical examination of the Greek words and phrases which refer to Jesus as "Lord" and relate Him to God in a most intimate and unique way he meticulously sums up:

> The reasoning is distinctly circular which denies to each of these passages in turn its natural meaning on the ground of lack of supporting usage, when this lack of supporting usage is created by a similar denial on the same ground of its natural meaning to each of the other passages. The ground of the denial in each case is merely the denial in the other cases. Meanwhile the usage is there, and is not thus to be denied away. If it may be, any usage whatever may be destroyed in the same manner.
>
> In these circumstances there seems no reason why the ordinary laws of grammar should not determine our understanding of II Thess. i. 12. We may set it down here, therefore, with its parallels in Tit. ii. 13 and II Pet. i. 1 in which the same general phrasing even more clearly carries this sense....
>
> In these passages the conjunction, in which God and Christ are brought together in the general formula which we are investigating, reaches its culmination in an express identification of them. We have seen that the two are not only united in this formula on terms of complete equality, but are treated as in some sense one. Grammatically at least, they constitute one "self" *(autos)* and they are presented in nearly every phraseology possible as the common source of Christian blessing and the unitary object of Christian prayer. Their formal identification would seem after this to be a matter of course, and we may be a little surprised that the recognition of it would be so strenuously resisted. The formal identification is

not acknowledged to be expressly made, those who find difficulty in believing that Christ is included by Paul in the actual Godhead may feel the way more or less open to explain away by one expedient or another the identity of the two, manifoldly implied in the general representation indeed, but not formally announced.

Expositor after expositor, at any rate, may be observed introducing into his reproduction of Paul's simple equalization, or rather, unification, of God and the Lord, qualifying phrases of his own which tend to adjust them to his personal way of thinking of the relations subsisting between the two.... It is most common, perhaps, to follow the path in which Lünemann walks, and to declare that Paul unites the two persons because Christ by His exaltation has been made for the time coregnant with God over the universe, or perhaps only over the Church.... An especially flagrant example of the substitution of quite alien phraseology for Paul's, in a professed restatement of his conception, is afforded by David Somerville in his Cunningham Lectures on "St. Paul's Conception of Christ." He tells us that Paul's "conjunction of God and Christ in his stated greetings to the churches indicated his belief that a co-partnership of Divine power and honor was included in the exaltation of Christ to be Lord." It obviously smacks, however, less of Paul than of Socinus to speak of the relation of Christ to God as a "copartnership of Divine power and honor," and of this co-partnership of Divine power and honor between them as resulting from Christ becoming Lord by His exaltation.[6]

At his death in 1921 Warfield was undoubtedly the foremost theologian in Calvinist circles.

Brief Bibliography

The Lord of Glory, New York, 1907; *The Plan of Salvation*, Philadelphia, 1915; *Counterfeit Miracles*, New York, 1918.

Following are volumes of published articles: *Revelation and Inspiration*, New York, 1927; *Biblical Doctrines*, New York, 1929; *Christology and Criticism*, New York, 1929; *Studies in Tertullian and Augustine*, New York, 1930; *Calvin and Calvinism*, New York, 1931; *Perfectionism*, New York, 1931, two volumes; *Critical Reviews*, New York, 1932; *Studies in Theology*, New York, 1932. In more recent years some of these volumes have been slightly revised and reissued under different titles.

Footnotes

1. "Inspiration and Criticism," *Revelation and Inspiration* (New York, 1927), pp. 395-96.
2. "Benjamin Breckenridge Warfield," *Princeton Theological Review*, xix (July, 1921), p. 386.
3. "Christian Supernaturalism," *Studies in Theology* (New York, 1932), p. 29.
4. "The Biblical Idea of Revelation," *Revelation and Inspiration*, p. 17.
5. *Studies in Perfectionism* (New York, 1931), volume I, p. 27.
6. *Biblical and Theological Studies* (Philadelphia, 1952), pp. 70-72.

53
Ernst Troeltsch

> *"The history of the Christian ethos becomes the story of a constantly renewed search for this compromise, and of fresh opposition to this spirit of compromise."*

J. Lawrence Burkholder

Ernst Troeltsch (1865-1923) was a German Theologian who taught at Heidelberg and at Berlin. His significance as a theologian lies in his appropriation of sociological categories for theology, and his understanding of the influence of history upon theology and Christian institutions. Although he was enough of a philosophical idealist to be concerned about the reality of the gospel in the abstract, he was, nevertheless, impressed by the endless concrete historical configurations of the gospel in the church. His major concern as a theologian was the adaptation of the church to culture and the influence of Christianity and culture upon one another.

His major publication is *The Social Teachings of the Christian Churches*, a monumental two-volume work in which he traces the changing forms of the church from its inception to modern times. This work is characterized by its sweeping generalizations and its sharp contrasts as epochs and ages of church history are compared and their inner rationales are explained in the light of sociological theory. His most famous delineations relate to the "church," the "sect," and the "mystical group." The "church" is the institution of grace whose purpose it is to embrace culture in its totality including entire populations. Troeltsch attempted to set forth the inner logic of the church in terms of the *corpus Christianum*. By comparison the "sect" is a voluntary association of believers who live according to a covenant, and who see themselves alongside the state and make no attempt to dominate society. The "mystical group" is a loosely organized group of

---

J. Lawrence Burkholder is President of Goshen College, Goshen, Ind. He received his BA from Goshen, his BD from Gettysburg Theological Seminary, and the ThM and ThD from Princeton Theological Seminary, the doctorate *summa cum laude*. For four years he was a relief administrator in the Far East, in India and China, and later in Vietnam. In 1970 he left his teaching post at Harvard (Victor S. Thomas Professor of Divinity) to accept the presidency of Goshen College. Among his writings may be mentioned: "There Is Hope for Indochina," *Theology Today* (Jl 1955); "The Anabaptist Vision of Discipleship," in Hershberger, *The Recovery of the Anabaptist Vision; The Church and Community;* and *Love and Justice in Mutual Aid*.

highly differentiated Christians who express the individualism and secularization of modernity.

The distinction between sect and church has become more or less standard among sociologists of religion even though the distinction is also criticized. It applies most directly to the European situation where Established and Free Churches exist side by side. In America, the "denomination" replaces the church and the sect in their original simplicity, and yet it is obvious that many of the characteristics of church and sect linger even yet in American churches.

Probably no single group has been more directly concerned with Troeltsch than the Mennonites. A number of Mennonite scholars have seen in Troeltsch's concept of the sect a helpful theological and sociological rationale for their denomination. This is not to say, however, that they are Troeltschians. Possibly Mennonites have tended to embrace Troeltsch's distinctions between the church and the sect without accepting his total position, because he showed that sectarianism could be accounted for not in terms of dissidence but in terms of an inner logic. Free Church sectarianism, in other words, is a respectable form of the gospel and must be respected as such. It is also to be noted that Troeltsch located Anabaptist beginnings with Conrad Grebel in Zürich in 1525, an interpretation which has been widely accepted by recent Anabaptist scholarship.

One of the problems which underlies Troeltsch's entire study is the problem of how the gospel of Jesus Christ could adjust to the world. This brings to the fore the problem of politics, power, justice, retribution, and war in relation to the absolute nonresistant love of Christ. That the church must come to terms with the world is obvious to any historian, but what it means to come to terms with the world is another thing. In an attempt to bridge the gap between "the gospel" and culture, Troeltsch introduces into ethical discussion the concept of "compromise." This term may not be the happiest one, since it gives the impression of capitulation to evil. Rather, Troeltsch used the term to describe the adjustment which the church makes when it accepts responsibility to the world, such responsibility being an implication of the "universality" of the gospel.

Through Troeltsch's influence such conceptions as "compromise" and "responsibility" are standard fare among a number of theologians, especially American ethicists—Reinhold Niebuhr in particular. Indeed, Troeltsch has had a greater influence upon American theologians than upon European theologians. Troeltsch is really the one who stands behind the vigorous "Christ and culture" discussion in Christian ethics and sociology.

Although Troeltsch was a theologian, he was not a typical German dogmatist. For one thing, he used sociological categories which he learned from Max Weber, with whom he lived for a while at Heidelberg. But more particularly his approach to theology was from the standpoint of the "history of religions." According to this standpoint, the absoluteness of Christianity is in doubt and "relativity" becomes essential to the system. Thus Troeltsch is noted for introducing into theology the fact of historical relativity, but what this really means for theology is a problem with which he wrestled but which he never solved before his untimely death at 58 in 1923.

One of the controversial themes surrounding Troeltsch is the origin and meaning of "modern times." The prevailing view among Troeltsch's friends and colleagues was that modernity is the product of the Reformation and to that extent it may be said to be Christian. Troeltsch countered in his *Protestantism and Progress* with the claim that Protestantism as set forth by Luther and the leading Reformers belongs to the church of the Middle Ages, and modernity looks not to the Reformation but to the Englightenment as its source. Troeltsch pointed in particular to the emphasis upon individuality and secularism as evidence of a spirit which is alien to Protestantism and other forms of traditional Christianity. Troeltsch saw in particular that the West was moving beyond the presuppositions of the *corpus Christianum*, and he used language to describe this movement with which we now associate Bonhoeffer.

Troeltsch was very pessimistic about the possibilities of traditional Christianity in the modern world. He saw within the restless spirit of man a continuous search for meaning, but he could not assure us that Christianity will always meet man's deepest needs, and certainly not traditional Christianity in its Protestant or Catholic forms. His final thoughts seem to have been that "nowhere does there exist an absolute Christian ethic," and for that matter the absoluteness of Christianity was for him similarly doubtful.

Bibliography

The best source on Troeltsch is his own writings, especially *The Social Teaching of the Christian Churches*.

The Bible contains truths to be believed, a salvation to be received, promises to be claimed, commandments to be obeyed, warnings to be heeded, experiences to be realized, and food for Christian growth.

54

Geo. R. Brunk I
1871-1938

J. C. Wenger

President D. H. Bender one time playfully referred to Geo. R. Brunk as the "tall sycamore." And in very truth, Bishop Geo. R. did stand tall in every way. Physically he was a giant—built on the proportions of President William Howard Taft, weighing about 275, with a huge head, neck, torso, arms, and legs. But he was also a giant in mind, with a massive intellect capable of seeing through complex issues and formulating an adequate solution for the difficulties involved. Above all, he was a spiritual giant, a man who knew the Lord and walked closely with Him through life in holiness and obedience.

The parents of Geo. R. were Henry G. Brunk (1836-1873) and Susan Heatwole (1840-1909), who were married in the Shenandoah Valley November 17, 1859. As a conscientious objector to participation in warfare, Henry G. fled north to Maryland during the Civil War, and later Susan bravely followed him—and successfully found him in Hagerstown. Later they located in Henry County, Illinois, and there Geo. R. was born the last day of the year 1871, the seventh of the eight children which Susan bore to Henry G. In 1873 the Brunks made the long trek to Marion County, Kansas, where Henry G. died of typhoid fever eight days after their arrival. And the father was followed in death in the next few months by Fannie, Sarah, and Henry G., Jr. The first child to die, however, was little John Albert, 1860-62, who lies buried

---

J. C. Wenger teaches in Goshen Biblical Seminary, and has made a study of the life and writings of Bishop Geo. R. Brunk.

in the Bank Cemetery west of Harrisonburg, Virginia. Susan went through many difficult trials in her 69 years.

Little Geo. R. as a small child saw his mother weep as she cut up the clothing of her beloved husband to make outfits for her little children. He was in the home when his older brother Joe climbed onto the kitchen table for the amputation of his badly mangled hand and part of an arm. He was put out of the home by his stepfather when still a boy, and his sensitive spirit ached for the fellowship of his dear mother. Adolescence, however, changed the homesickness into bitterness, perhaps with even some arrogance and waywardness. When Geo. R. was 17, God sent Evangelist John S. Coffman into the area. Geo. R. attended his meetings, accepted Christ as his personal Savior and Lord, and began to live the Christian life. But he received little or no pastoral care, and in the course of time, he was in a worse state than before conversion. Worst of all was the dreadful sense of hopelessness which came over him, for he was inclined to believe on the basis of Hebrews 6 that there was no hope of ever finding God again.

But God in His great compassion took steps to deliver the youth from his dreadful distress. He caused R. J. Heatwole, maternal uncle of Geo. R., to dream one night that he saw the devil binding his nephew George with a huge rope—and all the struggles of the youth were futile. The next day R. J. drove all day across the Kansas prairies to find his nephew. When R. J. shared his dream, Geo. R. stated openly, "Uncle Reuben, you have told me how I am better than I could tell you!" Geo. R. added that the worst thing of all was that there was no longer any hope for him.

"You're wrong!" said R. J. "Whenever a sinner turns to Jesus, He accepts him." And R. J. was so loving and so assuring that the youth was able to turn to the Savior in penitence and faith. As Geo. R. himself wrote later, "Through his help and guidance I was saved from absolute despair and, finally, brightly saved."

Not only did the angels in heaven rejoice, so did the members of the West Liberty Mennonite congregation near Inman in southwestern McPherson County, Kansas. In that church Geo. R., still single, was ordained to the ministry of the gospel on October 1, 1893, at 21 years of age. Immediately he threw himself into the work of God. He was actually intemperate in his study habits, frequently retiring only when the roosters began to crow in the early morning. And even more remarkably, five years later and still single, he was ordained as a bishop for the Spring Valley and Catlin congregations near Canton in McPherson County. In a remarkably short time the young leader was known all across the church, even as far west as the Willamette Valley of Oregon, as a sober, judicious, and spiritual man of God. The many series of meetings which he held were as much doctrinal and Bible study sessions as they were evangelistic in character. Many were the men and women who decided to become cross-bearing disciples of the lowly Nazarene as they listened to the gifted young man of God "open up" the Scriptures.

In the year 1900 Bishop Geo. R. was invited to come back to the area from which his parents had come, the beautiful valley of Virginia, and there he had enormous evangelistic success—as well as exercising a stabilizing influence from the Word of God on the members of the church. It was at the Lindale meetinghouse where he also, for the first time, laid eyes on Katie Wenger, 25, a girl who was destined to become his bride shortly—the date being July 15, 1900. On her picture (which he saved) he wrote: "Eureka!" (I have found her). This happy union was eventually blessed with four sons and five daughters. All four sons are ordained, three ministers and one bishop; one son-in-law was a college and seminary professor, one a minister, and one a bishop—as well as the editor of the organ founded by Geo. R., the *Sword and Trumpet*.

The base from which the young minister operated was McPherson County, Kansas, until 1907 when he and his family located at Protection in Comanche County. Three years later Geo. R. and family left for Fentress, Virginia, but for several reasons turned aside "temporarily" to the Warwick River congregation at Denbigh, Virginia (now a part of Newport News). His plan to locate on a farm near Spring City, Chester County, Pennsylvania, was never realized. He remained a farmer and fruit grower at Denbigh until his sudden and lamented death, April 30, 1938, when but 66.

Bishop Geo. R. made a great impact on the church as a minister, bishop, conference speaker and leader, and churchman in general. He wrote numerous articles for the several periodicals of his denomination, the *Herald of Truth*, the *Gospel Witness*, and their merger, the *Gospel Herald*. He also authored two effective books, *Rightly Dividing the Word (Gospel Synergism)* 1935, 1961, an exposition of the relation of the two Testaments; and *Ready Scriptural Reasons* (the current title being *Ready Bible Answers*, 1975). In these books we see the incisive mind of Bishop Geo. R. coming to grips with the basic issues in the Anabaptist-Mennonite tradition. He was a most effective "defender of the Old Faith." But his really huge literary contribution was the thousand-page ten volumes of the *Sword and Trumpet*, 1929-1938. He considered the "Trumpet" his "last stand" in his dying effort to convince his denomination that it must simply not go down the road of a lukewarm American Protestantism—for in very truth the Bible contains *Truths to be believed, a Salvation to be received, Promises to be claimed, Commandments to be obeyed, Warnings to be heeded, Experiences to be realized*, and *Food for Christian Growth*.

What then were the aspects of the "Old Faith" which Geo. R. saw as in danger? It would, of course, take a book to set these emphases forth adequately. But they included the following:

1. Perhaps it was the sensitive nature he had, perhaps partly the influence of his beloved mother, perhaps partly the influence of the sound old Methodist theologian, Richard Watson, whose *Theological Institutes* he devoured; but in the main it was the Bible itself which led Geo. R. to a lifelong emphasis on a *religion of the heart*. To use his words, Christ by His Spirit wishes to give to every believer a "sky-blue" Christian experience. With this blessed work of the Spirit as a foundation, all the commandments of the Word of God become a delight, for one is living to please his Lord. And without such a foundation in the heart, the Christian way of life becomes but legalism. God wants each Christian disciple to become a partaker of the divine nature. He needs to be "brightly saved" (another phrase of Geo. R.) and he needs to go on

steadily in a life of progressive surrender to the Lord, joyfully and blamelessly walking the narrow road which leads in the hereafter through the "Glory Gates."

2. Because Christians are in various stages of Christian maturity, there will always be a need for definite *disciplinary standards*—not that the Christian life is one of legalism, but rather that those wishing to follow the Savior faithfully ever stand in need of the faithful teaching of the Word—and what it asks of those who wish to be earnest sons and daughters of God. No disciple is a law unto himself. He is part of a band of pilgrims who are committed both to the Lord and to each other. They all stand in need of mutual admonition, mutual affirmation, mutual forgiveness, and mutual prayer. The disciple is not a spiritual "lone wolf"; he is much more a part of that spiritual army which is "marching upward" to the heavenly Zion.

3. According to Romans 12 the Christian shall be a suffering and nonresistant follower of the lowly Nazarene, of Him who accepted without even a verbal retort all the suffering from ridicule to crucifixion. Romans 13, however, recognizes that the sword worn by the officer of the law is no empty badge; it is a symbol of the power of the state to suppress crime and evil behavior by the threat of force. The only way these two chapters can be adequately interpreted—without weakening either of them—is to hold as did Geo. R. to the separation of church and state—a view set forth most effectively in the first formal group consensus by the Swiss Anabaptist "brothers and sisters" as they met at Schleitheim in Schaffhausen in 1527 and adopted unanimously the "Seven Articles." Church and state stand in contrast as to means of entrance, function, means of control, sanction, headship, and end. This means that the church does not try to force on the state the Christian ethic of love and nonresistance; and it means also that the state should not attempt to control the church. In the one case, Romans 13 would be violated, and in the other Romans 12. Nonresistant believers do not attempt to disarm the state. But Scofield's dispensationalism and "postponement" of the Sermon on the Mount attempted erroneously to arm the Christian with the weapons of the state.

4. Geo. R. feared like the plague any professed Christianity which did not call for and lead to a life of earnest obedience and faithfulness. To borrow a phrase from Hans Denck, a sixteenth-century Anabaptist: "No one can truly know Christ except he follow Him in life." Antinomianism—which means that it doesn't matter how one lives, just that he have "faith"—Geo. R. saw as a monstrous and devilish lie. According to the Word of God, those who continue in faith and obedience and heart holiness are safe in Christ. As Menno Simons, one of the favorite mentors of Geo. R., put it: "They can never be made to 'topple!'" But to teach "eternal security" for those living in sin and carelessness, even in gross carnality, was utter heresy, totally untrue, wickedly false. To combat this danger which Geo. R. saw as a threat to Mennonites who uncritically read periodicals which were "Calvinized," Geo. R. devoted enormous energy. It was a major concern in his book, *Ready Scriptural Reasons* (1926), and in the organ *The Sword and Trumpet*, which he founded in 1929 and edited with great vigor for ten years.

5. Living in the South after 1910, the sensitive spirit of Geo. R. caused his heart to ache for his black friends. Even in his youth in Kansas he tried to help his dear mother to break free from her racial prejudice. So when he moved to Virginia he was determined to treat his black friends as real persons, just as dear to God as any other race—and just as welcome in the body of Christ. He wrote to his sister in Kansas that he hoped to see black churches, even black bishops, in the Mennonite Church before he died. (His dream was almost realized, for the black minister, James Lark, 1888-1978, was ordained as the first black Mennonite bishop in 1945, just seven years after Geo. R. entered into rest with Christ.) He therefore gladly accepted invitations to preach for the blacks in Newport News, even though he reckoned seriously with the possibility of imprisonment, and he entertained blacks at his table, with the full awareness that racial bigots might well burn down his dwelling. For him, racial prejudice was simply unvarnished sin.

6. Geo. R. believed strongly that society had the right to vote a community, even the nation, "dry," and he himself would hurry halfway across the continent to be at the polls of his home community to vote against the saloon. He was happy with the Eighteenth Amendment, which made the manufacture, sale, and transportation of strong drink a crime, and he was deeply displeased with the oft-repeated statement that conditions were worse then than when liquor was once more legalized. He lifted his pen to warn his readers against the evils of social drinking, and at 52 even composed a vigorous poem, "Sunshine and Shadow," which begins with "A noble man, a lovely wife," and toward the end, as strong drink closed in for the kill, there were "Demons, demons everywhere, which claim his soul with black despair."

The religion of Geo R. was not so "heavenly" that he had no concern for social evils such as strong drink—or the cruelty of conscienceless financiers (See his account of a lawyer who went to the home of a silver-haired couple to evict them: *Faithfully, Geo. R.,* p. 159, and his moving poem, "Prayers I Don't Like to Hear," 1895, p. 50.)

7. Geo. R. had total confidence in Pastor John S. Coffman, who served in the early years as president of the board which controlled Elkhart Institute. But the school had not been very long in Goshen until he was looking at it with some concern. It is not easy to pinpoint the trouble. It was not that the Goshen leaders openly challenged the great doctrines of the Christian faith: the being and personality of the triune God, the creation of the universe and of man in the divine image, the fall of the original couple, the redemptive concern and activity of God, the fact of divine revelation, the supernatural birth and resurrection of the Lord Jesus, His atoning sacrifice on Golgotha, His personal return at the end of the world, and the like. Nor did the Goshen leaders reject believer's baptism, nonresistance, nor separation from the world—at least not explicitly. What grieved and troubled Geo. R. was a certain mild and noncommittal attitude on the part of some of the Goshen leaders. They seemed to assume that the fact that they were willing to make sacrifices to teach in a church college proved that they were sound members of the church. Geo. R. wanted to hear

them actively espousing, and teaching, and defending the great doctrines of the faith, as well as the "unpopular" doctrines which were somewhat unique to the Peace Churches—including nonconformity to the world. And in the end what may have appeared as a cantankerous trait in the "tall sycamore" proved to be an insightful discernment—for under the leadership of S. C. Yoder, Iowa bishop and president of the Board of Education, Goshen College was closed for a year and reopened under new leadership.

8. Although Geo. R. held to and defended the historic Mennonite practice of quietly voting at the polls, especially when moral or religious issues were involved, he did see his role as a Christian as essentially nonpolitical. But that did not mean that he was indifferent to world movements such as communism, which was openly atheistic and opposed to all the freedoms so dear to the hearts of those living in a democracy—which gives full freedom to the church for its evangelistic and nurture activities. Geo. R. was vigorously opposed to godless communism, and he did not hesitate to say so. He took an attitude of loyalty and respect toward those in power in the U.S. government, and gladly gave them the honor which Scripture enjoins. He saw church and state as institutions with quite diverse functions, but he felt that when a philosophy of government was being actively advocated by what appeared to him as men who would stop at nothing, even force, in their attitude of trying to take over control of the world, he could not remain silent. The free world had to be warned against such evil doctrines. People needed to see how anti-Christian the assumptions of communism were—as well as the methods. Someone needed to sound the trumpet and warn the people of the free world so that they would not be duped into accepting the deceptive doctrines of those who were out to destroy the church. At the same time, Geo. R. was a vigorous champion of nonresistant Christianity, for the "weapons" of Christian disciples are not swords of steel—yet their spiritual weapons are "mighty through God" to pull down the strongholds of evil and to demolish "every pretension that sets itself up against the knowledge of God" (2 Cor. 10:5, NIV).

It was a great day for the Mennonite Church when John S. Coffman led the young Geo. R., 17, to the feet of the Savior, a great day when his Uncle Reuben lifted him out of the pit of hopeless despair, a great day when he was ordained to the ministry, and a still greater day when he was made a bishop. For Geo. R. Brunk I was destined to be one of the most gifted and discerning leaders of the Mennonite Church in the first half of the twentieth century.

On one occasion, when he lay at the point of death, far from home and loved ones, and believing that he was about to die, Geo. R. bared his heart to his beloved Katie and his "precious children":

> I am painfully conscious of my own imperfections and unworthiness, and hope only in the mercy of God through the merits of our Lord Jesus Christ.
> I die in the faith as I preached it.
>
> A loving farewell,
> Papa

And after his lamented death on April 30, 1938, there was found among his papers words which remind one of Lincoln's poetic prose—words which could well be set in poetic lines:

> The evening shades are falling.
> My work is fragmentary
> and my strength is broken.
> I know that in the record
> of this life
> There will be much
> in need of pardon,
> And some for which
> I trust and hope
> There may also be
> the smile of divine approval.

Bibliography

See the writings of Geo. R. which are cited in this essay, the biography entitled *Faithfully, Geo. R.* (1978), and the sources cited in the biography, pp. 219, 220.

> "... Always in your heart be a
> preacher, first of all."

55
A. T. Robertson

W. R. Estep, Jr.

Archibald Thomas Robertson (1863-1934) may well have been the greatest Greek scholar of his age or of any other for that matter. Although he possessed a sense of destiny from his youth, he never dared to dream of himself in such grandiose terms. To the contrary, during his student years he was frequently subjected to periods of depression in which he wondered if the Lord could possibly use him in any capacity. Above all else, he was determined, with God's help, to preach the gospel at any cost. It was this unrelenting purpose that compelled him to refuse the invitation to join the faculty of Wake Forest College upon his graduation from that institution in 1885. Once enrolled in the Southern Baptist Theological Seminary, he applied himself in complete abandon to his studies—even to the detriment of his health. In spite of repeated bouts with illnesses, which caused him to despair of life itself, he so distinguished himself that he was invited to become a member of the faculty in October 1888, joining Dr. Broadus in teaching the New Testament. On the threshold of what became a forty-six-year teaching career, the young Professor of Greek and New Testament Interpretation wrote, "I am sure I do not know how to teach, but I am equally determined, by the grace of God, to learn how."

Professor Robertson seldom viewed himself as a teacher, preaching; but much more often as a preacher, teaching. He was a preacher long before he became a seminary professor, having delivered his first sermon to a Negro congregation when not quite seventeen years of age. Even though ordination did not come until July 29, 1888, just two months before he assumed his responsibilities with the seminary, he never relinquished this self-image. It is reflected in the advice he gave Dr. W. J. McGlothlin upon his selection as Professor of Church History, "Now, Mac," Dr. Robertson admonished, "you have been elected to be a teacher here. You must always in your heart be a preacher, first of all."

W. R. Estep, Jr., is Professor of Church History at Southwestern Baptist Theological Seminary. He received the BA from Berea College, the ThM from Southern Baptist Theological Seminary, and his ThD from Southwestern Baptist Theological Seminary. He was engaged in postgraduate studies both in Europe and in America. Among his writings are: *The Anabaptist Story, La Fe de los Apóstoles, Baptists and Christian Unity,* and *Colombia: Land of Conflict and Promise,* also many articles.

For young Archie Robertson the call of God to the gospel ministry was at the same time a call for thorough preparation. An education might have eluded the gifted young man if it had not been for F. M. Purefory, "a godly merchant" and some other friends in Statesville, North Carolina, who were determined that the young preacher would get that college education that his impoverished father could not provide. His father was a physician who was considered wealthy before the Civil War. The war left him bankrupt. He had land but no cash. In an attempt to improve his fortunes, his father moved the family from Virginia to North Carolina when Archie was twelve years of age. But here prosperity escaped him. However, the son was not denied his day of opportunity despite his father's destitution. After six years of exacting studies at Wake Forest Archie received both his Bachelor's and Master's degrees in 1885, graduating as valedictorian of his class. Even though Wake Forest was a relatively new and small Baptist school, its academic standards were the highest. And "Newish" Robertson, as he was known at Wake Forest, made the most of the stimulating intellectual atmosphere. Honors and medals became his usual trophies. He was so well prepared in Greek that during his first year in the seminary he took senior Greek. Assyrian and Patristic Greek were taken in the second year. In addition to Patristic Greek, in his third year, he embarked on a study of German theology and Coptic.

The years as a student at Wake Forest and Southern Seminary were, in some respects, the most important years of Robertson's life. These, indeed, were the formative years. At Wake Forest he developed an almost inexhaustible capacity for hard work which characterized his entire life. It was while in college that he was firmly grounded in a knowledge of the Greek language. His summers were spent preaching. Even though he suffered from a speech impediment which, at times, drove him to despair, neither his handicap nor a delicate physique which was frequently incapacited, could hold him back for long.

The year 1888 was a memorable one in the life of the young professor. Not only did it mark the beginning of his teaching ministry and ordination, it was the year Dwight L. Moody and Ira D. Sankey conducted a six weeks evangelistic campaign in Louisville. Robertson was impressed by Moody, of whom he wrote, "He breaks grammar all too much. But he has a grip on the Bible, human nature and God." Referring to Moody's sermon on the Holy Spirit, he remarked that it was the most enrapturing and heaven-inspiring discourse he had ever heard. Robertson was one of the counselors in the after-meeting. He reports that one evening he talked with a Universalist who was initially perfectly satisfied with himself. "After some time," Robertson writes, "I got him on his knees and persuaded him to pray. He arose with tears of joy in his eyes and said: 'I shall write my wife that I am a Christian.'"

His first task, as a teacher, was to assist his esteemed professor, Dr. John A. Broadus, in Greek and homiletics. Doubtless, it was Broadus who insisted that his young colleague study in Europe since his own year abroad had so enriched his knowledge of theology and the New Testament. From Germany, Robertson wrote of his determination to master the German language in order to use it as a tool during the upcoming fall term. A few months before Dr. Broadus died, Robertson married Broadus' youngest daughter, Ella, on November 22, 1894. His deep appreciation for his mentor and father-in-law was the occasion for the publication of the first of forty-five books. It was a biography entitled, *Life and Letters of John A. Broadus*. An examination of this book leaves one with the distinct impression that Broadus helped to shape the life and ministry of A. T. Robertson far more than perhaps either of them recognized. He shared Broadus' devotion to both biblical authority and thorough scholarship. Indeed, it was Broadus who first gave Robertson the opportunity to demonstrate his competence as a New Testament scholar when he asked him to prepare the critical notes for his *Harmony of the Gospels*. However, Robertson lived to surpass his beloved teacher in both popular acclaim as a preacher and in the quality as well as quantity of his literary production.

It was at Northfield that A. T. Robertson came into his own as an expository preacher. Here he took the bold innovative step of preaching with the Greek New Testament in hand. His penchant for scholarly accuracy was punctuated by keen humor and apt illustrations. Twelve summers, from 1911 to 1923, he preached and lectured at Northfield to thousands. Winona Lake, Princeton, as well as numerous pulpits and universities, vied for his services.

Today, however, almost four decades after his death, few remember Robertson, the preacher, but many still use the works of Robertson, the New Testament scholar. Dr. Robertson began writing his first volume at thirty-eight, and was in the process of making his own translation of the New Testament into English when death overtook him. In addition to his books, numerous articles were written for encyclopedias, scholarly journals, and Bible dictionaries. For a time he was manager of the *Review and Expositor* to which he contributed scores of book reviews. However, the work which served more than any other to establish his reputation as a scholar was his "Big Grammar." After twenty-six years of study which involved a year's research in England and Europe, *A Grammar of the Greek New Testament in Light of Historical Research* was finally ready for the publisher. The first edition which appeared in 1914 contained 1360 pages. In subsequent editions it grew to more than 1500 pages. The "Big Grammar" was received by scholarly circles around the world with a mixture of astonishment, praise, and gratitude. W. F. Moulton of Cambridge declared that it was "not only up to date, but was final on the New Testament." One European scholar declared it, in exaggerated praise, the one and only work of scholarship that the United States had ever produced! Doubtless it was Dr. Bob's *magnum opus*. To it he had devoted much of his life. In his mind it was a service rendered to the Lord. His attitude about such a work is clearly revealed in a phrase that was often on his lips. "I feel as truly led of the Holy Spirit when I am studying Greek roots as the preacher when he is preaching." However, his earlier grammars found a wider use by theological students. Before 1912, his *A Short Grammar of the Greek New Testament* had been translated into Italian, German, French, and Dutch. Many a minister has found his six-volume work, *Word Pictures in the*

New Testament, an invaluable aid to understanding and interpreting the New Testament Scriptures.

The primary task to which Dr. Robertson devoted most of his time was neither preaching nor writing, but teaching. He was, in some respects, a poor teacher. He broke all rules of pedagogy. Few students loved him, but all respected and feared him. He was referred to by his colleagues as "the seminary's official executioner of ministerial pride." The indolent or unprepared, the pretentious and ignorant, he exposed and proceeded to demolish with withering sarcasm. Some students left the seminary after such an encounter. Those who thought Dr. Bob was deliberately malicious were mistaken. His severity with the unprepared student can, in part be explained by the teacher's overwhelming sense of the importance of his task. He was determined to do everything possible to inculcate a thorough knowledge of the New Testament in his students, whom in very truth he actually loved.

Unfortunately, students frequently saw only one side of Dr. Bob's complex personality. Only a few knew of the more gentle aspects of his nature. The love with which he enveloped his family reveals the heart of the man. It was this same quality of gentleness that broke through in his preaching and teaching, particularly when he touched upon the Passion of our Lord. There is no doubt that in both his severity and compassion he felt himself a servant of God. This conviction drove him to be as severe with himself as he was with others. And thus it was when the end came, he was in the classroom, having just begun to lecture. Suddenly he did not feel well. The lecture was never completed. A few hours later the servant was called to meet his Lord and the day was done. The Christian who worshiped freely with those of many different creeds and confessions and who had done much to bring his own Baptist brethren together in the Baptist World Alliance had joined that unbroken fellowship.

Bibliography

Read the many volumes of Dr. Robertson himself.

"Only the Bible conveys a knowledge of God that is ... free from error ... and that answers to the spiritual needs of fallen man."

56
Louis Berkhof

George R. Brunk II

Louis Berkhof (1873-1957) served for thirty-eight years in a teaching career at Calvin Theological Seminary in Grand Rapids, Michigan, first as teacher of Biblical Studies in both Old and New Testament. Later (1926) he took up work in the department of Systematic Theology where he served until his retirement in 1944. During a part of this time he served also as president of the Seminary.

The influence of Dr. Berkhof reached far beyond his classroom activity by means of his off-campus lectures and his published writings. The "Stone Lectures" delivered at Princeton Theological Seminary, 1920-21, were later published under the title *The Kingdom of God* (1951). His classroom lectures were published in 1932 as a two-volume work titled *Reformed Dogmatics*. In 1941 these lectures were revised and published in a single volume of 784 pages as his *Systematic Theology*. This work is appreciated for its systematic arrangement of material for use in theological seminaries where it has been widely accepted all over America.

Dr. Berkhof was an ardent disciple of John Calvin making a strong defense for the Calvinistic predestinarian theology to the point of almost offending the milder men in that tradition. His writings show the influence of the Dutch Reformed theologians Abraham Kuyper and of Herman Bavinck—whose four-volume *Gereformeerde Dogmatiek* was particularly influential in Berkhof's thought. Fred H. Klooster says that "while his (Berkhof's) works are mainly devoted to setting forth positively the Reformed doctrine, this is always done with reference to the historical development of doctrine and with reference to the positions divergent from Reformed theology, especially the RC,

---

George R. Brunk II has served as Dean and Professor of Practical Theology in Eastern Mennonite Seminary in Virginia. He received the ThB from Eastern Mennonite College, the BA from the College of William and Mary, and the BD, ThM, and ThD from Union Theological Seminary (Richmond). Served for a time as a pastor in Newport News, Virginia. Has served extensively as an evangelist ("Brunk Revivals"), and Bible teacher. Associate editor of *The Sword and Trumpet*.

Arminian, and Liberal positions." Berkhof saw in the Neo-Orthodox theologians, Karl Barth and Emil Brunner, deviations from the historic orthodox Reformed theology of which he became such an able defender. Berkhof attempted to state and refute the various non-Calvinistic positions, the Arminian position in particular. In some instances he appears to have somewhat belabored his defense of the difficult doctrine of Reprobation.

In addition to his *Systematic Theology* Berkhof also wrote an *Introductory Volume to Systematic Theology*. His *History of Christian Doctrine* of 1937 gives a survey of the historical development of Christian doctrine from the days of the apostles to Albrecht Ritschl. He also wrote a *Manual of Christian Doctrine* for use on the college level. This was somewhat of a condensation of his vastly larger *Systematic Theology*. He later made a further revision of this for use on the high school level as a *Summary of Christian Doctrine*. Berkhof also wrote *The Assurance of Faith* (1928), *Vicarious Atonement Through Christ* (1936), *Principles of Biblical Interpretation* (1950), *Aspects of Liberalism* (1951), and *The Second Coming of Christ* (1953).

Bibliography

A good introduction to the thought of Berkhof is his *Systematic Theology*, first published in two volumes, later as one.

"No substitute will ever be found for the knowledge of the Word of God."[1]

57
Lewis Sperry Chafer

Henry J. Harder

His Life and Ministry

Lewis Sperry Chafer (1871-1952), founder and president for twenty-eight years of Dallas Theological Seminary, was born to the Reverend Thomas Franklin Chafer and Lois Lomira Sperry Chafer on February 27, 1871, at Rock Creek, Ashtabula County, Ohio. Dr. Chafer's paternal grandfather, William Chafer, was born in York, England. His maternal grandmother, Ann Sperry was of Irish descent. Dr. Chafer received his early education at the public schools in Rock Creek, and at the New Lyme Institute of New Lyme, Ohio, and Oberlin College and Conservatory of Music.

While teaching music at East Northfield Boys School, Dr. and Mrs. Chafer also took part in the service of music at the Moody Summer Bible Conferences. It was here that he learned to know Ira D. Sankey, D. B. Towner, George Stebbins, and many others in the field of music. He also came to know such evangelists, preachers, and teachers as Moody, Scofield, Morgan, and Griffith Thomas. Chafer was rapidly becoming known, not only as a musician, but also as an evangelist and Bible teacher. He concluded his teaching ministry at Northfield Boys School and gave his full time to public meetings and writing. His first book, *Outline Studies in the Science of Music*, was written while still at Northfield. His second book, *Satan*, appeared in 1909, and *True Evangelism* in 1911.

A close association between Chafer and C. I. Scofield developed. Scofield saw in Chafer the gifts of a Bible teacher. One morning in Scofield's study at what is now the Scofield Memorial Church in Dallas, Scofield laid his hands on Chafer and dedicated him to the service of the Lord as a Bible teacher. This was an experience of affirmation never to be forgotten by either of the men.

Henry J. Harder is pastor of the Central Mennonite Brethren Church in Shafter, Calif. He earned his ThB in the Pacific Bible Institute, also the AB; and the ThM and the ThD at the Dallas Theological Seminary. He also studied at the Pacific School of Religion and at the Hebrew Union College in Los Angeles. For many years he was Professor of Old Testament and Registrar of the Mennonite Brethren Biblical Seminary, Fresno, Calif.

In 1915 Chafer's book *The Kingdom in History and Prophecy* was published, and in 1916 came the book on *Salvation*. *He That Is Spiritual* reached the public in 1918, and in 1922 his work on *Grace* appeared.

In the winter of 1921, at a hotel in Atlanta, Georgia, Chafer met with Dr. Alexander B. Winchester, pastor of Knox Presbyterian Church in Toronto, and W. H. Griffith Thomas, former professor at Oxford University. After a day of prayer it was decided to announce their intention to found a school and that a suitable location was being sought. Two years later, while Chafer was conducting meetings at the First Presbyterian Church in Dallas, Dr. William M. Anderson, pastor of the church, suggested that the school be located in Dallas. Immediately a temporary board was organized. In 1924 the new school, known as the Evangelical Theological College, opened with a dozen students enrolled. Dr. Chafer with Dr. Anderson and Professor A. Perpetuo formed the resident faculty. Dr. W. H. Griffith Thomas was appointed to teach theology but died suddenly just before the school opened its doors. As a result of this sudden and tragic loss, Dr. Lewis Chafer took up the task of teaching theology, a task that shaped his teaching and preaching ministry for the years to follow. His book *Major Bible Themes* appeared in 1926. In the same year Wheaton College honored Chafer with the degree of Doctor of Divinity—the first of his three honorary degrees. In 1935 his last popular book, the *Ephesian Letter*, was published.

In 1937 Chafer began work on an unabridged *Systematic Theology*. Much of the material appeared first in *Bibliotheca Sacra*, the oldest theological quarterly in America, of which Chafer became the editor in 1940. The eight-volume *Systematic Theology* was finally published in 1948.

After an illness of eight weeks in the summer of 1952, on August 22 Dr. Chafer passed into the presence of the Lord whom he loved so well and served so long. He was 81. His was a long and faithful ministry as musician, evangelist, Bible teacher, theologian, writer, editor, and educator. His oral ministry covered a period of sixty years. His classroom ministry extended over a period of nearly forty years.

Dr. Chafer's Bible study was intensely inductive. He sought earnestly to make his *Systematic Theology* strictly biblical in its approach and content. Dr. Chafer once stated, "The very fact that I did not study a prescribed course in theology made it possible for me to approach the subject with an unprejudiced mind and to be concerned only with what the Bible actually teaches."[2]

His Theology

Chafer's major distinctive contributions lay in the areas of bibliology, Christology and soteriology, and ecclesiology and eschatology.

Bibliology

Perhaps nothing shaped Chafer's theology so much as his unswerving conviction in the absolute authority of the Bible and in the infallibility and inerrancy of its text. Coupled with this was the conviction that in order to arrive at the precise meaning of the text, certain rules of interpretation must be stringently followed and applied. The first hermeneutical rule listed by Chafer in his *Doctrinal Summarization* is that Scripture must be interpreted grammatically. As a result of this emphasis, Dallas Theological Seminary has over the years emphasized the study of the original languages and the application of this hermeneutical principle to the original text. Chafer states,

> Apart from the knowledge of the original languages in which the Bible was written, there can be no very accurate conclusions as to what a difficult passage teaches. For this reason the study of both Hebrew and Greek to the extent that worthy exegesis is one's own right is undertaken as most essential...."[3]

Christology and Soteriology

Chafer believed and taught that Christ is Deity in the full and absolute sense, and that He took upon Himself a perfect and complete human nature—that these two natures, the divine and the human, were united forever in the person of Christ. As for the death of Christ, Chafer taught that it was substitutionary, and that in its extent Scripture declares Christ's death to be for the whole world.

Relative to the five elective decrees of Calvinism, Chafer classified himself as a sublapsarion, i.e., a moderate Calvinist. The logical order of the divine decrees, which he found in Scripture are: (1) the decree to create all men, (2) the decree to permit the Fall, (3) the decree to elect those who believe, and to leave in just condemnation those who do not believe, (4) the decree to provide salvation for men, and (5) the decree to apply salvation to those who believe.

Chafer believed and taught that salvation was, in its entirety, a work of Jehovah (Jonah 2:9; Psalm 3:8):

> The truth that salvation is of Jehovah is sustained both by revelation and by reason. As for revelation, it is the testimony of the Scriptures, without exception, that every feature of man's salvation from its inception to the final perfection in heaven is a work of God for man and not a work of man for God.[4]

With respect to the human will, Chafer observes that

> ...God did not create the human will as an instrument to defeat Himself; it was created rather as a means by which He might realize His own worthy purposes.... God does not coerce the human will.... The divine invitation still is true that 'whosoever will may come.' However, it also is true that none will ever come apart from this divine call...[5]

Ecclesiology and Eschatology

Dr. Chafer's moderate dispensationalism (he strenuously opposed hyperdispensationalism) was especially evident in his approach to the doctrine of the church and in the doctrines of last things. He carefully distinguished God's purposes for the church and God's purposes for Israel. His hermeneutics did not allow him to confuse the two. The church is a new order or class of humanity, namely a redeemed company taken from both Jews and Gentiles, and, together with the resurrected Christ, form a new creation which is His body and His bride. This company is being called out in the present age which is bounded by the two advents of Christ—an age which was not unforeseen by God nor undetermined by Him, but which Chafer terms "intercalary" in that it was unforeseen by the prophets in the divine program for the Jews.

In his eschatology Chafer was pretribulational and premillennial. He taught that the church, which began at Pentecost, would be taken in rapture and translation prior to the establishment of Daniel's seventieth week (the tribulation). He taught that the tribulation will begin when the Antichrist makes a covenant with Israel (Dan. 9:27), that it will last a week of years (seven years), and that it will end with the second coming of Christ in judgment. At this time Christ will establish a reign of peace lasting for one thousand years (Rev. 20).

Chafer has given Christendom a massive and thorough theology, written from the stance of Dispensationalism.

Brief Bibliography

Bibliotheca Sacra, Dallas Theological Seminary. Since 1934 Dr. Chafer served on the staff of *Bibliotheca Sacra*, first as department editor in systematic theology, then as literary and managing editor from 1940. A wealth of material, relative to his thinking on particular theological issues, is given in this quarterly. A sketch of his life and ministry begins in the July-September, 1952, issue and concludes in the October-December, 1952, issue.

Chafer, Lewis Sperry, *Systematic Theology*. 8 vols.; Dallas: Dallas Seminary Press, 1948. The seven major divisions of *Systematic Theology* are completed in Chafer's first four volumes. Volume five concerns itself with *Christology* and volume six with *Pneumatology*. Volume seven continues his doctrinal summarization and volume eight the index. Also included in volume eight is a biographical sketch of the author by a close friend and associate Dr. C. F. Lincoln. The biography concludes with the year 1947, five years prior to Dr. Chafer's death.

Lincoln, C. F., *Lewis Sperry Chafer, Man of God*. This is a biographical pamphlet written by this close friend and associate of Dr. Chafer. It treats Dr. Chafer's life and ministry under the headings, A Man of Prayer, A Student of the Scriptures, An Exponent of Holy Writ, A Man Who Walked with God, and A Personal Worker.

Walvoord, John F., *The Life and Ministry of Lewis Sperry Chafer*. This is a reprint of an article which appeared in the *Sunday School Times*.

Footnotes

1. Lewis Sperry Chafer, *Systematic Theology*, I, p. vi.
2. Lewis Sperry Chafer, *Systematic Theology*, VIII, pp. 5-6.
3. Lewis Sperry Chafer, *Systematic Theology*, I, p. 118.
4. Lewis Sperry Chafer, *Systematic Theology*, III, p. 6.
5. Lewis Sperry Chafer, *Systematic Theology*, VII, p. 136.

> "Modern liberalism may be criticized (1) on the ground that it is unchristian and (2) on the ground that it is unscientific."

58
J. Gresham Machen

Grant M. Stoltzfus

The years of J. Gresham Machen (1881-1937) spanned a critical period in the life of American Protestantism. In his lifetime American society underwent change from rural to urban; from predominately Protestant to "post-Protestant"; from widespread acceptance of traditional biblical authority to the challenges of comparative religion, Darwinism, biblical criticism, and the social demands of a fermenting industrial order. Amidst the transitions and conflicts Machen is remembered as an exponent of an orthodox Christianity and for opposition to the growing centralization of government in an age of spreading technology.

A Baltimore-born bachelor, Machen was descended from families of English origin on both sides. He grew up to hold deep respect for Southern traditions and was a member of the Southern Presbyterian Church till his ordination in 1914 as a minister of the Presbyterian Church of the United States of America. At the early age of 18 he showed his attachment to the Gresham ancestral home in Macon, Georgia, when he described in lyrical language the "dear old home in the midst of waving magnolia trees and its fragrant roses ... the balmy southern air accented with flowers ... the real, old-fashioned, kind-hearted southern darkies ... the table groans with the weight of a Georgian supper."

Machen was the son of a successful lawyer and a mother who possessed great intellectual power and a strong Christian faith. His early education was strongly classical and in 1901 he graduated with honors from Johns Hopkins University, where he remained for a year of graduate study in the classics. In 1902 he entered Princeton Theological Seminary, "a gibraltar of orthodoxy and a school of eminent scholarship." He received a BD (1905) from the seminary, as well as an MA from the university (1904).

Grant M. Stoltzfus (1916-1974) was Professor of History at Eastern Mennonite College. He received the BA from Goshen College, the MA at the University of Pittsburgh, and the BD and ThD at Union Theological Seminary (Richmond). His most significant book is entitled *Mennonites of the Ohio and Eastern Conference*.

A year's study at the universities of Marburg and Göttingen brought him into clear confrontation with Wilhelm Herrmann of the Ritschlian school of theology. He was captivated by Herrmann's learning and warm personality but ultimately came to the conviction (which was to dominate his later life and thought) that here was a system of theology which, if it were to prevail, would be the death knell of historic Christianity.

Upon his return from Germany, he became an instructor and later assistant professor at Princeton Theological Seminary in the field of New Testament exegesis. He remained on the Princeton faculty from 1906 to 1929, interrupted only by a period of overseas service under the YMCA in World War I. As a teacher and preacher Machen acquired a reputation for clarity of expression and for powerful and analytical lectures and sermons.

The thought and influence of J. Gresham Machen are best understood in the context of the dichotomy that developed in American Protestantism in the later nineteenth and early twentieth century. It is commonly known as the "fundamentalist-modernist" controversy; it became a live issue in the major denominations and also in many smaller ones. It was Machen's alignment with conservative Christianity which made him become a great exponent, some say the most scholarly, of the "fundamentalist" side. (He preferred not to be called a "fundamentalist"; he regarded his version of Christianity to be rather that of historic Calvinism. For example, he was cautious in his views on the origin of the species. Though opposed to evolution to the extent of its involving a philosophy of materialism, he was too much the scholar to pose as a competent judge in such fields as biology and geology. He was also not a premillennialist.)

In the liberalism of his day Machen saw a deadly foe to the Christian faith, and from about 1912 onward his main preoccupation was to wage warfare against this peril to Christianity. In his own church the conflict became serious as the lines of battle were drawn in theological education, in its doctrinal beliefs, and in the policy that governed its foreign missions.

Machen's theology was built on a conception of the historical or factual nature of Christianity. In the first sentence of his inaugural address at Princeton he stated, "The student of the New Testament should be primarily an historian." It was his steadfast conviction that Christianity could hold its own under the scientific scrutiny to which modern man subjected it. He applied the historic and scientific method to biblical study and set forth his clear reasons for accepting and defending (1) the verbal and plenary inspiration of the Scriptures, (2) the virgin birth, (3) the deity of Christ, (4) the bodily resurrection, and (5) the miracles of Christ.

In defending the above Machen used the classroom, the printed page, and the pulpit. Later, he resorted to forming independent ecclesiastical organizations in the fields of theological education (the founding of Westminster Seminary in 1929), in missionary activity (the founding of the Independent Board for Presbyterian Foreign Missions in 1933), and in organizing a separate ecclesiastical body in 1936 (after being unfrocked for insubordination by his church).

In addition to these ecclesiastical efforts, Machen carried his views into the wider forum of American thought by writing articles for learned journals such as *The Annals* of the American Academy of Political and Social Science, *Forum, Survey Graphic,* and also for a leading newspaper, *The New York Times.* It is of interest to note that Walter Lippmann regarded Machen's *Christianity and Liberalism* as "an admirable book," praising it for its "acumen," and for being "the best popular argument produced in the controversy between Christianity and Liberalism." *The Literary Digest,* a leading national weekly newsmagazine, featured prominently the role and position of Machen in his criticism of the Presbyterian Board of Foreign Missions and of Mrs. Pearl S. Buck, a distinguished author and a missionary under the board, and one who held to what Machen viewed as unsound doctrines.

It is as a writer of books and articles that Machen can be studied today. His numerous works are largely apologetic. They are clearly documents of the time and show the battle scars of the fierce theological controversy that raged in his lifetime. Frequently the books grew out of lectures and sermons and, though popular in style, they contain the tightly reasoned arguments of a well-honed mind. Firm in his belief that historic Christian theology should understand and pervade contemporary culture, he opposed to the end what he considered dangerous concessions to liberalism—a viewpoint which he considered to be unchristian and a derivative of plain naturalism.

Machen's suspension from the ministry as a schismatic in 1935-1936, following the formality of a trial, led him to sever himself completely from his church and to form the Presbyterian Church of America, which later became the Orthodox Presbyterian Church. He died on January 1, 1937, while on a tour of the Midwest in the interests of the newly formed denomination.

Bibliographical Notes

A seminal work of J. Gresham Machen is his *Christianity and Liberalism* (1923) in which he makes perhaps the clearest statement of the antithesis between Christian orthodoxy and liberalism. In *The Origin of Paul's Religion* (1921), he treats the Christianity of Paul as being in accord with historic reality. His *magnum opus, The Virgin Birth of Jesus Christ* (1930: second edition, 1932), is the fruitage of long years of biblical and historical studies. A lucid statement on the intellectual content of Christian belief, *What Is Faith?* (1925), presents his firm reply to the charge that Christianity is anti-intellectual. For a succinct and readable summary of Machen's views one can refer to the series of radio addresses which were given in 1935 and published in *The Christian Faith in the Modern World* (1936).

Other major works include *God Transcendent and Other Sermons* (1949), *The Christian View of Man* (1949), *The Literature and History of New Testament Times* (1915), and *What Is Christianity?* (1951).

For a sympathetic and thorough biography the reader should consult N. B. Stonehouse, *J. Gresham Machen: A Biographical Memoir* (1954). An autobiographical sketch appears in Vergilius Ferm, ed., *Contemporary American Theology* (1932). An indispensable source for understanding the internal life of the Presbyterian Church is Lefferts A. Loetscher, *The Broadening Church: A Study of Theological Issues in the Presbyterian Church Since 1869.* The chapters dealing with the 1920s set forth the role of Machen in clear context; the book contains a valuable summary of the transitions of the Presbyterian Church in rapid social and intellectual changes.

The life and thought of Machen have been the topics for at least two graduate theses: Dallas M. Roark, "J. Gresham Machen and His Desire to Maintain a Doctrinally True Presbyterian Church" (typed PhD thesis, University of Iowa, 1963) and Charles William McNutt, "The Fundamentalism of J. Gresham Machen" (typed ThM thesis, Union Theological Seminary at Richmond, 1952).

"Was sagt das Wort?" (What does the Word say?)

59
A. H. Unruh

A. J. Klassen

Abraham Heinrich Unruh was born in a small village in the Russian Crimea on April 5, 1878, the seventh child in a family of ten. His father, Heinrich Benjamin Unruh, an elder in the Mennonite Church, died when his son was only five years old. Young Abraham was adopted and educated by his uncle, a teacher in a *Zentralschule* (high school) and minister in the Mennonite Church. He completed high school at fifteen and enrolled in the pedagogical classes in Halbstadt. Upon graduation two years later young Unruh launched out on a teaching career that was to span sixty years in Russia, Canada, and the United States.

His first year of teaching was marked by a great turning point in his life: he found salvation in Christ and became a member of the Mennonite Brethren Church. His desire to serve Christ found expression in conducting children's services and youth meetings on Sunday afternoons. At the turn of the century he married Katharine Toews. Six of their children reached adulthood. Ordination to the ministry at the age of 26 led to a very fruitful combination of teaching and preaching. He served as instructor in German and religion at a middle school *(Kommerzschule)* for some nine years. During World War I he was a medical corpsman in the Red Cross. Upon his discharge he returned to the middle school and served as principal for two years.

In 1920 he became an instructor at the Tschongraw Bible School, the first Mennonite Brethren institution of its kind, modeled after the Baptist *Predigerseminar* in Hamburg. When the government closed the institution in 1924 Unruh sensed that time for the Christian ministry in Russia was running out, so he emigrated to Canada with his family, settling in Winkler, Manitoba. Here he founded the Peniel Bible School and became a much appreciated instructor, adviser, and confidant to many young people during his nineteen-year tenure. His travels in support of the school took him across Canada and the

---

A. J. Klassen has served as Dean and Professor of Theology in the Mennonite Brethren Biblical Seminary in California. He received the BA at the University of British Columbia, the MA at the Wheaton Graduate School of Theology, the BD at Goshen Biblical Seminary, the STM at Union College, and the PhD from the Claremont Graduate School. He and N. P. Springer are coauthors of a massive two-volume *Mennonite Bibliography*.

United States. Thus he became a leading figure in the General Conference of the Mennonite Brethren, and beyond it. (One of his admirers was Harold S. Bender.) Tabor College granted him the BTh degree, and Bethel College honored him with a DD in 1938. The Canadian conference called him to be the first president of the Mennonite Brethren Bible College in 1944, where he served as professor for ten years.

Although he took graduate studies in Russian, mathematics, and music, he was largely a self-taught man, but well acquainted with the teachings of the Reformers, the Anabaptists, and such modern theologians as Barth and Brunner. However, Bible teaching and expository preaching were his first love and his greatest contribution to the brotherhood. A colleague eloquently describes him as a "master of the expositional sermon." Twenty-three consecutive appearances at the annual Winnipeg Bible conferences testify to his ability. He aimed to convey a message rather than an elaborate outline, and was more concerned that his listeners remember the text than his sermon. He was concerned to address the whole person, not only to enlighten the mind and to stir the emotion, but also to move the will. On one occasion a prominent personality complimented him with "I admire your oratorical talent," to which Unruh replied: "I would much rather you admired my Lord Jesus." Popular demand prompted the publication of some of his choice sermon outlines in *Zwei-und-fünfzig Predigentwürfe.*

Unruh was not a scientific theologian, or a theoretical dogmatician, but a thoroughly biblical theologian. His book studies: *Der Prophet Jesaja* [The Prophet Isaiah], *Der ewige Sohn Gottes: Erbauliche Vorträge aus dem Hebräerbrief* [The Eternal Son of God: Edifying Lectures from the Hebrew Letter], and *Einundfünfzig Vorträge über das Buch der Offenbarung* [Fifty-one Messages on the Apocalypse], are excellent examples of expository preaching at its best.

His preaching strongly underlined the final authority of Scriptures. Since he never had opportunity to master the original languages, he carefully compared translations and frequently asked his colleagues "How does this passage read in the original? I don't want to be in error." In the best Mennonite Brethren tradition he often asked the penetrating question "Was sagt das Wort?" (What does the Word say?) and insisted on its application to faith and life. He frequently warned fellow ministers against diluting the authority of Scripture by offering an admixture of personal opinion and biblical truth.

Unruh understood the church to be the body of Christ. The ultimate goal of the Christian should be to glorify Christ in the church. This view of the church led him to relate his own denomination to other evangelical groups. He understood the Mennonite Brethren contribution to be in three areas: biblical thinking *(Denken),* a scripturally oriented church life, and a sober social life.

It is quite natural that the Christian life and ethics held a prominent place in Unruh's theology. He insisted that theology must find practical application in life. Thus he spoke to such issues as the generation gap, salvation, Christian nurture, Christian maturity, church discipline, sanctification, and separation. True Christians will experience both the forgiving and disciplining grace of God. However, discipline must be redemptive and must be carried out in a spirit of meekness, love, and compassion. He stressed the need for nonconformity, and warned against carnality. His insistence on practical application led to stressing a healthy balance in both the message and performance of music, the need for psychology and pedagogy in education, the role of science and the Bible in a balanced view of life, the importance of dogma and ethics in preaching, and the interrelationship of preservation and sanctification in Christian living.

Unruh was remarkably open to new trends of thought. He was confident that his younger colleagues would benefit through advanced theological study. He also advocated theological study abroad. Instead of viewing European theology as a threat, he held that the cross-fertilization of American and European theology would lead to a fruitful synthesis.

Unruh tended to be a "middle of the road" theologian. He was well aware of the inroads that certain eschatological interpretations were making into the Mennonite Brethren Church, and critically analyzed their implications in a study conference paper, "Die Grundzeuge der Theologie der Vaeter der M.B. Gemeinde" [The Theology of the M.B. Founding Fathers], based on the *Confession of Faith.* When interest in the minutiae of prophecy and dispensationalism ran high, he firmly held to the traditional premillennial interpretation, but warned against dangerous intellectual "additions" to the Revelation.

Unruh's biographer characterizes him as an intercessor, teacher, preacher, and writer. His writings include numerous sermons that appeared in the periodicals, *Zionsbote, Mennonitische Rundschau,* and the *Voice,* also a handful of pamphlets compiled for classroom use, curriculum materials for Sunday school, *Die Antwort* (a monthly paper for preachers), exegetical series, and sermon outlines.

Although not a trained historiographer, he deeply appreciated history, especially the history of his own denomination. He was much concerned about individuals who ignored their own historical roots and thereby neglected their spiritual heritage. The Mennonite Brethren Church is indebted to him for preserving and transmitting their historical heritage in his *magnum opus: Die Geschichte der Mennoniten Bruedergemeinde* [History of the M.B. Brotherhood], 1954, 847 pages.

Unruh began his last sermon on January 6, 1961, the 101st anniversary of his own denomination. A sudden illness prevented him from completing the message. He died on January 15, 1961.

Brief Bibliography

Primary sources by A. H. Unruh:
1. *Die Mennonitische Bibelschule in Tschongraw*
2. *Eine Anleitung für die Lehrer der Sonntagsschule*
3. *Leitfaden für den Religionsunterricht*
4. *Nikodemus: Wie kommt man ins Reich Gottes?*
5. *Zweindfünfzig Predigtenwürfe*
6. *Gottes Wort als Wegweiser für die Gemeindezucht*

7. *Des Herrn Mahnung an die Gemeinde der Endzeit*
8. *Der ewige Sohn Gottes (Erbauliche Vorträge aus dem Hebräerbrief)*
9. *Der Prophet Jesaja (Der erste Teil ist ins Englische Übersetzt worden)*
10. *Einundfünfzig Vorträge über das Buch der Offenbarung*
11. *Die Geschichte der Mennoniten-Brüdergemeinde*
12. *Die Antwort*, edited by A. H. Unruh
13. *Zeugne's der Schrift*, co-edited by A. H. Unruh

Secondary Sources:
1. Ewert, "In Memoriam: A. H. Unruh, DD, 1878-1961," *The Voice*, (Jan.-Feb., 1961), pp. 1-2.
2. Toews, H. P., *A. H. Unruh's Lebensgeschichte.*
3. Toews, J. A., "A. H. Unruh, D.D.: Christian Educator and Practical Theologian," *Mennonite Brethren Herald* (Oct. 21, 1968), pp. 13-51.

> "The wealth of the church does not rest in vast cathedrals nor in the majestic notes of organs but in the words of Jesus: 'Behold, I stand at the door and knock.'"

60
Karl Heim

H. D. Burkholder

Karl Heim was born at Frauenzimmern, Württemberg, Germany, January 20, 1874. As a young man he studied at the Tübingen School of Theology. Active in church ministries, he soon became involved in the German Christian Student Movement. As an assistant to John R. Mott he always sought to confront men with the claims of Christ. He was secretary of that organization from 1899 to 1902. In 1903 he became a tutor at the Theological Seminary of the Silesian Church.

He taught systematic theology at the University at Halle from 1907-14. From 1914-20 he served in a similar capacity at the University of Münster. In 1920 he became the Professor of Systematic Theology at Tübingen, his alma mater.

Heim was a master in the pulpit. When he delivered the sermon in the Stiftskirche in Tübingen, the building was filled to capacity. Among his most ardent listeners were the humble peasant-folk of that area.

As a lecturer he participated in many conventions throughout the world, including China and the United States. In 1935 he delivered the Sprunt Lectures at the Union Theological Seminary, Richmond, Virginia.

After a rich life of teaching, preaching, and writing, he died August 30, 1958. The tributes given to him, in the memorial service in Stiftskirche, included his large range of interests as theologian, philosopher, musician, painter, swimmer, and mountaineer.

Of the many religious voices which rose above the whirl of ideas in postwar Germany, the two most significant were those of Karl Barth and Karl Heim. The name of Barth is well known to those who have an

---

H. D. Burkholder graduated from Moody Bible Institute, received the BA and MA from George Pepperdine College, and the BD and DD from the Reformed Episcopal Seminary; he did additional study at Willamette University. He has served as Vice-President, as Dean of Men, and as President of Grace Bible Institute in Omaha. More recently he has been Director of the Pastoral Ministries Department. He has had wide pastoral experience, and has traveled extensively in many lands. He is the author of *A History of the Pacific District Conference*. He is presently pastoring a Mennonite Church at Elbing, Kan.

interest in recent theological thought. The name Heim, the elder of the two, is still comparatively unknown in this country. Within Germany itself, his works have received an equal response to those of Barth.

Heim's main interest has been in the area of apologetics. While Barth is a prophet who shakes men's hearts by a language that is often defiant and violent in paradox, Heim is the thinker who from the quietness of his study challenges the minds of men with God's call for decision. He had great influence on the younger generation at the University of Tübingen.

As a writer, the first book to attract attention was *Das Weltbild der Zukunft* (The Idea of the Universe in the Coming Time) published in 1904.

His writings are marked by a freshness and originality of thought and expression. In 1931 Heim launched a six-volume project called *The Christian Faith and Contemporary Thought.* The series was completed in 1952.

The first volume, *Glaube und Denken*, translated as *God Transcendent*, dealt almost entirely with the theistic foundation of the Christian faith, namely, the doctrine of God. In *Jesus the Lord* he attempts to answer the question: "Is Jesus Christ merely a great personality of the past or is He the living Lord who can tell us with authority what we are to do about the burning questions of the present?" The book draws the inescapable conclusion that man has no hope unless he receives help from someone else, namely, Jesus the Lord. In *Jesus the World's Perfecter* we have a fuller account of the words and deeds of Jesus. He presents our Lord as One engaged in conflict with satanic power. Central to his discussion of the atonement is his emphasis on the objective significance of the work of Christ.

The second coming of Christ is not a matter of world progress toward some far-off divine event. However, it will be of such a nature that all men will see it. Heim's view invites us to take seriously the language of the Book of Revelation, which portrays the conflict between the exalted Christ and the kingdoms of this world.

Christian Faith and Natural Science presents a new kind of apologetics. Here we have the author's attempt to understand the divine transcendence, and the nature and function of science. This volume, like the others, helps to confirm one's faith in divine revelation, not against the findings of science, but in the light of them. Heim refuses to sell out the miraculous or to liberalize the Christian faith.

The Transformation of the Scientific World View calls attention to the breakdown of Newtonian physics and the apparent disappearance of the law of causality as traditionally understood. From this he draws certain conclusions which he considers of apologetic value for the development of a Christian world view. The only absolute which is left is a transcendent God who is the Head of all creation and who puts His claim upon every member of the human race.

It is encouraging to see a competent scholar, prompted by a deep appreciation for scientific research, develop a system which keeps God at the center of things. Heim was once praised by Albert Einstein for his insight into the theory of relativity.

The final book in his six-volume project, *The World: Its Creation and Consummation*, was completed in 1952. In this volume he correlates the biblical view of creation with modern cosmology and biology. He speaks of man as the crown of earthly being. He states that the order of creation in Genesis is in accord with the findings of science. He also correlates biblical eschatology with the scientific anticipation of the world's end. By the law of entrophy we are taught that death awaits the universe.

Heim concluded his lifework with the following statement: "The aim of the whole project from the beginning was to proclaim the Gospel of the redeeming power of Christ to a world which to a large extent rejects and contests the Gospel" (p. 151). Heim always sought a way to make the Christian faith relevant to the modern mind. The very fact that his last three volumes dealt with modern science is an indication of what he believed to be the concern of modern thinking.

Today innumerable theologians in Britain and America, as well as the continent of Europe, acknowledge their indebtedness to this profound and versatile thinker. Few people realize that his last books were written in his eighties while suffering from a heart disease.

Heim's name will live chiefly perhaps through his great distinction in the field of the philosophy of religion, but also because of his work as a Christian apologist. Harold S. Bender sat in his classes and deeply appreciated him as a profound intellectual with a firm faith in Christ.

Some historians have referred to him as one of the greatest theologians of the Lutheran Church. He has also been classified as the most modern representative of the Pietism of Württemberg.

Brief Bibliography

Books:
God Transcendent: Charles Scribner's Sons, New York, 1936; *Jesus, the Lord:* Fortress Press, Philadelphia, Pa., 1961; *Jesus, the World's Perfector:* Fortress Press, Philadelphia, Pa., 1961; *The World: Its Creation and Consummation:* Fortress Press, Philadelphia, Pa., 1962; *Christian Faith and Natural Science:* Harper Bros., New York, 1953; *The Transformation of the Scientific World View:* Harper Bros., New York, 1953; *The Gospel of the Cross:* Zondervan, Grand Rapids, Mich., 1937.

Magazine Articles:
Homer, P. L., "Karl Heim and Sacrifice of Intellect," *Lutheran Quarterly* 6:207-19, August 1954; Wittemore, R. C., "Karl Heim: panentheism and the space of God," *Concordia Theological Monthly*, 30:824-37, November 1959; *Lutheran Quarterly* 15:250-65, August 1965, "Main types of the doctrine of the atonement," Karl Heim; Barker, E., "Germany's new religion," *Spectator* 159:306-7, August 20, 1937; *International Review of Missions* 17:133-44, January 1928, "Message of the New Testament to the non-Christian world," Karl Heim.

61
Karl Barth

Clarence Bauman

Karl Barth (1886-1968) has exerted the greatest single influence upon Protestant thought in this century. Whether one welcomes or opposes his ideas, no one who wishes to understand contemporary theology can afford to ignore them. To comprehend his thought is an arduous but not unrewarding task.

Barth cannot be understood apart from his involvement in the historical and cultural developments of the twentieth century, for his theology is the product of his dialogue with its scientific and philosophic movements. At confirmation young Karl, already wrestling with the medieval proofs for God's existence and the orthodox theories of inspiration, resolved to be a theologian. At university his leading lights were Kant and Schleiermacher. After studying at Bern, Berlin, Tübingen, and Marburg, Barth was ordained in 1908 at the age of twenty-two. Following a brief stint as journalist in Marburg, he was appointed vicar in Geneva. From there he transferred to the parish at Safenwil in Aargau, Switzerland, where he labored ten decisive years exegeting the Book of Romans and comparing notes with his colleague Edward Thurneysen on the opposite side of the mountain. Together they frequently journeyed to Bad Boll in Württemberg to hear Christian Blumhardt proclaim the message of the kingdom of God and to observe how this great preacher brought the compassion of God to bear upon the daily life of man in all its redeeming power.

In his exegetical work on Romans Barth desperately sought answers to the critical atheism of modern man. Like the sudden clang of a bell the publication of his *Römerbrief* in 1919 startled much of the Western world. Two years later he accepted a lectureship at the University of Göttingen without, however, neglecting the pulpit ministry which he always considered "the proper arena of the kingdom of God." From 1925 to 1930 Barth was professor at Münster, where he published a volume of essays and the *Prolegomenon* to his

---

Clarence Bauman is Professor of Theology and Ethics in the Associated Mennonite Biblical Seminaries, Elkhart, Indiana. He received the BA from the University of British Columbia, the BD from Fuller Theological Seminary, the Dr. Theol. from the University of Bonn, and the PhD from the University of Edinburgh. He is the author of a definitive work, *Gewaltlosigkeit im Taeufertum*.

dogmatics. For the next five years Barth transferred to Bonn, where he witnessed Hitler's rise to power and tyranny. For refusing to swear the Hitler oath, Barth was exiled from Germany in 1935. He took refuge in Basel, the city of his birth, from where he gave leadership to the German *Kirchenkampf* and the Swiss Resistance Movement. In the course of teaching three decades at Basel, Barth produced the formidable thirteen-volume *Church Dogmatics*, the most massive work of its kind since the Middle Ages, although unfinished.

In the first instance Barth's theology was a theology of correction directed against the old liberal emphasis on the immanence of God which minimized the "otherness" of God and practically affirmed the deity of man. Barth confronted the chronic presumption of the evolutionary ideal of man saving himself with the radical gospel dualism of the righteousness of God over against the sinfulness of man. Up to this point continental theology regarded itself as the inner aspect of culture, as that which gave coherent expression to the liberal humanist spirit. Barth, however, discovered the strange new world of the Bible which claims to be the primary Word of God and, as such, challenges all the scientific presuppositions of liberalism. Barth's insistence that obedience to the Word of God frees the theologian from all presuppositions resulted in a Copernican revolution in theology—which in turn inspired Bonhoeffer to explore the meaning of this freedom for Christian discipleship.

Second, Barth attacked the "religious experience" which Schleiermacher (1768-1834) (the so-called father of liberal theology) had advocated, as an altogether inadequate basis for bridging the gap between earth and heaven. For when religious experience becomes the cult of one's own enjoyment and self-sufficiency, it has degenerated into a cancerous subjectivism by which man tries to survive spiritually by feeding on his own ideas as a sheep caught in a snowdrift tries to survive by feeding on its own wool. Barth maintains that encounter with the Word of God takes us beyond subjective experience to a concrete encounter with God Himself. The moment religion takes joy in its existence and considers itself indispensable, it falls away from its inner character and ceases to be the truth. In fact, religion has a right to exist only to the extent that it calls in question its self-evidence. But the moment organized religion becomes self-consciously self-evident, it has become irreligion—an existentialist critique which Barth applied to the cultivation and perpetuation of sacramental rites, liturgical forms, and devotional exercises, all of which may become barriers between the soul and God.

Third, early Barthian theology was a theology of crisis. The term "crisis" speaks of the strain and agony of the war years. Man stood condemned to death with his questions about the good, for he was powerless to do the good in a world so desperately in need of the good. Amid despair of life and anxiety unto death the gracious YES of God in the paradox of the gospel suddenly became clearly intelligible and infinitely relevant. In the whole unbearable situation the church's conscience revived. Amidst the inescapable severity of his doom man came upon the reality of God. One of Barth's early essays reflects the existential mood of this crisis as follows: "We meet our doom upon the rock of the imperishable truth, but that is the only way we can be saved from the sea of appearance and delusion.... It is because God Himself and God alone lends our life its possibility that it becomes so impossible for us to live. And it is because God says YES to us that the NO of existence here is so fundamental and so inescapable."

Fourth, by far the most significant feature of Barth's theology is his persistent emphasis on the centrality of the incarnation as the supreme act of God in history. For Barth the Christ event is the rationale of *Heilsgeschichte* and the meaning of being. Barth is the most vigorous opponent of Bultmann's attempt to demythologize the objective content of the Christ event as a determinant of existential self-understanding. Barth rejects Bultmann's reduction of the gospel to a secular existentialism as the "Babylonian captivity" of theology to a particular philosophy. Likewise, Barth takes issue with the "quest for the historical Jesus" which sought to go behind the "Easter faith" of the early church to discern the uniqueness of Jesus prior to and apart from His resurrection. For Barth all such historical investigations are illegitimate because the object of our faith is not the bare historicity of Jesus stripped of all His acts and promises but the gloriously resurrected Christ clothed with His gospel. According to Barth, the truth of Jesus Christ is not one truth among others but the primary and ultimate truth, for in Him God has created all things. Together with the whole cosmos every man exists not apart from but in Him, whether he is aware of it or not and whether he rejects or accepts his election in Him who is the axis of all things in heaven and on earth. Therefore Barth refuses to develop either a theology or an anthropology apart from Christology.

Foremost of Barth's personal characteristics is his searching and questioning mind, his relentless capacity for self-examination and his ruthless critical encounter based on an uncanny ability to thoroughly sound out his opponents. In addition, Barth is known for his openness to change with the changing situation, to constantly shift his emphasis depending on the partner in dialogue. Furthermore, there is Barth's redeeming joy and humor: the satisfaction with which he observes that *homo sapiens* is the only being accustomed to laugh (and to smoke!), the merriment with which he wrote about the angels while casting side glances at the demons because of their bad smell, his satisfaction at giving Mozart the Mason a place among the Church Fathers, the silver thread of sheer fun that characterizes his account of eighteenth-and-nineteenth-century theologians, the rich spice of humor in his angry *Nein* to Emil Brunner, and last, but not least, the pure delight of his intellectual enjoyment of God.

Of all the critiques leveled at the content and method of Barth's dogmatics perhaps the most discerning is the charge of Christomonism. Since Barth's Christology literally includes everything from creation to redemption, it includes within *Heilsgeschichte* all of secular history, thereby denying its reality and in effect short-circuiting the mission of the church in the world. Barth's all-inclusive Christology tends to blur the distinction between what God *is* and what God *does*, so that, in turn, the distinction between creation and reconciliation loses its meaning. When anthropology becomes Christology on the grounds that all men are crucified, converted, sanctified, and glorified in Jesus Christ irrespective whether they believe it or not, the resulting ontological identification of mankind with the humanity of God in Christ can be as misleading as the humanistic liberal Pelagianism which Barth's Christomonistic expansion of the doctrine of election was meant to correct. Of course, Barth does not deny the reality of personal Christian life and hope, but he reacts against any tendency toward Pietism and existentialism lest Christian faith become a subjective repetition of what happened objectively once for all in Christ.

Furthermore, Fundamentalists are offended by Barth's claim that the Bible's inspiration lies not in its other-worldliness but in its function as witness, and that the Bible's authority lies not in its infallibility but in the power of the Spirit to communicate life. Liberals, on the other hand, are apprehensive of Barth's rejection of natural theology. The orthodox Reformed take issue with his view of election and his critique of infant baptism. Conservatives see in his somewhat modalistic view of the Trinity a new Unitarianism of the second person. Evangelicals express misgiving over his relegation of the Genesis account to the literary category of *Saga* and question the adequacy of defining the resurrection as *Geschichte* rather than *Historia*. Skeptics fail to be convinced by the logic of his principle of presupposition, and mystics are unhappy with his method of analogy.

For all of them the value of Barth's dogmatics lies in its stimulus and experimental nature that challenges us to find our own way through this maze of theological problems which are resolved neither by the ignorant nor by the slothful but only by those for whom the critical challenge of theology has become the subject of labor and the object of prayer.

Brief Bibliography

Karl Barth's *magnum opus* is *Die kirchliche Dogmatik* (EVZ-Verlag Zürich) translated *Church Dogmatics* (Edinburgh 1936 f.), comprising thirteen books, the last of which (published 1968) is an unprecedented defense of believers baptism. Perhaps a good place to begin is with the *Ethics* (Vol. III, Part 4) or with the *Doctrine of God* (Vol. II, Part 1). For purposes of orientation, the guide by Otto Weber, *Karl Barth's Church Dogmatics, An Introductory Report* (London, 1933) is helpful. Of the many surveys, the one by G. C. Berkouwer, *The Triumph of Grace in the Theology of Karl Barth* (London, 1956) is very lucid and positive. Of Barth's many critics, three very discerning ones are Hans Urs von Balthasar, *Karl Barth: Darstellung und Deutung seiner Theologie* (Köln, 1951); Hans Küng, *Rechtfertigung: Die Lehre Karl Barths und eine katholische Besinnung* (Einsiedeln, 1957); and Klaas v. Runia, *Karl Barth's Doctrine of the Holy Scriptures*. Though any selection of the hundreds of definitive theological books and articles Barth has written over the years is arbitrary I mention one classic, *Credo. A Presentation of the chief problems of Dogmatics with reference to the Apostles' Creed* (London, 1936) and one volume of essays, *Against the Stream: Shorter Post-War Writings, 1946-52* (London, 1954).

62
Rudolf Bultmann

> "God meets man in the here and now and offers him a new self-understanding."

David Schroeder

Rudolf Bultmann was born on August 20, 1884, at Wiefelstede in Oldenburg, Germany. His early life was influenced by the Pietism of his grandfather and the moderate Lutheranism of his father, who was the Protestant pastor in Oldenburg. His basic education Bultmann received at the *Gymnasium* in Oldenburg. He received his degree in Marburg in 1910 after having studied at Tübingen, Berlin, and Marburg. In 1916 he became *extra-ordinarius* professor in Breslau. In 1920-21 he taught at Giessen and in 1921 he took up his post in Marburg, where he remained till his retirement. Though Bultmann's dissertation on *The Style of Pauline Preaching and the Cynic-Stoic Diatribe* was published in 1910, most of his writings, except for book reviews and articles, date from 1921 to the present. It is presumed that he did not publish earlier because he disagreed with the "liberal" theology of his teachers but he had not yet fully worked out the details of his own theological position until that time.

Some of Bultmann's works are considered to be monuments of biblical scholarship and stand as milestones in the different areas of New Testament studies. In the study of the history and background of the Gospels, he has contributed *Die Geschichte der synoptischen Tradition*, a form-critical study of the origin of the synoptic Gospels, published in 1921; in the field of exegesis, his commentary on the Gospel of John is unsurpassed; in biblical theology, his *Theologie des Neuen Testaments* breaks new ground in the understanding of the theology of the early church. His writings in the area of hermeneutics, i.e., the method of interpreting Scripture, have drawn him into repeated and heated controversy with other theologians. The debate was touched off by his article on demythologizing the Scriptures published in a volume on *Offenbarung und Heilsgeschehen* entitled "Neues Testament und Mythologie" (New Testament and Mythology). The debates have been published in six volumes of *Kerygma and Mythos* (1933-63).

David Schroeder is Professor of New Testament and Philosophy in the Canadian Mennonite Bible College, Winnipeg. He received the B Th from the Mennonite Brethren Bible College, the AB from Bethel College, the BD from the Mennonite Biblical Seminary, the D Th from the University of Hamburg, and the MA from the University of Western Ontario. Has served in a pastorate. His writings include *Learning to Know the Bible*.

To understand Bultmann we need to understand in what way he continues and in what way he corrects the theological approaches that preceded him. Three such approaches are of interest in this respect. There was, first of all, the attempt in the eighteenth and nineteenth century to rigorously apply historical methodology in the study of the biblical documents. This led to the attempt to regain and expound the life of the historical Jesus, freed from all embellishments the gospel writers might have given his life because of dogmas they now held. Yet at the end of several hundred years, it had to be conceded that to take a purely historical approach to the Gospels was not sufficient. A different approach was taken by Reitzenstein, Bousset, and others, referred to as the "history-of-religions" (religionsgeschichtliche) approach to the Gospels. In this instance, the unity between Jesus and Paul was questioned, and the differences between Jesus and Paul, as well as the differences between Paul and Judaism, were explained with reference to an increasing contact with Hellenism. Reitzenstein looked for the origins of Paul's religion in the religious *gnosis* of the Middle East, and Bousset sought it in the Hellenistic mystery cults. But all such explanations did not account for the power of the gospel.

Yet another approach was taken by Albert Schweitzer. He interpreted Jesus and Paul in strictly Jewish terms and saw them as being entirely dominated by the eschatological dogma of Jewish apocalypse. For Jesus the "Eschaton" still lay in the future and for Paul it had begun with Jesus' death and resurrection, according to Schweitzer. Bultmann in some ways affirms aspects of all three positions. He accepts as legitimate the rigorous historical criticism of the biblical writings. But his application of this method leads him more to the early church and its beliefs about Jesus than to the historical Jesus.

His use of the form-critical method in the study of the synoptics causes him to incorporate much of the history-of-religions approach in outlining the history of the synoptic Gospels. Any new elements in the Gospels and in Paul beyond Judaism are explained in terms of a synthesis of Jewish apocalypticism and Hellenistic mystery cults. But again, though he accepts this, he does not view the Gospels as simply a natural development but as *Kerygma* (proclamation of Christ). Bultmann goes beyond the history-of-religions approach when he agrees with Schweitzer in holding that the preaching of Jesus and Paul has a common base within an eschatological world view. It is therefore not enough simply to use historical-critical methods to inform us about what Jesus and Paul preached; the Word must be interpreted as Kerygma.

The historical method, for example, can describe what Jesus proclaimed: that the kingdom is at hand! But phenomonologically, said Bultmann, this is an apocalyptic myth that has not been fulfilled. What we must do now, according to Bultmann, is to interpret the real meaning of this Word. What Jesus' proclamation means to say is that God in Jesus is calling men to make a radical decision for Him as over against the World. It is in very truth God's address to man, here and now!

It is at this point that Bultmann's contribution to the method of interpreting Scripture must be considered, that is, his program of "demythologization" of Scripture. Simply stated, Bultmann holds that the biblical writers had one view or image of the world, while we today have quite a different image of the world. The Kerygma, though spoken in terms of one image, must now be stated in terms of another image of the world, namely, that of our own. Bultmann claims that the image of the world held by the biblical writers was essentially a mythological view of the world, whereas ours today is conditioned by modern science. This being the case, Bultmann believes that we should not attempt to perpetuate the mythological image of the world in our preaching; we must demythologize the Word. We do this by restating the Kerygma in terms of our own image of the World. The proper way to demythologize the New Testament is *not to remove* accounts in which heaven and hell, or spirits, etc., are mentioned, but to *get at the message* or kernel of meaning of these accounts so that their real intention is revealed. In this way Bultmann believes the text will confront us as an actual Word from God today. It will bring us into an actual moment of decision—a confrontation.

Bultmann's approach to the text of Scripture then involves three basic steps. 1) Historical analysis. His approach here leans heavily on the form-critical method as seen in his analysis of the history of the synoptic Gospels. 2) The biblical accounts must be demythologized—i.e., understood in terms of the modern image of the world. Rather than center on the virgin birth as a historical event, for example, we must understand what it intends to say: that God really entered history and is "with man." 3) Place ourselves obediently under the Word. If the text is rightly interpreted it becomes God's Word to us; it is Kerygma, and demands our response. Jesus is not the originator of a religion but the last Word of God to man.

Any criticism of Bultmann's theology must reckon fully with the great contribution he has made to biblical studies. Nevertheless, he has not been without his serious critics. (1) He is criticized for still following too much the history-of-religion approach in his understanding of the Gospels. (2) His program of demythologization assumes too much that we now have a correct world view, and that we can successfully translate the real meaning of the Gospel accounts into our world view without loss. (3) His own world view is shaped too much by the existentialism of Heidegger. (4) It is probably the case that to translate the Kerygma into our own world view as he suggests is to make too little of the historical events through which God revealed Himself to man. Especially, since the central event is Jesus as the incarnate Son of God, Bultmann's teaching has the effect of undercutting the historical aspects of God's revelation of Himself.

Bibliography

Bultmann, R., *Die Geschichte der synoptischen Tradition*, Göttingen, Vandenhoeck und Ruprecht, 1921; English translation by John Marsh *The History of the Synoptic Tradition*, Oxford, Basil Blackwell, 1963.

————, *Glauben und Verstehen, Gesammelte Aufsaetze*, Tübingen, J. C. B. Mohr, Vol. 1-4, 1933 to 1965.

————, *Das Evangelium des Johannes, Kritisch-exegetischer Kom-*

mentar ueber das Neue Testament, Vandenhoeck und Ruprecht, 1941. English translation by G. Beasley-Murray in preparation, Oxford, Basil Blackwell.

―――――, *Kerygma and Myth,* H. W. Bartsch, ed. New York, Harper Torchbook, 1966.

―――――, *The Theology of the New Testament.* Translation by Kendrick Grobel, New York, Charles Scribners, Vol. I (1951), Vol. II (1955) and London, SCM I (1952) II (1952).

―――――, *Jesus Christ and Mythology,* New York, Scribner's 1958; London, SCM 1960.

Kegley, C. W., ed. *The Theology of Rudolf Bultmann,* London, SCM 1966; New York, Harper & Row 1966. This book gives various reviews of Bultmann's theology and also gives a complete bibliography of Bultmann's writings.

Schmithals, Walter, *An Introduction to the Theology of Rudolf Bultmann* Minneapolis, Augsburg Publishing House, 1968. Translated from the German by John Bowden. This is the most detailed and careful introduction to Bultmann's work and theology.

> *"The way to achieve grace is to perform with love and cheerfulness that which is smallest, indeed that which is lowliest, as though it were something great—also performing something great as though it were something small."*

63

Christian Neff

Gerhard Hein

I. Out of his life

Christian Neff was born on February 18, 1863, at Hemshof (today a part of Ludwigshafen on the Rhine). His parents were Peter Neff, a farmer, and Barbara nee Schowalter, widowed Stauffer. His paternal as well as maternal ancestors belonged to that group of Mennonites who in the seventeenth century had been driven out of Switzerland because of their Anabaptist faith and had found a new home in the Rhenish Palatinate of South Germany. His great-great-grandfather, Johann Peter Neff, as well as his great-grandfather, Peter Neff, were already ministers in their home congregation of Assenheim (today a part of Friedelsheim). His grandfather, Abraham Neff, was the leader *(Vorsteher)* of this congregation. His father, Peter Neff, came to Hemshof through his marriage to the widowed Barbara Stauffer.

Christian Neff grew up in a large Mennonite family. Besides his twin brother (Johannes) he had three other brothers (Peter, Abraham, and Philipp), one sister (Elise) and two older stepbrothers (Heinrich and Jakob Stauffer). Abraham Neff, a watchmaker, migrated to America and Jakob Stauffer moved to Galicia. The worldwide connections of the Neff-Stauffer family may have served to widen the horizons of young Christian Neff. In spite of this, he is, however, characterized since his youth by a strong relationship to his home and a deep attachment to the Mennonites of the Palatinate, from whom he originated.

Gerhard Hein was born November 20, 1905, in Galyschewo at Dawlekanowo, Ufa, Russia. In 1925 he went to Germany to study, becoming a student of theology at Göttingen, Tübingen, Münster, and Leipzig. He served as assistant pastor with Christian Neff for four years, then pastor at Sembach, at Berlin, and at Monsheim. He has served as editor of *Junge Gemeinde*, of *Der Mennonit*, of Volume IV of the *Mennonitisches Lexikon*, and of the *Mennonitischer Gemeinde-Kalender*. He has been chairman of the Mennonite Historical Society and of the German Mennonite Mission Committee. This essay was translated into English by Professor Gerhard Reimer of Goshen College.

Christian Neff received his early education in the primary school *(Volksschule)* and then continued at the grammar school *(Lateinschule)* in Ludwigshafen. In the meantime he spent some time at the Mennonite *Heimschule* at Weierhof (1874-75), the location of his later activities. Here he received lasting impressions of Mennonite ministers and teachers (Thomas Löwenberg, Samuel Blickensdörfer, Heinrich Risser, and David Krehbiel). After that he attended the *Realschule* in Landau and the *Gymnasium* in Speyer, from which he graduated in 1883. As he admitted himself, he would now very much have liked to study history, which, however, in the eyes of his father seemed too much of a "risk" for a future life appointment. He decided, therefore, to pursue theology and studied successively at the universities of Erlangen, Berlin, and Tübingen, then returning to Erlangen again.

In 1887, together with six other candidates in theology, he took the Protestant pastor's examination *(Pfarramtsexamen)*. Christian Neff later wrote a vivid description of his youth and student years in his autobiography, which has been published several times since his death (see *Mennonitische Geschichtsblätter* (1949), pp. 2-6, and *Mennonitischer Gemeinde-Kalender* (1951), pp. 18-21. On October 30, 1887, Christian Neff was elected as a minister in the Mennonite congregation at Weierhof in the Palatinate. He was ordained on the third Advent of the same year.

After two years, on December 28, 1889, he was married to Babette Christine Krehbiel of Weierhof, who stood by him as a faithful marriage partner and active co-worker in their home as well as in the congregation. The marriage was blessed with six children, of whom three daughters (Dora, Thilde, and Ina) and one son (Hans) are still living (1969); one daughter died at the age of thirty and a small son at the age of four and a half years. The father survived the mother by nine years; she died on October 10, 1937, and he on December 30, 1946. Both lie buried in the old cemetery in Weierhof.

II. Out of his activities

A) At Weierhof and among the German Mennonites

For almost sixty years Christian Neff dedicated his energies and talents with unusual loyalty and devotion to the congregation at Weierhof, in the heart of the Rhenish Palatinate. Already toward the end of the seventeenth century a small Mennonite congregation had formed here, which gradually increased in size through natural generation, as well as through the arrival of Mennonite families from other areas. Until the beginning of the nineteenth century this congregation was served by lay ministers from its own ranks. In 1837 a new church came into being under the vigorous minister, Hermann Reeder. Christian Neff lived to see not only the fiftieth but also the hundredth anniversary of this congregation and as a teacher at the *Heimschule* contributed not a little to the fact that Weierhof developed into the intellectual center for all of the Mennonite church of Germany. The weekly Sunday services at Weierhof and at the affiliated congregation at Uffhofen, the religious training of youth, baptismal instruction, and the pastoral care of the scattered church members were serious and heartfelt concerns of Christian Neff. His sermons were always carefully prepared and related to life. At times Bible studies were held. The winter Bible courses at Weierhof became especially appreciated throughout the church. He invited Mennonite, as well as non-Mennonite evangelists, for these courses. Youth instruction in Bible was supplemented with intensive instruction in Mennonite history. He gave preparatory instruction to over 400 baptismal candidates. During the course of a year all the members of his congregation were visited one or more times. During his earlier years he did this by foot or by horse and buggy, and later with his car, which he gladly placed in the service of the church as he ministered to the scattered congregation.

His love for the brotherhood was by no means limited to his own congregation; it radiated far beyond that—first of all to the surrounding congregations of the Palatinate and Hesse, whose stability and coherence lay close to his heart from the beginning, then also to the Mennonite congregations on the east side of the Rhine, whom he brought together with those of the west side in the Conference of the Mennonites of South Germany, and beyond this also to the total German Mennonite church in both East and West. At numerous conferences he conducted biblical-theological and historical lectures. He also committed himself wholeheartedly to Mennonite relief and welfare work and to the support of missions. For half a century he was at the very center of the total activity of the entire German Mennonite church. Through his unselfish and winning manner he earned and richly deserved the trust of all.

B) In historical research and within the worldwide brotherhood

Of special merit is the Anabaptist-Mennonite research of Christian Neff, and his initiative in promoting the Mennonite World Conference. His research significantly began in his home territory: in Speyer, Heidelberg, and Karlsruhe. Here he discovered important sources concerning the history of the Anabaptist-Mennonites of the Palatinate and South Germany. He carefully copied these sources, utilized them, and in part also published them. Beginning in 1893 Christian Hege of Frankfurt/Main was his co-worker in scholarly research. When Hege undertook a study of the Mennonites of the Palatinate *(Täufer in der Kurpfalz)*, Neff very selflessly permitted him to use all his source materials. Neff limited himself to individual historical articles in Mennonite periodicals: in *Der Mennonitische Gemeinde-Kalender*, in *Die Mennonitische Jugendwarte*, and finally in the *Mennonitisches Lexikon*, the German Mennonite encyclopedia. (A bibliography of all the publications of Christian Neff is found in the *Festschrift* for the occasion of his seventieth birthday, pp. 89-96, and, with some additions, also in *Mennonitische Geschichtsblätter*, 1949, pp. 11-13.)

Christian Hege and Christian Neff together founded the *Mennonitisches Lexikon*, of which the first installment was released in 1913 after many years of preparatory work. Even though the two editors could not complete this task (Christian Hege died in 1943), it is, nevertheless, to their honor that they courageously undertook this task, completed over half of it, and laid down definite lines for its completion. Also the American *Mennonite Encyclopedia* (four volumes) is based to a considerable extent on their preparatory work. In recognition of his scholarly research Neff received an honorary doctorate in theology from the Faculty of Protestant Theology of the University of Zurich on the occasion of the first Mennonite World Conference, 1925. Christian Neff and Christian Hege were also the co-founders of the Mennonite Historical Society *(Mennonitischer Geschichtsverein)*.

Although the idea of a Mennonite World Conference had occasionally been expressed earlier by others, it was, however, Christian Neff who gave reality to this dream on the occasion of the four-hundredth anniversary of the existence of Anabaptist congregations. It was also he who edited a valuable commemorative publication of historical contributions (the *Gedenkschrift)* resulting from this conference. Christian Neff was also decisively involved in the preparation for and the carrying out of both of the next world conferences— the World Relief Conference in Danzig in 1930 and the Mennonite World Conference in Amsterdam in 1936—as well as in the publication of the respective reports. He did, however, not live to see the Fourth World Conference after World War II in 1948, which met in North America. In concluding, it must also be noted that in 1913 Christian Neff undertook a trip to America from which he returned with a wealth of impressions and ideas. He had been especially impressed by the Mennonite schools and the quality of the Mennonite congregational life in North America. Later many visitors from America, as well as from other European countries, found their way to Weierhof, which had become almost a shrine. Christian Neff is one of the most important and best-known Mennonite personalities of the past several centuries.

Bibliographical Note

See the data and bibliography on Dr. Neff in *The Mennonite Encyclopedia*, III, 820; photo on p. 13 of the illustrations.

"Deep within us all there is an amazing inner sanctuary of the soul, a holy place, a Divine Center, a speaking Voice, to which we may continuously return. Eternity is at our hearts, pressing upon our time-torn lives, warming us with intimations of an astounding destiny, calling us home unto Itself. Yielding to these persuasions, gladly committing ourselves in body and soul, utterly and completely to the Light Within, is the beginning of true life."[1]

64

Thomas R. Kelly
Prophet of Inward Obedience

T. Canby Jones

As Thomas Kelly (1893-1941) sat on the porch with Rufus Jones, on the day that he began his year of graduate study in philosophy at Haverford College, he said to his teacher, "I'm just going to make my life a miracle!" It was only in the last three years of Thomas Kelly's life that the miracle came to fulfillment. This writer knew him only during those final years.

Native of southwestern Ohio, Tom Kelly was reared in an ardently evangelical Quaker home, fell in love with chemistry during his four years at Wilmington College, then turned to philosophy at Haverford. Just ask some of his cronies at Hartford Seminary—his three years there were a lark! On graduation he married Lael Macy and returned to teach at Wilmington. Disillusioned with the Midwest he returned to

---

T. Canby Jones, a member of the Society of Friends, is Professor of Religion and Philosophy in Wilmington College in Ohio, and a Visiting Lecturer at the Earlham School of Religion in Indiana. He received the AB from Haverford College, the BD from Yale University Divinity School, and also from Yale the PhD with a dissertation on *George Fox's Teaching on Redemption and Salvation*. He has been editor of *Quaker Religious Thought*, and is currently chairman of the Quaker Theological Discussion Group. He is a Vice-Chairman of the American Section of the Friends World Committee. One of his more recent works is a book, *George Fox's Attitude Toward War*.

245

earn his PhD at Hartford in 1924. Fifteen months of work with the new Friends Center in Berlin turned his life around. In the lives of convinced postwar German Friends he found a depth and authenticity he felt almost totally lacking in his American evangelical Quaker heritage.

As he returned to America to teach philosophy at Earlham College, Richmond, Indiana, he burned for two things, to reinterpret Quaker faith for modern man, and to become second to none in academic scholarship. The zest for further scholarship took him to Harvard, where he pursued a second PhD even to the publication of his thesis. But during his oral defense of his thesis he suffered a mental and emotional blackout and was failed. This shattering of his self-image as a scholar led to near suicide. During the ensuing months this cataclysm also led to a genuine conversion and a total life reorientation. The objective realist philosopher with theories *about* many things was transformed into an *authentic* who had unmistakable and direct acquaintance with God. I once heard Richard Niebuhr say that philosophers who turn Christian theologian are among the greatest. Such was Thomas Kelly. In the years that I knew him, he bubbled over with joy. Suave and debonair Haverford students couldn't accept such authenticity and joy. They felt threatened by it. But for those of us who met weekly in his home to feast on classics of Christian devotion, especially his favorite, Jean Nicholas Grou, Tom's joyful freedom was meat and drink to our souls. His little book, *A Testament of Devotion*, is already a classic, in a class with Thomas a Kempis. Another volume of his writings, *The Eternal Promise*, has recently been published. A companion volume, *A Biography of Thomas Kelly*, written by his son, Richard M. Kelly, which documents his father's conversion, appeared at the same time.

Among the main themes of Thomas Kelly's thought I see first an Augustinian emphasis on God, "God the initiator, God the aggressor, God the seeker, God the stirrer into life, God the ground of our obedience, God the giver of power to become the children of God."[2] Thomas Kelly stresses that seekers are already finders for:

> He has *already* been showing Himself to you, in your very impulse to seek Him. Did *you* start to search for Him? He *started you* on the search for Him, and lovingly, anxiously, tenderly guides you to Himself.
>
> You knock on heaven's gate, because He has already been standing at the door knocking within you, disquieting you and calling you to arise and seek your Father's house.[3]

For Thomas Kelly the important question was not so much a theoretical belief in God but "*yielding* your lives to Him."[4]

Cited in the quotation at the beginning of this essay is Thomas Kelly's next major theme. Deep within, in the hidden recesses of our being, lies a holy place where we meet God face to face. But belief in a point of contact is not enough. "It is a matter of daily, hourly going down into the Shekinah of the soul, in that silence, to find yourselves continually recreated...."[5]

Religion, therefore for Thomas Kelly, is no mere luxury or peripheral experience. "Religion is the lifeblood of the full self, the deepest necessity, the most imperious hunger of man. You and I are not our full selves until we are in God's Presence and He is visibly in us...."[6] Thomas Kelly had no patience with religion as a dull habit. He championed it as an acute fever. There is "no substitute for *immediacy* of revelation.... Religion is in nothing outward.... Religion is *inward*, it arises in immediacy of relation with God."[7] With inner ear attuned and "in expectancy directed to the still small voice within," Kelly calls us to "live a listening life."[8]

But the whole point of listening is hearing, obeying, total commitment. By "continuous and quiet *willing* away of our lives, utter dedication of will, utter surrender of oneself into God's care ..."[9] Thomas Kelly calls to us, "Commit your lives in unreserved obedience to him."[10] He continues:

> The life that intends to be wholly obedient, wholly submissive, wholly listening, is astonishing in its completeness. Its joys are ravishing, its peace profound, its humility the deepest, its power world-shaking, its love enveloping, its simplicity that of a trusting child. It is the life and power in which the prophets and apostles lived.[11]

Thomas Kelly's name for this kind of life is *holy obedience*. In it we carry out God's "slightest wish, his faintest breathing ... gladly, urgently, promptly one leaps to do His bidding, ready to run and not be weary and to walk and not faint."[12]

Obviously a life of inward obedience is one of constant prayer and enkindled worship. Prayer without ceasing is possible because there is a way of living our lives on two levels at once. On one level we are fully occupied, "but deep within ... at a profounder level, we may also be in prayer and adoration, song and worship and a gentle receptiveness to divine breathings."[13] At first we alternate between levels, but dawning simultaneity leads to constant cosmic awareness, "hid with Christ in God."

Thomas Kelly describes five levels of inner prayer: *inward oblation*, pouring oneself out before God; *inward song, inward listening, inward carrying*, and *infused prayer*. In the latter God takes over the spirit and mind of one of us and speaks His Word through us to our fellows. Not only are we transported as words not of our making pour through us but all who hear are caught up into His presence.[14]

Thomas Kelly calls worship "group mysticism" in which "an objective dynamic Presence enfolds us all, nourishes our souls.... The burning bush has been kindled in our midst, and we stand together on holy ground."[15] The ground, foundation, and experience of all worship, Kelly insists, is "the Real Presence of God ... just as firm and solid as the belief of Roman Catholics in the Real Presence in the host."[16]

The fruits of a life of inward obedience are manifold. The first is *joy*, joy unspeakable and full of glory. Poking fun at our overseriousness Kelly explodes, "I'd rather be a jolly St. Francis hymning his canticle to the sun than a dour old sobersides Quaker whose diet would appear to have been spiritual persimmons."[17] Next come *hu-*

mility and *holiness*. Far from being a doormat, the humble person is one who exhibits a boldness, an unconcern about what others say, with eye so fixed on God he sees only Him in all things. Likewise the obedient yearn "to become pure in heart, even as He is pure, with all the energy of their souls." Gratitude for the love, "the blinding purity of God in Christ, how captivating, how alluring, how compelling it is."[18]

A fourth fruit is an astonishing *simplification* of life. No longer does a whole committee of selves argue for a share of our distraught time and energy. Tasks sort themselves out by divine priorities. We learn that "we cannot die on *every* cross, nor are we expected to."[19] But one of Thomas Kelly's most helpful insights is his promise of *victory through suffering*. After a visit to Nazi Germany in 1938 he was convinced that all the plagues of Egypt were once again loosed upon the world, condemning men to "hopeless, hopeless despair," or to a kind of redemptive suffering which sublimates anguish into a sacrament, which finds release and peace on the yonder side of the valley of the shadow. The key for Thomas Kelly to the sacrament of suffering was Psalm 126: "They that go forth in tears, bearing the seed for sowing, shall doubtless come again with shouts of joy, bearing their sheaves with them."[20] The seed for sowing is radiant faith. "The way of holy obedience leads out from the heart of God and extends through the Valley of the Shadow."[21]

Thomas Kelly had a great concern for those of us who loved him and shared his vision that we should become "Publishers of Truth," like the early Quakers. With a soul-shaking discovery of God's power in our lives, complete dedication to human renewal and to each other, now is the time, says Kelly, in the words of George Fox to "sound, sound abroad, you faithful servants of the Lord ... to the awakening and raising of the dead."[22] Such sensitized souls will not only renew mankind but stamp out war. "Do you see war as a giant, iniquitous, futile, unchristian system? Then hurl yourself against it, in full blindness to the seeming impossibility of the task. For if God be for us, who can be against us.... There are no impossibles to those who in supreme dedication, are rooted deep in the Eternal Love."[23]

Astonishingly, the morning of the day on which he suffered a massive heart attack (and died within moments of its onset), Thomas Kelly had exclaimed to his wife, "Today will be the greatest day of my life."[24] In the face of the bitter and desolate tears I shed that night, what an amazing statement!

A sign of Thomas Kelly's greatness as a prophet of inward obedience was the simple directness of his appeal. Here is a concluding example:

> To you in this room who are seekers, to you, young and old who have toiled all night and caught nothing, but who want to launch out into the deep and let down your nets.... I want to speak, as simply, as tenderly, as clearly as I can. For God can be found. There is a last Rock for your souls, a resting place of absolute peace and joy and power and radiance.... There is a Divine Center into which your life can slip, a new and absolute orientation to God, a Center where you live with Him, and out from which you see all of life, through new radiant vision, tinged with new sorrows and new pangs, new joys unspeakable and full of glory.[25]

Footnotes

1. Thomas R. Kelly, *A Testament of Devotion*, New York: Harper & Row, 1941, p. 29.
2. *Ibid.*, p. 52.
3, 4. Thomas R. Kelly, *The Eternal Promise*, New York: Harper & Row, 1966, p. 105.
5. *Ibid.*
6. *Ibid.*, p. 112.
7. *Ibid.*, p. 53.
8. Thomas R. Kelly, "Have You Ever Seen a Miracle?" Unpublished MSS, p. 5.
9. *Ibid.*, p. 8.
10. *Testament of Devotion*, p. 52.
11. *Ibid.*, p. 54-55.
12. *Ibid.*, p. 58.
13. *Ibid.*, p. 35.
14. Thomas R. Kelly, *The Reality of the Spiritual World*, Wallingford, Pendle Hill, 1942, p. 46-53.
15. *Eternal Promise*, p. 72.
16. *Ibid.*, pp. 79, 81.
17. *Testament of Devotion*, p. 92.
18. *Ibid.*, p. 65.
19. *Ibid.*, p. 109.
20. *Eternal Promise*, pp. 41-42.
21. *Testament of Devotion*, p. 71.
22. *Eternal Promise*, pp. 90-94.
23. "Have You Ever Seen a Miracle?" p. 13.
24. Richard M. Kelly, *Thomas Kelly, A Biography*, New York: Harper & Row, 1966, p. 122.
25. *Eternal Promise*, p. 102.

"His main concerns are with Christian ethics, the Christian understanding of history, and the Christian doctrine of man."[1]

65

Reinhold Niebuhr
Christian Idealism and
Political Realism

John H. Redekop

Reinhold Niebuhr (1892-1971) was born in Wright City, Missouri, son of a clergyman in the Lutheran Church. His education included Elmhurst College (1910), Eden Theological Seminary (1913), BD, Yale Divinity School (1914), MA at the same institution (1915), DD, Eden Theological Seminary (1930). It is probably noteworthy that although he never completed a PhD, more PhD dissertations have been written about him than about any other American theologian.

In 1915 Niebuhr was ordained to the ministry of the (Lutheran) Evangelical Synod of North America. He then served as pastor in a low-income area of Detroit from 1915 to 1928. Following this period of pastoral service he was invited to join the faculty of Union Theological Seminary in New York from which he retired in 1960. However, he was long a leader in theological as well as political thought and discussion.

Niebuhr's earliest writings reflect moderate religious "liberalism" and social idealism. With increased experience and reflection he gradually reoriented his thinking and slowly became much more orthodox theologically and realistic socially. Significantly, he finally terminated his membership in the Socialist Party in June 1940. His experience at the Bethel Evangelical Church in Detroit gave rise to his first major literary work, *Leaves from the Notebook of a Tamed Cynic* (1929). Probably his best-known book, *Moral Man and Immoral Society* (1932), emphasized the universality of sinful self-love, especially in corporate structures. Having terminated his earlier toying with Marxist radicalism, Niebuhr quickly became a strong and eloquent critic of all forms of totalitarianism. Even responsible socialism lost most of its appeal for him.

John H. Redekop is Associate Professor of Political Science, Waterloo Lutheran University. He received the BA and the B Ed from the University of British Columbia, the MA from the University of California, and the PhD from the University of Washington. He authored *The American Far Right, Approaches to Canadian Politics, Labor Problems in Canadian Perspective, The Star-Spangled Banner*, and *Making Political Decisions*.

Although all of Reinhold Niebuhr's writings reflect theological thought he became increasingly concerned with historicity and the relationships of human power structures, especially political, with Christian ethics. His major works in this area include *Christianity and Power Politics* (1940), *The Children of Light and the Children of Darkness* (1944), *Discerning the Signs of the Times* (1946), *Faith and History* (1949), *The Irony of American History* (1952), *The Self and the Dramas of History* (1955), and his very influential, *The Structure of Nations and Empires* (1959), which more or less culminates and systematizes his views on historicity, human nature, and the problems related to power.

Niebuhr's theology is expressed best in *The Nature and Destiny of Man* (2 volumes, 1941-1943). This statement of his position brought him fairly close to the Continental school represented by Karl Barth and Emil Brunner, although he always remained very critical of both, partly because he felt that they were still too orthodox and too conservative. In North America, Niebuhr is commonly referred to as the leading spokesman of Neo-Orthodoxy but a more appropriate term is Neo-Reformation Theology. There are, after all, many kinds of orthodoxies, both Christian and non-Christian. (Furthermore, "Neo-Orthodox" is widely used as an emotionally charged label of opprobrium.)

Specifically, Niebuhr worked hard and long at trying to reinvigorate Christendom with the essential doctrines of the major Protestant Reformers, especially those of Luther and Calvin. However, he was critical of Calvin's ethical stance which, he alleges, is derived almost entirely from the Old Testament rather than the New. He argues that it lacks the compassion of Jesus and is much too individualistic. Transferred to the realm of economics and politics, it has, he feels, produced an exploitative, insensitive, and at times even an intolerant, *laissez faire* power structure. Aside from this basic criticism of Calvinist ethics, Niebuhr has generally emphasized the same theological tenets stressed by the Great Reformers, but significantly he has added an eloquent and passionate concern for the expression of Christian love in terms of justice. He insists that Christianity is intrinsically comprehensive in scope and relevance.

In part Niebuhr's later theology, as already implied, constitutes a clear-cut rejection of liberal optimism about human nature, social evolution, and historical development. He rejects the notion of gradualism; in its stead he posits discontinuity and points to the seriousness of man's plight. His involvement with a largely untamed capitalism during his early pastorate is relevant in this connection. Niebuhr also categorically rejects any liberalistic attempt to define God in terms of reason, universal law, or philosophy. He admits that it is rationally absurd to believe that God is a person, but insists that such a belief is nevertheless valid, and it actually constitutes an essential element of the Christian faith. There is no solution, he believes, to the rational problems associated with the premise that there is a personal God who must be thought of in terms of both structure and freedom. No theological or other system of thought, he suggests, can do justice to both notions.

In Niebuhr's writings, God is depicted as loving, merciful, and perpetually relevant, but also as mysterious, transcendental, and remote. In keeping with his genuinely Christocentric approach, Niebuhr asserts that God has revealed both His love and His righteousness through the divine Christ. While tending to avoid the more evangelical terms of "conversion" and "rebirth," as well as the essentially Anabaptist emphasis on an unqualified discipleship (see J. H. Yoder's article), Niebuhr underscores the fact that Christians are exclusively dependent on Christ's righteousness rather than their own. In contrast to an earlier liberal emphasis on humanism, Niebuhr again makes almighty God central, supremely holy, and worthy of genuine reverence and worship. The fact that the human mind is incapable of comprehending such a God is presented not as a valid indictment of Christianity but as a crucial part of the Christian faith.

Concerning Niebuhr's doctrine of man we again encounter an allegedly irresolvable dilemma. Man is partly rational, and his life directed by his own moral choice, but his nature is also partly determined; he is free, but he is also a slave to sin. Niebuhr, while acknowledging both the possibilities and limitations of human nature, unhesitatingly asserts that all men are guilty and stand under God's judgment. His classic observation in this regard is that "man's capacity for justice makes democracy possible; but his inclination to injustice makes democracy necessary."

Frequently Niebuhr stresses man's propensity to grasp power—to reveal his sinful pride by claiming and trying to be greater and better than he is. The result of this tendency, explains Niebuhr, is an increased sense of guilt, insecurity, and further self-assertion. This desperate struggle for worldly power proceeds unabated. As the central fact of personal existence it becomes crucial in the realm of group pressures, especially in the form of nationalistic fervor.

Comparatively little has been written by Niebuhr about the creative potential and reconciling functions of the church. Much of his commentary on the organized church is highly critical. He accuses it of frequently shielding, even justifying, man's inherent pride by the use of sentimental generalities, platitudes, or apathy. "Conventional and graceless legalism," as well as "religious fanaticism" and all forms of pretention are roundly condemned. But to set his criticisms in perspective he reminds his readers that he makes "no apology for being critical of what I love."

Perhaps the greatest shortcoming in Niebuhr's widely scattered comments on the church is his hesitation to express explicitly and systematically the traits, functions, and ultimate essence of the "true church" in terms of any historic institution. He sees the Christian church variously as a "community of hopeful believers," a "community of forgiven sinners," or a "curiously mixed body" of those who are self-righteous and those who "live by a broken spirit and contrite heart." In any event, it should impinge upon all human enterprise. He sees the church as being peculiarly tempted to pray, "Lord, I thank thee that I am not as other institutions." Always he urges the church to seek relevancy—and his widespread dissent has indeed served a constructive purpose.

Much attention is given to critical studies of the Bible and of

Christianity generally but Niebuhr and his fellow Neo-Reformation theologians constantly stress biblical authority. However, it is not always clear to what extent Niebuhr speaks symbolically or when he assumes biblical statements to have a symbolic meaning. Certainly he would not identify fully with a conservative literalist interpretation.

Perhaps Niebuhr's greatest significance lies in his role as a social critic who has sought to restate traditional biblical principles in forms relevant to the crucial issues of contemporary society. His wide practical interests throughout his long and impressive ministry have concentrated primarily in political, social, and economic reform. He has given us vigorous warnings against viewing oversimplified and legalistic solutions to social problems as being either Christian or adequate. He is emphatic in asserting that it is a false Christianity which adheres to neutrality when issues of justice are at stake. However, it is probably fair to suggest that on balance Niebuhr's pungent and incisive criticisms and warnings are not always matched by consistent, positive prescriptions. For instance, he suggests that "the ultimate exercise of responsibility may involve the guilt of the destruction of life" (Ernest W. Lefever, *The World Crisis and American Responsibility*, p. 34).

Niebuhr has frequently been criticized for asserting, "We now know that we cannot be responsible without guilt." It would appear that despite his long and dedicated attempt to derive a consistent code of ethics from "Agape"—sacrificial, sin-bearing, other-oriented love— he has not fully succeeded. His ethical system seems to reflect considerable compromise in the name of relevance, rather than the unqualified obedience intrinsic to true Christian discipleship.

For better or worse, Niebuhr has come to the conclusion that there are no solutions to the "great social problems within history." However, he insists that it is incumbent upon mankind, and especially Christians, to strive for such proximate public justice as is attainable and to live by the ethic of love in personal relationships.

The pioneering impact of Reinhold Niebuhr on the contemporary world can hardly be overstressed. His influence cuts across national boundaries, the lines of academic disciplines, and, of course, denominational distinctions. Interest in theology, ethics, social problems, and Christian responsibility has increased immeasurably as a result of his penetrating insights, devastating criticisms, and provocative assertions. He has done much to shake especially the North American "religious establishment," including its evangelical wing, out of a lamentable complacency. Many critics have faulted Niebuhr either for departing from a narrow literalism or for undermining religious liberalism, but whatever their view, they cannot deny that his powerful affirmations of biblical truths have had a wholesome leavening effect. Truly, his has been, and continues to be, a much-needed prophetic voice.

Brief Bibliography

The best source for Reinhold Niebuhr's thought is, of course, his own prolific pen. A listing of his books and major articles would fill several pages. His most influential works have already been cited. Some significant secondary sources, many of which include further bibliographies, are the following:

June Bingham. *Courage to Change: An Introduction to the Life and Thought of Reinhold Niebuhr,* 1961. An easy-to-read but not superficial introduction for the beginning student. Its 400 pages present a balanced account.

Edward J. Carnell. *The Theology of Reinhold Niebuhr,* (1950) 1960. A critical and penetrating analysis by a noted conservative thinker.

Gordon Harland. *The Thought of Reinhold Niebuhr,* 1960. One of the best works on Niebuhr's views on love and justice. Part Two analyzes Niebuhr's thoughts on politics, war and peace, economics, race, etc.

Charles W. Kegley & Robert W. Bretall, eds. *Reinhold Niebuhr: His Religious, Social and Political Thought,* 1956. Aside from the many stimulating ideas presented in the various articles, this work is useful because it contains a full bibliography to 1956.

D. B. Robertson, ed. *Essays in Applied Christianity by Reinhold Niebuhr,* 1959. This is by far the best work dealing with Niebuhr's views on the church, Roman Catholicism, and Ecumenism.

Paul Tillich, John C. Bennett, Hans J. Morgenthau. *Reinhold Niebuhr: A Prophetic Voice in Our Time* (Essays in Tribute), 1962. The three major essays included in this volume draw attention to Niebuhr's major contributions, as well as to some shortcomings. They are noteworthy not only in their own right but because of the status of their authors.

John H. Yoder. *Reinhold Niebuhr and Christian Pacifism,* Zeist, The Netherlands, 1954. A perceptive and stimulating critique.

Footnote

1. L. Harold DeWolf, *Present Trends in Christian Thought,* p. 86.

"If you continue to love Jesus, nothing much can go wrong with you, and I hope you may always do so."

66

Logic and Fantasy:
The World of
C. S. Lewis

Clyde S. Kilby

That remark may sound like a fond old grandmother's, but it was written to a little girl by one of the most brilliant men of our time. The man was Clive Staples Lewis, distinguished professor at Oxford and Cambridge universities and author of more than forty books. It was written less than a month before his death on November 22, 1963, the same afternoon President John F. Kennedy was assassinated.

C. S. Lewis did not easily come to so simple and straightforward a faith. Born in Ireland, he learned simple goodness from his first nursemaid; but afterward, through the influence of a well-meaning but wrongheaded school matron, he turned atheist. His father was a successful but eccentric Irish solicitor, and his mother was a cheerful and wise woman who early started her son off in the study of French and Latin. But neither parent was noteworthy for the sort of deep faith that eventually was to characterize their son.

Nor had the parents two other deep strains that came to mark their son's outlook. The first was a romantic strain of longing for an indefinable but intense thing called joy. The second was just the opposite—a mind trained razor-sharp in logic. In the course of time the British *Guardian* said that following the train of an argument by Lewis was "like watching a master chess player who makes a seemingly trivial and unimportant move which ten minutes later turns out to be a stroke of genius." The *New York Times* spoke of one of his books as possessing "a brevity comparable to St. Paul's" and an argument "distilled to the unanswerable."

Clyde S. Kilby has served as Professor of English in Wheaton College. He received the AB from the University of Arkansas, the AM from the University of Minnesota, and the PhD from the New York University. Among his books are *Poetry and Life*, *Minority of One*, *The Christian World of C. S. Lewis*, and coauthor with Douglas Gilbert of *C. S. Lewis: Images of his World*. Lewis was born November 29, 1898.

Reprinted from *Christian Action*, January 1969. Copyright © 1968 by Graded Press. Used by permission.

The romantic strain in Lewis was associated with the green Castlereagh Hills, which Lewis and his brother Warren could see from their nursery window, and with a toy garden of moss, twigs, and flowers made by Warren on the lid of a can. Later this tendency came to include a profound love of Norse legend, the "Ring" cycle of Richard Wagner's operas, and the entire world of Norse mythology. The logician strain is best seen in Lewis the lecturer and biblical apologist. For instance, at the beginning of his book *The Problem of Pain* (The Macmillan Company, 1944) he makes out a better, or at least a more succinct, case for atheism than Bertrand Russell ever did, and then he proceeds to demolish that case. But it should be said that nearly always the romantic and the logical are combined both in his books and in his whole way of thought.

The big house to which his family moved when he was seven years old helped to shape Lewis's love of solitude. It was a place of "long corridors, empty sunlit rooms, upstair indoor silences, attics explored in solitude, distant noises of gurgling cisterns and pipes, and the noise of wind under the tiles." There on long rainy afternoons he and his brother read among the hundreds of books with which every room downstairs was filled. Clive began early to write stories of animals, including chivalrous mice, and finally set out to do a full, fanciful history of Animal-land complete with maps and drawings.

This happy childhood experience was cruelly broken by the death of his mother when he was ten years old. Her illness marked the first real religious experience he had. He prayed that she would be healed. But at this time he thought of God as a magician who would heal his mother's cancer and then go away.

Afterward he was taught a more substantial notion of God in the English boarding school to which, dressed in uncomfortable clothes, bowler hat, and tight, unyielding shoes, he was sent by his father. At first he fervently hated both England and the bad food, cold beds, and horrid sanitation of the school. He described his teacher, called Oldie by the boys, as likely to come in after breakfast and, looking over the little group, say, "Oh, there you are, Rees, you horrid boy. If I'm not too tired I shall give you a good drubbing this afternoon." Yet here he did find people talking about Christianity as though they believed it, and the little boy struggled, yet unsuccessfully, to gain a realization of God. The best thing about his school life was the anticipation of the holidays—the trip home to Ireland and the long days full of play, good reading, cycling, and solitude.

Later in other English schools he learned a love of that country's beautiful landscape and the raw and brutal tyranny of older boys over younger ones, of rampant homosexuality, of a brash and silly sophistication in ideas, clothes, and women. In short, he learned a system of education calculated, as he put it, to make genuinely uneducated prigs and highbrows. For the rest of his life he never missed an opportunity to satirize this sort of school system as one calculated more to fill the country with "a bitter, truculent, skeptical, debunking and cynical *intelligentsia*" than to make good citizens.

In these days Lewis, as college students often do, was living in many different worlds. His private world was still that of "Northerness" and joy. At the same time he was now an atheist and was trying to incorporate his ideas around that pole of conviction. "I maintained that God did not exist. I was also very angry with God for not existing. I was equally angry with Him for creating a world."[1]

Increasingly sick of college life, Lewis persuaded his father to let him prepare for the university under the tutelage of W. T. Kirkpatrick in Surrey. Almost from the minute he first met this man Lewis's intellectual life underwent a sharp change. The tall, shabbily dressed man with Franz Joseph whiskers met the boy at the railway station, took his hand in an iron grip, and as they walked away promptly pounced upon Lewis for a passing remark about the unexpected "wildness" of the Surrey landscape. "Stop!" he shouted to the fifteen-year-old boy. "What do you mean by wildness and what ground had you for not expecting it?" After further questions, he asked, "Do you not see, then, that you had no right to have any opinion whatever on the subject?"

This was the beginning of a training in logical thought the like of which had not often occurred before. The "Old Knock," as he was called, was the very personification of reason and trained his increasingly adept student in the practice of a relentlessly logical handling of ideas. Finally the time came when the pupil could stand up to the master. Lewis found that Kirkpatrick was an atheist and was glad to have his own atheism bolstered by that of his tutor, but the time came when the Old Knock's ubiquitous logic actually put Lewis on the road to God.

Lewis tells how on the first school day the Old Knock sat down with his pupil and without a word of introduction read aloud in Greek the first twenty lines or so of Homer's *Iliad* and translated with very few explanations about a hundred lines. He told his understudy to dig in, and it was not long until Lewis was beginning to think in Greek. And so it was with Latin and other languages. Years later Lewis looked back at this time as one of the happiest periods of his life.

His childhood love of nature was continued in the intimate landscape of Surrey with its dingles, copses, and little valleys and with quiet saunters under great trees. He had a happiness that seemed of another world.

By the age of sixteen he had already begun to feel a deep-seated antipathy to the shallow "getting and spending" that occupied people's lives, to ideas of collectivism, of modern education, of inflated desires caused by false advertising, of slanted news, of built-in obsolescence in manufacturing, and of the whole scheme of "getting ahead" in the world. Even more he began to be alarmed about modern movements such as logical positivism, Freudianism, relativism, scientism, sexual frankness that resulted only in more and worse sexual deviation, "modernism" in religion and the contradictory idea of inevitable improvement from natural causes, and the increasing feeling of hopelessness in society. He felt that even democracy itself was taking the impossible road of trying to make men equal rather than providing a way for men clearly unequal to live together in peace.

Lewis had hardly passed his examinations for admission to Oxford when he was called into the war then raging. He enlisted as a second lieutenant in the Somerset Light Infantry, and on his nineteenth birthday he found himself in the front-line trenches of France. Five months later, in April 1918, he was wounded in battle, and sent back to London for recuperation. Even earlier Lewis had heard the distant baying of the Hound of Heaven, and now in a long period given almost wholly to wide reading he had the opportunity to learn more about writers such as G. K. Chesterton and George MacDonald. Through them the Hound drew nearer and made it clear enough that Lewis was his prey.

Early in 1919 Lewis was back at University College, Oxford. There he met men of high intellect who were Christians, or at least theistic, in their thinking. One of them, Owen Barfield, was destined to be his lifelong friend. Barfield had read, said Lewis, all the right books but had got the wrong things out of them. Lengthy and warm debates with Barfield and others forced him to a careful reexamination of the foundations of his atheism. Meanwhile Lewis went on to highest honors, taught for a year at University College, and then was chosen a Fellow of Magdalen College, a position he was to hold for thirty years.

Lewis continued to be troubled by what looked like the finger of God pointing directly at him. On the one side were Christian colleagues and on the other side one shattering experience with "the hardest boiled of all the atheists" he had known. This man sat in Lewis's room before the fire and finally blurted out, "Rum thing.... All that stuff of Frazer's about the Dying God. Rum thing. It almost looks as if it had really happened once." So a second atheist was added to the Old Knock in the process of turning Lewis toward God. Lewis's account of how God finally came to him must be read just as he puts it:

> You must picture me alone in that room in Magdalen, night after night, feeling, whenever my mind lifted even for a second from my work, the steady, unrelenting approach of Him whom I so earnestly desired not to meet. That which I greatly feared had at last come upon me.... I gave in, and admitted that God was God, and knelt and prayed: perhaps, that night, the most dejected and reluctant convert in all England. I did not then see what is now the most shining and obvious thing; the Divine humility which will accept a convert even on such terms.[2]

The rest of his life was to consist of teaching and writing. If that seems a dull business, remember that Lewis's adventures among ideas were as exciting as the exploits of a big game hunter or an Alpine climber. He became one of the great teachers of his time. His lectures were always crowded. One of his students said that he had at his fingertips more knowledge than he had ever known in any other scholar, and another said that Lewis had "the most exact and penetrating mind" he had ever encountered.

Lewis's conversion brought to him the long-sought joy, and soon he was writing books about Christianity. Millions of copies of them have been sold. Though many of his books treat their subjects directly, such as *Miracles* (The Macmillan Company, 1947), *The Problem of Pain* (The Macmillan Company, 1944), and *Mere Christianity* (The Macmillan Company, 1952), perhaps his best-loved books are of the creative variety. Would you like to make a trip to hell and examine its fondest hopes and its strategy for winning souls? Would you care to know the subtleties of Satan that surround you and are intent at this moment on destroying you? Would you care to learn what happens to a particular imp who lets a soul slip through his fingers into the hands of the "Enemy"? If so, you can go to Lewis's most popular (though he himself did not at all feel his best) book, *The Screwtape Letters* (The Macmillan Company, 1942).

Or would you like to take a bus trip with people going from hell to heaven and hear the earnest appeal of celestial beings for them to come in and listen to their excuses for not doing so? You can hear the claims of people who do not believe in heaven, even one famous preacher, while they are looking at a part of its glory. You can meet the man who has "done his best" all his life and now wants what he thinks is due him. Or you can meet the man who thinks heaven is just another trick of "the Management." Or you can meet the woman who on earth hounded her husband literally to death in her efforts to promote him in business and society and refuses heaven unless she will be allowed there to take charge of him again. If you would like to observe that, as Lewis insists, people in hell really choose that malign place, you can read it all in *The Great Divorce* (The Macmillan Company, 1946).

Or if you would rather take a space journey, you can go to an unfallen planet and there see another Eve undergoing the temptation to disobey. There a very evil man and a good one meet this lady in her own glorious surroundings and each endeavors to persuade her to his viewpoint. The reader has an intimate and startling experience of what Eden and the temptation might have been like and of the far-reaching and subtle grounds of that temptation. All this is in *Perelandra* (The Macmillan Company, 1944).

Or one may go to Lewis's seven much-loved stories for children and discover not only charming adventures but also little episodes that put the gospel clearer than many a sermon. In one of them, for instance, a little girl wants a drink of water but finds the lion, Aslan (Christ), between her and the water.

"Are you not thirsty?" said the Lion.

"I'm *dying* of thirst," said Jill.

"Then drink," said the Lion.

"May I — could I — would you mind going away while I do?" said Jill.

The Lion answered this only by a look and a very low growl....

"I daren't come and drink," said Jill.

"Then you will die of thirst," said the Lion.

"Oh, dear!" said Jill, coming another step nearer. "I suppose I must go and look for another stream then."

"There is no other stream," said the Lion.[3]

In another of the books the idea that a Christian lives in daily contact with God is suggested when the youngsters, voyaging into a far-off country, come upon a place where a sumptuous table is set. They inquire and learn that it is Aslan's table.

"Why is it called Aslan's table?" asked Lucy presently.

"It is set here by his bidding...."
"But how does the food *keep?*" asked the practical Eustace.
"It is eaten, and renewed, every day," said the girl...."[4]

And we could hardly imagine a finer depiction of the necessity for divine salvation than that in another of the children's books. A boy called Eustace Scrubb had accidentally gone along on *The Voyage of the Dawn Treader*. He hated the other children and made all the trouble he could. When they came to an uninhabited island far away, he ran off from the group and in the course of events was turned into a dragon. Shocked through and through to realize his terrible condition, he longed to be a boy again (and a good one). In his terror, he remembered that snakes cast off their skins and thought it might also be true of dragons. He finally got a rent made and managed to slip off his entire skin. He was happy until he looked in a well of water and found another skin on his body that was just as ugly and knobbly as the first. Again he managed to pull off this skin, but again underneath was another that was no better. Finally Aslan said, "You will have to let me undress you." Eustace was afraid of Aslan's claws, but being desperate now for relief, he lay down and let Aslan take over.

This is how Eustace told the story to his friends later:

"The very first tear he made was so deep that I thought it had gone right into my heart. And when he began pulling the skin off, it hurt worse than anything I've ever felt...."

"Well, he pulled the beastly stuff right off—just as I thought I'd done it myself the other three times, only they hadn't hurt—and there it was lying on the grass: only ever so much thicker, and darker, and more knobbly looking than the others had been."[5]

Afterward Aslan bathed him in the water (baptism) and dressed him in clothes, and Eustace never again was the cantankerous child he had been.

A truly fresh air blows through Lewis's books. Though his ideas are profound, his words are as simple as can be. One American who visited Lewis summarized him well. "You find yourself using his ideas and forgetting that they are his. His mind seems a colossal picture-making machine, and each picture reduces a great and terrible theological abstraction to the clarity of a Gospel parable. He moves in on you, and possesses the stray ends of your imagination, not by the color and fire of his intellectual pyrotechnics, as his enemies assert, but rather by the simple reality of his service to your spirit." Like the greatest writers, he knew how to take simple things and make them illustrate profound things.

He was anything but a solemn, long-faced saint. In fact, he once said, "I'm not the religious type." He once went to address a congregation wearing a lounge coat, slacks, and tennis shoes. He had little use for hymns and hated organ music. He usually attended the early service in his little parish church in order to have a minimum of music and sermon. He so ardently loved the outdoors that on one particularly beautiful day he stood outside and dictated to his secretary through the open window. He loved sitting with friends and swapping jokes. It was his "unsaintly" attitude, together with his unanswerable logic, that made him, as Chad Walsh says, the apostle to the skeptics. One of them said, "His books exposed the shallowness of our atheist prejudices; his vision illumined the Mystery which lay behind the appearances of daily life."

In a BBC address, Lewis said, "All I'm doing is to get people to face the facts—to understand the questions which Christianity claims to answer."

C. E. M. Joad, professor of philosophy at the University of London, said of Lewis, "He had the rare gift of being able to make righteousness readable." Like St. Augustine, Lewis was deeply convinced that no man will ever find rest until he rests in God, indeed that a man will never really be a man until he recognizes God's rights to him. The only real face is the face turned in contrition and gratitude to God.

Perhaps his greatest fear had to do with the ease and subtlety with which even a man's best acts become tinged with selfishness. Though always perhaps a bit more decent than the average man, Lewis says that when he examined himself before God about the time of his conversion, he found within what appalled him, "a zoo of lusts, a bedlam of ambitions, a nursery of fears, a harem of fondled hatreds." He saw the necessity for a Christian to commit himself anew every morning to God and really to live the life commanded. "Nothing you have not given away will ever be yours," he said. Also, "Until you have given yourself up to Him you will never have any real self." He believed that God calls Christians to perfection and that the whole of life is a preparation for even further training in the next until God fulfills quite literally His promise of perfection.

What Lewis genuinely believed in and attempted to practice was a life of holiness. He saw true holiness not as a dull and negative sort of thing but as something irresistible, and he believed that if even ten percent of Christians had holiness the world speedily would be converted. One close friend said that he saw in Lewis what he had never seen in any other man—"in Lewis the natural and the supernatural seemed to be one, to flow one into the other." Lewis did not have many enemies, but some of those he had simply could not understand a man, and especially a man as lively as he, seriously intent on holiness.

The wide range of interest in Lewis is suggested by two letters I happened to receive in the same mail. One was from a Boston wool merchant who said, "I am frank to admit no Christian writer has made the contribution to my own faith and my ability to defend the Christian position that Lewis has." He said he had given away many of Lewis's books to people in spiritual need.

The other letter was from a teacher in New Jersey who was reading Lewis's *The Lion, the Witch and the Wardrobe* (The Macmillan Company, 1951), to her third-graders. She had come to the point where the lion Aslan allowed himself to be killed by his enemies to save a bad boy's life. "The attitude of the room," said this teacher, "was worship, holiness. The rare impression of that moment will never leave me. When I had finished the chapter about Aslan's death the room was in stunned disbelief. Aslan dead! And then a child who had read further said, 'Don't give up—something wonderful is going to happen.' It crept through the room and sighs issued. The little people had caught glimpses of the very real, the miracle of spiritual understanding."

During the last eight years of his life Lewis moved from Oxford to Cambridge, but he never gave up his beloved house four miles east of Oxford. During this period, when he was fifty-eight, he married Helen Joy Gresham and had a little more than three blissful years before his wife died of cancer. His own physical troubles steadily increased and on July 15, 1963, about three months before his actual death, he went into a coma during which he had such a glimpse of the glory ahead that he was disappointed to awaken on earth. Afterward he wrote a friend that he thought Lazarus was really the first martyr because of being brought back and having his "dying to do again." No one can read Lewis's numerous accounts of the glories and joys of heaven without anticipating the abundant entrance this great and good man had into that realm. He was buried in the churchyard of his small parish church a half mile from his home.

One of the world's greatest scholars in his chosen field and great-minded in all his thoughts, he was nevertheless a man who rejoiced in the simple things of earth and who from the heart believed that God was alive and really meant what He had said to men.

Footnotes

1. From *Surprised by Joy*, by C. S. Lewis (Harcourt, Brace and Company, 1955), p. 115.
2. From *Surprised by Joy*, by C. S. Lewis, pp. 228-29.
3. From *The Silver Chair*, by C. S. Lewis (The Macmillan Company, 1953), p. 17.
4. From *The Voyage of the Dawn Treader*, by C. S. Lewis (The Macmillan Company, 1952), pp. 169-70.
5. From *Voyage of the Dawn Treader*, by C. S. Lewis, pp. 89-90.

"I wish I could have done more. But it is very rewarding to know that I gave 25 years in India. I'd do it again if I could." (Her testimony at 91.)

67

Florence Cooprider Friesen, MD

J. C. Wenger

A wedding took place in Kansas in 1878. A former Hoosier, Matthias Cooprider, already twice widowed, took as his bride, a Virginian, a widow named Susan Heatwole Brunk. Both the bride and groom already had families. And the strangest events followed in due time. Cooprider joined the Mennonite Church of his wife, and eventually was chosen as a Mennonite preacher. And two of his sons married two of Susan's daughters! The older Cooprider son, John A., chose as his bride Henrietta, an older sister of George R. Brunk I, later a mighty pillar in the Mennonite Church—bishop, editor, author, churchman, and father of a distinguished family (see his biography, *Faithfully, Geo. R.*, Sword and Trumpet, 1978.)

John A. and Henrietta Brunk Cooprider were blessed with seven children. The second child, a girl, was born January 6, 1887, and at this writing is still living, age 94. Her name was Florence Cooprider, and she was a freckled, shy, and brilliant farm girl. As a child she dreaded to see visitors come, for she feared they would comment on her freckles. God must have been speaking to Florence and to her younger sister, Stella (later the wife of Bishop Allen H. Erb, the longtime Superintendent of the La Junta Hospital in Colorado), for in 1906 they both enrolled in the Academy Department of Goshen College, then a junior college at Goshen, Indiana.

During the course of her studies at Goshen, Florence heard a missionary widow describe the deep need of the people in India, in particular of the need of a woman doctor because so few of the women in that land would consent to see a man doctor. Shortly after that, the pastor of the College Mennonite Church at Goshen asked Florence whether she would consider going to India as a physician. Soon the burden to go began to rest on her. She prayed earnestly for God to guide her, and eventually clearly felt that she ought to go. She finished the academy course at Goshen at 24, and that fall enrolled in the medical college of the University of Illinois in Chicago for a four-year course of concentrated study. There were about a hundred men in the

---

J.C. Wenger teaches in the Goshen Biblical Seminary.

class, and three women! But Florence was the kind of person who commanded the respect of the students, and she got along well with the group. (It was only a short time after she was admitted, however, that the Medical School began to require college study as a prerequisite.)

Late in 1978 Stephanie Mason interviewed Dr. Florence—then almost 92 years of age—and published an excellent account of the interview in the *Hesston Record*, Hesston, Kansas, issue of December 14, 1978. Florence told the reporter how her mother simply could not imagine her Florence taking up medicine when she couldn't bear to kill even a chicken! (Florence had then mustered her courage, and the next time her mother needed to have some chickens killed, Florence rose to the occasion and dispatched them—all three! So she *was* able to stand the sight of blood!)

Dr. Florence served her year as an intern at the Women's Hospital in the City of Brotherly Love, Philadelphia. But before leaving for India she took yet another year of Advanced Bible Study in Hesston College in Kansas, 1915-16. Finally, in the fall of 1916 she sailed for India. She rather dreaded the six-week ocean voyage all alone. But God took care of that problem also. She discovered as they sailed from Vancouver that a party of missionaries were on the ship—missionaries from a Peace Church at that (Church of Brethren), so she had delightful fellowship all the way to Bombay! From Bombay she took a train for Dhamtari, and arrived there safe and sound. It will be recalled that the entire trip took place during World War I.

At Dhamtari there was a primitive healing center known as a hospital, but she was the only doctor there. And so whether a patient came in with hookworm infestation, or leprosy, or cholera; or a woman was brought in who could not deliver her child; or a child was admitted with an ugly gash from the teeth of a wolf—it was up to Dr. Cooprider to rise to the occasion. She had come far from the days of her youth in Kansas when her mother thought she could not bear to face the sight of blood. Much harder than individual tragedies was the experience of seeing vast numbers of people die in famine conditions—people who were in no way able to avert famine conditions.

One of the India missionaries impressed her as particularly effective in the work of the Gospel. She wrote to her folks that P. A. Friesen, originally from an Evangelical Mennonite Brethren congregation in Mountain Lake, Minnesota, "is one of the best evangelists we have. He knows how to get next to the hearts of these villagers like no one else." Unfortunately, after bearing seven children (one of which was lost in death), missionary P. A.'s wife, Helena, nee Hiebert, followed her daughter in death.

The spring of 1922, Dr. Cooprider returned to Kansas for a well-deserved furlough. By that time, missionary P. A. was a lonely man, with five children to care for, ages three to twenty. He, of course, saw the sterling character and the beautiful faith and life of the lady doctor, and he must have used his skills to win the heart of his younger colleague, Dr. Cooprider. For one thing, he pointed out to her that marriage would make her a better missionary! And so they were married at Hesston on August 24, 1922, and suddenly she was the mother of his five children. P. A. and Florence later became the parents of two additional children: Paul A. and Grace Elizabeth. In 1924, when Paul was but two months of age, the Friesens returned to India—and in very truth they did make a tremendous team. P. A. preached to the roadside clinic people, and she ministered to their illnesses. They often started out early in the day, and P. A. sang and preached before she attended to the illnesses of the many people who came for help. The health officials of the British government were favorably impressed with her clinics. She also established a Leper Clinic at Shantipur—work which their son John later took charge of. Dr. Florence did many operations, especially cataract operations.

When P. A. was 62, and she was 54, they returned to the States, and settled in Denver—he as a pastor and she as a hostess to the nursing students from the La Junta School of Nursing in Colorado who came to Denver to "affiliate." Five years later, he took over the pastorate of an emerging church in Greensburg, Kansas. (And I have the most delightful memory of serving at that church, then meeting in a schoolhouse in March 1946.) The Friesens were then living in the basement of the schoolhouse. And Dr. Florence could not wait for a hospital to be established—she delivered many babies in that humble home.

Her final stint as a physician took place at Hesston, Kansas, where she established an office in 1953, and which she maintained until her sister Stella came there, dying with cancer. She then closed her office and cared for her until she was delivered from her suffering by departing to be with the Lord—which is "better by far."

Finally, in 1961, the Friesens entered Schowalter Villa at Hesston, where P.A. suffered a stroke, and died at 88 on October 28, 1967. By that time Florence was almost 81, and had lived with her beloved Peter for forty-five years. In 1971 the Mennonite Medical Association honored her with a plaque. In 1972 she sent me the reprinted life story of her grandmother, Susan Heatwole Brunk Cooprider, a moving account written by her sister Stella. And when she heard that I was working on the biography of her uncle Geo. R., she again got in touch. No wonder the editors of *Who's Who Among the Mennonites*, A. Warkentin and Melvin Gingerich, included both missionaries P. A. and Dr. Florence for separate entries in their useful reference work.

Today Dr. Friesen, in her tenth decade, is busy knitting gifts for grandchildren, making afghans for the MCC Relief Sale, and making bandages for lepers in India. She wonders where the past twenty years have gone! Best of all, she has never ceased to show love for people. She has kept the "first love," which in her academy days caused her to dedicate her life to meeting the needs of those for whom her Master shed His precious blood. "She hath done what she could!"

"Jesus is Lord. Go make disciples."

68

Harold S. Bender

Guy F. Hershberger

Harold S. Bender summarized his own theology in two sentences inscribed on the walls of the former chapel of Goshen Biblical Seminary: *Jesus is Lord. Go therefore and make disciples.* His lifelong emphasis by word and deed on these two basic concepts, the lordship of Christ and Christian Discipleship, was instrumental in arousing the worldwide Mennonite brotherhood from a moribund traditionalism for a reorientation of its thought and life, a recovery of its sense of mission, and a renewal of its encounter with Christendom and with the world. The following essay is an attempt to summarize some major motifs of Harold S. Bender (1897-1962).

Basic to these concepts as Bender understood them is the fact of the incarnation, the identification of the Word-become-flesh with sinful humanity. Back of this is the Hebrew concept of "corporate personality," the solidarity of the individual with his community. In Hebrew-Christian thinking, unlike modern individualism which rests on Greek thought, the individual represents not only himself, but the people as a whole. When one member suffers the whole body suffers with him. Whatever a man does, whether right or wrong, the entire race is affected. As Achan's sin disgraced all Israel, so Adam the representative of corporate humanity involved the entire race.

If this is true, however, the obverse is also true. If the corporate body can be betrayed by its representative it can also be redeemed by its representative. This is what was accomplished through the incarnation and the earthly ministry of Jesus. As a true representative of humanity Christ hungered and suffered as other men while ministering to their every need. His love went out to His sinful fellowmen, yet without sin on His own part. His life was in perfect obedience to the great commandments, to love God with all one's being and to love one's

---

Guy F. Hershberger is Professor Emeritus of History in Goshen College. He received the BS from Hesston College, the MA and PhD from the University of Iowa, and also studied at the University of Chicago and the University of Michigan. He is a former editor of *The Mennonite Quarterly Review*, and he taught for decades at Goshen College while Harold S. Bender was Dean. Among Dr. Hershberger's books are: Editor, *Harold S. Bender;* Editor, *The Recovery of the Anabaptist Vision; War, Peace, and Nonresistance;* and *The Way of the Cross in Human Relations.* He was long the Executive Secretary of the Committee on Peace and Social Relations of his denomination.

neighbor as oneself. When sinners reviled Him He reviled not again.

Atonement for human sin does not derive from a legal transaction designed to satisfy the demands of a capricious God and symbolized by a ceremonial sacrifice on an altar of fire. It derives from the living sacrifice of a will in perfect submission to the will of God, holy and acceptable to Him, doing justice, loving mercy, walking humbly with Him, and symbolized in that dramatic moment when, even as the quarreling Twelve were arguing among themselves as to who should be greatest, He girded Himself with a towel and stooped to wash their feet. This was the cross life of Christ by means of which He earned the right to the cross of Calvary which was but the logical sequence, the crowning experience, of what had gone before. This was the great reconciliation, the human will at-one with the will of God.

The *great* crowning achievement, however, was yet to come: the Jesus of history became the risen, the living Lord, triumphant over death, hell, and the grave, and now the Head of the church, the Ruler of the cosmos, seated at the right hand of the Father. As Bender says, throughout the pages of the New Testament that lordship is proclaimed, the lordship of Him who is Lord of lords and King of kings, at whose name every knee shall bow, and every tongue confess that Jesus Christ is Lord to the glory of God the Father. This is He of whom Paul said: "If you confess with your lips that Jesus is Lord and believe in your heart that God raised him from the dead, you will be saved" (Rom. 10:9).

But what does it mean to confess Jesus as Lord? It means something more than believing *on* Christ, more than a mere intellectual assent. It is believing *in* Christ or *into* Christ, *a union with Christ* (Rom. 6:5), an identification of the believer's will with that of Christ, the two grown together "in complete renunciation of the dominion of sin." "Faith, then, is our total response to God's act in Christ, repenting, believing, trusting, obeying, loving. This decisive act on our part permits the penetration of Christ to the very roots of our selfhood." This is receiving the grace of God. Not a grace passively received through the instrumentality of the sacraments. Nor a cheap grace whose end is a mere inner repose of the soul. But the enabling grace of God commissioning the believer with the ministry of reconciliation, the Holy Spirit empowering him to go forth as an ambassador for Christ, carrying on His work in the world (2 Cor. 5:18-21; 6:1). The believer's will, voluntarily captive to Christ, is crucified with Him, dead unto sin. In its stead a new will has risen up, a new man in whom the will of Christ and the will of the believer are one. This is the making of a Christian. This is the foundation of Christian discipleship.

And what is Christian discipleship? It is entering into the same experience with Christ as He walked the way of the cross in Judea and Galilee, the way of the basin and the towel. It is to have the mind of Christ; to walk with Him who suffered, leaving us an example that we should follow in His steps. It is to take the way of love and nonresistance in union with Him who when reviled reviled not again. For when He bore our sins on the tree He did so not only that there might be an inner peace in our soul and that some day we might be with Him in heaven, but that we might live unto righteousness here and now. Christian discipleship means to be raised in newness of life which we with Menno Simons can say from the heart and demonstrate in real life that the regenerated do not go to war, nor engage in strife. "They are the children of peace who have beaten their swords into plowshares and their spears into pruning hooks, and know of no war."

Christian discipleship is a holy obedience, springing not from legal requirements, but arising from the holy commitment of union with Christ. When God was in Christ reconciling the world to Himself, His victory over sin and death was a moral achievement which entered into the spiritual history of the race. Christian discipleship means entrance into this historic stream. It is "to fling oneself without reserve into the stream of forces issuing from Christ's supreme moral achievement." As disciples of Christ we cannot take His place in the work of redemption, but we must take our place as His followers, as laborers together with Him, sharing in the love which prompted Him to sacrifice His love for sinful humanity.

Here again the Christian concept of corporate personality plays its role. As Bender reminds us so forcibly, the Christian disciple is not merely an individual. As in the case of the 120 in the upper room in Jerusalem, he is one of a band of disciples in solidarity with each other and with their Lord, awaiting "the great and manifest day," receiving their Great Commission to go forth in his work with power. The disciples are the body of Christ. He is the head of the body. The church is a brotherhood whose unity derives from Christ the Head. Each disciple is a saint, sanctified for the ministry of the gift with which he has been endowed. True, there are prophets, evangelists, apostles, pastors, and teachers, but these are names of functions, not titles of status, and their common function is to equip the saints—each saint individually and all unitedly—that the body of Christ, the church, may go on to maturity and perfection (Eph. 4:11-12).

The church is a visible holy community, known as such to the Lord, to each other, and to the world about them, and symbolized in the communion service which is neither a mere memorial service nor a mere sacrament dispensing the grace of heaven through the transformation of bread and wine into the flesh and blood of Christ's physical body. It is the Lord's Supper, the priestly community under the headship of Christ the high priest, experiencing and declaring its solidarity with Him and with one another.

As a student both of the New Testament church and of the Anabaptist search for the restitution of the church, Harold Bender was in full accord with the words of Walter Rauschenbusch when, in speaking of the Anabaptist communion service, he said: "As in the primitive church, their service was preceded by searching of heart and reconciliation, so that all might be one in Christ. As in the upper room at Jerusalem, they acted in full view of death, and their main thought was to gain strength for imprisonment and torture by once more touching the garment-hem of their Lord. They often dwelt on the fact that many grains of wheat had been crushed and had felt the heat of the oven to make this bread, and many berries of the vine had been pressed in the wine-press to make this wine; in the same way the followers of Christ must pass through affliction and persecution in order to form the body of the Lord."

The church of Christ, however, is more than a holy community observing the Lord's Supper in an upper room. It is a holy community on the march, "fighting the good fight of faith," as Bender said it in a sermon based on 1 Timothy 6:12. This is what it means to lay hold on eternal life. It is to join the forces of God's redeeming power which "has entered the world in Christ to do battle with the hosts of wickedness." It is "enlisting under the banner of the King of kings and fighting the battles of the Lord here and now until He comes again." It is to reject the "balcony perspective" of Christianity, passively enjoying the grace of God in one's own heart, taking no part in the stream of life below, "coldly indifferent to the desperate shape of things today."

The good confession, laying hold on eternal life, fighting the good fight of faith, is to acknowledge Christ as Lord and to follow Him in obedient discipleship. The fight of faith is a spiritual warfare, not a carnal one. It is to fight against evil with weapons of love. It is "to follow him in tribulation, to suffer unto blood ... to stand before the authorities and say what the Holy Spirit says to witness against the unrighteousness, hate, greed, exploitation and injustice to one another, to do so in the name of Christ. If we confess him as Lord we may not shrink from this prophetic mission.... If we confess him as Lord we must become peacemakers in a world of conflict and strife in the name of the Prince of Peace.... This is what we say when we confess Jesus as Lord."

The good confession of the incarnate Christ, the solidarity of the human Jesus with all mankind, His life of sacrificial service; the way of the basin and the towel leading to the cross; the new man in Christ, crucified, buried, and risen with Him, in total allegiance to him who is Lord of lords and King of kings; the response of the *Koinonia* church, its members in solidarity with their Lord and with each other, in unreserved commitment to full discipleship; the enlistment of the united holy community in the good fight of faith, running with perseverance the race set before it; looking to the pioneer and perfecter of the faith, who in disarming principalities and powers, and triumphing over them shall bring all things to their consummation and make all things new, whence he shall reign forever and ever! This was Harold S. Bender's concept of the Christian faith and life.

Crucial in the development of Bender's faith was a solid, well-integrated, liberal education, followed by thorough biblical studies and church history on the deeper level, in the course of which, although always sensitively conscious of the church universal, he developed a deep conviction as to the normative character of the apostolic church, with Anabaptism as his second point of reference. He had the advantage of a home and church environment in which, even if the nature of the Anabaptist heritage was not fully understood, it was nevertheless cherished with a degree of comprehension sufficient to encourage the entrance of the student on the road to a career in which he was destined to rediscover the deeper meaning of that heritage not only for his own Mennonite brotherhood but for the ecumenical church as well.

Bender's scholarly efforts were devoted to the writing of Anabaptist history and to its use as "an instrument for evangelism in the truest and best sense," to which forty-two volumes (by the end of 1968) of the *Mennonite Quarterly Review*, the four-volume *Mennonite Encyclopedia* (with numerous articles on theological topics), his books, and numerous articles in periodicals are a monumental testimony. As an educator his diligent efforts to put the Christian faith into "every place in the curriculum where interpretation of the data of experience enters in" had a significant influence not only in the college which he served as dean, but in Mennonite higher education generally, and beyond. As seminary dean his aim was to make that seminary a school of the Bible, a school of true disciples, of apostles, evangelists, and prophets, a school of pastors, teachers, and scholars devoted to the church, "a school which ... with the soundest historical and biblical scholarship will seek to appreciate the great heritage which has come down from the founders and martyrs through the past four centuries, and to expound it and interpret it to the present generation so effectively and so attractively that it may become more of a living and powerful force for the present age and its needs."

That the effectiveness and attractiveness of the exposition and interpretation of which Bender spoke in 1944 has come in good measure to be realized is to be seen not only in the growing influence of Bender's vision in Mennonite schools and colleges in North America and beyond, including the Mennonite seminary in Paraguay in South America and the Bienenberg Bible School in Europe, and in the formation of the Associated Mennonite Biblical Seminaries in 1958, bringing together the seminary programs of the two largest American Mennonite groups. It is to be seen even more significantly, perhaps, in the manner in which the worldwide Mennonite brotherhood in and through its various conference groups, its mission, service, and peace teaching programs, its inter-Mennonite cooperative work on various levels, including the Mennonite Central Committee and the Mennonite World Conference, has come to place increasing emphasis upon the lordship of Christ and Christian discipleship, not only by evangelism through proclamation, but also through the witness of brotherhood action in community services, mutual aid, race relations, and the Christian peace witness at home and abroad. This in turn has opened the door to conversations on peace and related questions on the ecumenical level, as in the Puidoux and Prague conferences in Europe, and in encounters with various sections of the National Association of Evangelicals and the National and World Councils of Churches.

The contribution of Harold S. Bender was well summarized in a statement by Chester K. Lehman: "His explication of the Lordship of Christ and of the nature of the church as the people of God has given new direction to Mennonite theology. The legalistic and hierarchical trends of modern Mennonitism should give way to the New Testament concept of the church." Professor H. W. Meihuizen, a Dutch Mennonite, says: "He was able to bring together 'Menno's people' ... in such a way that they learned to esteem each other.... He regarded the entire range of Mennonites as his people and therefore he was able to acquire an inalienable place in their hearts." Heinz Kloppenburg, German state-church leader: "It was a call to the origins of our faith when Harold S. Bender and his friends came to Europe to ask us whether we should not reopen the discussion that had been interrupted for nearly 400 years ... to ask ... how the challenge of the Prince of Peace could be brought forward to the continental churches, which for too long a time had been much too closely associated with the state and the world's philosophy of power."

Capsule statements such as these are characteristic of Bender's own capacity for formulating his convictions in brief, succinct clarifying statements. One little book, *These Are My People*; one sermon, "Fight the Good Fight of Faith"; and his Seventh Mennonite World Conference address, "Who Is the Lord?" written from a hospital bed in the last weeks of his life, these three in themselves are an excellent summary of the theological contribution of Harold S. Bender, Dean of Goshen College and its Bible School, 1931-44, and of the Goshen Biblical Seminary, 1944-62.

Brief Bibliography

The chief writings of Harold S. Bender were: *Old Testament Law and History, Conrad Grebel, These Are My People* (a monograph on the church), and Editor, *The Mennonite Encyclopedia*, 4 volumes. He edited the first 35 volumes of *The Mennonite Quarterly Review*, and he compiled a bibliographical work, *Two Centuries of American Mennonite Literature*. Among his briefer works may be mentioned *Menno Simon's Life and Writings* (with John Horsch), *The Anabaptist Vision*, and *Biblical Revelation and Inspiration*.

After his death his friends issued a series of essays on his life, thought, and work entitled *Harold S. Bender: Educator, Historian, Churchman*, 1964.

> "My upbringing had given me a definite attitude regarding the struggle which goes on perpetually in the human spirit and in society as to whether the Gospel demand shall be adjusted to the outward circumstances or the recalcitrant reality shall be made to conform to the high ethical demand."[1]

69
Abraham Johannes Muste

J. R. Burkholder

To include A. J. Muste (1885-1967) in a book about theologians is to make a special kind of judgment about the nature of theologizing. Certainly A. J. (as he was always called) never thought of himself as a theologian, nor did he receive public acclaim as such. In his multifaceted career, he was minister, teacher, labor organizer, civil rights leader, but above all, the foremost radical pacifist of his time. He has been variously described as "peace agitator," "fighting reconciler," and "man of conscience." But if the professional definition of "theologian" includes those who have thought long and hard and profoundly about the meaning of man's existence in God's world, then A. J. surely qualifies. His life bears testimony to the quality of conviction that characterized the biblical Abraham, whose figure Muste frequently evokes in writing about response to the divine command, and whose namesake he was.

Because it is his life, as much or more than his writings, that reveals Muste's pilgrimage of faith, it is necessary to give more attention to biography than is the rule in this book. Born in Holland, young A. J. came with his family to the United States in 1891, settling in Grand Rapids, Michigan. Nurtured in the strict Calvinist orthodoxy of the Dutch Reformed Church, he recalls in autobiographical sketches the awesome experience of Sunday church attendance, employing the imagery of Hebrews 12:22-23. He attended Hope College, distinguished himself as an orator, and graduated in 1905 as class valedictorian.

J. R. Burkholder is Professor of Religion in Goshen College. It was from Goshen that he received the BA, the BD from Goshen Biblical Seminary, and the PhD from Harvard University. He was for a number of years a missionary in Brazil, then a pastor in Philadelphia. He is much interested in peace and biblical nonresistance as understood in the Anabaptist-Mennonite tradition.

In 1909, upon graduation from the denominational seminary at New Brunswick, New Jersey, Muste was ordained to the ministry of the Reformed Church. That same year he married Anna Huizenga, who was to be his devoted companion until her death in 1954. During his first pastorate in New York City, study at Union Theological Seminary (BD, *magna cum laude*, 1913) and experience in the Lower East Side slums broadened his intellectual horizons and made him aware of the need for drastic social change. His political radicalism was expressed in his vote for the Socialist Presidential candidate Eugene Debs, in 1912; Muste never voted for a candidate of the major parties. No longer comfortable with Calvinist dogma, he resigned his pastorate in 1914 and moved to the Central Congregational Church of Newtonville, Massachusetts.

With the outbreak of World War I in Europe, Muste was led, through the study of the Bible, Christian mystics, and the Quakers, to an uncompromising pacifist stand. The congregation appeared to tolerate his views until the United States entered the war. But it soon became clear that most American Christians agreed with Theodore Roosevelt that "the clergyman who does not put the flag above the church had better close his church, and keep it closed." In 1917, the Mustes were forced to leave Newtonville, and thus began the radical phase of his career.

In the next months, he worked with the American Civil Liberties Union, served a Friends Meeting in Providence, and, with his family and dedicated friends, formed the "Comradeship," a pacifist communitarian fellowship in Boston. Involvement in the bitter textile strike at Lawrence, Massachusetts, in 1919, where A. J. counseled nonviolence in the face of massive official brutality, led to his work as a labor organizer, teacher, and later director of the Brookwood Labor College, a post he held until 1933. During the 20s, he continued his association with the Quakers and was active in the Fellowship of Reconciliation, a religious pacifist organization.

But his growing disillusionment over the possibilities for peaceful social change led to the study of Marxism and fascination for a time with the communist revolution. Critical of the churches, he abandoned his Christian pacifism and became, in his phrase, a "Trotskyist Marxist-Leninist," founding the revolutionary American Workers Party in 1933. Several years of controversial political activity followed.

The "detour to the left," however, was destined to be no more than a detour. Muste writes of his "reconversion" as he sat in the empty church of St. Sulpice in Paris in 1936:

> Somehow, almost from the moment I came into the sanctuary, a deep and what I can only describe as a singing peace came over me.... I seated myself on a bench and looked toward the altar and the cross. I felt, "This is where you belong, in the church, not outside it."[2]

Before the year was over, Muste was back in action with the F.O.R. (Fellowship of Reconciliation), the organization that claimed his loyalties and provided the context for the rest of his life. As writer, speaker, and demonstrator, he put his words and body on the line against war, the draft, racial segregation, and other forms of inhumanity, all through the war years and beyond.

After retirement from the post of F.O.R. executive secretary in 1953, he continued to protest injustice and violence. War taxes, civil defense, nuclear testing, missile bases—all these and more were targets of his frequent acts of civil disobedience. In the months before his death at the age of 82, he traveled to both Saigon and Hanoi in unrelenting witness to the way of peace.

During these decades, Muste published the books and essays from which one may seek to distill a theology. His writings are for the most part "tracts for the times," offering prophetic criticism of American life and arguing for social justice by nonviolent means. But A. J., while not a systematic thinker, was more than a polemical gadfly. While he seldom spoke explicitly as a churchman, his writings probe the meaning of events, and evaluate man and society, from a deeply religious viewpoint. It was his genius to be able to move freely between the realms of the secular and sacred, to speak both to the Marxist and to the Methodist. His personal commitment, however, was unequivocal:

> I am a Christian believer. I was brought up in the Christian church. After some years during which I was a thorough-going Marxist-Leninist, renouncing all religion as "opiate of the people" and the church as nothing but a bulwark of a reactionary status quo, I returned to the church and to faith in the love of God as revealed in Jesus Christ as the one means of salvation for the individual and for mankind.[3]

As far as precise theological statement is concerned, A. J. had no interest in intellectual activity for its own sake. He read widely in the field, however, and demonstrated his ability to match the theologians at their own level in his debates with such worthies as Reinhold Niebuhr and his analyses of ecumenical pronouncements on war and peace. He had little patience with what he regarded as the neo-orthodox "theology of despair," arguing on the basis of the New Testament that man, though justified, is not doomed to remain in his sins.

> The word of forgiveness is necessarily accompanied by the charge. "Go and sin no more." Forgiveness in its most basic aspect means this: that God will not let us drop out of the moral universe; he will not free us from the requirement that we be his children reborn in Christ.[4]

It is this deep conviction of a moral universe in which men can become new creatures that grounds A. J.'s stubborn faith and resolute action. Man comes to know God as Father only when he begins to live and to act as the son of such a Father. At the moment of moral decision, man comes into relation with the living God. But, although Muste's beliefs might be characterized as "liberal," he is anything but a simple optimist. Both in his self-understanding and in his prophetic pronouncements, the note of humility and of judgment is sounded.

> I was self-sufficient in 1929. Now I know that I was not and am not; that I live by the grace of God and stand straightest when I am on my knees.[5]

Unless men are prepared to a significant degree to accept the laws of God and the spirit of Christ as the way of life for nations as well as individuals, there is no hope for us.[6]

His constant challenge was for the church to become truly the church, for Christians to follow their Master in renouncing warfare and exploitation, and to make nonviolence a pervasive way of life. Muste, however, had no illusions about quick success:

> Pacifism cannot guarantee a cheap and painless solution. Life is dynamic and unpredictable. We have to make the leap of faith. We have to risk failure and stark defeat. The Cross is central.[7]

But beyond the cross, a symbol recurring frequently in Muste's writing, there is the sustaining vision of the holy community.

> Abraham went out looking for a city which existed—and yet had to be brought into existence. It was the perfect and holy city—which had to be built and whose "builder and maker is God." Precisely because it was God who built the city, it could be built only by Abraham's faith and labor.[8]

Footnotes & Bibliography

1. Nat Hentoff, editor, *The Essays of A. J. Muste* (Indianapolis: Bobbs-Merrill, 1967), p. 46.
2. Nat Hentoff, *Peace Agitator: The Story of A. J. Muste* (New York: Macmillan, 1963), pp. 97-98.
3. A. J. Muste, *Non-violence in an Aggressive World* (New York: Harper and Brothers, 1940), p. 11.
4. *Essays of A. J. Muste*, p. 319.
5. *Ibid.*, p. 208.
6. A. J. Muste, *Not By Might* (New York: Harper and Brothers, 1947), p. 133.
7. *Ibid.*, p. 85.
8. *Essays*, p. 415.

> *"He is a confessional Theologian, yet he insists that the Scriptures must judge the confessions."*

70

Gerritt Cornelius Berkouwer

Archie Penner

G. C. Berkouwer (1903-   ), contemporary Dutch theologian and previous pastor, was reared in a devout Reformed home and church in the Netherlands. From his earliest years, he thus drank deeply at the springs of the thought and moods of the Calvinism of his time in his native country. As one gathers from his writings, he became a deeply committed Christian. His commitment and dedication can best be described as first to Christ and then to his confessional, Reformed faith and his tasks as pastor and theologian.

Berkouwer, was long the Professor of Systematic Theology at the Free University of Amsterdam. Occupying this position since 1945, he is the fourth in a line of distinguished orthodox Dutch theologians. First was Abraham Kuyper; both a theologian and a statesman, who was responsible for the founding of this university (1880). He was also a leader involved in the formation of the seceding Reformed Churches of the Netherlands (1892). These developments and Abraham Kuyper expressed reaction against the liberalism and modernism which had largely become acceptable in leading circles of the Dutch church of the time.

Falling heir to Dr. Kuyper was Hermann Bavinck, a theologian in his own right. Then came Hepp who pursued a scholastic approach in his theology. Berkouwer, the fourth in this line, studied theology under Hepp. He inherited Hepp's position but did not adopt his theological method.

Professor Berkouwer strikes the reader as staunchly evangelical. At the same time his theology is confessional. He thus writes from within the context of classical Dutch Reformed thought. As a confessional theologian, he is thoroughly familiar with creeds and confessions of the church. He considers them a significant dimension of Christian theology. However, what Berkouwer does not want to do is to subject the Scriptures to the confessions. In fact, he takes the posi-

---

Archie Penner is Professor of Religion in Malone College. He is an ordained minister. He received his BA from Goshen College, the BD from Goshen Biblical Seminary, the MA from Wheaton College, and the PhD from the State University of Iowa. He is the author of *The New Testament, the Christian and the State*.

tion that the confessions must be subject to the Scriptures, and the Scriptures must judge the confessions. "... dogma is in the church, which in turn is subject ... to the Word" (*The Person of Christ*, p. 91). Again, "For the church there is but one terminal point and but one limit: ... this revelation of him ..." (*ibid.*, p. 97).

To be a practical theologian is Berkouwer's aim and task. Theology is not meant to be for the purpose of speculative mental gymnastics. It is not for logic but for faith that theology must exist. It must be kept concrete and unphilosophical so that it can be of the fullest service to a preaching, listening, believing, worshiping church.

Further, Berkouwer can be characterized as a polemical theologian. There are two features in his writings which make him a polemicist. First, he is in almost constant conversation in his writings with the thinkers of the church in the past and in the present. He argues with them. He sifts. He distills. And as he does so, the reader is struck with his accomplished fairness and kindliness of spirit. This is polemics at its best.

This theologian's specifically polemical books are the second feature. The Swiss theologian, Karl Barth, and the Roman Catholic Church are his formidable opponents. With Barth, he enters into critical conversation in his book, *The Triumph of Grace*.... Two noble features seem to show themselves in this book. First the critic listens sympathetically, and endeavors to obtain the clearest understanding of his opponent's position. Second, he "attacks" him in what the opponent actually tries to say, not the results which the critic might think would be the logical outcome of the assumptions underlying the other's position. Berkouwer employs this kind of critical treatment of Barth. This does not mean that he uncritically accepts Barth. On the contrary, he criticizes him severely.

Among other questions, Berkouwer feels that Barth's view of sin is not wholly biblical. He fears that the gospel must lose its fuller meaning and effectiveness when Barth's view of sin is accepted. Again, there is the question of an implicit universalism. Berkouwer does not charge the Swiss theologian with universalism. However, he does feel that it can hardly be avoided in Barth's thought. These criticisms reveal some of the Dutchman's own biblical and theological positions.

In his polemical conversation with the Roman Catholic Church, he does not deal with peripheral problems. Rather, he plunges into the very center of his conflict with Rome. Rome's claims to authority, the place of the Scriptures, and the cult of Mary in her theology are carefully and critically discussed in his books on Roman Catholicism. He concludes that if weighed on the scales of grace, Rome is found wanting. But this does not rob Berkouwer of hope because wherever the Bible is open the unexpected can happen.

In spite of Berkouwer's frankness and his vigorous Protestant theological views, the Church of Rome seemed pleased with his analysis. His objectivity and fairness won for him an official invitation as observer at the Second Vatican Council in Rome.

As an ecumenically minded evangelical, Berkouwer will not close his mind to any development in better understanding and closer fellowship among communions. But he faces squarely the fundamental problems of theology which ecumenicity entails. The Scriptures define ecumenicity for him.

Berkouwer endeavors to be a relevant theologian. He has not developed a new theology, nor does he intend to do so. However, since he has come to the Free University of Amsterdam, wafts of new theological breezes have been noticed. Some welcome modifications and clarifications have been advanced. If some of the older Reformed theologians seem to have given occasion to the view that in some sense God is responsible for sin and evil, Berkouwer will have none of it. "Theology may not say anything that would put the mystery of evil somewhere within the will of God."

Again, there is a healthy approach to Calvinism's view of election. It is not a hidden decree to Berkouwer. Those who accept grace at the "foot of the cross" know their election by faith. Neither is election "a brute decree of a merely sovereign Deity." It is rather the personal, gracious deed of a loving God. On the other hand, he seems to break the grip of double predestination by holding that rejection of the sinner is the divine response to sin.

Justification and sanctification are inseparable in Berkouwer's view. Both the fact that the sinner is *accepted* as righteous in Christ, and that he is *made* pure and holy in life are part of the same grace, and throughout life related to the same exercise of faith. Man needs accepting and forgiving grace, as well as purifying grace, at every moment of his life, as much at the end and the middle of his Christian life as at the beginning.

It will be remembered, in conclusion, that these are but a few of the major contributions which Berkouwer is making to present evangelical theological thought. He has tried to base all of his thought on careful and faithful exegesis of the Scriptures. However, he would want his readers to remember that his understanding of the Christian faith is organically related to the historic Reformed thought.

Brief Bibliography

Berkhouwer has written some three dozen theological books in Dutch, of which twelve are in his *Dogmatics* series. The following ten *Studies in the Dogmatics* volumes are available in English: *The Providence of God; Faith and Sanctification, Faith and Justification, Faith and Perseverance, The Person of Christ, General Revelation, Divine Election, Man: The Image of God, The Work of Christ,* and *The Sacraments.*

For a full list of his works in English, see *Books in Print.*

> "All theological questions and answers are meaningful only within the framework of the history which God has with humanity and through humanity with his whole creation—the history moving toward a future still hidden from the world but already revealed in Jesus Christ."

71

Wolfhart Pannenberg

Helmut Harder

Wolfhart Pannenberg (1928-   ) is a German theologian who represents a new turn in theology since the middle of the twentieth century. Before that time the theological scene had been influenced very much by the theological work of Rudolf Bultmann and Karl Barth. Although Pannenberg has been one of Barth's students, and was also very much influenced by Bultmann, he is convinced that the time has come for theology to move beyond the guidelines set by these two great theologians of the earlier half of our century.

Pannenberg is not alone in this new movement. Other theologians also felt as he did. In the early 1950s a group of four students of theology at Heidelberg, who had studied under Bultmann, began to meet together to discuss and question the theological assumptions of their teacher. They were joined almost immediately by Wolfhart Pannenberg, who came to study at Heidelberg after one year as a student of Barth at Basel. Pannenberg soon became the most articulate spokesman and prolific writer in the group. The viewpoints of the "Pannenberg group" were first published formally in a monograph entitled *Offenbarung als Geschichte* (1961). An English translation has appeared recently under the title *Revelation as History*.

The Pannenberg movement is related, though less directly, to the work of other post-Bultmannian and post-Barthian scholars. The work of this loosely related group has come to be known as the "theology of hope," and is represented by such men as Johannes B. Metz and Jürgen Moltmann in addition to Pannenberg. Although these scholars are from continental Europe, there has been interest in

---

Helmut Harder is Professor of Theology in the Canadian Mennonite Bible College, Winnipeg. He received the AB from McMaster University, the BD from Mennonite Biblical Seminary, the M Th from St. Johns College, and the ThD from the University of Toronto.

the "theology of hope" movement in America as well. Both Pannenberg and Moltmann have lectured in American universities for extended periods of time in recent years. Furthermore, the third volume of *New Frontiers in Theology*, edited by James M. Robinson and John B. Cobb of the Southern California School of Theology at Claremont, and entitled *Theology as History*, is devoted to a discussion of the views of Pannenberg.

What are the views of Pannenberg? The key word for Pannenberg is history. It is his contention that with Bultmann, Barth, and others, theology has too much lost its historical foundation. He is devoted to explicating a theology which will be firmly based upon history. The term "history," of course, does not refer only to facts about what has happened in the past, as we usually think of this. This is only a small part of what Pannenberg means by history. His idea of history is much richer than this. History is a dynamic force which grasps man and catches him up into the movement of life by pushing him from the past and pulling him into the future. Man finds himself caught up in a movement which is hastening toward an end—the end of history. With this basic starting point, Pannenberg develops his understanding of the Christian faith and his interpretation of the Bible.

What does Pannenberg say about the revelation of God? The process of history, or better, the dynamic movement of history, reflects the self-revelation of God. In the very movement of history God reveals Himself. The events of history are His speaking and His acting. Such a revelation of God is to be thought of as indirect. That is, it is not that history is God. Rather, the events of history throw light back upon God, and thus reveal Him to us.

Since history is still running its course, it follows that the revelation of God is in a sense not yet complete. We do not know everything there is to know about God because He is still in the process of creating events through which we further get to know Him. The full knowledge of God would require that all of His acts be known. This is why Pannenberg says that there are still things about God that we do not yet know. This is also why he says that the fullness of God will be known to us only at the end of history. The future still has some things to tell us.

This view of revelation is therefore different from that of Barth. Barth would hold that God was revealed in His fullness in individual acts in the past, specifically in the incarnation. Pannenberg's view is also different from that of Rudolf Bultmann, who would hold that God can reveal Himself more or less fully in the one master existential decision which a Christian makes in the present day. Pannenberg does not tie revelation exclusively to any one event, but to the whole of history.

The question now arises: How does Jesus Christ fit into the picture? Was Christ not the full revelation of God? Pannenberg speaks of Christ as the full revelation of God in a modified sense. Certainly He is the full revelation of God as far as Israel is concerned, since He brought the formal history of Israel to a close. He did this when he fulfilled their highest expectations as the Messiah. Also, Jesus Christ is the full revelation of God in the sense that through Christ, God revealed

Himself fully as the God of the whole world—not only as the God of Israel. Furthermore, Christ is the full revelation of God in the sense that the resurrection shows what will befall all men. But beyond this the Christian still awaits a fuller revelation of God. This is seen in the fact that Jesus spoke certain promises which have not yet been fulfilled. That is, the fullness of revelation requires also the future. The Christ-event affords certain guidelines for faith, but the full story will become evident only when history has run its course.

What does this mean for faith? Faith has two directions or perspectives. On the one hand, faith is based firmly on what has happened in the past. Men look at past events, and the way in which God has been working becomes evident to them. They see how God has made Himself known, and thus they come to know what God is like. The Christ-event is particularly impressive as a guide to an understanding God. On the other hand, faith is also based on a hope of what God will yet bring in the future. Men live by the expectation that the promises and anticipations given in the past will be fully realized in the future. The key promise is contained in the event of the resurrection. The resurrection, as an "end" to Jesus' own history, gives the Christian some idea of his own "end." Thus faith is based on both the evidence of history and trust in the future.

This view of faith is different from that of Bultmann. For Bultmann the Christian has faith in the proclamation of the church. For him, the Christian believes in Christ because the disciples and the early church believed in Christ. But for Pannenberg belief in Christ is based upon the Christ-event itself. That is, faith finds its basis, its very foundation, in the historical Jesus, both in the evidence that Jesus was a historical figure in the past, and in the firm trust that He will appear again in history. There is another major contrast between Bultmann and Pannenberg. In Bultmann's view, man's self-conscious faith relation to God causes him to select certain facts which he then claims as acts of God for his salvation. In Pannenberg's view, all of history, including, of course, those events which the Christian faith has emphasized, draw man into the movement of faith, and impart to him his union with God and his salvation.

Anyone who reads the writings of Pannenberg will find some viewpoints which will have a familiar ring, and others will sound strange and new. This is to be expected of any theologian who engages in the formidable task of seeking to formulate the relationship between the historic Christian faith and the mood of the times in which we live. Pannenberg offers the Christian a way of speaking about his faith which will preserve the historical foundation of the faith, and at the same time temper this with an openness to the new events which crowd in upon man from day to day.

Bibliography

Representative of the many books by Pannenberg now in English translation are *Basic Questions in Theology; Jesus: God and Man; Theology and the Kingdom of God; What Is Man; Spirit, Faith, and Church;* (Editor) *Revelation as History;* Pannenberg, et al., *Historical and Hermeneutical Journal for Theology and Church.* (See *Books in Print.*)

72
Women in the Anabaptist/Mennonite Tradition

Esther K. Augsburger

During the 16th-century Reformation, the Free Church movement came to birth with a special emphasis on the community of believers. In these congregations there was an outstanding expression of freedom which involved women in responsible positions along with the men in the life of the church. The Baptist historian, Roland Bainton, points out that, whereas women in Catholic and Protestant churches were still treated in a very medieval manner, there was among the Anabaptists a great degree of freedom.

Women were actively involved in the movement. They were commissioned as deaconesses, Bible teachers, and further evidence of their active participation is the fact that in *Martyrs Mirror*, the major volume on the Christian martyrs of the 16th century, one out of every three martyrs was a woman.

They had an amazing grasp of the Scriptures, as evidenced in their many writings from prison. In the accounts of their responses to their interrogators, they quoted line upon line of Scriptures from memory. They were not permitted Bibles in prison, therefore their Bible knowledge was established before their capture.

Numerous women in the 16th century taught and nurtured new believers, engaged in theological discourses with church leaders, held positions in the church, and contributed to literary works printed for distribution and used as church hymns. This tradition can be exemplified by the following accounts of several women of that century who made outstanding contributions to the church and brief biographies of several women from the 20th century who were faithful servants for Christ.

Esther K. Augsburger is the wife of Dr. Myron S. Augsburger, the mother of three children, John, Michael, and Marcia, and a free-lance artist. She was born in India, of missionary parents, participated with her husband in ministry and evangelism, and taught at Eastern Mennonite High School. Her life has been dedicated to Christ and His church. She has served her denomination also as President of the Virginia Mennonite Conference WMSC for a term, and as speaker for various women's groups. She is the author of a devotional guide for women, *Women Expendable for Christ*. Her academic training includes a Master of Arts, with additional postgraduate study.

Elizabeth Dirks (1549) was the first Mennonite deaconess. She worked so closely with Menno Simons that when she was arrested they thought they had taken Menno's wife. She was drowned for her faith on May 27, 1549, at Leeuwarden, Friesland.

Elizabeth, who came from a wealthy family, was taken to live in a convent when she was a young child to learn the arts and the Latin language.

By accident one day Elizabeth found a Latin New Testament in the convent, which she read ardently and thought about much. As a result she became dissatisfied with her life as a Catholic. Her honest questions resulted in imprisonment for a year on suspicion of heresy. Since the nuns favored her, they petitioned for and secured her release on the condition that she would be under their constant supervision.

She became increasingly disturbed by her way of life there, by the emptiness she felt, and by the discovery that many of the doctrines she was taught in the convent seemed contrary to the Scripture. So Elizabeth made an agreement with the milkmaid of the convent to exchange clothes one morning. Disguised as a milkmaid, she made her escape.

She went to live with an Anabaptist family in Leer, where she studied the Scriptures and was baptized. Later she went to live with an Anbaptist widow whose name was Hadewijk, from whose home she went in and out to work with Menno Simons until her death. The most detailed account of her imprisonment, interrogation, and torture can be found in *Martyrs Mirror* on page 582.

Elizabeth was significantly involved in the church by teaching, visiting, and writing. A song was written on her death, "Twas ein maechdeken van teder leden Elizabeth dat was horen naem." It is found in the *Het Offer des Heeren* (1562) and also in the *Ausbund,* number 13. She composed a song which was included in *Sommige Stichtelycke Leidekens (Hoorn,* 1618).

(*The Mennonite Encyclopedia,* Vol. II, p. 185.)

Magdalena Pappenheim was one of three significant Pappenheim sisters of a manorial family of lords in the 16th century from South Germany. Magdalena was a nun of the Benedictine order in the convent at Urspring, Swabia. However, she left the convent to join Schwenkfeld, an association which never materialized. Instead she developed an association with Pilgram Marpeck, the great Anabaptist leader. She became a significant literary figure, corresponding on theological issues with both Marpeck and Schwenkfeld, and functioned as a go-between in their communication and discussion. Their discourse centered around the doctrine of Christ and man's nature and sinfulness, and on the importance of baptism and the Lord's Supper.

Magdalena wrote Schwenkfeld a pointed letter of criticism and declined any further association with him. To which Schwenkfeld replied on August 21, 1542, expressing regret that she was no longer interested in working with him. He explained that he was not preaching a "proud Christ" and criticized Marpeck's writings. He accused her of relying on Marpeck's opinion of him rather than reading his books for herself. He engaged her in a debate he had with Marpeck on the question of whether Christ could have sinned. Schwenkfeld frequently wrote to her on other controversial issues to influence her away from Marpeck, and to Marpeck accusing him of deprecating him to Magdalena and thus arresting her growth.

Her intense involvement in such discourses is evidence of her intellectual and spiritual insights on the theological issues with which the church leaders at that time were struggling.

Magdelena died in 1571.

(*The Mennonite Encycopedia*, Vol. IV, p. 115.)

Anneken Jans inherited a considerable fortune. She came from Rotterdam, Holland, and was married to Arent Jans. They were baptized together in their home in Brielle, Holland.

Anneken was an avid follower of David Joris, an Anabaptist preacher at the time. Historical writings allude to her many gifts and strong influence on Joris by her keen insights into the Scriptures. However, shortly after her death, Joris backslid from the faith and moved to Basel, Switzerland, to live under an assumed name to avoid identity and persecution.

Anneken and her husband, under pressure of persecution, had, at the early age of twenty-four, relinquished all their possessions for their faith and fled to England. A short time later, Arent died. Two years later Anneken, with her 15-month-old son, Esaias, returned to Holland in order to settle her financial affairs and to meet David Joris in the small town of Delft. On the way to Rotterdam, as Anneken was stepping into the boat for Delft, along with a sister in the church as a traveling companion, she was arrested. She was gifted in music and was heard singing a hymn. For this she was charged with sectarianism. She openly confessed her faith in Christ and was sent to prison.

Anneken's numerous letters from prison have been a significant contribution to the early Anabaptists and are recorded in the historical manuscripts. One of these letters was beautifully written to the wavering David Joris: "For as the rain refreshes the earth and the dew refreshes the flowers of the field and gives them a fragrance dear to men, so your admonition, preaching, and instruction gives men life, food, and taste, though it contains no high wisdom, and shows them the way of perfect wisdom of God, whereby they grow into the stature of a perfect man in Christ Jesus, our Lord.

"O thou sanctified of the Lord, be brave, let nothing dismay you; yet a little while, and He will come and show us a sample of His glory, for the judgment of the world, but to His and our glorification" *(The Mennonite Encyclopedia,* Vol. I, p. 127).

One of the most significant manuscripts is the will Anneken wrote to her son Esaias from prison *(Martyrs Mirror,* pp. 453, 454). It was printed in 1539 and reprinted many times. It was included in the oldest (1562) editions of the Dutch *Martyr Book, Het Offer des Heeren,* and in all the martyr books following. One writer makes the following comment:

> The testament is one of those broadside and short popular writings which, scattered among the people by hundreds and thousands after

1520, have in part been destroyed and burned, but often carefully preserved and passed on from generation to generation as a precious heirloom.

Another writer judged it to be "one of the most worthy witnesses of the self-denying, sacrificing, steadfast piety of the Anabaptists." It contains a glorious confession of faith and evidence of faithful mother love.

An unknown poet included part of the will in a song found in the *Ausbund* (number 18) and other Anabaptist hymnbooks.

Anneken authored a song early enough to be included in David Joris's *Geestelyck Liedtbocxken* (Royal Library in the Hague) and later in Menno Simons' songbooks. It begins: "I hear the trumpets blow . . ." which is unusual in Mennonite martyr literature because one finds unmistakably the thought of vengeance—the saints are to wash their feet in the blood of the ungodly and are prompted to play a new song on their harps because God "comes to pay, to punish the ungodly."

Following about a year in prison, Anneken was drowned for her faith at the young age of 28. On her way to the execution she pleaded for someone in the crowd to adopt her son. A poor baker with six children volunteered and his whole family benefited from the wealth which was reclaimed and became theirs with the son Esaias.

(*The Mennonite Encyclopedia*, Vol. I, pp. 126, 127, and *Martyrs Mirror*, pp. 453, 454.)

Jebarbi Ma brings us to the 20th century to a most outstanding Bible woman in the Mennonite Church of India. She served in the early 1900s and was the mother of the first ordained Mennonite Indian pastor, John Haidar.

As a young Muhammadan widow, Jebarbi was hired to be the cook for a family of the Pentecostal Mission, which was located next to the Mennonite Mission in central India. It was unusual for a woman to be engaged as cook, but it must have been in God's providence that Jebarbi was hired to this position.

As was the practice of the missionary family, Jebarbi and all the servants were expected to gather each morning for Bible reading and prayer before beginning the work of the day. Jebarbi was instructed to prepare breakfast first, then to place it in the warmer to be served after "prayers." However, the first morning she simply remained in the kitchen and did not go. The missionary explained at breakfast that part of her job requirements was to attend prayers. Again the next morning she stayed in the kitchen. After some time the missionary told her she would either join them at prayers or they would need to find another cook.

Jebarbi was struggling to support her twelve-year-old son John, ten-year-old daughter, Miriam, and herself. She needed the job desperately, so she unwillingly promised to thereafter attend morning prayers. The next morning she arrived in the kitchen early as usual and prepared the breakfast, but when the bell rang for the gathering, she deliberately left the eggs and toast on the old wood stove and went to the meeting. Following prayers the family sat up to eat their breakfast of burnt eggs and charred toast. They quietly ate without one word of complaint. Jebarbi was so overtaken by this demonstration of patience and love that in tears she ran to her mistress, embraced her, and apoligized. Jebarbi became a Christian that very morning.

The Muhammadan people of her village were much angered by her commitment to Christianity. While Jebarbi was at work, they kidnapped her two children, kept them in their village, and tried to turn them against her. They taught John to hide each morning behind a tree along the road which Jebarbi walked to work and to throw stones at her and call abusive names. Each morning she would stop and tenderly express her love to John, urging him to go along home with her. After several days of this, John burst into tears, ran from behind the tree to his mother, and went back to live with her again. Miriam also returned later.

Jebarbi was made Bible woman in the Pentecostal Mission. This involved village evangelism, teaching, and ministering to needs of the people in the church (as perhaps a deaconess would). A few years later the Pentecostal Mission was forced to close because of lack of funds and Jebarbi went to Dhamtari, where she became a member of the Mennonite Church. She grew to become an outstanding leader among the Bible women and was much loved and highly respected by all who knew her.

(This story was related to me by my beloved father, Lloy Kniss, who knew Jebarbi Ma and also worked with her son John in India.)

Sarah Hahn Lapp was known, loved, and admired as "Auntie Lapp" by the writer, as she was by so many people in almost forty-two years of service.

She was born in 1869, married, and went with her husband, Mahlon C. Lapp, to the mission field in Central India. Mahlon was the first moderator of the India Mennonite Conference and was the only bishop of the church from 1908 to 1916. He died in 1923 of a paralysis at a hospital in Calcutta, but Sarah stayed on in the work for nineteen more years.

Actually, Sarah became a missionary "statesman" for the Mennonite Church. She served the longest of any other missionary in the India Mennonite Mission, which dated from 1901 to 1942, for five full seven-year terms. Coordinating and directing the work of the Indian Bible women, she gave direction to this evangelistic outreach among women. John Lapp, in his book *The Mennonite Church in India*, describes her well: "Sarah Lapp stands out as one of the most extraordinary of all the missionaries. Rarely ill during her long career, she stayed in India nineteen years after her husband's death. Her greatest achievement was with the Bible women with whom she virtually lived during her fifth term in India." She also spent many years at Balodgahan working with the boarding school girls.

She was one of those women who, in spite of very small stature and a quiet, unimposing manner, commanded a deep respect from all who knew her. In fact, the Indian people revered and almost worshiped her as a true saint.

She was highly respected both at home and abroad. The children of Bishop George R. Brunk of Denbigh, Virginia, recall that Sarah Lapp on furlough was the very first woman their father invited into the pulpit to bring the message on Sunday morning.

Undaunted in spirit, motivated by the love of Christ, she had a vision for the future of the church in India. Seeking ways by which the church could be indigenous, her role was an enabling mission, a support role of service to and through others whose work she enhanced. But with this she was a leader, setting the pace by her own spirit, dedication, and efficiency. She stands in the train of those whom the Apostle Paul greeted in Romans 16: "women who work hard in the Lord" (16:12).

Annie C. Funk was a new name to the writer until recently when the following inscription on a memorial tombstone was brought to her attention while visiting in the small town of Bally, Pennsylvania.

Erected by
The Eastern District Conference
of the Mennonite Church
in memory of
ANNIE C. FUNK
Missionary in India 1906-1912
Daughter of
James B. and Susan Funk
Born April 12, 1874, Died April 15, 1912
Aged 38 years and 3 days

She was coming home on her first furlough when death overtook her in the wreck of the steamship *Titanic*, off the coast of Newfoundland.

Her life was one of service in the spirit of the Master—"not to be ministered to but to minister."

The account of Annie's life and service was found in the General Conference *Mennonite Year Book of 1912* in an article by Anthony S. Shelly, who was then the pastor of the congregation.

The story of her life expresses strength, courage, genuine humility, and sacrificial living. Her unusual death epitomized the essence of her life. She was already in a lifeboat with a small child whose mother was left standing on the deck of the sinking *Titanic*, holding her small baby in her arms. This part of the story was described in a British newspaper following the incident. Annie's dramatic courage and love were described by Shelly: "Her last act of unselfish love on earth was to surrender her place in one of the lifeboats to another woman in order that the latter's little children might not be left without the needful tender care of a mother."

Annie grew up in Bucks County, Pennsylvania, and was a member of the Bally General Conference Mennonite Church. Her letter of response to the call from the Mission Board to go to India expresses her dedication and sensitivity to God's will:

> It is now a week since I was home and we talked about India. I am just a step further now than I was then. Several years ago I promised the Lord that if the way would open to go to the foreign field, I would do my duty.
>
> Ever since I came to know Jesus as my personal Savior and to realize what He did for me, *I longed to give the message.* Now the door is open wide enough for me to do my duty to the extent of *being willing* to go. If, the Board does not see fit to send me, then the answer is plain. He can use me better somewhere else.

She reached Janjgir, India, a few days before Christmas, 1906. Letters express her love and compassion for the people of India and her eagerness to get to the work for which she went. Before completing language school, she began the task of starting a school for girls. She describes the difficulties of building the schoolhouse without complaint, but with trust in God. She gives endearing descriptions of the women of the village, the pleasure of sewing for two little girls with leprosy, and the joy of bringing a young couple from Dhamtari to join the teaching staff.

The school was opened July 1908 about which she writes: "I am so glad to get to work even if it is with some misgivings. Village schools are somewhat hard to manage but it is such a blessed thought that if we are in His hands He will guide. I do not expect an easy time, but I do expect some joy in it, which will outweigh the dark days."

Annie must have had an unusually "bubbling" personality. On receipt of a Friendship Calendar from her church at home she writes: "I almost walked on air coming back from the post office. I just felt like hugging the love messages with Bible verses, religious admonitions, humor, and familiar faces as well as some new ones."

She was blessed with unusually good health and never seemed to mind the heat as the other missionaries did. She wrote to friends that the hot season only made her lazy. With untiring energy she rode many miles of rugged roads on her bicycle which was a gift from a Sunday school at home.

Many letters and testimonies from fellow missionaries in India confirm the fact that Annie Funk was one of God's choice servants in that faraway land.

After six years on the field she left for the homeland, being advised to do so on account of the illness of her mother. But she never reached her earthly home. From London she took passage on the *Titanic* which (it was thought) could never sink. She was to have traveled from London on the *S.S. Haverford* but erroneous information from the travel line caused the change. On that fateful journey the magnificent ship struck an iceberg and sank, carrying this servant of the Lord and 1516 others to a watery grave.

Annie Funk's death dramatically illustrated the character of her life—she always gave consideration first to the welfare of others. She leaves a rich legacy of love and inspiration for unselfish sacrificial living.

www.ingramcontent.com/pod-product-compliance
Lightning Source LLC
Chambersburg PA
CBHW070238230426
43664CB00014B/2346